Effectiveness and Reform of the United Nations Development Programme (UNDP)

EFFECTIVENESS AND REFORM OF THE UNITED NATIONS DEVELOPMENT PROGRAMME (UNDP)

STEPHAN KLINGEBIEL

FRANK CASS
LONDON • PORTLAND, OR
Published in association with the
German Development Institute, Berlin

First published in 1999 in Great Britain by
FRANK CASS PUBLISHERS
Newbury House, 900 Eastern Avenue,
London IG2 7HH

and in the United States of America by
FRANK CASS PUBLISHERS
c/o ISBS
5804 N.E. Hassalo Street
Portland, Oregon 97213-3644

Website http://ww.frankcass.com

British Library Cataloguing in Publication Data

Klingebiel, Stephan
Effectiveness and reform of the United Nations Development Programme. – (GDI book series ; no. 13)
1. United Nations Development Programme. Office of Development Studies – Evaluation 2. United Nations Development Programme. Office of Development Studies – Reform
I. Title
338.9

ISBN 0-7146-4972-4 (cloth)
ISBN 0-7146-8032-X (paper)

Library of Congress Cataloging-in-Publication Data

Klingebiel, Stephan.
Effectiveness and reform of the United Nations Development Programme (UNDP) / Stephan Klingebiel.
p. cm. — (GDI book series, ISSN 1460-4175 ; no. 13)
Includes bibliographical references (p.).
ISBN 0-7146-4972-4 (cloth). — ISBN 0-7146-8032-X (paper)
1. United Nations Development Programme. 2. United Nations—Economic assistance. I. Title. II. Series.
HC60.K534 1999
338.91—dc21 98-52087
CIP

Printed and bound in Great Britain by
Antony Rowe Ltd, Chippenham, Wilts

Preface

This study contains the findings of independent research I have undertaken as a member of the professional staff of the German Development Institute (GDI).

A number of people have contributed to the study in many ways. I would like to thank all those who agreed to be interviewed and gave their advice. This applies especially to the management and staff of the United Nations Development Programme (UNDP), the representatives of the UN missions located in New York, or the delegates on UNDP's Executive Board, and the relevant staff members of the Federal Ministry for Economic Cooperation and Development and the Foreign Office in Bonn. I received valuable suggestions and advice from colleagues at the GDI, particularly Dr. Guido Ashoff. For the technical preparation of the manuscript and for helping to make the text more readable I would especially like to thank Waltraud Phaneuf and Ingrid Sattler-Panjatan. The excellent translation of the study into English was made by Rodney Sayer.

I owe a special debt of gratitude to Heike Henn for her constructive criticism of the contents and for her practical support.

The study has been accepted by the Gerhard Mercator University of Duisburg as a doctoral thesis. For overseeing my work on this thesis and for their important suggestions my sincere thanks go to Professors Franz Nuscheler and Peter Meyns.

Berlin, summer 1998 Stephan Klingebiel

Summary of Contents

Abbreviations		
Summary		I
Part I	**Introduction**	**1**
Part II	**Theoretical and Conceptual Foundations**	**21**
1	Effectiveness of International Organizations	21
2	The Development Policy Debate on the Role of Technical Cooperation	34
Part III	**UNDP: Reform Debate, Reform Measures and Development Options**	**64**
1	UN Development Cooperation: State of the Reform Debate and Relevance to UNDP	64
2	Need to Reform UNDP	102
3	Concepts for the Reform of UNDP	150
4	Measures to Reform UNDP	173
5	Profile of a More Effective UNDP	240
6	Positions of the Most Important Actors on the Reform Process and on the Prospects for UNDP's Reform	266
7	Options and Scenarios for the Future Development of UNDP	279
Part IV	**Conclusions**	**292**
1	Introduction	292

2 Conclusions for the Debate on the Effectiveness of International Organizations 293

3 Conclusions for the Debate on Technical Cooperation 294

4 Conclusions for the Reform and Effectiveness of UNDP and UN Development Cooperation 297

Notes 306

Bibliography 343

Annex 383

Contents

Abbreviations

Summary I

Part I Introduction 1

1 Background to the Problem 1

2 Objectives and Structure of the Study and Questions to be Answered 4

3 Research and Literature 9

4 Explanations and Definitions 13

5 Methodological Approach and Sources 18

Part II Theoretical and Conceptual Foundations 21

1 Effectiveness of International Organizations 21

1.1 Introduction 21

1.2 International Organizations and Factors Influencing Their Effectiveness 23

1.2.1 Premises and Concept of Effectiveness 23

1.2.2 Levels of and Factors Influencing Effectiveness 24

1.3 Conclusions for the Study 32

2 The Development Policy Debate on the Role of Technical Cooperation 34

2.1 Introduction 34

2.2 Foundations for the Debate on Technical Cooperation 36

2.2.1 Definition and Clarification 36

2.2.2	Instruments, Characteristics and Scale of Technical Cooperation	38
2.3	State of the Debate on Technical Cooperation	41
2.3.1	Criticism of Technical Cooperation	41
2.3.2	Proposals and Methods for the Reform of Technical Cooperation	51
2.4	Conclusions for the Study	59
Part III	**UNDP: Reform Debate, Reform Measures and Development Options**	**64**
1	**UN Development Cooperation: State of the Reform Debate and Relevance to UNDP**	**64**
1.1	Introduction	64
1.2	Basics	66
1.2.1	The UN's Development Policy and Development Cooperation: Historical Background	66
1.2.2	UNDP's Role and its Functions for UN Development Cooperation	69
1.3	Reform of UN Development Cooperation	72
1.3.1	Need for Reforms	72
1.3.2	Reform Concepts and Initiatives	85
1.3.3	Past Reform Measures	89
1.3.4	Views on the Reform Debate	95
1.4	Conclusions	97
1.4.1	Political Dimensions and Implications of the Reform Debate	97
1.4.2	Analysis of the Reform Debate and Implications for UNDP	100
2	**Need to Reform UNDP**	**102**
2.1	Introduction	102
2.2	Need for Reform: Shortcomings	103
2.2.1	Shortcomings at Conceptual Level	104
2.2.2	Shortcomings at Structural and Policy Level	114

2.2.2.1	Financing	114
2.2.2.2	Coordination	129
2.2.2.3	Country Programming	133
2.2.2.4	Assumption of Implementing Functions	135
2.2.2.5	Political Guidance by the Governing Council, or Executive Board	136
2.2.3	Shortcomings at Administration and Implementation Level	137
2.3	Comparative Advantages	145
2.4	Conclusions	147
3	**Concepts for the Reform of UNDP**	**150**
3.1	Introduction	150
3.2	Selected Reform Concepts	151
3.2.1	Jackson Report	151
3.2.2	The Future Role of UNDP in World Development	153
3.2.3	*UNDP in Action*	154
3.2.4	UNDP and World Development by the Year 2000	157
3.2.5	Kienbaum Report	158
3.2.6	UNDP's Effectiveness at Country Level	159
3.2.7	Nordic UN Project	162
3.2.8	Quo Vadis, UNDP	164
3.2.9	*A Charter for Change*	165
3.2.10	*A Comparative Assessment*	167
3.2.11	*Assessment of UNDP*	168
3.2.12	Speth Initiative	170
3.3	Conclusions	171
4	**Measures to Reform UNDP**	**173**
4.1	Introduction	173
4.2	Reform Process	174
4.2.1	Terms of Reference	174
4.2.2	Foundations and Phases of Reform	175
4.3	Levels of Reform	179
4.3.1	Conceptual Level	179

4.3.2	Structural and Policy Level	193
4.3.3	Administration and Implementation Level	219
4.4	Conclusions	236
5	**Profile of a More Effective UNDP**	**240**
5.1	Introduction	240
5.2	Premises	240
5.3	Elements of a More Effective UNDP	243
5.3.1	Substantive Tasks	244
5.3.2	Functional Elements and Service Functions for UN Development Cooperation	253
5.3.3	Elements in the Creation of the Profile and the Improvement of Quality	256
5.4	Conclusions	263
6	**Positions of the Most Important Actors on the Reform Process and on the Prospects for UNDP's Reform**	**266**
6.1	Introduction	266
6.2	Positions of Important Groups of Actors	267
6.2.1	Positions of the Industrialized Countries	267
6.2.2	Positions of the Programme Countries	270
6.2.3	Positions of the UN and UN System	274
6.3	Conclusions	276
7	**Options and Scenarios for the Future Development of UNDP**	**279**
7.1	Introduction	279
7.2	Premises on the Future Development of UNDP	279
7.3	Scenarios	283
7.4	Conclusions	291

Part IV Conclusions 292

1 Introduction 292

2 Conclusions for the Debate on the Effectiveness of International Organizations 293

3 Conclusions for the Debate on Technical Cooperation 294

4 Conclusions for the Reform and Effectiveness of UNDP and UN Development Cooperation 297

Notes 306

Bibliography 343

Annex 383

Annex I UNDP: Main Features and Structures 385

Annex II Resolution 2029 (XX): Consolidation of the Special Fund and the Expanded Programme of Technical Assistance in a United Nations Development Programme 391

Annex III Resolution 2688 (XXV): The Capacity of the United Nations Development System 396

Annex IV Mission Statement of the United Nations Development Programme 410

Boxes in the text

1 Typologization of the effectiveness of international organizations 25

2 Eritrea and the international donor community: criticism of the present development cooperation model 50

3 The DAC principles for the reorientation of technical cooperation 53

4	UN Secretary-General Kofi Annan's reform efforts and initiatives	92
5	National Technical Co-operation Assessment and Programme (NaTCAP)	109
6	*Failing the World's Poor* - an analysis by the Heritage Foundation	155
7	The UN world conferences of the 1990s	250

Figures in the text

1	Structure of the United Nations	14
2	Theoretical approaches to international organizations	22
3	Factors influencing the effectiveness of international organizations	33
4	Principal shortcomings of UN development cooperation in the 1990s	84
5	Non-core resources as a proportion of total UNDP resources	122
6	UNDP Organizational Chart	139
7	UNDP's main deficiencies in the 1990s	149
8	Elements of the UNDP core mission	183
9	Governance	189
10	Reform measures at structural and policy level	218
11	Outline of a new organizational structure for UNDP	231
12	Reform measures at administration and implementation level	235
13	UNDP's most important reform measures since the beginning of the 1990s	239
14	Elements of a more effective UNDP	265

Tables in the text

1	Sectoral breakdown of UNDP interventions	106
2	Tendencies in the quality of project design	110
3	Quality of UNDP projects based on evaluations studied	112
4	Net disbursements by multilateral agencies on concessional terms	116
5	UNDP's financial resources, revenue from 1991 to 1996	117
6	Main contributors to UNDP's core resources	120
7	Regional distribution of UNDP resources (core and non-core) on the basis of current operations	124
8	Expenditure on the UN system's grant-based operational development activities	127
9	UNDP's largest executing agencies, 1988-1996	144
10	Substantive classification of UNDP projects and programmes approved in 1994 and 1995	187
11	Financing lines of the Target for Resource Assignments from the Core (TRAC) system and distribution of the resources	212
12	Resources entered on TRAC Lines 1.1.1 and 1.1.2, 1997 - 1999	214
13	Average financial volume and number of current UNDP operations	226

Abbreviations

A	(General) Assembly
ACC	Administrative Committee on Co-ordination
BMZ	German Ministry for Economic Cooperation and Development (Bundesministerium für wirtschaftliche Zusammenarbeit und Entwicklung)
BPPS	Bureau of Policy and Programme Support
BREA	Bureau for Resources and External Affairs
CCF	Country Cooperation Framework
CCPOQ	Consultative Committee on Programme and Operational Questions
CDA	Capacity Development Assistance
CG	Consultative Group
CP	Country Programme
CPMP	Country Programme Management Plan
CRP	Conference Room Paper
CSN	Country Strategy Note
CSO	Civil Society Organization
DAC	Development Assistance Committee
DANIDA	Danish International Development Agency
DC	Development Cooperation
DDSMS	Department for Development Support and Management Services
DGVN	German United Nations Association (Deutsche Gesellschaft für die Vereinten Nationen)
DP	Development Programme
DRM	Division for Resources Mobilization
DSE	German Foundation for International Development (Deutsche Stiftung für internationale Entwicklung)
E / ECOSOC	Economic and Social Council

EB	Executive Board
EC	European Community
ECDPM	European Centre for Development Policy Management
EPTA	Expanded Programme of Technical Assistance
ESA	European Space Agency
EU	European Union
FAO	Food and Agriculture Organization
FC	Financial Cooperation
G 7	Group of Seven
G 8	Group of Eight
GATT	General Agreement on Tariffs and Trade
GC	Governing Council
GEF	Global Environmental Facility
GTZ	German Agency for Technical Cooperation (Deutsche Gesellschaft für Technische Zusammenarbeit)
HDR	Human Development Report
HQ	Headquarters
IAEA	International Atomic Energy Agency
IBRD	International Bank for Reconstruction and Development
ID	Institutional Development
IDA	International Development Association
IDTA	Institutional Development Technical Assistance
IGO	Intergovernmental Organization
ILO	International Labour Organization
IMF	International Monetary Fund
INGO	International Non-Governmental Organization
IO	Internationale Organisation(en) / International Organization
IPF	Indicative Planning Figure

JCDP	Joint Consultative Group on Policy
JIU	Joint Inspection Unit
LDC	Less Developed Country
LLDC	Least Developed Country
MDB	Multilateral Development Bank
NaTCADS	National Capacity Policies and Programmes
NaTCAP	National Technical Cooperation Assessment and Programme
NEX	National Execution
NGO	Non-Governmental Organization
NHDR	National Human Development Report
OAU	Organization of African Unity
ODA	Offical Development Assistance
ODC	Overseas Development Council
ODI	Overseas Development Institute
ODS	Office of Development Policy Studies
OECD	Organization for Economic Cooperation and Development
OESP	Office of Evaluation and Strategic Planning
OPEC	Organization of Petroleum Exporting Countries
OPS	Office for Project Services
OUNS	Office of UN System Support and Services
PSDA	Programme Support and Development Activities
PSI	Poverty Strategies Initiative
RC	Resident Co-ordinator
ResRep / RR	Resident Representative
RMT	Resource Mobilization Target
RT	Round Table
SF	Special Fund
SHD	Sustainable Human Development
SIP	Sector Investment Programme

SPPD	System for Policy and Programme Development
SUNFED	Special United Nations Fund for Economic Development
TA	Technical Assistance
TAL	(Freestanding) Technical Assistance Loans
TC	Technical Co-operation
TCDC	Technical Cooperation among Developing Countries
TCP	Technical Co-operation Programming
TCPFD	Technical Co-operation Framework Statement
TRAC	Target for Resource Assignments from the Core
UIA	Union of International Associations
UK	United Kingdom
UN / U.N.	United Nations
UNA	United Nations Association
UNAIDS	United Nations Programme on HIV/AIDS
UNCDF	United Nations Capital Development Fund
UNCHS	United Nations Centre for Human Settlements
UNCTAD	United Nations Conference on Trade and Development
UNDAF	United Nations Development Assistance Framework
UNDCP	United Nations International Drug Control Programme
UNDG	United Nations Development Group
UNDP	United Nations Development Programme
UNEP	United Nations Environment Programme
UNESCO	United Nations Educational, Scientific and Cultural Organization
UNFPA	United Nations Population Fund

UNFSTD	United Nations Fund for Sience and Technology for Development
UNHCR	United Nations High Commissioner for Refugees
UNICEF	United Nations Children's Fund
UNIDO	United Nations Industrial Development Organization
UNIFEM	United Nations Development Fund for Women
UNOPS	United Nations Office for Project Services
UNRFNRE	United Nations Revolving Fund for Natural Resources Exploration
UNSIA	United Nations Special Initiative on Africa
UNSO	United Nations Sudano-Sahelian Office
UNV	United Nations Volunteers
U.S. / US	United States
USA	United States of America
USAID	United States Agency for International Development
WB	World Bank / Weltbank
WFP	World Food Programme
WHO	World Health Organization
WSSD	World Summit for Social Development

Summary

1 Goals of the Study and the Problems Addressed

The study "Effectiveness and Reform of UNDP" is intended as a constructive contribution to the current debate on the reform of UNDP and thus to the debate on the reform of UN development cooperation as a whole. Reference will also be made in this context to ways of improving the design of international development cooperation.

Above all, the study considers the following questions:

- What stage has been reached in the debate on the reform of UN development cooperation as a whole?
- What aspects of UNDP are in greatest need of reform, and what are the most important challenges it faces?
- What UNDP reforms have been initiated in the 1990s, and how can they be rated?
- In addition to the reforms already launched, in what spheres and in what form should adjustment efforts be made with a view to creating a UNDP that is more effective in development policy terms?
- What are the chances of establishing a UNDP that is more effective in development policy terms?

The project is based on assumptions in two theoretical or conceptual debates, which will be discussed first:

- The question of the effectiveness of international organizations is considered against the background of the debate on the theory of political science and international relations as a discipline.
- One of the questions discussed in the development policy debate on technical cooperation concerns the shortcomings of technical cooperation and the role it might play in the future.

2 Effectiveness of International Organizations

The state of the debate on the theory of political science as it relates to international organizations is only partly satisfactory. The formation of a theory is generally fragmented and has a low level of generalization. The question of the effectiveness of international organizations has yet to be adequately considered; however, it has attracted greater interest since the 1980s in the context of the "regime approach". With few exceptions the debate on theory has also paid little attention to the ability of international organizations to adapt and reform.

Several categories can be deduced from a number of theoretical papers for research on the effectiveness of international organizations. This study develops from them an analytical framework for empirical research. The framework includes various factors of relevance to the effectiveness of international organizations. These factors are typologically ascribed to one of the following three levels: (a) a conceptual level, (b) a structural and policy level, and (c) an administrative and implementation level.

3 Debate on Technical Cooperation

The 1990s have seen the beginning of an intensive debate on the purpose, shortcomings and effectiveness of technical cooperation; this debate is important for UNDP, since it is one of the main pillars of multilateral technical cooperation.

In terms of its goal of capacity-building and so eventually making itself superfluous, technical cooperation has been largely ineffective in the past, and results have been disappointing. Principally to blame for this are the following factors: (1) the donor-driven system, (2) input orientation, (3) the absence of a strategic line, (4) deficient project design, (5) excessive employment of foreign experts and advisers, (6) inadequate cost awareness, and (7) structural shortcomings in the recipient countries.

For remedying these shortcomings, there are various problem-solving approaches at conceptual level; they are described, for example, in "Principles for New Orientations in Technical Cooperation" by the OECD's Development Assistance Committee (DAC) (greater use of local know-how, more appropriate project design, etc.). So far, however, the practical application of problem-solving approaches by the donors has been unsatisfactory.

For development policy in the 1990s technical cooperation primarily means capacity-building. Capacity-building is complex and difficult, since it entails contributions to independent and effective institutional structures and to the development of specific conditions. Attention is increasingly turning here to factors that are important for the political environment and good governance (democratic procedures and institutions, human rights, violent conflicts, civil society, etc.). Where these tasks are concerned, multilateral technical cooperation has certain advantages (because of its universal structures, neutral approach, more limited self-interest, etc.). The international debate on technical cooperation has so far paid little attention to the question whether a new division of labour among the various donor institutions would be wise; account should also be taken in this context of the growing competition from the World Bank in the technical cooperation field.

4 State of the Debate on the Reform of UN Development Cooperation as a Whole and its Significance for UNDP

The debate on the effectiveness and reform of UNDP must be seen against the background of UN development cooperation as a whole, since UNDP is expected to perform major UN-wide planning and co-ordination tasks.

Broadly speaking, five main problem areas can be identified for UN development cooperation:

- poor political control and coordination within the UN,
- inadequate mechanisms and instruments for coordination between the UN and its specialized agencies,
- the proliferation of UN operational development institutions,
- the poor quality of development policy and inadequate cost awareness,
- the inadequate and unstable financial endowment of the UN funds and programmes.

In the 1990s there have been several proposals for reforms (including the Nordic UN Project and an EU initiative), and some action has been taken (conversion of the Governing Councils into smaller Executive Boards, etc.); UN Secretary-General Kofi Annan is very keen to see reform. Efforts so far have failed, however, to lay the foundations for dealing with the structural shortcomings. For this the UN member countries are themselves primarily to blame, since they have been unable to reach agreement on major areas of reform and often show little commitment to reform ("UN bashing", etc.).

5 The Need for the Reform of UNDP

The main challenges facing UN development cooperation are closely related to the need to reform UNDP. A need to reform UNDP in the 1990s can be identified at three different levels:

- At conceptual level the main shortcomings are an unsatisfactory substantive profile and, to some extent, the inadequate account taken of the conclusions drawn in the debate on technical cooperation.

- At structural and policy level the most serious problems are due to the poor functioning of the coordinating mechanisms, especially at country level (Resident Coordinator system) and also at headquarters level. As regards funding, it can be said that the existing mechanism (voluntary contributions) does not provide a sufficiently stable and predictable base and that the increase in earmarked funds (non-core resources) at the expense of funds for the core programme (core resources) is leading to growing "bilateralization", causing a lack of transparency and impairing the appropriate use of resources for development; furthermore, the UN's financial volume is small in absolute terms (core resources in 1996: US $ 850 m) and shrinking in real terms. Other major shortcomings are, or were, to be found in the original country programming procedure, which did not offer any development policy incentives because the allocation mechanisms were quasi-automatic, and in the limited ability of the Governing Council, or Executive Board, to exercise political control (micro-management, inadequate strategic prescriptions, etc.).
- At the level of administration and implementation complex problems connected with the quality of project planning and implementation (insignificance due to "projectitis", dependence on executing agencies, etc.), the increase in implementing activities undertaken by UNDP itself and the monitoring and evaluation system can be identified. Additional difficulties are posed by the need to reform administrative and staff structures and conditions.

These shortcomings have led to UNDP being regarded in the past predominantly as a weak actor in the development field, with an imprecise substantive profile, no clearly defined functions and inadequate implementing instruments. Besides its shortcomings, however, UNDP has some major advantages over other donors (such as pronounced ownership in the programme countries, very good representation at country level).

6 Concepts for the Reform of UNDP

In the 1970s, 1980s and 1990s there have been a number of analyses and reform concepts relating partly or entirely to UNDP. The best known of these and the one that had the greatest impact is the Jackson Report, which was submitted in 1969. The recommendations it contained were reflected in the resolution on which UNDP is largely based ("Consensus Resolution"). In the 1990s major analyses have been undertaken or commissioned by various Scandinavian countries (the Nordic UN Project, studies by DANIDA and the Centre for Development Research, etc.), the Overseas Development Council and UNDP itself.

These analyses and concepts generally come to the conclusion that UNDP needs to be reformed (which will also be in the interests of UN development cooperation as a whole). Reforms should be undertaken with the aim of strengthening UNDP in the core functions it performs.

7 Measures Taken to Reform UNDP in the 1990s

Since the first half of the 1990s there has been a complex process of reorganizing and reforming UNDP. This process, which has yet to be completed, includes decisions and reform efforts by various UN bodies (General Assembly, Secretary-General, UNDP's Governing Council, or Executive Board, and its Administrator) relating to (1) the whole of the UN, (2) all UN funds and programmes or (3) UNDP alone.

The most important of the reforms so far undertaken or launched are the following:

– At conceptual level the emphasis is on the definition of a core mission ("*to assist countries in their endeavour to achieve sustainable human development*") and the drafting of a mission statement. From this UNDP has deduced its principal goals, focus areas and patterns of intervention.

- At structural and policy level measures have been or are being taken, for instance, to strengthen the Resident Coordinator system (by having a larger pool of candidates, for example) and to improve the coordination of UN activities at headquarters level (principally through the establishment of a United Nations Development Group convened by the UNDP Administrator). Other steps concern the replacement of the current country programming procedure, which now partly operates with development policy incentives (the size of the financial volume may therefore vary) and the conversion of the Governing Council into a smaller Executive Board. The programme coherence of all UN funds and programmes is also to be increased through the establishment of a common programme framework (United Nations Development Assistance Framework - UNDAF), although it leaves the various agencies considerable room for manoeuvre. Efforts are also being made to improve the financial situation.
- At the level of administration and implementation efforts are primarily aimed at strengthening the programme approach, increasing the number of projects and programmes implemented by programme countries on their own responsibility (national execution), improving and strengthening the evaluation instrument and turning implementing capacities into a separate entity. Attempts are also being made to restructure and decentralize organization, and steps are being taken to reduce staff numbers and administrative costs.

The UNDP reform process includes many elements that change structures: UNDP's profile has changed significantly in many areas in the 1990s, largely for the better. The measures hitherto taken are appropriate because they concern the main shortcomings and it is realized or expected that they will help to increase the effectiveness of UNDP and its measures in the development field and to reduce costs considerably. Various reforms have, however, yet to prove their worth (e.g. the programming procedure and the operationalization and clearer definition of the core mission) or have proved to be not or not entirely suitable. Furthermore, little or nothing appropriate has so far been done to remedy some of the main shortcomings. This is particularly true of the coordinating mechanisms at country and headquarters level (no effective coordinating instruments or incentives, continued institutional fragmentation) and of the questions concerning financial endowment and funding mechanisms. Various reform measures are also having an impact on other agencies of the UN system (e.g. the increase in national execution has implications for the traditional executing agencies).

8 Profile of a More Effective UNDP

To create a UNDP that is more effective in development policy terms, current efforts need to be joined by clarification of future priorities and reforms. The strategy proposed here is not guided by the political feasibility of possible reforms, but it is largely based on the UNDP reform process in the 1990s and in some areas follows on from the overall reform of UN development cooperation. It is inappropriate and unnecessary to "invent" a new UNDP and to "discover" new niches: the existing approaches and the needs arising from the UN tasks and the development debate must be integrated into a coherent strategy.

A reform strategy of this kind should place the emphasis on three elements: (1) UNDP's substantive terms of reference, (2) the functional tasks and services performed for UN development cooperation as a whole and (3) elements for the attainment of the substantive and functional profile and for development quality assurance.

- Proceeding from the two concepts of sustainable human development and capacity-building, UNDP might place the emphasis on three areas. This should lead to clear substantive focusing and concentration of the core resources currently available. Firstly, good governance, crisis prevention and the consolidation of peace should become its most important substantive concerns. This range of tasks is very important in development terms: as a UN agency, UNDP has a particular legitimation in these areas; there are also links with other UN agencies (e.g. the UN Commissioner for Human Rights) and sound foundations on which to build, partly because of the network of country offices. Secondly, UNDP should help to ensure that the conclusions drawn at the UN world conferences in the 1990s are implemented effectively and efficiently; to this end, one of its main tasks at international and especially national level should be systematic follow-up (i.e. implementation of the conclusions through purposeful capacity-building). Thirdly, the goal should be as extensive coordination of development cooperation as possible and its effective management by the programme countries themselves; UNDP can help to develop suitable capacities for this purpose.

– In the case of functional tasks and services for the UN the emphasis is on three aspects. Firstly, the institutional structure of UN development cooperation and UNDP's position at headquarters level should be changed. Above all, it would be advisable in this context to integrate most UN funds and programmes (and other technical cooperation funds of the UN system) into UNDP's main programme. It would also be appropriate for UNDP to be given effective decision-making powers for the coordinating tasks (especially in the United Nations Development Group). Secondly, the reform of the Resident Coordinator system should be stepped up and activities that hinder the Resident Coordinator in the performance of neutral tasks (e.g. UNDP-specific fund-raising) should be excluded. Thirdly, a single country-related programming document should in principle be submitted for UN development cooperation on the basis of the United Nations Development Assistance Framework.

– In the case of the elements for attaining the profile and quality assurance the aim should be a single, more decisive Executive Board for all UN funds and programmes, the further development of innovative technical cooperation approaches (national execution, NaTCAP (National Technical Cooperation Assessment and

Programme), greater involvement of non-governmental actors, etc.), graduating mechanisms for the country-related differentiation of technical cooperation conditions, the expansion of development policy incentives in country programming and the linking of technical cooperation measures to non-operational UN policies.

Where finances are concerned, a significantly larger volume (US $ 4 - 5 bn) should, if possible, eventually be made available through transfers and some additional funding; these resources should also be provided on a more stable basis. To achieve this objective, various measures will need to be taken in the short, medium and long term; they include improved information and lobbying work directed at the traditional main contributors, the involvement of "emerging donors", the conversion of the financing mechanism to a multiannual basis, the establishment of financing funds earmarked for development purposes (model: Global Environmental Facility) and finally, innovative financing approaches.

9 Views of the Leading Actors on the UNDP Reform Process

The behaviour of the main actors in the reform debate is characterized by heterogeneous interests and often unclear conceptual ideas on UNDP's future role:

- The industrialized countries are generally agreed on the need to place greater emphasis on and expand UNDP's guiding and coordinating role. They also advocate better performance, greater accountability and increased efficiency. A generally favourable view is taken of the UNDP reforms in the 1990s. Despite this, resources have been cut, severely in come cases (owing, among other things, to domestic budget problems), or future cutbacks are likely. The most controversial issues for the group of industrialized countries are the question of funding (scale, mechanisms and burden-sharing among the contributing countries) and the assessment of UNDP from the political and development angles.

- The developing countries as a group show little interest in the current UNDP reform process. Their position is essentially shaped by the assumption that the present structure of the UN funds and programmes needs to be preserved to safeguard the current scale of resources; they believe that UNDP reforms should above all lead to better financial endowment. They also welcome reforms that lead to the programme countries taking greater responsibility for measures, but reject the idea that a higher priority should be given to development in the use of resources.
- There is no uniform UN position on the debate on the reform of UNDP; the positions of the vast majority of the UN agencies active in the development cooperation field are in fact geared to safeguarding their identity and preserving their autonomy. In practice, this means there is little or no acceptance of UNDP's task of playing a coordinating role.

10 Options and Scenarios for the Future Development of UNDP

A wide variety of factors is likely to influence the future development of UNDP and its environment (the future of development cooperation as a whole, the role of multilateral development cooperation, the reform of the UN, etc.). Against this background very different options are in principle conceivable for a medium- to long-term time horizon (about 5 to 12 years). They are considered here in five scenarios:

- In the first scenario it is assumed that UNDP abandons functional tasks and services for the UN and instead evolves into an agency that defines itself primarily in terms of a substantive mandate. Its substantive task might be kept relatively general (capacity-building at national level or something similar) or related to a specific subject area (such as good governance, crisis prevention and the consolidation of peace). Focusing on substantive issues would have major implications for UNDP since it would have to be joined by an institutional adjustment (i.e. a reduction in size) and, above all, other agencies would have to take over and finance the general coordinating tasks at headquarters level and the Resident Coordinator system.

- In the second scenario it is assumed that UNDP focuses on its general service functions for UN development cooperation and no longer concerns itself with specific substantive issues. This option might have the advantage of enabling UNDP to be very independent in performing, coordinating and monitoring tasks for the overall system (honest broker). It would be particularly dependent on effective enforcement instruments since there would be less potential for exercising influence in the form of financial resources for UNDP programmes and of know-how.
- In the third scenario it is assumed that UNDP would place the emphasis on assisting bilateral donors with the management and implementation of development cooperation measures. Measures for specific purposes (in the sense of trust funds) would then become the main task. This approach might be of interest, for example, to small and medium-sized countries among the traditional donors and to emerging donors without development cooperation structures of their own. The crucial disadvantages of this option would be the resulting "bilateralization" of UNDP and some duplication of tasks with other UN bodies (especially the United Nations Office for Project Services).
- In the fourth scenario it is assumed that the reform process that has already been launched is continued and intensified (roughly along the lines of the profile of a more effective UNDP developed here); in other words, further substantive focusing, strengthened functional activities and improved quality standards, an increase in financial resources, etc. might be achieved. While the requirements this would entail would be relatively difficult to satisfy,

they would help to bring about a significant improvement in UNDP's effectiveness.

- In the fifth and final scenario it is assumed that the leading contributing countries would reduce their political and financial commitment to UNDP (in order, for example, to strengthen their bilateral development cooperation or to relieve the pressure on their own budgets) and that other sources of funding do not exist. Such conduct would have a wide range of sometimes highly adverse effects on the coordination of UN and other development cooperation activities, especially at country level, but also at headquarters level, on the account taken of subject areas in operational work (crisis prevention, good governance, etc.) and on innovative approaches to development. A major forum that enables programme countries to participate in decision-making and share responsibility on a largely equal footing would also be lost in the operational sphere of development.

The scenarios discussed above show that evolution along the lines of the fourth scenario would be most beneficial to the programme and main contributing countries because it would make for a significant improvement in effectiveness in development terms. However, it is also quite conceivable that, despite the successful continuation and intensification of UNDP's reform orientation, UN member countries would refuse to give their political and financial support because of short-term interests (e.g. a preference for bilateral channels owing to economic self-interest, budgetary problems, the UN's public image).

11 Conclusions

The factors and effectiveness levels that have been developed against the background of the debate on the theory of political science as it relates to international organizations have proved to be an appropriate analytical framework for this study. The role of international organizations and the importance of their capacity for reform should attract greater attention in the debate on theory in the future.

It has been possible to derive from the international debate on technical cooperation some important assessment criteria for the study of UNDP. In general, the debate reveals that technical cooperation needs to be geared far more closely to its real objective (i.e. capacity-building) and set out in a phasing-out strategy. To judge from the debate on technical cooperation, UNDP's activities are impressive (national execution, ownership, the NaTCAP process, etc.). UNDP should seek to become a think tank and form an important pillar for technical cooperation in the international debate on development.

All in all, UN development cooperation is in clear need of reform. Strategies aimed at remedying the deficiencies must also be directed primarily at UNDP, which can and must play a key role in reforms.

In the 1990s UNDP has begun an intensive reform process. In many areas it bears little resemblance to the UNDP of ten or so years ago, having generally managed to change into a more efficient actor in the development field.

The reform process so far must be applauded, since it has followed an appropriate course; however, it is by no means over, and needs to be stepped up and extended to include areas that are not yet covered. The question of funding, one of the most controversial issues, could become a key question in future reforms (e.g. incentives for reforms).

Although the UNDP reforms are viewed favourably by a majority of the member countries, they are not sufficiently acknowledged and rewarded. A dilemma to be seen here is that, despite the changes for the better, commitment is waning in several cases.

In both the programme countries and the main contributing countries there is a need for greater awareness of the "costs" in development terms that will arise if UNDP is weakened further rather than strengthened (especially because of a shortage of funds and a lack of willingness to accept reform). On the whole, many member countries do not have any clear ideas how and with what instruments and resources UNDP should operate in the future. In addition, the division of labour between UNDP or the UN on the one hand and the World Bank (and other donors) on the other needs to be discussed in view of the changing environment (growing importance of technical cooperation, etc.).

Attaching greater importance to UNDP and the whole of UN development cooperation and giving it a better profile at the same time would be a good thing for the international development debate and especially for practical work at country level. A strengthened UNDP can make a decisive contribution to the application of multilateral principles and innovative approaches in development policy and to more effective development cooperation.

Part I Introduction

1 Background to the Problem

This study was undertaken against the background of the wide-ranging debate on the shortcomings, effectiveness and reform of the United Nations' development cooperation, a debate that has been going on for several decades. Symbolic of this debate is the *Capacity Study* (UN Document: DP/5) (also known as the *Jackson Report*) published in 1969; the current reform debate that began in the early 1990s was largely prompted by the *Nordic UN Project*.[1] The debate on reforms has been unable in the past to bring about any adjustments that all the important groupings of UN member states regard as adequate. A consensus has yet to be reached by the various actors on many important aspects of the reform.

Since the early 1990s the environment for UN development cooperation and, therefore, the debate on reforms has changed in many respects. Not least because of mounting problems over the financing of *official development assistance* (ODA) a more intensive and more goal-oriented debate has been conducted on the future role of multilateral development cooperation,[2] its effectiveness and structural shortcomings and the sharing of national development cooperation budgets between bi- and multilateral channels.[3] The role of the UN institutions, their tasks, activities, organizational structure and resource endowment are particularly important in this context since they represent the central pillar of multilateral technical cooperation and are under far greater pressure to adjust and reform than the international development banks[4], and especially the World Bank group. One of the main changes to the environment has been the end of the East-West conflict. This has presented UN development cooperation with not only additional opportunities but also additional risks. On the positive side are the greater opportunities for taking action in politically sensitive areas (such as human rights and participation). On the negative side there is the declining political will of some countries to commit themselves to UN development cooperation, to which greater strategic importance was attached during the Cold War. At the same time, there are signs of growing expectancy that UN development cooperation will turn to issues that are of special cross-frontier interest (such global public goods as the environment, peace/war and migration).

The options open to UN development cooperation are often directly influenced by the general political climate at the UN (e.g. Kofi Annan's reform policy). Many fundamental aspects of the United Nations are of relevance in the UN development cooperation bodies. Thus questions concerning representation (How many delegations can be represented on a board without jeopardizing its ability to function? Can civil society groups communicate directly with the UN?), political neutrality (What development criteria and conditions are inconsistent with the principle of neutrality?) and universality (To what extent can UN development cooperation be concentrated on certain groups of countries?) are very important.

The new environment for UN development cooperation in the second half of the 1990s may mark the beginning of a radical break with existing structures. Many donors are politically determined to reduce the financing of the UN's operational development cooperation activities significantly unless there are signs in the foreseeable future of the reform producing definite results.[5] The World Bank, on the other hand, is indicating its willingness to continue expanding in the field of technical cooperation. The *Strategic Compact* (World Bank 1997b, 1997c) it submitted in 1997 can be seen as a clear sign of this.

The United Nations Development Programme (UNDP) plays a key role in the United Nations' development cooperation and the debate on its reform. Crucial functions were assigned to UNDP when it was first established: it is the main financing, coordinating and controlling body for the UN's operational development tasks. At no time in its history, however, has UNDP ever succeeded in performing these tasks adequately. In the past it has in fact been regarded as a weak development institution, partly because of its poor annual resource endowment of well under US $ 1 billion (mid-1990s). The large donor countries in particular have emphasized its poor performance, excessively low standards and inadequate accountability. Governments of developing countries, on the other hand, appreciate the allocation of funds with comparatively few conditions attached and the greater opportunities for political participation than other development institutions permit. However, they have been critical of the inadequate financial endowment, which makes it impossible for much of the UNDP mandate to be carried out. In the international development debate UNDP has been able to attract some attention primarily through the annual *Human Development Report*, which first appeared in 1990. In the first half of the 1990s at least, the concept of *sustainable human development* (SHD) partly developed and propagated by the *Human Development Report* and UNDP was frequently seen as a criticism of the World Bank as the dominant development policy think tank and of its development paradigms.

The *Human Development Report* should not, however, be equated with UNDP and its policy. The political disputes in UNDP's Governing Council in the early 1990s in fact clearly reflected the absence of a political majority in favour of a UNDP that endorses the *Human Development Report* in conceptual and practical terms.

As early as the 1970s and 1980s there were discussions on the re-structuring or comprehensive reform of UNDP, and some action was taken to this end. The debate has become far more topical and dynamic in the 1990s. Two tendencies are evident in this context. Firstly, the pressure for reform has become even greater. Since the early 1990s the debate has been revived mainly by the "like-minded countries"[6] with various analyses and proposals for reforms. The mid-1990s saw further initiatives emerging from the group of donor countries, such as the Group of 7 at the Lyon summit meeting in 1996 and the European Union in December 1996 (see section III.1). Secondly, UNDP has come to play something of an "anticipatory role" in that it has itself stimulated the reform debate and undertaken reform measures. This is particularly true of the period since UNDP Administrator James Gustave Speth took office (in 1993).

The reform debate to date and the reforms that have so far been launched leave a number of important questions open, since what constitutes an appropriate direction for the reform to take remains a contentious issue and the reform measures continue to be fragmentary. As the interests of the various actors differ, it has, moreover, yet to be clarified what form a consensus and future tasks might take and what the relationship with other actors in the development field in and outside the United Nations should be. What profile a future UNDP is to have is therefore a question of the utmost importance and still very much on the agenda.

Besides the factors referred to above, there is another important reason for analysing UNDP's future tasks within the donor group: fundamental criticism has been levelled at and arguments have been advanced against the instrument of technical cooperation (TC) during the development debate since the late 1980s. Doubt is expressed particularly about the effectiveness and sustainability of TC. The 1980s and 1990s have also shown, however, that development is often primarily obstructed not by lack of finances but by institutional and structural problems. The associated questions mainly concern areas of TC activity. In the 1980s, for example, there were several cases of structural adjustment programmes failing because of weak national institutions and structures; in the 1990s growing attention has been paid to the dimensions of *good governance*. Against this background too, it is important to consider the question of the need to adjust the objectives, role and practical form of UNDP's technical cooperation.

2 Objectives and Structure of the Study and Questions to be Answered

Objectives

The aim of the study is to contribute to selected aspects of the current debate on the reform of the United Nations' development cooperation. It focuses in this context on an analysis of the reform processes at UNDP, a profile for a UNDP that is effective in the field of development policy and the attitude of the most important political actors in this respect. The study "cuts across" the reform debates often conducted within the UN and governments, which are guided by the limits to the terms of reference of individual UN bodies. It is not confined to aspects that fall directly within UNDP's terms of reference (Administrator and Executive Board / EB or Governing Council / GC): it also considers questions that are important for UNDP's effectiveness in the development field, but are the responsibility of the UN General Assembly, the Economic and Social Council (ECOSOC) or the UN Secretary-General.

The study proceeds from various assumptions adopted during the debate on the effectiveness of international organizations based on the theory of political science and from specific conclusions drawn during the development debate on technical cooperation. A further aim is to contribute to the development of effectiveness criteria and to the conceptual debate on development policy.

From the various objectives it is clear that the study seeks to address different groups in both the academic and the practical development environment and in the policy sphere ("decision-makers"); in other words, an attempt is also made in this study to forge links between aspects of the debate which are otherwise regarded as largely unrelated.

Questions to be answered

In line with the objectives referred to above, the study seeks to answer a number of questions:

1. In the theoretical debate in this study on the basis of political science the main question is what pointers it includes that enable factors and criteria of relevance to the effectiveness of international organizations to be identified.

2. When analysing the debate on technical cooperation, the study mainly considers two questions:

- What role can and should TC play in development cooperation in the future?
- Can specific conclusions be drawn from the international TC debate that include pointers to the possible substance of TC or to appropriate functions to be performed by multilateral donors in this sphere? This question is important primarily in the context of conceptual aspects of UNDP and substantive dimensions of the UNDP reform process.

3. The study focuses on five questions concerning the reform of UNDP:
   - What stage has the debate on the reform of UN development cooperation as a whole reached, and what is its relevance to UNDP?
   - What is in most urgent need of reform, and what are the main challenges for UNDP? Existing shortcomings and current reform plans and initiatives are to be considered in this context.
   - What reforms have hitherto been initiated in the 1990s, and how should they be rated? The aim here is both to take stock of reforms that are planned or have already been undertaken and to determine whether sufficient progress has so far been made in reforming UNDP.
   - What changes and reforms - if necessary in addition to the reforms already launched - might UNDP undergo to alleviate current problems and to enable account to be taken of recent conclusions drawn during the TC debate?
   - How should the political chances of establishing a more effective UNDP be rated, and what are the prospects of reforms succeeding?

Although the study touches on questions and aspects relating to UNDP's internal organization and management, it will not focus on these subjects.

For the purposes of the study a further substantive restriction is appropriate and necessary. The United Nations' relief and emergency aid and its relationship with long-term development cooperation is a substantively and institutionally difficult issue, which also affects UNDP. Although this debate is not ignored here, it is mentioned only where necessary. A satisfactory and more thorough discussion of this issue is not therefore possible in this study.

Finally, it should be emphasized that the study is not comparative in design and does not therefore make any comparisons with bilateral or other multilateral donors. This needs to be stressed because industrialized countries are calling for extensive and sometimes excessive reforms and efforts from UNDP and the UN as a whole and often express conflicting expectations (such as calls for improved efficiency on the one hand and for procurement orders or staffing decisions in favour of their own nationals on the other) that would be politically unacceptable at national level and cannot or can hardly be fulfilled in practice.

The study focuses on the 1990s. It has been possible to take account of events in the UN and UNDP reform debate until the end of August 1997. Decisions taken by UNDP's Executive Board up to and including January 1998 have not fundamentally changed the overall picture of the UNDP process.[1]

Structure

The objectives and questions that have been presented determine the structure of the study. This introduction is followed by three main chapters (II, III and IV) and an annex.

Chapter II considers the theoretical and conceptual foundations and attempts to develop analytical and assessment criteria on the basis of two strands of discussion and to find general references for the classification of the empirical subject of the study. The first part of the chapter (II.1) considers the effectiveness of international organizations. The second (II.2) concerns the debate on the role of technical cooperation. It begins by looking at the basic shortcomings of technical cooperation and then considers approaches to solving the current problems.

Chapter III covers the reform debate and the measures being taken to reform UN development cooperation, and especially UNDP. Section III.1 begins by reviewing the debate on the reform of UN development cooperation as a whole. It analyses the most serious problems and evaluates the current state of the reform debate and reforms undertaken in this area. Section III.2 provides an analysis of UNDP's main shortcomings and weaknesses in the 1990s. This analysis of the problems forms an important starting point and basis of assessment for the subsequent stages of the study. This is followed by a rough appraisal of concepts and initiatives that have been geared to a reform of UNDP in the past (section III.3). UNDP reform measures in the 1990s are carefully analysed in section III.4. The various reform elements and their implementation are described, discussed and evaluated. This is followed by the development of elements that are also appropriate and necessary if a more effective UNDP is to be created (section III.5). The aim here is to profile a UNDP that is strengthened and innovative in development policy terms. Section III.6 considers the positions and interests of the main actors vis-à-vis UNDP and its reform process. Finally, in section III.7, options and scenarios for UNDP's future development are outlined and discussed, the emphasis being on UNDP's future environment and on variants of change and reform.

Chapter IV draws conclusions from the whole study for the debate on the effectiveness of international organizations, the debate on technical cooperation and the reform of UN development cooperation and UNDP.

The annex gives a brief description of the main features and structure of UNDP. This description is suitable as an introduction to the general discussion of UNDP. It has been included as an annex to ease the burden on the part devoted to analysis. The annex also contains three basic documents on UNDP (see contents) to which reference is frequently made in the text.

3 Research and Literature

Research and literature on the effectiveness of international organizations on the basis of the theory of political science

The research and literature on the debate on international organizations can be roughly described as follows: the theoretical debate on international organizations forms part of the debate on international relations. It is treated in the literature predominantly in this form; in other words, chapters or something similar are often devoted to international organizations in the literature. There are also various case studies of international organizations. Little attention has generally been paid in the past to the question of their effectiveness.

The results of the theoretical debate on international organizations are relatively well documented and appraised. A good review of the current state of the debate can be found in the papers or works by Archer (1992), Groom / Taylor (eds.) (1990), Kohler-Koch (ed.) (1989), Krasner (ed.) (1983), Rittberger (1994) and Rittberger (ed.) (1993). The journal *International Organization* is a particularly important fund of information on the state of research. Extensive empirical material can be found in the several volumes of the *Yearbook of International Organizations.*[1]

A good overview of the present state of the debate and of focal areas of research in the whole discipline of international relations in the 1990s is provided by Burchill et al. (1996), Lehmkuhl (1996) and Meyers (1994), among others.

Research and literature on technical cooperation

The research and literature on the debate on technical cooperation in the context of development policy can be divided into two strands. The first covers practical experience at project level, i.e. it concerns individual projects, programmes, countries, etc. of which evaluations and other studies have been made. There are many studies at this practical level. Studies of this kind have been partly evaluated in cross-section analyses.[2] The majority of studies geared to the practical side were commissioned, financed or carried out by the institutions concerned.

The second strand includes the debate on development policy, which avails itself of practical experience but largely abstracts from it. It consists of general papers on the debate concerning the conception of development policy or specifically the TC debate, examples being the studies by Cassen (1994), Berg (1993), Bossuyt / Laporte / van Hoek (1995), Betz (1996) and Brüne (1996).

Research and literature on the debate on the reform of the United Nations' development cooperation

In view of the actors involved and the intricate areas covered the whole debate on the reform of the United Nations is extremely complex and touches on a wide range of politically sensitive issues and problems. The UN's development cooperation, or its operational activities in the area of development policy, is only one of various topics in this context (e.g. peace-keeping, peace-making, human rights).

Independent research and literature fail to cope adequately with this complex situation in many respects. This means that, while many publications and studies have been devoted to the overall reform of the United Nations, there are many wide gaps where the UN's development cooperation is concerned, one reason being that many analyses consider the UN's economic and social fields rather superficially, distinctions that should be made between operational and non-operational development activities are not adequately respected and fundamental organizational issues (e.g. the relationship between the UN and its specialized agencies) are not considered in sufficient depth in many studies.

Many, though not all, of the most important publications and studies of the debate on the reform of the United Nations' development cooperation are directly linked to the UN, having, for example, been commissioned by the UN or written by insiders.

A good overview or analysis of the whole subject of the reform of the United Nations can be found, for example, in the papers or works of the following: Bertrand (1986, 1993b, 1995), Childers / Urquhart (1994), Dicke (1995), Hüfner (ed.) (1994) and Hüfner (ed.) (1995).

The few good analyses of the debate on the reform of UN development cooperation include Beigbeder (1995), Singer / Jolly (1995), Gwin / Williams (1996), Renninger (1987), Nordic UN Project (1991b, 1996) and Rudischhauser (1997). Much of the Jackson Report (DP/5) also remains topical. Other, older studies of UN development cooperation that similarly provide important background information and insights are the paper by Kirdar (1966) and the volume edited by Mangone (ed.) (1966).

Further important sources of information on the process and substance of the reforms are the many mimeographed documents and official records of the United Nations, which contain a wealth of material on the subject; they include the UN Secretary-General's progress reports on the implementation of resolutions adopted by the General Assembly[3] and the UN Secretariat's annual report on the United Nations' operational activities in the development policy field.

Research and literature on UNDP and its reform

Independent studies have hitherto paid relatively little attention to UNDP and the debate on its reform. Apart from showing some interest in the *Human Development Report*, most donor countries, research institutes and groups engaged in the debate on development policy have failed to consider UNDP in any depth. There are very few studies of the type that has been drawn up on bilateral and other multilateral donors (e.g. German development cooperation, the EU or the World Bank group). However, a small number of studies on UNDP, its activities and various aspects of its reform have been commissioned by the UNDP itself or by individual UN member countries. A problem often encountered in this context is that studies focus on the responsibility of a given actor (e.g. the UNDP Administrator's or UNDP Executive Board's reform efforts) without forging a link with the processes of change initiated by the UN General Assembly and the UN Secretary-General.

The following publications and studies provide an overview of the state of the debate and various relevant aspects of UNDP and its reform: Centre for Development Research (1996), Danida (1991c, 1996b), Sahlmann / Blank (1995), and Ahlberg / Løvbraek (1985).

Added to this, numerous official UNDP papers have been published as mimeographed documents or official records; UNDP also publishes various series, annual reports and individual publications. Many other official documents - particularly of the UN Secretary-General, the UN General Assembly and ECOSOC - refer directly or indirectly to UNDP. Finally, there are innumerable internal UNDP documents (memoranda, opinions, drafts, etc.), which are not as a rule freely accessible.

4 Explanations and Definitions

Agreement needs to be reached on the meaning of a number of basic concepts if this study is to be understood. The terms "UN and UN system", "economic and social field", "operational and non-operational activities / UN development cooperation", "UN funds and programmes", "reform" and "country categories related to development cooperation" will therefore be briefly explained or defined. The terms "effectiveness" and "technical cooperation" will not be defined here, since this is done in some depth in sections II.1 and II.2. Where development cooperation terms are used without further explanation, reference should be made to the definitions given by the Development Assistance Committee (DAC) of the Organization for Economic Cooperation and Development (OECD);[1] for terminology relating to the UN and UN system the explanations in the relevant works[2] should be consulted. A number of UNDP-specific terms relating to instruments, procedures and concepts are to be found in various glossaries that have appeared in UNDP publications.[3]

UN and UN system

The term "United Nations" (UN) covers only the UN's principal organs (General Assembly, Security Council, Economic and Social Council, Trusteeship Council, International Court of Justice, Secretariat) and their numerous special and subsidiary organs (e.g. the General Assembly's and ECOSOC's various committees, and such bodies as UNDP, the United Nations Children Fund / UNICEF, etc.).

In addition to the UN bodies referred to above, the term "UN system" embraces the 18 specialized agencies (including the World Bank group, International Monetary Fund (IMF), International Labour Organization (ILO), Food and Agriculture Organization (FAO), World Health Organization (WHO), United Nations Educational, Scientific and Cultural Organization (UNESCO) and United Nations Industrial Development Organization (UNIDO)). The specialized agencies are

Figure 1: Structure of the United Nation

Source: based on Ministry of Foreign Affairs (1996), p. 8; NGLS (1997), p.. xiii

not UN organs, but legally independent organizations, each with its own budget. Pursuant to the UN Charter,[4] they have a formally regulated relationship with the UN, although this gives the UN very little opportunity to influence them.[5]

Economic and social field

In UN terminology all the UN's development activities form part of the economic and social field, which is guided by the provisions of the UN Charter.[6] The economic and social field includes both operational and non-operational activities. It is, however, generally understood to be more comprehensive than development policy.

Operational and non-operational development activities / UN development cooperation[7]

In the sphere of development policy a distinction is normally made in the UN debate between non-operational and operational activities. Non-operational tasks are also known as normative functions.

- Non-operational activities are advisory, normative and standard-setting functions (e.g. resolutions on development policy objectives and strategies). The UN General Assembly and ECOSOC, for example, are primarily concerned with such questions. The UN world conferences in the 1990s have similarly focused on standard-setting and values.
- The UN's operational activities in the field of development cooperation are announced at the annual United Nations Pledging Conferences for Development Activities and undertaken by the UN funds and programmes. They are projects and programmes directly associated with development cooperation measures. The UN funds and programmes (UNDP, UNICEF, United Nations Population Fund (UNFPA), United Nations Environment Programme (UNEP), etc.) are particularly active in this sphere.

Unless otherwise stated, operational and non-operational activities as used in this study always mean activities forming part of the UN development policy.

The terms "UN development cooperation" and "operational development activities of the UN" are used as synonyms in this study.

UN funds and programmes

By analogy with United Nations terminology, the term "UN funds and programmes" means the operational development institutions listed by the UN General Assembly for participation in the annual UN Pledging Conferences for Development Activities. The five largest UN funds and programmes (in terms of financial volume) are UNDP, the World Food Programme (WFP), UNICEF, UNFPA and the Office of the UN High Commissioner for Refugees (UNHCR).[8]

Reform

In the United Nations context the term "reform" has an extremely wide range of meanings and connotations.[9] For the purposes of this study it will be taken to mean intended changes with greater effectiveness and/or efficiency as their goal. Ideally, these changes either develop in an evolutionary process or cause a relatively abrupt and comprehensive transformation as a result of a deliberate intervention. The changes may have been preceded by a learning process, or the reforms are primarily a reflection of adaptive behaviour.[10] The goal of reforms must be, qualitatively and/or quantitatively, to bring about a significant difference from the current situation; this is often a question of political assessment. Reforms may aim at different levels; a concept that differentiates various levels is developed in section II.1 and applied in this study.

Of particular importance for reforms are the political processes that bring about and accompany the changes, the effects, the results achieved and their evaluation.

Country categories related to development cooperation

In this study the term "developing countries" covers countries included by the DAC/OECD in the "DAC List of Aid Recipients" under the heading "Aid to Developing Countries and Territories"; in other words, what these countries receive can be recognized as official development assistance (ODA). The term "transforming countries" as used here comprises the other countries on the DAC list referred to above; although this group of countries also receive assistance that is statistically recorded, it is not recognized as ODA.[11]

The terms "donor", "recipient", "contributor" and "programme country" are also used in this study in line with international usage.[12]

- The term "donor" means a country or multilateral institution that provides aid within the framework of development cooperation.
- The term "recipient" means a country that is intended to benefit from development cooperation.
- In the UNDP context the term "contributor" means a country that contributes to the various financing options (core and non-core resources). Unlike many other development cooperation structures, UNDP receives contributions not only from industrialized countries but also from developing countries. There is thus a blend of "contributors" and "programme countries".
- "Programme countries" in the context of the debate on UNDP are countries where projects or programmes (often generally known as "interventions" in UNDP usage) are implemented. In the UNDP context there is no difference between "programme country" and "recipient country".

5 Methodological Approach and Sources

This study is based on various methodological approaches. They include the evaluation of primary and secondary sources and standardized and open interviews conducted during research trips; the standardized interviews were based on an interview guide. Most were fairly exhaustive, lasting 45 - 90 minutes; it was also possible to conduct such interviews with high-ranking representatives, especially at UNDP.

The chapter on the effectiveness of international organizations is based on the relevant literature, including in particular theoretical studies by political scientists and some theory-led empirical research work in this field.

The part concerning the debate on the conception of development policy / technical cooperation is based first and foremost on the evaluation of primary and secondary sources, meaning that, besides relevant studies on the subject, a number of pertinent documents drawn up by development institutions (the OECD's Development Assistance Committee, the World Bank, etc.) have been evaluated. These primary sources include, in particular, evaluations and cross-section evaluations of technical cooperation or certain aspects of technical cooperation. The findings of research studies (secondary sources) have also been evaluated and included. In addition, interviews on various topical aspects of this development debate were conducted with relevant experts or representatives of pertinent development institutions. They included representatives of the following institutions:

- the Overseas Development Council (ODC), Washington,
- the World Bank, Washington, and
- UNDP, New York.

The comments (especially those in section III.1) on the United Nations, the UN reform process and the operational development activities are based mainly on a wide range of primary sources (especially documents of the UN General Assembly, ECOSOC and the UN Secretariat) and the evaluation of relevant secondary literature. Interviews were also conducted with representatives of the UN Secretariat[1] and various operational UN bodies (the United Nations Office for Project Services (UNOPS) and the United Nations Development Fund for Women (UNIFEM)).

The chapter on UNDP is based on the evaluation particularly of primary sources, some secondary sources and numerous interviews with representatives of UNDP, representatives of various governments and experts from a number of development institutions.

The primary sources are UNDP's official documents, which appear in UN publications, and many internal documents. The examination of a wide range of relevant internal documents was particularly helpful since it made for a far better understanding of the problems relating to many aspects of the subject and gave access to various substantive positions.

The interviews conducted within the UNDP administration and with representatives of the member states on the UNDP Executive Board are also particularly important. They concentrated on the following aspects, possibly depending on the specific functions of the interviewee (e.g. with the focus on financial resources or evaluations):

- questions of principle as regards UNDP's tasks and functions,
- UNDP's main shortcomings,
- current reform efforts,
- any additional reforms required,
- UNDP's external relationship with the UN's other bodies and its specialized agencies.

UNDP staff members from all relevant organizational units were interviewed.[2] At UNDP's managerial level lengthy interviews were conducted not only with the Administrator but also with two Assistant Administrators and various high-ranking advisers.

Representatives of 12 of the member states represented on the Executive Board were interviewed.[3] In particular, it proved possible to interview the representatives of all but one[4] of the members providing the President[5] and Vice-Presidents[6] of the Executive Board in 1997 on behalf of their respective groups of countries:

- Argentina,
- People's Republic of China,
- France,
- Germany,
- Indonesia,
- Japan,
- Norway,
- Romania,
- Sweden,
- United Kingdom,
- USA and
- Zambia.

An interview was also conducted with the representative of Denmark, which, though not a member of the Executive Board in 1997, pursues a particularly active UNDP policy as a donor country.

Part II Theoretical and Conceptual Foundations

1 Effectiveness of International Organizations

1.1 Introduction

This section considers the effectiveness of international organizations (IOs). Particular account will be taken in this context of the debate on the theory of political science and on international relations as a discipline. The main aim is to find pointers to help answer the following question: what conditions and criteria relevant to the effectiveness of IOs can be identified?

Identifying and systematizing factors that are, or may be, important for the effectiveness of IOs is particularly relevant as an analytical framework for the empirical study of UN development cooperation and of UNDP.

The state of the general debate among political scientists on IOs can be considered no more than very briefly in this study.[1] It must generally be regarded as unsatisfactory, however. With the existing approaches (see Figure 2) it has so far proved impossible adequately to cover and explain the actual situation; a convincing and closed theory or conception does not yet exist. This is due to many factors. The number of possible significant variables and plausible hypotheses influencing the existence, behaviour, effectiveness, impact, etc. of IOs is enormous. Existing IOs also differ widely (substance, goals, members, etc.). Together with each organization's very specific environment, this makes general statements difficult. An added factor is that few empirical data are available to enable approaches to an explanation to be examined and verified.[2]

The most important innovative role in the debate since the early 1980s has been played by the *regime approach*, which can be ascribed to neo-institutionalism. Unlike older institutionalist studies, the regime debate differs fundamentally from legalistic or historical-descriptive analyses of institutions (Keck 1991, p. 635; Rittberger 1994, p. 85). In contrast, the regime analysis seeks

- to explain how cooperation between states is possible under conditions of international anarchy - *governance without government* (Müller 1995, p. 384; Lehmkuhl 1960, p. 255),
- to explain decision-making processes within regimes (Rittberger 1994, p. 85),
- to determine the effectiveness, impacts and output of regimes (Efinger et al. 1990, p. 264; Rittberger 1994, p. 85) and
- to define the proportion of international regimes as intervening variables in international relations (Wolf 1994, pp. 422 f).

Early research on IOs concentrated on their institutional origins, organizational development and objectives. It was generally regarded as descriptive and lacking in theory.[3] The main question as to the effectiveness of IOs and their impact on international relations (Gallarotti 1991, pp. 184 f.) has - with a few exceptions - been considered in any depth only in connection with the debate on international regimes, but so far inadequately even in this context.

Figure 2: Theoretical approaches to international organizations

Realistic approaches	Cooperation and globalization approaches	Structuralist approaches
- Realism - Neo-realism	- (Neo-)functionalism - Federalism - Transactionism - Analysis of interdependence - Globalism - Multilateralism - (Neo-)institutionalism	- Marxism - Imperialism - Dependence theories

1.2 International Organizations and Factors Influencing Their Effectiveness

1.2.1 Premises and Concept of Effectiveness

Premises

The following comments on the effectiveness of international organizations are based on three premises in particular.

- The theoretical debate has hitherto paid too little attention to the effectiveness of international organizations (Archer 1992; Groom / Taylor (eds) 1990; Rittberger 1994). This is true both of factors that influence effectiveness positively and of factors that influence it negatively.[4] What studies there are are often geared to specific organizational factors or focus on certain dimensions of effectiveness.[5]
- A thorough analysis of factors influencing effectiveness may help to enable a number of general and abstracting statements on IOs to be made. They will make it possible for pointers to be given to political decision-making processes and so to policy formulation. Expectations of possible findings should not be pitched too high, however, since IOs and their effectiveness are not determined by automatic processes.
- A general answer cannot, on the other hand, be given to the question: how effective are international organizations? Their effectiveness varies widely in quantitative and qualitative terms. In each case a complex package of possible factors and different environmental conditions has to be analysed.

Concept of Effectiveness

If the analysis is to be understood, the term "effectiveness" needs to be defined. In general, effectiveness can be taken to mean the extent to which a goal is achieved or

> "*(...) simply a measure of the role that institutions play as determinants of the content of individual and collective behavior.*"[6]

In this study international organizations will be described as effective if they are able to bring about behavioural changes in actors, to contribute to goal attainment or to influence the structures for controlling and processing the policy environment.

Besides the question whether the goals pursued are attained (output), the relationship between goals and the means used to attain them (input) is of interest. However, this dimension of the appropriateness of the means used is normally distinguished from effectiveness by the term *efficiency*.

1.2.2 Levels of and Factors Influencing Effectiveness

The effectiveness of an international organization depends on certain factors. These factors are also of crucial importance for the quality and degree of goal attainment. In the following the factors that appear relevant to the effectiveness of IOs will be identified and discussed. An attempt will thus be made to systematize and complement the conclusions found in the literature (see also Box 1). The conceptual framework sought in this way is summarized in Figure 3.

The various factors influencing effectiveness will be ascribed typologically to one of the following three levels:

- a conception level,
- a structure and policy level and
- an administration and implementation level.

These three levels are explained and discussed in greater depth below.

Box 1: Typologization of the effectiveness of international organizations

The authors who have attempted to contribute to the typologization of factors influencing the effectiveness of international organizations include Young, Dicke and Haas:

I. Young seeks *"... factors that enhance or diminish the role of institutions as determinants of behavior at the international level."* (Young 1992, p. 175). He identifies a total of seven factors:
   (1) *"The effectiveness of international institutions varies directly with the ease of monitoring or verifying compliance with their principal behavioral prescriptions."*
   (2) *"The effectiveness of international institutions is a function of the robustness of the social-choice mechanisms they employ."*
   (3) *"The effectiveness of international institutions varies directly with the stringency of acknowledged rules governing changes in their substantive provisions."*
   (4) *"The effectiveness of international institutions varies directly with the capacity of governments of members to implement their provisions."*
   (5) *"Sharp asymmetries in the distribution of power (in the material sense) among participants circumscribe the effectiveness of international institutions."*
   (6) *"The effectiveness of international institutions varies directly with the level of interdependence among the participants."*
   (7) *"International institutions cannot remain effective for long after the erosion or collapse of their intellectual substructures."*

II. Taking the UN as his example, Dicke (1994, p. 310) makes a distinction between the following dimensions, to which he again ascribes various factors:
   (1) internal organizational structure,
   (2) member states and
   (3) international system.

III. On the basis of three types (setting, power and behaviour) Haas (1990, pp. 63 ff.) discusses a number of variables that account for the differences among IOs. They are:
   (1) *Setting*
      - *ideological consensus,*
      - *representation,*
      - *autonomy of secretariat,*
      - *status of experts.*
   (2) *Power*
      - *revenue base,*
      - *administration,*
      - *monitoring of compliance.*
   (3) *Behaviour*
      - *voting,*
      - *budgeting,*
      - *personnel recruitment,*
      - *role of NGOs,*
      - *leadership of executive head.*

Conception Level

The conception level concerns the general principles and objectives of an international organization and of the area of policy in which it is, or seeks to be, effective. Three factors are relevant at this level: (1) ideologies and values, (2) structure of the member states' interests and (3) adaptability and capacity for reform.

1. Ideologies and values may be the decisive fundamental requirement. Questions concerning the member states' agreement or disagreement on values play a decisive role in this context. It can be assumed, for example, that in many problem areas of international policy the closer an international organization comes to universal membership, the less consensus there will be on values. There is thus more agreement on values in a human rights organization at regional level in Europe or sub-Saharan Africa than at international level in the UN framework. The debates on development policy at UN level in the 1970s and 1980s were relatively ineffective because fundamental political disputes did not permit a consensus to be reached between the major political groupings.

   It can therefore be argued that conditions for IOs to be effective tend to be more favourable where they operate on a relatively homogeneous basis in terms of ideologies and values.[7]

2. The structure of the member states' interests may influence or dominate the effectiveness of an IO in very different ways. An attempt to pursue selective interests of individual member states or groups within an IO may lead to its legitimacy being undermined or questioned, thus impairing its effectiveness.[8]

   A completely different variant has the hegemonic position of a country or a group of members possibly improving an international organization's effectiveness through the assertion of their interests. In terms of theoretical approaches to hegemonic stability, then, one premise must be that IOs can emerge and be effective primarily when there is a *hegemon* (state or coalition of states) to bear at least a disproportionate share of the cost of institutionalization (Keohane 1989, pp. 74 ff.). This may partly compensate for the structural disadvantages of IOs as compared to nation states (no territorial base and no direct access to resources, especially financial resources).[9] A decline in hegemony may therefore result in instability as IOs weaken or collapse.

"*It leads, first and foremost, to the proposition that intergovernmental organizations will loom large at the international level if and when they serve the interests of powerful states or coalitions of states and these states provide adequate resources to support their initiatives.*"(Young 1995, p. 202)

Examples of IOs that are highly effective (a reference in this context to their ability to assert themselves externally and to their internal efficiency) because of hegemonic stability are the World Bank (IBRD and IDA) and the International Monetary Fund. The effectiveness of these institutions is largely based on the specific interests of some industrialized countries rather than the strength of the interests of all their member states. In contrast, there are, for example, no selective interests capable of being asserted in the context of UN development cooperation. In the past stalemate has been reached because the industrialized countries form an economically strong minority and the developing countries an economically weaker majority.

Power politics in the form of member states trying to assert their selective interests in or through international organizations may thus be an important factor in explaining effectiveness.

3. Effectiveness at conception level also very much depends on whether the various IOs succeed in adjusting to the changing environment as regards tasks and objectives and area of policy. This process may vary in form and intensity. Adaptability or capacity for reform is thus of prime importance. The aim is to ensure that an international organization is able to internalize new problems and tasks and that this ability is endorsed by the actors (especially the member states). Rigid structures that lead to pronounced inertia are thus a possible cause of the limited effectiveness of IOs.

The World Bank can again be cited as an example of an IO that is adaptable and capable of reform. While it was initially the World Bank's task to promote the reconstruction of countries devastated in the Second World War, it has increasingly become, especially since the 1960s, a development institution operating not in Western Europe but in developing countries. The development policy paradigms adopted by the World Bank in the 1970s, 1980s and 1990s have also undergone various fundamental changes.

Policy and Structure Level

The policy and structure level concerns fundamental aspects of an international organization's institutional structures, political decision-making processes and resource endowment. It is decisive for the operationalization of many aspects of the conception level.

A total of five factors are relevant to the policy and structure level: (1) representation, (2) decision-making, (3) degree of autonomy, (4) revenue base and (5) adaptability and capacity for reform.

1. Representation (Keohane 1990, p. 750) may influence effectiveness in various ways. Important dimensions in this context are (a) the number of states represented, (b) the criteria by which the status of the member states is determined (equality of states, economic strength, political significance, etc.) and (c) the involvement and status of non-governmental actors.

   The high degree of representation (i.e. number of states) in the UN's development bodies is, for example, seen as one of the main causes of their limited effectiveness (sections III.1 and III.2).

2. Where votes are weighted in the decision-making process, there is a close link to representation, since this may have a major impact on status and means of exercising influence. Equally common are other decision-making mechanisms based on different majorities or the principle of consensus, the aim of which is to preclude any inferiority in voting that is considered unacceptable by one or

more member states. An example of this is the "right of veto" which the permanent members of the UN Security Council enjoy.

3. The degree of autonomy indicates the extent to which an international organization is able to take decisions and alter its own rules without having to involve outsiders and obtain their consent.[10] Autonomy is therefore particularly important as regards an international organization's ability to assert itself, the binding nature of its activities and decisions and its flexibility in adjusting and undertaking reforms.

4. The revenue base is relevant to effectiveness and - indirectly at least - influences the IO's autonomy. The possible variants for financing an IO include a fixed scale of contributions to its annual budget, voluntary contributions, negotiated contributions, capital shares and tax revenue. This determines, for example, the scale of the IO's operational activities and how far they can be planned, which may in turn have an effect on the IO's ability to assert itself. Arguments along these lines are advanced to explain, for example, the relative weakness or strength of the UN's or World Bank's development cooperation.[11]

5. Effectiveness at policy and structure level also depends very largely on whether an IO succeeds in bringing about adjustment and reform processes with a view to maintaining or improving its effectiveness. This level thus entails processes of change that affect fundamental structural and political aspects and have been discussed here as determinants of effectiveness. In principle, another question of relevance in this context is whether a new international organization stands a better chance of coping successfully with the tasks and challenges it faces than a reformed international organization.[12]

Administration and Implementation Level

At the administration and implementation level the following four factors have a considerable bearing on effectiveness: (1) management/administration, (2) staff, (3) monitoring and evaluation and (4) adaptability and capacity for reform.

1. Where management and administration are concerned, the main aim is to identify management methods and administrative structures that permit and enable a high level of effectiveness to be achieved. This involves such aspects as organizational efficiency, the institutionalization of permanent learning mechanisms and administrative processes that cause little friction and consume little time.[13]

2. As regards staffing, effectiveness is influenced primarily by the selection of personnel. There are various options in this respect: an international organization may select its staff by reference to quality criteria, it may be guided by the nationality of candidates, or selection may give way to the secondment of staff by the member states. Many IOs (explicitly or implicitly) adopt a mixed approach. A criticism often levelled at the UN's development agencies, for example, is that too little importance is attached to qualifications when staff are selected (section III.1.).

3. Monitoring and evaluation are among the most important factors if it is to be possible to make case-by-case or ongoing checks and performance appraisals and to derive benefit from experience at all levels (conception, political planning and control and implementation). IOs may use monitoring and evaluation instruments in systematic and/or ongoing fashion or on a case-by-case basis, or they may do without them.

4. Effectiveness at administration and implementation level in turn depends very largely on whether an IO succeeds in carrying adjustment and reform processes at this level with a view to maintaining or improving effectiveness.

Adaptability and Capacity for Reform as a Cross-section Dimension of the Effectiveness of International Organizations

As shown above, adaptability and capacity for reform are of the utmost importance for the effectiveness of international organizations. This is true both of the various levels discussed above and of an international organization's overall effectiveness. An unchanging international organization cannot continue to be effective in a changing environment. Although goals and tasks, structures and political processes and management and administration are different levels, they are all under pressure to change. Adaptability and capacity for reform may therefore be seen as one of the main cross-section dimensions.

However, adaptability and capacity for reform cannot be ends in themselves. In the final analysis it is only in combination with other factors that they should indicate whether effectiveness can or should be improved on the basis of potential for adaptation and reform. They thus form an important and necessary precondition for the effectiveness of an international organization. In themselves, on the other hand, they say nothing about the direction and envisaged objective of the changes. Substantive features and orientation of reforms are therefore be among the main elements that ultimately remain essential for evaluation.

The debate on the theory of IOs on the basis of political science has so far paid little attention to adaptability and capacity for reform. Ernst B. Haas's study *When Knowledge is Power* (Haas 1990) is an important exception[14] in that it analyses different models of IOs on the basis of the distinction Haas introduces between adaptation and learning.[15] Although the informative value of his research is relatively limited where his goal is concerned,[16] Haas can be credited with playing a major role in the introduction of typological questions and differentiations and in the inclusion of certain central aspects of the subject in subsequent studies.[17]

Changes and reforms of IOs are complex processes, which may take many different forms. The only examples that will be given here are the UN on the one hand and the EC, or EU, on the other. Since it was founded in 1945, the UN has not undergone a comprehensive reform in the sense of a change of constitution through a formal reform of its Charter.[18] Nonetheless, the UN is engaged in a permanent process of change. As Dicke has said:

> "*Irrespective of whether and to what extent there will be a revision of the Charter in the foreseeable future, the organization's capacity for reform in the sense of its adaptation to new and growing tasks can be seen as one of the most important criteria of its effectiveness.*" (Dicke 1994, p. 362)

The EC, or EU, on the other hand, has not only concluded supplementary treaties on the accession of new Member States but has in the past shown itself capable of making other changes which have altered its institutional structures fundamentally (treaties on common institutions and direct elections to the European Parliament, the Single European Act establishing the European Union, etc.) (Rittberger 1994, p. 92).

The range of IOs is on the whole extremely wide when it comes to processes of change. Adaptation or reform may be slow, incremental and lacking in transparency, or it may be transparent and explicit as a result of decisions on redefinition or reorganization. All international organizations are subject to such processes.

1.3 Conclusions for the Study

The formation of a theory on international organizations based on political science is generally characterized by a low degree of generalization. To a limited extent the theoretical debate permits deductions and pointers for political analysis and practice. With the aid of the development and discussion of the three levels presented above (conception level, structure and policy level and administration and implementation level) and the various factors influencing effectiveness this study attempts to identify, against the background of the theoretical debate, dimensions and criteria that have an informative

Figure 3: Factors influencing the effectiveness of international organizations

Level	Relevant factors	Possible variations of degree
Conceptual level	- Ideologies and values - Structure of member states' interests - Adaptability and capacity for reform	- Consensus or dissension among the member states on values - Selective or common interests - Ability to internalize new tasks or inertia
Structure and policy level	- Representation - Decision-making - Degree of autonomy - Revenue base - Adaptability and capacity for reform	- Equality of member states or qualifying features (based on economic strength, population, etc.); only governmental or also non-governmental representation - Simply majority, qualified majority or consensus; qualifying voting features (i.e. weighting of votes based on economic strength, population, etc.) - Degree of rule-changing possibilities with regard to own international organization - Annual budget, voluntary contributions, capital shares or tax revenue - Ability to internalize new challenges or inertia
Administration and implementation level	- Management / administration - Staff - Monitoring and evaluation - Adaptability and capacity for reform	- Centralized or decentralized organizational structures - Staff selected on basis of quality criteria or nationality or seconded by member states - Systematic or case-by-case/ad hoc account taken or neglect of experience - Ability to internalize new challenges or inertia

value of kinds for IOs (categories of analysis). They will prove useful in practice in that they are able to provide points of departure for political analyses and political evaluations.

The debate on the factors influencing effectiveness has shown that the adaptability of IOs and their capacity for reform play a special role at both conception level and structure and policy level and also at administration and implementation level. The theoretical debate on IOs on the basis of political science has hitherto paid little attention to this dimension. It is an aspect to which particular attention will be paid during this study.

2 The Development Policy Debate on the Role of Technical Cooperation

2.1 Introduction

Background

Since the first half of the 1990s there has been an intensive international debate on the fundamental purpose, shortcomings, effectiveness and future role of technical cooperation (TC). This debate raises questions that touch on the whole of development cooperation and the related debates[1] on general conditions, successes and failures, the effectiveness and efficiency of development cooperation, etc.

In the debate on technical cooperation two papers have attracted particular attention and respect: the study *Rethinking Technical Co-operation, Reforms for Capacity-Building in Africa* by Elliot J. Berg (Berg 1993), published in 1993, which is closely associated with UNDP's Regional Bureau for Africa, and the address entitled *Capacity-Building: the Missing Link in African Development* given by Edward Jaycox (Jaycox 1993), Vice-President (African Region) of the World Bank, in May 1993.

UNDP and people who can be attributed to the UNDP environment have taken a very active part in the international TC debate over and above the Berg study. Examples are the joint UNDP/World Bank paper *Toward Improving the Effectiveness of Technical Cooperation* (UNDP / World Bank 1995), UNDP's co-organizer role in the high-level seminar *Improving the Effectiveness of Technical Co-operation in the 1990s* (OECD 1995b) and the contributions to the debate by Fukuda-Parr (1995) and Sirleaf (1996). Through the NaTCAP (*National Technical Cooperation Assessment and Programme*) process[2] UNDP has also played a major part in ensuring that since the mid-1980s many developing countries have taken stock of their institutional capacities and analysed the role of TC. In many countries this has revealed shortcomings in TC.

The international TC debate cooperation is particularly important for UNDP. It is one of the leading TC donors and performs vital co-ordinating functions for the whole UN system in this sphere. Any criticism of TC is thus a criticism of UNDP. UNDP in particular must therefore seek to reform and adjust to take account of new findings on development policy.

Objectives

This section sets out to evaluate the current international debate on technical cooperation in terms of the following questions:

1. What role can and should TC play in the context of development cooperation in the future? This question is of prime importance for the present study, since UNDP's tasks are geared to TC. The international TC debate can therefore be seen as an overarching conceptual frame of reference that is also applicable to UNDP.

2. Can inferences that include pointers to possible substance and to appropriate functions and instruments of multilateral donors in the TC sphere be drawn from the international TC debate? This question is relevant primarily to conceptual aspects of UNDP and

substantive dimensions of the UNDP reform process and will be taken up again later in this study.

Before the above questions can be discussed, the general state and most important substantive aspects of the TC debate need to be considered.

2.2 Foundations for the Debate on Technical Cooperation

2.2.1 Definition and Clarification

In the international TC debate there is general agreement on what is meant by technical cooperation.[3] A sound foundation is laid by the definition in *Principles for New Orientations in Technical Co-operation* published by the OECD in 1991:

> "*Technical Co-operation (TC) encompasses the whole range of assistance activities designed to develop human resources through improvement in the level of skills, knowledge, technical know-how and productive aptitudes of the population in a developing country. A particularly important objective of technical co-operation is institutional development based on human resources development, that is, to contribute to the strengthening and improved functioning of the effective management and operation of an economy and of society more generally, from government ministries, local administrative structures, over hospitals and schools to private enterprises. Human resources development is a prerequisite for institution-building. Capacity-building for improved policy analysis and development management by the core government institutions is of special importance.*" (OECD 1995a, p. 1)

Reduced to an even shorter formula, technical cooperation can be taken to mean development cooperation activities that seek to improve the skills of people and institutions.

Some donors make a distinction between technical assistance (TA) and technical cooperation (TC) (Berg 1993, pp. 43 ff.; Elshorst 1995, p. 296). Where the choice of term is based on a conscious distinction, technical assistance means an activity intended to support and accompany investment, especially through financial cooperation (FC). In this case TC paves the way for or accompanies FC and is consequently subordinate to it (Mitzlaff / Vermehren 1993, p. 582). Technical cooperation, on the other hand, places the emphasis on the independent role and function of measures designed to develop human resources; in some cases it is therefore also known as *free-standing technical co-operation*. While Berg[4] maintains that it is now rare for a distinction to be made between technical assistance and technical cooperation, Elshorst sees it as one of the main outcomes of the TC debate.

> "*Critical discussion of technical cooperation in international fora over recent years had produced some key results, one of which being the distinction between technical assistance, which is understood as a means of preparing and accompanying investments, and technical cooperation, which is defined as the joint effort to improve institutions and build capacities, a venture worthwhile in itself and which goes beyond the confines of investment only.*" (Elshorst 1995, p. 296)

This distinction also has some similarity with that made by the World Bank, although the latter proceeds from the concept of technical assistance.[5] It distinguishes two forms of TA: first, the use of consultants and advisers to fill short-term gaps in local capacities; second, TA in *institutional development* (ID),[6] meaning a process designed for the long term.

The conference on *Improving the Effectiveness of Technical Co-operation in the 1990s* jointly organized by the OECD, the World Bank and UNDP (Paris, 1994) similarly attempted to clarify the definitions. The participants in the conference agreed to specify technical cooperation and interpret it more narrowly along the lines suggested by UNDP Administrator James Speth. It was consequently defined as "*support for national capacity-building*".[7]

This study will be guided by a narrower definition of technical co-operation, which assumes that it makes its own contribution to the improvement of human and institutional resources; TC contributions in support of FC are not therefore meant unless otherwise stated.

The term *institution-building* is often used in the literature to mean the same as *capacity-building* or something similar. To clarify the situation, it is therefore worth briefly considering what the two terms capacity-building and institution-building[8] have in common and how they differ. By analogy with the definition undertaken by UNDP,[9] it will be assumed here that the terms institution-building and capacity-building are not identical in meaning; however, they have a number of common features. In general, institution-building is more closely geared to the development of a given institution and so fairly specific as an intervention. Capacity-building, on the other hand, also deliberately seeks to involve the environment of the institutions concerned. Capacity-building is thus broader and more ambitious than institution-building and so may also be more diffuse and less transparent and entail more risks.

> "*Although institution-building and capacity-building do not refer to identical activities, there is considerable overlap between them. Institution-building refers to the development of particular institutions, their human resources, equipment, organization, management and administration. Capacity-building is concerned with a broader set of activities, involving support for human resource development, organizational strengthening and the emergence of an overall policy environment that is conducive to development.*" (DP/1992/23, p. 3)

2.2.2 Instruments, Characteristics and Scale of Technical Cooperation

Together with financial cooperation, technical cooperation forms the instrumental foundations of international development cooperation. TC is mostly provided in the form of grants, the grant element thus being

100%. However, the World Bank in particular also uses credits for *free-standing technical cooperation* in its funding activities (Raphaeli 1996, pp. 226 f.); this means that the developing countries concerned cannot obtain this TC free of charge.[10] Most bilateral TC consists of tied contributions (UNDP / World Bank 1995, p. 18), the developing countries concerned being required to use services (primarily personnel) and goods from the donor country. Multilateral TC, on the other hand, is not, as a rule, tied.

Various instruments are used in TC, particular among them being the following (OECD 1995a, p. 1):

- training schemes,
- the provision of national or expatriate experts,
- policy and technical advice,
- assistance with the preparation and carrying out of studies and surveys,
- contributions to science, research and technological development.

The instruments of TC are used at various levels of intervention, normally in different combinations. A distinction can be made between the following levels (Weiter 1995, pp. 310 f.):

- an individual level, where the aim is to improve the skills of one or more people,
- an organizational level, at which various measures are taken to improve the activities of the organizations concerned, and
- a structural level, where the emphasis is on promoting coordination among various institutions and groups.

TC plays a special role primarily in countries that have limited potential in terms of human resources and a weak institutional structure. Countries in sub-Saharan Africa are therefore the most important partners for this type of development cooperation (Sirleaf 1996, p. 59; Jaycox 1993; World Bank 1996a, p. 1). The significance of TC in sub-

Saharan Africa has grown in recent years not least because of the structural adjustment processes[11] that began in the 1980s and the institutional requirements that accompanied them.

Each year more than US $ 4 billion goes to Africa in the form of TC.[12] The arithmetical TC amounts per inhabitant are substantial in some cases. In the Cape Verde Islands, Botswana, Madagascar, Djibouti and the Seychelles, for example, they range from US $ 46 to 134 (Sirleaf 1996, p. 59). The number of expatriate experts working in sub-Saharan Africa is estimated at 80,000 (Bossuyt / Laporte / van Hoek 1995, p. 11).

At some US $ 12 to 18 billion, TC accounts for about a third of all official development assistance (ODA), which amounted to US $ 58.9 billion in 1995. Originally, the UN system emerged as the most important source of technical cooperation; today the lead in this area is taken by the bilateral donors (DP/1990/9, p. 78).

In 1995 TC accounted for US $ 14.3 billion of the 40.6 billion contributed in bilateral development cooperation (net disbursements) (OECD 1997a, pp. A2 and A11). The largest TC donors are the USA (US $ 2.6 billion), France (US $ 2.5 billion), Germany (US $ 2.5 billion) and Japan (US $ 2.4 billion). All other bilateral donors reported TC amounts usually well below US $ 1 billion (see the data in OECD 1997a, p. A11). Owing to the differences in the definition of TC, however, the comparability of these data with data provided by other development cooperation institutions is limited. In particular, the OECD data concern only free-standing technical cooperation based on grants; they do not therefore include, for example, TC measures in support of FC or TC on a credit basis (Berg 1993, p. 71).

The scale of the UN's TC can be put at about US $ 3 to 3.5 billion p.a. in the first half of the 1990s; TC data on the UN are primarily available from the ECOSOC's reports on *Operational Activities of the United Nations for International Development*. These reports reveal that UN expenditure on operational development cooperation activities in grant form totalled US $ 4.6 billion in 1994.[13] However, this figure does not consist entirely of TC contributions. Most WFP measures in particular comprise humanitarian activities (1994: US $ 1.01 billion); they are joined by humanitarian activities of other UN agencies (1994: US $ 253.3 million) (E/1996/64/Add. 2, p. 38). Assuming that most other measures consist of TC, we arrive at the above annual figure of US $ 3 to 3.5 billion.

The World Bank's tasks are primarily concerned with financial co-operation; nonetheless, a number of project components and specific measures must be ascribed to the TC spectrum. In past decades the World Bank has been able to expand its TC activities considerably, especially compared to UNDP. The volume of its TC was very small in the 1960s and was greatly increased in the 1970s, 1980s and 1990s.[14]

The World Bank puts the present scale of its TC at an average of 10% of funds disbursed. In the 1995 calendar year this was equivalent to US $ 1.9 billion. Of this, US $ 1.3 billion was used in connection with investment or economic reform programmes, the other US $ 0.6 billion being spent on individual TC projects (World Bank 1996, p. 45). In the past ten years the World Bank has increased spending on its own TC measures and on TC in support of FC (World Bank 1996a, p. 4; Raphaeli 1996, p. 225). In the World Bank reform document *Strategic Compact* (World Bank 1997b, 1997c) submitted in 1997 it formulated objectives for further expansion in the field of TC.

All in all, the range of TC donors has widened significantly in the past few decades. The international development banks are also becoming increasingly active in technical cooperation.

2.3 State of the Debate on Technical Cooperation

2.3.1 Criticism of Technical Cooperation

Technical cooperation has been under pressure since the late 1980s. While the Cassen Report[15] was relatively moderate in its criticism, many other observers and practitioners of the donor institutions have been far more outspoken in questioning the usefulness of TC in the 1990s.

The most important criticism levelled at TC is that it is often not effective enough. In sub-Saharan Africa its limited effectiveness is particularly evident from its failure to develop adequate local structures in the various countries. TC's actual goal of making itself "superfluous" by establishing independent, functioning institutions and structures has not been achieved.

Scepticism about the effectiveness of TC is expressed primarily by the donors themselves. Like the World Bank, many donor institutions, donor countries and developing countries take a negative view:

> "*Outcomes have varied widely, but overall the efficacy and cost-effectiveness of TA has been disappointing, especially in sub-Saharan Africa.*" (World Bank 1996a, p. 4)

A few conclusions drawn in World Bank evaluations will be given here as examples.[16] Of the 1,689 World Bank projects that were approved from 1971 to 1991 and sought to promote institutional development, only 29%, according to the Evaluation Department, made a substantial contribution to the project objective.[17] A 1997 evaluation referred to *"poor performance by free-standing technical assistance loans"* (Baser / Morgan 1997, p. i); only 19% of the measures concerned were rated satisfactory by this study.

Studies (UNDP 1995g, pp. 77 ff.; UNDP 1997d, pp. 109 ff.) on UNDP's project portfolio similarly indicate shortcomings and unsatisfactory results. The performance criteria of which they take account include institution-building, outputs, immediate objectives, impact on target groups and sustainability; project design is also evaluated. The statements in this UNDP study, which are based on an analysis with a number of weaknesses, place the majority of the projects in the medium evaluation range (of three possible options) where all criteria are concerned.[18]

Many evaluations of TC conclude not only that its effectiveness is limited or that it has no effect at all, but that in many cases it even helps to make the situation worse. Jaycox remarks:

> "*Now it's my contention that the donors and African governments together have in effect undermined capacity in Africa; they are undermining it faster than they are building it, or at least as fast.*"[19]

Examples and exemplary analyses of the use and effects of TC show how in need of adjustment are the existing structures and practical application of TC:

> "*In Bangladesh, for example, 25 projects funded by 15 different donors and undertaken in eight different ministries each set up its own administration, thereby contributing to high overhead costs because each donor preferred to negotiate bilaterally with a particular ministry. In such cases the identification of a project is really a collusive exercise between a donor and a supervising ministry, not an outcome of popular demand.*" (UNDP / World Bank 1995, pp. 18 f.)

The unfavourable assessments were backed by numerous evaluations and other studies. This is true of the information provided both by donor institutions and countries and by the developing countries concerned.[20]

There are many reasons for criticizing TC. The location (actor concerned, academic criticism, etc.), perspective ("donor" or "recipient") and empirical background determine what points and issues are referred to or emphasized. However, there is quite considerable overlapping or similarity in the criticisms voiced. Accordingly, the following factors can primarily be blamed for the lack of effectiveness or for counterproductive effects:[21]

- donor-driven system,
- input orientation,

- absence of strategic alignment,
- deficient project design,
- excessive employment of expatriate experts and advisers,
- insufficient cost-awareness and
- structural shortcomings in the recipient countries.

Before the factors referred to, which help to impair effectiveness, are discussed in greater depth, it should be pointed out that the criticism of TC - much of which this study endorses - is a statement of a general nature. This is not to deny the favourable effects of TC or, in the broader sense, of development cooperation as a whole. There is evidence both of success at the level of individual projects[22] and of positive contributions to development cooperation at more highly aggregated levels.[23] The main argument advanced here, on the other hand, is that one of TC's essential objectives has not been achieved despite partial successes: TC has not resulted in its being possible to develop local capacities, which are indispensable for the sustained success of the development process.

Donor-driven system

In many cases TC measures are attuned to the priorities, interests and logic of the various donors rather than those of the recipients. The inherent donor-driven system of TC is therefore one of the key problems.[24]

> "*Although one should avoid generalisations, much of the TC is donor driven rather than guided by well defined needs and priorities expressed by the recipient country. Projects are often generated from within aid agencies or from foreign experts in the field* (...)" (Bossuyt / Laporte / van Hoek 1995, p. 23)

There are many examples to show that, if this is accompanied by a lack of commitment and ownership[25] on the recipient side, the TC measure is very likely to fail.[26]

As TC measures are primarily needed in developing countries that have no more than weak structures (administration, know-how, etc.), the countries concerned do not as a rule have the necessary capacities to exercise any appreciable influence on individual TC measures, the priorities set or the form taken by the project. The countries of sub-Saharan Africa, where frequently more than 50% of investment projects are financed with development cooperation resources (Sirleaf 1996, p. 60), are particularly lacking in adequate structures for the relatively independent control of the planning, implementation and monitoring processes.

TC measures therefore often fail to conform to domestic priorities:[27] ownership of projects is consequently not very pronounced, or is non-existent. Recipient countries are often forced to play a passive role in these processes. Referring to UNDP, or the UN, Griffin and McKinley say curtly of the structure of the traditional TC system:

> "*The system was supply-driven: the agencies supplied the experts, UNDP paid the bills, and the developing countries were the passive recipients*." (Griffin / McKinley 1996, p. 12)

Input orientation

TC measures are often heavily input-oriented (Fukuda-Parr 1995, pp. 64 f.; Berg 1993, pp. 5 f.). The emphasis is not on the goal to be achieved but on what the donor is able to provide. This may have a major influence on the choice of problem areas and the solutions available.

The offer of TC is usually linked to employment of the donor country's or institution's experts and advisers. This may give rise to serious problems since, while expatriate experts (employed without a training component for local experts) may provisionally help to close any gap that may exist, they do not provide a lasting solution. Problems may also be caused by the employment of expatriate personnel even though local know-how is available.[28]

Components of TC projects that are meant to contribute to capacity- or institution-building are crucially important for the sustainability of the measures taken, since they are the actual structure-forming factor. Components of this kind are, however, often absent or play no more than a secondary role (Sirleaf 1996, p. 60).

Absence of strategic alignment

Many TC measures are not based on adequate conceptual ideas for integrating TC measures into more comprehensive development strategies. They are often small and very small measures that bear little or no relation to the identified development objectives.

> "*There has been a generalised 'lack of strategic vision and definition' of what these programmes were intended to achieve.*" (Bossuyt / Laporte / van Hoek 1995, p. 17)

Many TC projects are therefore fragmented and lack datum lines.[29] The effectiveness of many measures compared to the objectives set is also often barely discernible or cannot be gauged, since specific objectives or objectives that can be operationalized have not been formulated (Berg 1993, p. 15).

Deficient project design

The implementation and supervision of many TC measures are poor. This can be ascribed to deficient project design, which may have resulted in the measures being overly complex, too many actors being involved and a high degree of domestic management skills and capacities being required. The World Bank's experience, for example, has shown the following to be important dimensions of the problem (Baser / Morgan 1997, pp. 12 f.):

- inadequate consideration given to the environment,
- overly ambitious and complex goals set for TC measures,
- largely inappropriate strategies (given the environment and objectives),
- inappropriate methodological foundations for the design of TC,
- unsatisfactory management (especially as regards the involvement of local structures and capacities) and
- limited ability to relate the above factors one to another.

Excessive employment of expatriate experts and advisers

Much of the criticism levelled at TC is directly or indirectly associated with the employment of expatriate experts and advisers,[30] who usually come from the donor countries in connection with bilateral development cooperation. Jaycox describes and assesses the causes as follows:

> "*We supply technical assistance because we want our projects to succeed, but we do not trust local talent to do the job. We still believe that our projects and programmes are not going to succeed without a big injection of expatriate personnel. I consider this attitude to be both fatalistic and non-productive; it is seal-defeating in the long run.*" (Jaycox, in: OECD 1995b, p. 24)

Many experts from the various donor countries do indeed continue to be employed in the context of TC in the 1990s. While there was a serious shortage of suitable experts in most developing countries when development cooperation began in the 1960s, the situation, though varying from one region to another, is very different today. There are now numerous local experts who cannot find appropriate employment (Mezger / Urban / Warth 1994, p. 3). Mezger / Urban / Warth therefore conclude in their study that TC is in serious need of adjustment:

> *"TC represents a burden today, because it is partly maintained in its old form, although the context for which it was intended has changed radically in almost every country - from a situation in which there was a shortage of qualified local experts to one in which there is a surplus."* (Mezger / Urban / Warth 1994, p. 4)

The criticism of the practice of employing expatriate personnel for TC measures has various relevant aspects:

- Expatriate advisers and experts are expensive. It is estimated that 70 - 80% of TC funds are spent on them (Bossuyt / Laporte / van Hoek 1995, p. 11).
- The employment of expatriate advisers and experts often leads to glaring disparities between their incomes and those of local experts and civil servants in the developing countries concerned.[31] The ratio of local salaries to what international consultants receive is sometimes 1 : 500 (Baser / Morgan 1997, p. 22). Disparities between the salaries of expatriate staff and those of the counterpart's personnel may lead to problems and tensions within TC projects (Berg 1993, p. 9).
- The subsidiarity principle in development cooperation[32] is not respected, or respected no more than selectively, expatriate advisers and experts sometimes being employed even when local personnel are available.
- Expatriate personnel are comparatively less familiar with the environment (culture, language, etc.).
- The "tied" nature of potential experts and advisers seriously restricts the choice of candidates and may therefore result in suboptimal solutions, even with regard to the quality of the services provided.

Insufficient cost-awareness

Neither recipient nor donor countries are as a rule sufficiently aware of the costs involved in TC. Neither side is clearly accountable for the wide range of financial costs:

> "*Under the present conditions of aid dispensation, neither the donor nor the recipients really feel they are in charge* (...)" (Museveni 1995, p. 9)

In the past donors have paid little or no attention to effectiveness or goal achievement in relation to the use of funds. Where the various programme countries are concerned, one of the main problems is that TC is available free of charge; only in the rarest of cases has willingness to pay been examined or adequately considered as a dimension.

The donor institutions and the relevant institutions of the developing countries concerned often overlook important aspects in this context. It is frequently forgotten that (Sobhan 1995; Bossuyt / Laporte / van Hoek 1995, p. 11; UNDP / World Bank 1995, pp. 21 f.)

- TC causes direct costs when it is provided on the basis of credits,
- indirect costs are incurred as a result of counterpart activities (accommodation, absorption of local personnel in the administration of development cooperation, etc.) and
- opportunity costs play a part in connection with TC measures.

It should also be borne in mind that the comparatively high incomes of international consultants do not automatically guarantee high quality and effectiveness: *"Simply put, many high-priced TA personnel have done questionable work despite their high costs."* (Baser / Morgan 1997, p. 22)

Box 2: Eritrea and the international donor community: criticism of the present development cooperation model

Shortly after gaining its independence (1993), Eritrea demanded in unusually open and tough language that the donors agree to a relationship more akin to a partnership and abandon procedures and mechanisms that do nothing for development. The Eritrean government was particularly critical of technical cooperation.

At the first meeting of the Consultative Group for Eritrea set up by the World Bank, which was held in Paris in December 1994, the Eritrean government submitted a document entitled *"Partnership in Development"* (Government of Eritrea 1994). In it the Eritrean government, which is considered extremely "development-oriented", emphasizes its interest in any foreign aid as long as it does not harm the country's sovereignty and the independence of its decision-making. The document is highly critical of the following aspects of development cooperation:

- Partnership: the traditional relationship of partners in development cooperation *"(...) disregards the fact that the issues being addressed by external assistance are of equal, if not of greater, concern to the country being assisted, and that their resolution would be enhanced if it plays a focal role in articulating and prioritizing the problems and in designing and implementing their solutions. (...) This requires a fundamental reassessment and reformulation of relationship between the parties to reflect this new character."*
- Principles of technical cooperation: *"It is not on the question of indiscriminate assignment of expatriate personnel that we have reservations. In the extreme case, there is a tendency to field experts and gather them in project units outside the bureaucratic structure making little contribution to institution-building. Where this is not the case, expatriate personnel are still very expensive and use up a lot of aid money. (...) Ideally, funds earmarked for technical assistance should be directly transferred to the concerned country as budgetary support for it to decide how to spend it to build its capacity."*
- Provision of development cooperation: *"External assistance is usually delivered in tied forms. Tied external assistance places two kinds of restrictions: restrictions on where the assistance could be spent and restrictions on how the assistance can be used."*
- Delays: *"(...) even though we realize the need for various administrative hurdles that externally financed programmes have to pass through before they become operational, we wonder if some of the procedures could not be streamlined, and if the establishment of a local office would not help solve some bottlenecks thus obviating the need for frequent contacts with headquarters."*
- Coordination: *"We are aware of the importance of proper coordination, firstly, as a means of disseminating government's strategies and priorities so that potential partners are in a good position to identify areas which they would like to support; secondly, to ensure that partner commitments are synchronized and tied together in a logical and comprehensive manner; and finally, to follow up on commitments and undertakings of the government and of partners."* The Eritrean government therefore makes the coordination of development cooperation the responsibility of the President's Office.

Structural shortcomings in the recipient countries

One of the main causes of the poor effectiveness of TC lies in the structures of the developing countries themselves (again, especially in sub-Saharan Africa). TC is an extremely complex process in which an ambitious objective is pursued. If effective action is to be taken in the context of TC, an institutional environment that enables the skills of people and institutions to be developed and strengthened tends to be needed. Put simply, TC therefore presupposes what it seeks as its goal.

> "*Perhaps there is a logical inconsistency in expecting an agency which lacks basic skills or experience to be able to articulate technical cooperation needs, supervise and guide the activities of technical cooperation personnel, and critically review and utilise their output.*" (Raphaeli 1996, p. 232)

Weak and inadequate structures in the developing countries concerned therefore have a decisive influence on the success of projects. Despite careful preparation and implementation, TC measures may remain ineffective owing to an unfavourable environment (Bossuyt / Laporte / van Hoek 1995, pp. 18 f.; Sirleaf 1996, p. 60), perhaps because a counterpart institution lacks the necessary "development orientation" or because the recipient government regards actual TC activities as insignificant and, faced with, say, budgetary problems, places the emphasis on "hard" TC provisions (such as equipment and cars).

2.3.2 Proposals and Methods for the Reform of Technical Cooperation

An essential feature of the international TC debate is its relatively marked practical orientation. This is particularly evident from the fact that criticism of TC is joined by specific proposals for reforms.

In 1991 the OECD's Development Assistance Committee (DAC) adopted some principles on the reorientation of technical cooperation (OECD 1995a). Against the background of the Berg study (1993) and the Jaycox address (also 1993) an initiative for the more rapid implementation of the DAC principles was launched. In this context a high-level seminar that was jointly organized by the DAC, UNDP and the World Bank and drew up recommendations, was held in 1994. A further practical outcome of the seminar was the establishment of a *Network on Technical Co-operation Effectiveness* to examine and test proposals for the reform of TC.[33]

Reference can also be made to many other international events, reports and other publications[34] that have given the TC debate a significant boost. They include the round table *Partnership in Development Co-operation: Combining Recipient Responsibility with Donor Accountability* (1994) held by the European Centre for Development Policy Management (ECDPM) and the international round tables (in 1989 and 1995) arranged by the German Foundation for International Development (DSE) for the discussion of *The Future of Technical Cooperation* and *Potential and Use of National Capacities and the Role of the Foreign Expert in Future Development Cooperation.*

A consensus on the direction it is felt reforms should take can be detected in the initiatives and publications[35] referred to above. It is agreed that their aim should be "capacity-building". This term is an attempt to summarize the main substance and tasks behind the findings and outcomes of the recent TC debate.[36] It means that TC efforts must be designed primarily to ensure that donors do not themselves offer solutions to existing problems but support the efforts of institutions in the developing countries concerned and promote the necessary structures.

The TC debate has produced some important conclusions and problem-solving approaches, which relate to the following aspects: (1) the functional objectives of TC, (2) the substantive tasks of TC, (3) project design, (4) the use of local know-how, (5) cost awareness and (6) impact indicators. These points will be explained and discussed in the following sections. Besides this action to adjust existing TC structures and approaches, more fundamental adjustments to the (7) TC instruments and approaches should be considered; a broad consensus has, however, yet to be reached on this in the development debate.

Box 3: The DAC principles for the reorientation of technical cooperation
The principles for the reorientation of technical cooperation drawn up by the DAC in 1991 • provide for TC to pursue the strategic objective of the long-term development and expansion of local capacities rather than demonstrable achievements in the short term; • place the emphasis in all phases of TC on the central role to be played by the developing countries; • underline the importance of improved planning; • encourage more ownership on the part of the developing countries during all phases of TC; • emphasize the key importance for sustainable development and self-reliance of long-term institution-building; • take account of the need for TC in the private sector; • advocate the employment of more local experts; • define objectives in terms of results to be achieved rather than inputs required; • underline the need for greater attention to be paid to the cost and cost-effectiveness of TC.

Functional objectives of TC

The goal of TC must be to make long-term contributions to capacity-building in the various developing countries. The recipient countries must therefore play a central role, which means greater independence and, therefore, more responsibility for them. The following criteria and objectives should be borne in mind in this context:

- TC must be determined not by available and possible inputs from the donors but by the goals and results to be achieved.
- TC must demonstrate a high degree of recipient ownership and, where possible, autonomy, both being particularly vital if the measures are to be sustainable.[37]

- TC must form part of a phasing-out strategy from the outset.
- Openings for TC must be sought at different levels (individuals, institutions, structures), with sufficient account taken of decentralized and non-governmental actors.

Casting the recipient country in a far more important role in the planning, implementation and monitoring of TC may help to create a new image of TC and development cooperation as a result of the transfer of additional "rights" (i.e. means of exercising influence) and the programme countries' assumption of significantly more responsibilities, and this may help to overcome traditional approaches to aid. The donors must pay more attention than in the past to the question of how and by whom on the recipient side the need for and interest in TC are formulated.

Substantive tasks of TC

In technical cooperation growing emphasis is being placed on questions and problems relating to society as a whole, which are pushing technical tasks in the narrower sense into the background. Past experience of development cooperation indicates that, like the macroeconomic environment that is considered so important, a crucial role should be assigned to societal, political and institutional structures.[38] The aim here is to lay country-wide institutional and political foundations for the private and public actors at national level and to share tasks between central and subordinate (provincial, district, etc.) structures. The policies associated with this are often referred to in the 1990s development debate as "development orientation" and good governance.

Specifically, TC actors in the 1990s have increasingly tried to develop strategies and solutions for such all-important societal and political aspects as democratization, human rights, civil society, participation, crisis prevention and the consolidation of peace (UNDP 1997b; Zell 1997; Heinz 1994; Waller 1996). The actors to be approached in this context are in the public sector (not only the executive but increasingly the judiciary and legislature) and the private sector (such actors in civil society as the media and non-governmental organizations).

Conceptually, the TC activities of the 1990s increasingly form part of the efforts to find answers to global problems and cross-frontier challenges. Such terms and approaches as "sustainable development" and "global public goods" are very important in this context.

Project design

There are many ways of improving the planning and implementation of TC measures through project design, examples being

- a substantial increase in training for local capacities in the case of TC projects;
- a comprehensive programme approach rather than the planning and implementation of TC measures in isolation; this includes comprehensive coordination of the measures of different donors; ideally, the programme countries themselves should coordinate development cooperation and TC;
- greater attention paid to terms of reference and the whole preparation of (external or local) personnel;
- the clarification and less ambitious definition of the objectives of measures;
- the devotion of more energy to ensuring the quality of TC measures.

Using local know-how

The present use of donor-country know-how should be reviewed with the aim of achieving a significant reduction by comparison with available local capacities. This is primarily true of expatriate experts, although a distinction should be made between different areas and forms of the employment of experts.[39] More of them should come from the various developing countries or from third countries (preferably in the same region). Generally speaking, all the staffing options and alternatives should be weighed up in any TC measure, and decisions on the employment of expatriate experts should be made with care, with the aims of the measure, other impacts and the cost dimension taken into account. Where local or regional know-how is available, there are likely to be few appropriate openings for employing experts from donor countries. Appropriate exceptions to this principle might arise, for example, where a measure concerns sensitive political issues in, say, the human rights sphere. In such cases it may be expedient or even necessary to employ someone who is, or appears to be, impartial. Even then, however, it should be asked, if only because of the cost involved, how far internationally available experts can be employed.

Greater cost awareness

There is also a general need for greater cost awareness on the part of donor and recipient institutions. Improvements can be achieved primarily through savings arising from the increased employment of local and regional experts. Besides this, incentive structures that reveal the direct and indirect costs incurred by the programme countries are appropriate and necessary. Market mechanisms that make for greater transparency of the opportunity costs of technical cooperation or enable TC "taxes" to be introduced (e.g. ministries benefiting from TC measures pay a "tax" to the finance ministry so that opportunity costs are included) may, for example,[40] help to prevent direct TC expenditure and indirect costs from arising.

Impact indicators[41]

As a rule, clear impact indicators are methodologically far more difficult to identify for TC measures than for FC investment projects. In many cases indicators related to TC also allow of many interpretations and may therefore lead to disputed evaluations. Nonetheless, there is a major need to develop evaluation criteria and apply them to measures that are geared to capacity-building. Past experience in particular has shown that the absence of (suitable) indicators has been partly to blame for the emergence or exacerbation of problems relating to the objectives, design, ownership, etc. of TC measures. Appropriate indicators may make a valuable contribution to the planning of suitable measures and to their implementation, monitoring and evaluation.

Reform of the TC instruments and TC approach

Besides the areas referred to above, where there is potential for improving TC that can be tapped within existing structures, more fundamental adjustments should be discussed. To overcome existing shortcomings of TC, three options, which are not necessarily mutually exclusive and are geared in some respects to more fundamental reforms of TC instruments or the TC approach,[42] will be considered here:

- First, the *development fund models* can provide some important ideas in this context. Development funds enable a relatively wide range of projects to be promoted and financed by local structures acting on their own responsibility. They represent a link between donors on the one hand and projects and project partners on the other. The donors' role is confined to (partly) financing and possibly advising the fund. The development fund itself is administered by local groups and institutions autonomously and on their own responsibility (project selection, etc.); there are now various models of such funds, with different features (proximity to the programme country's administration, etc.).[43] As a rule, much is expected of the funds: strong ownership where local structures are concerned, pronounced needs-orientation, participatory approach, etc.
- Second, it may be useful in this context to consider ways of overcoming the traditional distinction between TC and FC, there being parallels here with the development funds discussed above. Various studies in the past have already indicated that the distinction between TC and FC did not emerge because of the structures in the developing countries:

"A separation between capital and technical assistance has no structural analogy in the economies of the recipient countries." (DP/1990/9, p. 35)

Taking UNDP as an example, Griffin / McKinley (1996, pp. 11 ff.), for instance, have argued that it should develop into an institution that makes untied funds available to programme countries in grant form. The developing countries concerned could buy services as and when they were required. However, these services would not necessarily need to comply with the traditional definitions of TC, i.e. they might well include forms typical of FC if they appeared appropriate for the solution of given problems.

A latent danger with this option is likely to be that, if TC and FC were merged, too little importance would be attached to the original components of independent TC in the sense of capacity-building. This might be a major cause of the failure of combined measures.

– Third, the concept of *sector investment programmes* (SIPs) developed by the World Bank in the mid-1990s seizes on important aspects of the TC debate (ownership, etc.).[44] This is particularly clear from the six main elements that make up the SIP approach. Sector investment programmes[45]

  (a) cover government capital and consumption expenditure in a sector or functional area,

  (b) are based on a long-term strategy,

  (c) are formulated by local actors ("local stakeholders in the driver's seat"),

  (d) are to be supported by all donors,

  (e) are assisted by the donors on the basis of a uniform procedure and

  (f) are planned, implemented and controlled not by expatriate experts but by local experts ("minimal long-term foreign technical assistance").

It should be borne in mind, however, that the SIP concept does not place the emphasis primarily on institutions, human capital or capacity-building. Consequently, some questions that play an important part against the background of the TC debate still await satisfactory answers. Seen from the angle of the Network on Technical Co-operation (DAC/OECD), they are as follows:

"- *Who leads the process of formulating SIPs?*
- *What is the time-frame?*
- *What are the respective roles of donors and host governments?*"[46]

The World Bank is planning to use SIPs on a fairly large scale; the 15 SIPs under way in sub-Saharan Africa at the beginning of 1997 are to be joined by another 50 by the end of 1998 (Hubert 1997, p. 81).

2.4 Conclusions for the Study

It is both appropriate and important that the shortcomings of TC and the reform options have been debated since the late 1980s. The debate has gained in that it has led to a self-critical and systematic appraisal, especially among the donors, but the practical implementation of the results poses serious problems. Given the major importance of the issue for the whole of development cooperation and the lack of interest the donor institutions have shown in the problems in the past, the TC debate is essential.[47]

During the overall international debate on development cooperation and TC there have been waves of "rediscovered" issues. The TC debate of the 1990s, the identification of problems, the development of problem-solving approaches, etc. are closely linked to the changing environment and a changing image of development cooperation and TC. It must also be emphasized, however, that a number of TC problems only appear to have been "rediscovered" and that many of the problem-solving approaches which appear appropriate have already been propagated. The resolution *New Dimensions in Technical Co-operation* (Resolution 3405, XXX) adopted by the UN General Assembly as long ago as 1975 and the UNDP Administrator's 1976 report entitled *Implementation of New Dimensions in Technical Co-operation* (DP/220) include such headings as *Increased use of national capability*, *The use of local resources through subcontracts and the hiring of locally available consultants*, *National project management*, *Execution by Governments and institutions* and *Towards a more result-oriented approach in technical co-operation*.

One of the decisive questions in the TC debate thus concerns the political willingness and ability of the donor countries and institutions to accept change: *"Are donors ready to change?"* (Guehenno / Pio 1997, p. 10)

However, this does not make the international TC debate of the 1990s superfluous. Previous TC debates obviously attracted too little interest and met with little response. Cassen states in his report, for example, that mention of TC is comparatively rare in the literature on the efficiency of development cooperation (Cassen 1990, p. 261). Yet it is not only because of the long-standing nature of the problems diagnosed that the subject needs to be considered: the general environment in the second half of the 1990s compared to previous decades has changed significantly in many respects, the availability of local know-how being an example. The basic view of what constitutes TC and what it is meant to achieve has also changed fundamentally in the 1990s.[48]

Against this background various conclusions can be drawn for this study:

1. The conceptual results of the TC debate in the 1990s can be rated positively.

   In themselves the 1991 DAC principles for the reorientation of technical cooperation provide a conceptually suitable basis which, though undoubtedly complemented by later contributions to the debate, has not been fundamentally questioned. Its main features have so far been able to prove their worth.

   Many donors have reacted to the TC debate with specific concepts and other papers that reflect the need for debate - adapted to the prevailing situation. In its first two years (1995 and 1996) the still young *International Journal of Technical Co-operation* published many documents on the subject (from the Asian Development Bank, Australia, Germany, the United Kingdom, Sweden and the USA, for example). The UN too takes an explicit interest in the current state of the debate in its reports (E/1997/65/Add. 3; UN 1997d, paras 10 ff.). This can at least be seen as an indication that the donors are making a scrupulous conceptual analysis of TC.

2. The conceptual image of technical cooperation in the second half of the 1990s differs fundamentally from that of previous decades (Baser / Morgan 1997, p. 5; Berg 1993, pp. 64 ff.). In the 1950s and 1960s TC was a means of helping to close gaps in the countries concerned through the direct provision or transfer of technical know-how. In the 1970s and 1980s came the growing realization that, if the success of TC was to be sustained, greater account must be taken of institutional structures and conditions. In the 1980s and the first half of the 1990s TC increasingly entailed institutional development efforts associated with comprehensive reforms in the countries concerned (structural adjustment programmes, democratization efforts, privatization programmes, etc.). Since the early/mid-1990s there has also been an increase in conceptual and methodological efforts to see TC not as a "transfer" but as a contribution to independent capacity-building.[49]

   Today TC is generally expected to help create sustainable institutional and know-how-related conditions without which progress in any area of development is impossible. TC goes well beyond technical know-how and technical effectiveness.

3. Capacity-building must be one of the main aims of TC. However, this aim needs to be clarified so that differences from traditional TC with problems attached can be identified below a general level of objectives.

   In other words, although the TC debate can be generally regarded as fruitful, its actual impact so far has been scarcely tangible. An important and clear example is the World Bank's free-standing technical assistance. An evaluation completed in 1997 found the performance of this instrument to be particularly poor, making this the least effective area at the World Bank (Baser / Morgan 1997, p. 1).

Given the known shortcomings (World Bank 1990), it is remarkable that the World Bank has been unable to make any progress with its TC in the 1990s. Instead, the scale and nature of its TC problems in 1997 have been similar to those a decade earlier.[50]

Although the TC debate has generally produced plausible results, which have found relatively wide acceptance and a broad consensus among most donors, they have not led to a situation where the conceptual findings on instruments (Fukuda-Parr 1995, p. 65) have been implemented at operational level in the donor institutions' practical TC work:

> *"Yet, a critical shortage of clear understandings of how to mould the often promising recommendations and guidelines into operational guidance still remains."* (Brigaldino 1995, p. 115)

An example of the failure hitherto to implement these findings is the employment of expatriate experts. Although a uniform trend is not discernible among the various donors, since both increases and decreases are to be seen in this sphere, the overall data reveal an increase in the number of expatriate experts employed (International Round Table 1995, p. 279).

4. In some areas of TC multilateral donors are able to offer advantages that bilateral donors cannot offer.[51] This is particularly true of
   - the employment of experts, which is based far less on nationality in the case of multilateral institutions (i.e. no "tying" of experts),
   - the good external structure of multilateral institutions, with their field offices,[52] which increase their familiarity with the ideas and priorities of the programme countries,
   - the special mandate and the mechanism for coordinating contributions to development cooperation[53] and
   - (in the UN's case) greater legitimacy to take action in areas (human rights, participation, etc.) that are politically sensitive and more controversial, but have been agreed and sanctioned by consensus in international agreements;[54] some bilateral donors

have serious credibility problems because they are alleged to apply double standards.

5. The performance of TC tasks has often been poor in the past. This is particularly true of the World Bank, which does not have an adequate "TC culture", despite its efforts to continue expanding free-standing technical cooperation:

   "Technical assistance is not a core competence in the Bank. Staff often view it as a second-class activity. TALs cannot compare in size and importance with other resource flows. They fit uneasily into the Bank's analytical culture and are less rooted in its traditions. As a result, TA loses its professional status, little research is dedicated to it, and staff develop a sense of boredom and fatalism about it." (Baser / Morgan 1997, p. ii.)

   It must be assumed that the demands on TC so far revealed by the debate cannot or can hardly be appropriately met by the whole range of donors. A new division of labour among the donors should be sought in this respect (the task and role of UNDP included), with the aim of achieving a necessary specialization effect in TC. The international TC debate has hitherto paid little attention to this aspect.

6. Where technical cooperation instruments and procedures are concerned, innovative approaches that help to preclude the present shortcomings should be sought. Appropriate options based on the output dimension should be sought. This includes the following elements:

   – a programme-oriented and coordinated approach is essential;
   – where TC procedures and instruments are concerned, the cost dimension must become a relevant factor through payment from a fund endowed with limited resources, for example;
   – TC providers must hold their own in the market as regards the prices and quality of their products;
   – the range of TC offered must be flexible enough to meet needs in each case, regardless of institutional or instrumental definitions; needs must determine supply, not vice versa.

All in all, the development debate is evidence of the major importance of technical cooperation. High-quality TC is necessary and appropriate in these circumstances. Some helpful and satisfactory problem-solving approaches are available to increase its effectiveness. The debate on UNDP's effectiveness and reform must therefore take adequate account of these aspects.

Part III UNDP: Reform Debate, Reform Measures and Development Options

1 UN Development Cooperation: State of the Reform Debate and Relevance to UNDP

1.1 Introduction

Background

The debate on the reform of UN development cooperation is only one part of a far more comprehensive debate on the reform of the UN as a whole, which includes aspects of the UN Security Council, the regular UN budget and the UN Charter. The link between the general reform of the UN on the one hand and the debate on the reform of UN development cooperation on the other is only partly direct; what cannot be overlooked, however, is that the political environment and political climate surrounding overarching aspects of the reform of the UN certainly have an influence on UN development cooperation and vice versa. An example is the debate in Germany in late 1996 concerning the country's possible withdrawal from UNIDO. The arguments with which it was conducted not only concerned UNIDO and its tasks and activities: it also took account of the possible implications of a withdrawal from UNIDO for Germany's application for a permanent seat on the UN Security Council.[1]

The debate on the need and options for the reform of UN development cooperation has continued for several decades now. Although adjustments have repeatedly been sought and sometimes made, a situation that all concerned consider satisfactory has still to be found. The effectiveness in development terms of the UN's operational activities and thus of one of the main pillars of multilateral technical cooperation suffers as a result. Political willingness - especially on the part of many donor countries - to become involved in development within the UN is also affected. Combined with the persistent problems that many industrialized countries are having with their budgets, this has done a great deal significantly to increase the pressure for the reform of UN development cooperation in the 1990s.

> *"The UN programmes and funds are affected not only by the general decline in development assistance but also by the associated drive for greater effectiveness and value for money."* (ODI 1997, p. 4)

An understanding of the debate on the reform of UN development cooperation is vital if the debate on UNDP is to be understood; conversely, the debate on the reform of UNDP is highly relevant to the whole of UN development cooperation. UN development cooperation is the immediate and narrower framework within which UNDP has its place; the UN's economic and social sphere is the larger framework within which UNDP is located or undertakes its activities. It is very important for the analysis that adequate account is taken of the interactions and linkages.

Objective

The aim of this chapter is to analyse and evaluate the debate on the reform of the United Nations' development cooperation. This is intended to reveal overarching aspects of the reform debate and the importance and place of UNDP in the debate on the reform of UN development cooperation. The analysis will therefore focus on the following:

- the most serious deficiencies in UN development cooperation (need for reforms),
- current reform concepts and initiatives,
- reform measures and efforts undertaken in the past and
- the basic positions of the most important actors.

1.2 Basics

1.2.1 The UN's Development Policy and Development Cooperation: Historical Background

The history of the UN essentially mirrors world policy.[2]

> *"The state or performance of the international organizations in general and the United Nations in particular has always been a direct reflection of the political and psychological mood and constellation of the international community."* (Van Agt 1994, p. 3)

In these circumstances analyses, initiatives, conclusions and demands concerning the shortcomings and reform of the UN have always depended largely on international conditions and developments. This study cannot consider the various phases of the UN's development and its environment in any depth. However, some important stages will be outlined to enable the times at which the reform debates occurred to be identified. Particular account will be taken of aspects that have been important for the UN's development policy and development cooperation:

- *From 1945 until the mid-1950s*: In the first phase of its existence the UN's policy was influenced particularly by the Cold War and US dominance. The Cold War resulted in the UN being de facto incapable of taking action to maintain international peace and security (Article 1 of the UN Charter) (owing, among other things, to the Soviet Union's use of its veto in the Security Council and the isolation of the Soviet Union and other socialist countries by the West). The superpowers also largely decided on the admission or rejection of new members against the backcloth of the East-West conflict, which meant that for a time (September 1950 to December 1955) it became politically impossible for new members to be admitted to the UN (Unser 1997, p. 318). The Soviet Union refused to participate in many of the UN's specialized agencies and aid programmes (e.g. the Expanded Programme of Technical Assistance - EPTA) (Hüfner 1991a, p. 12; Unser 1997, pp. 318 ff.). The USA's dominant role was particularly evident from the political supremacy that led to the West having a majority in the General Assembly and elsewhere[3] and from the major importance of the USA's financial contributions to the UN budget (initially 49.89% of total UN contributions[4]).

- *From the mid-1950s until the first half of the 1960s*: In its second phase, when there was a slight easing of the international tension[5] between the political blocs, the UN played a more active role. The admission of 20 new member states (in 1955) was an important sign of this. The Soviet Union began to participate in UN specialized agencies and aid programmes. The importance attached to and the perception of development problems also grew as the process of decolonization gathered pace.

- *From the first half of the 1960s until the early 1970s*: By the early 1970s the UN had achieved - with a few exceptions - its goal of universality. In 1970 it had 127 member countries. Major issues of international peace (e.g. the Vietnam war) were usually dealt with outside the UN. The East-West conflict was increasingly eclipsed within the UN by the North-South conflict and singled out for special attention by the developing countries. Many of the UN's development bodies were established at this time (WFP, UNCTAD, UNIDO, UNFPA, etc.). In 1961 the General Assembly proclaimed a *First United Nations Development Decade*.

- *From the early until the late 1970s*: Outside the Security Council the developing countries largely determined the UN agenda by a two-thirds majority. This was reflected, for example, in the *Char-*

ter of Economic Rights and Duties of States adopted by the General Assembly in 1974 and the calls for a *New International Economic Order* at two special sessions of the General Assembly (1974 and 1975) (Dadzie 1993, pp. 300 ff.; Unser 1997, pp. 325 ff.).

- *From the early until the late 1980s*: For the UN the 1980s were characterized by a "crisis of multilateralism". This crisis was largely due to a US policy that had been highly critical of the UN since the mid-1970s and even more so since 1981 under President Reagan.[6] This attitude was clearly demonstrated, for example, by the USA's Permanent Representative to the UN (Jeane Kirkpatrick, for further information see Gerson 1991), by its growing arrears of contributions to the UN budget (the *Kassebaum Amendment*[7]), by its withdrawal from UN bodies (ILO and UNESCO), temporarily in some cases, and by threats of withdrawal. The UN's financial situation came to a head in the mid-1980s, when it faced its most serious financial crisis (Unser 1997, pp. 330 f.), which also gave rise to an intensive debate on the need to reform the UN.
- *Since the late 1980s*: In connection with the events that led to the end of the East-West conflict, especially after 1987, UN activities in the sphere of international security increased sharply.[8] With the *Agenda for Peace*, the *Agenda for Development*[9] and the impending *Agenda for Democratization* (Rudischhauser 1997, p. 133), UN Secretary-General Boutros Boutros-Ghali demonstrated the UN's clear will to act in important areas of international policy. The UN has faced up to global problems in the 1990s with a series of world conferences, for example.

Since the early 1990s an initially positive view taken of the UN's future role in world politics ("Renaissance of the UN") by the international media and large sections of the public has, however, given way to an increasingly sceptical attitude towards the UN. The reform debates and efforts have also been stepped up in the UN's economic and social sphere because of mounting financial problems.

The pressure on UN development cooperation that has increased especially in the 1990s. Reductions in ODA have also had an impact on UN funds and programmes. In addition, there have been more calls for greater effectiveness and efficiency ("value for money"). Some "like-minded countries" launched various new reform efforts in the first half of the 1990s.

With the withdrawal of certain UN members from a number of agencies in the UN system, there is a growing danger of the UN being subjected to more selective interests in the field of development cooperation too ("UN à la carte").

Kofi Annan, UN Secretary-General since January 1997, is stepping up the pace of reform significantly. It was not least the hope that he would be able to force through substantial reforms that ensured his election as Secretary-General and the USA's support.

In view of the very different phases the UN has passed through and the highly complex problems arising in each, this study will focus on the recent past, with the emphasis on the period since 1987/89, when the reform debate can be said to have entered a new phase.[10] This decision is essentially prompted by three factors: firstly, the UN's financial crisis has assumed very serious proportions since the late 1980s, which has led to a considerable rise in the pressure for reform. Secondly, the prospects for more fundamental reforms have improved significantly with the end of the East-West conflict. Thirdly, the current debate on the reform of the economic and social sphere has found greater political support as a result of various initiatives (especially the Nordic UN Project[11]).

1.2.2 UNDP's Role and its Functions for UN Development Cooperation

The debate on the reform of UNDP is closely linked to the debate on the reform of other UN institutions and the whole of the UN development cooperation system. Two factors are decisive in this context. Firstly, as a subsidiary organ, UNDP is subordinate or attached to other UN organs. Reforms that affect the United Nations as a whole or individual UN organs to which UNDP is attached may therefore have direct implications for UNDP. Secondly, its mandate is such that UNDP performs important functions for all operational activities in the area of UN development cooperation. Reforms geared to UNDP are therefore likely to lead to changes for other UN agencies.

UNDP as a subsidiary organ

The UN General Assembly established UNDP by adopting Resolution 2029 (XX) in 1965.[12] The UNDP sprang from the merging of the Expanded Programme of Technical Assistance (EPTA) and the Special Fund (SF). With the 1970 Consensus Resolution,[13] which emerged against the background of the Jackson Report, the General Assembly enlarged and clarified UNDP's foundations. The Consensus Resolution designated UNDP as the central element of the UN system's technical cooperation. It sets out the most important principles, procedures, etc. (e.g. the indicative planning figure).

UNDP is a subsidiary organ of the General Assembly. It is administered under the authority of ECOSOC and the General Assembly (UNDP 1994a, p. 1, Sect. 1000) and is composed of an Executive Board,[14] an Administrator and his staff.

> *"The General Assembly sets the overall policy of UNDP. The Economic and Social Council is responsible for the formulation of the general rules and principles which govern the administration and operations of UNDP."* (UNDP 1994a, p. 1, Sect. 1000).

UNDP is required to submit reports to ECOSOC. ECOSOC forwards the reports to the General Assembly. At the level of the UN's main organs UNDP thus has links both to the General Assembly and to ECOSOC. It cooperates with various bodies of these two main organs, such as the General Assembly's Second Main Committee and various bodies of the standing committees and functional commissions, which are responsible for specific tasks.

UNDP is not superior to other subsidiary organs, especially other UN funds and programmes, but is formally on an equal footing with them within the UN structure.[15]

UNDP tasks for operational development activities

UNDP's most important tasks extend to all the operational development cooperation activities of the UN and part of the UN system. It was created as the single, central body for financing and coordinating the United Nations' technical cooperation (Sahlmann 1991, pp. 895 f.). Many of its services are thus "outwardly" oriented.

For a long time UNDP was the largest operational development cooperation body within the UN (in terms of available financial volume). It still has the broadest mandate and a multisectoral task within the system of UN agencies engaged in technical cooperation. In principle, this gives rise to a number of different functions, which will be discussed in greater depth below. They comprise the following:

- Funding role: UNDP is generally meant to serve as the single financing instrument for operational development activities. In return, the bodies that engage in operations act as executing agencies.[16]
- Coordinating function at country level: At country level UNDP in principle plays a special role in the coordination of the UN's operational activities. Of crucial importance in this context is that, as a rule, the UNDP's Resident Representative (RR) is also appointed as the UN's Resident Coordinator (RC) and as such performs vital coordinating functions for operational development cooperation activities. In addition, the Consensus Resolution provides for UNDP to play a coordinating role in country programming.[17] UNDP is also responsible for the round tables, the country-related development cooperation coordination mechanism.
- Coordinating function at headquarters level: UNDP also plays a coordinating role between the headquarters of the UN funds and

programmes and other operational bodies in the UN system. This role is largely linked to the financing function and country-related coordination.

1.3 Reform of UN Development Cooperation

1.3.1 Need for Reforms

There is no generally accepted list or analysis of the most important shortcomings of UN development cooperation. The assessments, evaluations and appraisals of existing problems very largely depend on the angle from which they are viewed by the various actors.

For this and later sections distinctions need to be made to permit substantive and problem-related differentiation of the subject matter of the study with the aid of various levels of analysis. Section II.1 has developed and discussed factors relating to the effectiveness of international organizations. These factors can be used for this aspect of the study through the identification of certain levels and elements of analysis with the aid of this systematology:

- The conceptual level concerns the substantive orientation and objectives of UN development cooperation.
- At structural and policy level account is primarily taken of the following elements: the mandate and foundations of UN development cooperation, institutional and structural aspects of the division of labour and authority among various agencies of the UN system, political decision-making and guidance, questions of coordination at political level among the UN agencies and the financial endowment.
- The administration and implementation level mainly concerns aspects of internal organization and management, staff recruitment and training, the implementation of measures and coordination at the level of implementation.

Conceptual Level

(a) "Gap-filling function"

One of the main criticisms of UN development cooperation is that it does not have a sufficiently clear substantive profile. The argument that the UN's operational activities are composed of a largely unconnected bundle of organizations and tasks is very important in this context. There are various reasons for endorsing this view. The UN was initially conceived as a political forum:

> *"The UN was originally designed as a system of political assemblies for its members to discuss and solve common problems."* (Nordic UN Project 1991b, p. 13)

Operational activities were therefore taken on gradually and, to some extent, unsystematically. This process was not based on a viable concept: it consisted of filling "gaps", i.e. tasks that had not been specifically assigned to other organizations. In the past UN members have therefore tended to "load" (Sahlmann 1987, p. 91) the UN with numerous new tasks and problems, while "ejecting" it from central areas of international development cooperation (especially development financing).[18]

(b) Absence of congruent, appropriate and realistic objectives

A criticism often levelled at the general substantive orientation of the UN's operational development activities is that it lacks sufficiently clear or appropriate objectives. The absence of substantive priorities is therefore seen as a particularly serious shortcoming;[19] it has been proposed, for example, that UN development cooperation should be focused on "poverty alleviation" as a possible common task (Jolly 1995, pp. 11 f.). Bertrand in particular is also critical of inappropriate objectives; the difference between the objectives set and practice results, he claims, in a serious "lack of realism" (Bertrand 1995, pp. 74 ff.).

(c) Absence of future orientation for the UN's technical cooperation

In the operational sphere of development the UN's activities are almost entirely confined to technical cooperation and food aid / humanitarian assistance. The role played by technical cooperation has, however, shrunk considerably over the years. For one thing, its importance has waned. For another, the tasks it entails have been increasingly taken over by the international development banks, which see serious obstacles to development in the non-monetary sphere (institutions, know-how, etc.). So far the UN's conceptual reaction has been inadequate.[20]

(d) New challenges after the East-West conflict

The UN has also been heavily criticized for making unsatisfactory attempts to adjust operational development cooperation to new challenges now that the East-West conflict is over.[21] The criticism related to such questions as how to respond to new challenges and opportunities for democratization and demilitarization, the aid fatigue tendencies of the 1990s and the growing globalization and what role to assign to the UN in this context.

There is in this connection a particularly serious need for conceptual and practical clarification of the relationship and stronger links between humanitarian assistance and development cooperation oriented towards the long term (UN 1996c, pp. 12 ff.; Nordic UN Project 1996, p. 18).

Structural and Policy Level

(a) Proliferation of UN agencies and fragmentation of tasks

The wide variety of UN funds and programmes and other organs, committees, etc. concerned with development cooperation issues has led to considerable fragmentation[22] and impairment of operational activities.

The proliferation tendency in the past was one of the main causes of a number of structural problems. Besides the resulting coordination problems for the UN and the individual member states, such added difficulties as duplication of effort, fragmentation of tasks and unproductive competition for financial resources arise.

Gwin and Williams emphasize the USA's role in connection with the emergence of the fragmented network of development institutions of the UN and the whole UN system:

> *"It must be recognized, however, that the current critiques of the decentralized, sprawling, international development system are calling into question a central feature of the postwar institutional architecture for which the United States was a principal proponent. The United States insisted upon autonomy for the specialized agencies. It was also U.S. policy to retain a distinction between the technical assistance activities of the U.N. agencies and the capital investment programs of the World Bank."* (Gwin / Williams 1996, p. 113)

When listing the "most important" UN bodies in his draft *Agenda for Development*, the UN Secretary-General included 105 entities (comprising nine of the General Assembly, 73 of ECOSOC and 23 other UN programmes, organs and funds) concerned with aspects of the economic and social sphere and the protection of human rights.[23]

(b) Overlapping of lines of authority and mandates[24]

The fragmentation of tasks has been largely to blame for the overlapping of the mandates originally handed down to UN agencies and for mandates no longer being considered adequate. The original lines separating, say, standard-setting and operational agencies in the UN system have become blurred; similarly, financing and implementing tasks, some of which are separate, are now often hardly discernible in the form originally envisaged. The sectoral focus areas of individual UN institutions are also becoming increasingly unclear, and there is frequently keen competition for operations of a multisectoral nature, because the agencies have an interest in running such projects.

(c) Inadequate political guidance of UN development cooperation

Poor political guidance of UN development cooperation is evident primarily from the absence of a coordinated, integrated approach as the conceptual basis for operational activities. ECOSOC is particularly to blame for this:[25]

> *"ECOSOC has problems in providing effective leadership for the operational organs under its authority."* (Nordic UN Project 1991b, p. 37)

It has not succeeded in obtaining binding decision-making power (corresponding to the Security Council's, for example). Its work is taken up with coordinating tasks, little time being devoted to the consideration of substantive issues (Tomuschat 1996, p. 9; Dias 1994). The large number of member states represented in ECOSOC (54) is regarded as a serious structural shortcoming.

Further problems are encountered in the General Assembly and at the level of subordinate or supplementary UN bodies (e.g. the General Assembly's Second and Third Committees). As the bodies supervising the UN funds and programmes also normally have separate and fairly infrequent meetings (Gwin 1995, p. 99), political guidance functions can be performed only on a limited scale.

(d) Poor coordination of UN development cooperation by UN bodies[26]

A major consequence of the lack of political guidance is the inadequate coordination of the many UN agencies in the economic and social field. It is particularly clear from past experience that ECOSOC has hitherto been unable to perform this management task properly.[27] The coordination problems at the UN may absorb considerable administrative and political capacities, especially in developing countries whose dependence on development cooperation is relatively pronounced, and pose serious difficulties for domestic structures, especially when other multilateral and bilateral donors similarly take little interest in a coordinated approach.

> *"It is the poorest countries with high dependence on external aid that are victimized by the lack of coherence among the many U.N. and other donor entities that largely overwhelm weak governments with separate agency program criteria, administrative procedures, and competitively guarded institutional identities."* (Gwin / Williams 1996, p. 123)

ECOSOC was created as a forum for political debate. The mandate defined in the UN Charter does not therefore refer to suitable instruments for ensuring or permitting the adequate performance of the coordinating task within the UN (Nordic UN Project 1991b, pp. 34 ff.). The work of the Administrative Committee on Co-ordination (ACC) set up as long ago as 1946 specifically to ease the burden on ECOSOC in this respect is similarly unsatisfactory (ODI 1987, p. 3; Ministry of Foreign Affairs and Trade 1996, p. 144). It is

> *"... too large and uneven in its composition, too broad in its scope and too infrequent in its holding of meetings to serve as much more than a general information exchange."* (North South Roundtable 1991, p. 21)

Coordination within the UN and the whole UN system cannot be an end in itself: it must be an instrument for achieving objectives (McLaren 1987, p. 393; Jolly 1995, p. 14). The objectives are particularly apparent from the current problems facing UN development cooperation; in other words, what is needed is improvement in the setting of priorities, standardized and coordinated procedures (if only to ease the pressure on the programme countries), simplified structures and the reduction of costs. The UN, and especially its economic and social fields, have been endowed with a decentralized structure (Gordenker 1995). This may have advantages (small administrative units, selective participation by countries in certain UN agencies, pluralist institutions, etc.), but it presupposes functioning coordination mechanisms capable of effectively precluding excessive diffusion tendencies and overly inconsistent action.

(e) Coordination between the UN and its specialized agencies[28]

A specific coordination problem is also to be seen in the relationship between the UN - and especially ECOSOC - and the specialized agencies. Given the central roles played by the World Bank group and the International Monetary Fund in international development co-operation and in development policy, particular importance must be attached to this relationship. Although the UN Charter (Chapter IX) describes the specialized agencies as being attached to ECOSOC and the General Assembly, they act de facto autonomously and do not participate in the coordination procedures for which provision is made. The IMF and World Bank

> *"... no longer respect even their own special agreements with the UN or invite the UN Secretary-General to their most important meetings, whereas they naturally insist on addressing the UN every year. Their membership of the system of United Nations is therefore almost a fiction."* (Childers 1994, p. 22)

Although the World Bank and IMF maintain they are prepared to co-operate with the UN, they also make it clear that they will not be bound or coordinated by it (Jolly 1995, pp. 12 f.). There has thus been no adequately coordinated approach to development or appropriate common action since the UN and the specialized agencies were established.

(f) Poor coordination within the administrations of the various UN member states[29]

Another important factor to be considered in the context of the coordination problem is the UN member states' behaviour, since the representatives of a member country's government often fail to speak with "one voice": responsibilities and terms of reference are fragmented. The fragmentation of the UN's bodies is thus mirrored in many capitals. The foreign ministries are responsible for giving general instructions to their permanent representatives at the UN, but other instructions often come from the various government departments. This greatly increases the likelihood and danger, for example, of a country's delegates expressing different views on given subjects in different UN bodies.

(g) Financing mechanisms and financial volume

There are various, sometimes linked problems as regards financial resources for UN development cooperation.

The first problem concerns the financing mechanisms and the structure of the financial resources. Basically, there are three types of financing within the UN:

- the regular UN budget,
- extraordinary contributions and
- voluntary contributions by the member states.[30]

Apart from relatively small amounts of resources,[31] the UN's operational development activities are financed from voluntary contributions. This financing mechanism has specific weaknesses. As voluntary contributions are committed annually at the United Nations Pledging Conference for Development Activities, a particular problem that arises is that there is no reliable and sustained financial base and the short-term thinking and interests of individual contributing countries may have a major influence (e.g. in the event of budget problems). This seriously affects the ability of the UN agencies concerned to plan ahead and the continuity of their activities. Owing to the system of voluntary contributions, the UN's operational development activities have also come to depend on a relatively small group of countries.[32]

A second difficulty as regards the structure of financial resources is that opportunities for spending the money available and the flexibility with which it may be spent on development are declining significantly in the various UN agencies. A fundamental distinction must be made between core and non-core resources where member states' contributions are concerned. While core resources are spent in accordance with the priorities, programming procedures, etc. of the UN agency concerned, the spending of non-core resources (e.g. trust funds, cost-sharing resources) is subject to certain conditions or restrictions imposed by the donors or programme countries (in the case of government cost-sharing resources).[33] The proportion of core resources available to various UN development cooperation agencies has fallen sharply over the years, from 97.9% (1973 - 1975) to 50.8% (1995) in UNDP's case and from 90.1 to 53.4% over the same period in UNICEF's case.[34]

> *"If taken to an extreme, excessive reliance on non-core resources could distort national and global priorities and affect the multilateral and universal character of the United Nations system."* (UN 1997c, para. 28)

A third point is that the concept of the central financing of UN development cooperation through UNDP (funding role) is being increasingly eroded. A growing proportion of contributions is no longer channelled through UNDP but paid directly to the various UN funds and programmes and other TC agencies in the UN system. In the past the resources available to the WFP, for example, has sometimes exceeded UNDP's volume. This tendency makes it far harder to adopt a coordinated approach towards countries and regions.

A fourth problem concerns the actual volume of resources. The figures compiled by DAC/OECD reveal the following: expenditure on UN development cooperation in 1995 amounted to US $ 5.877bn (net disbursements), equivalent to 9.98% of all ODA (US $ 58.94bn) and to 30.14% of multilateral ODA (US $ 19.5bn).[35] The UN Secretary-General puts the annual volume of resources passing through the UN funds and programmes from 1994 to 1996 at US $ 4.3 - 4.5bn (UN 1997c). Taken together, the UN's development cooperation agencies are thus comparable to a medium-sized donor. However, they have difficulty in attracting additional resources, partly because of their limited significance and impact. Singer refers in this context to the danger of a "vicious circle" (Singer 1995, p. 38).

As regards the volume of resources in absolute terms there is no evidence of an above-average decline in ODA in the first half of the 1990s,[36] but sharply growing pressure on the financial situation is to be seen. At the same time there is far greater demand (E/1995/98, p. 14) for UN technical cooperation (from the group of transforming economies, for example), which cannot be met.

Administration and Implementation Level

(a) Shortcomings in the quality and significance of development co-operation measures

A number of shortcomings can be identified in the actual planning and implementation of operational development measures, there being clear parallels with the general debate on technical cooperation (absence of strategic orientation, poor project design, etc.). Besides the coordination problem, which also arises at this level, the following are important in this context:

- The operations often consist of small, unrelated projects. A given focus or a substantive connection cannot therefore be recognized in many cases. As a rule, there is no policy dialogue or influence on certain policies and general conditions.[37]
- UNDP in particular is used for "gap-filling" or as "donor of last resort" to finance operations that other donors are not assisting. This may mean assisting operations with a low development priority.[38]
- Expatriate experts are often preferred to local expertise. This may result in operations being too expensive and not sufficiently adapted to local conditions (Nordic UN project 1990a, pp. 19 ff.).

– Operations frequently take too long to plan and implement and are not appropriate to needs (Koetz / Otte 1992, pp. 187 f.; Nordic UN Project 1990a, pp. 20 f.).

(b) Coordination problems at implementation level

Coordination is particularly deficient in the case of the country programmes and the UN agencies' field offices. In the past country programmes were meant to be the real planning documents for development cooperation with the various developing countries. They were drawn up by UNDP and were intended to be a "frame of reference" (UNDP 1993b, Sect. 20200 ff.) for the UN's technical cooperation. The documents failed, however, to achieve this goal of coherence and coordination (Nordic UN Project 1990a, p. 28). Country programming has undergone various structural changes (including the introduction of the Country Strategy Note - CSN) since the early 1990s.[39]

The on-the-spot coordination of the UN's various operational activities is usually poor, since in many countries UN agencies each maintain several offices and have separate programming, documentation and decision-making procedures; the Resident Coordinators' options and requirements are inadequate in this context. Even in cases where UN agencies have their offices "under one roof", efforts to coordinate their activities and those of the government concerned are hampered by uncoordinated procedures; to some extent, agencies of the UN system in fact compete with one another (e.g. in the search for suitable projects) in the various countries (Childers / Urquhart 1994, p. 90; Danida 1991a, pp. xiii ff.; Koetz / Otte 1992, p. 186).

(c) Administrative inefficiency

A shortcoming to which reference is frequently made is the administrative inefficiency that is reflected in complex administrative structures, slow work flows and, consequently, high administrative costs. UN bodies are generally assumed to be highly bureaucratic.

> *"At headquarters bureaucratic procedures are gaining ground."* (Ministry for Foreign Affairs (Netherlands) 1991, p. 288)

As examples Koetz / Otte (1992, pp. 186 ff.) refer to the small proportion of development cooperation resources actually reaching the developing countries and to the cost of the field offices, which have risen far more quickly than available financial resources. Commenting on assessment by the programme countries, an expert report states:

> *"When viewed in the light of pressing needs of the countries, the United Nations system was generally considered slow in its response."* (DP/1990/9, p. 47)

(d) Poor cost awareness

It is also frequently assumed that the UN is guilty of limited cost awareness, waste and even, in some instances, particularly widespread corruption.[40] Although the UN has had various instruments for exercising control in the past (audits, evaluations and monitoring), it did not have an effective internal auditing system until 1994 (Paschke 1996, p. 43). Commenting from his experience of corruption, embezzlement and waste, however, the Under-Secretary-General responsible for internal oversight services says in qualification:

> *"... the United Nations are no better or worse in this respect than the average comparable public organization ..."* (Paschke 1996, p. 43)

(e) Skill shortages and overstaffing[41]

Past practice shows that, when recruiting and making other decisions on staff, the UN has often failed to take anything like adequate account of criteria relating to competence and experience. Many posts are thus filled with underqualified people. Added to this, some areas of

Figure 4: Principal shortcomings of UN development cooperation in the 1990s

Level	Area
Conceptual level	1. "Gap-filling" function in international development cooperation 2. Absence of congruent, appropriate and realistic objectives 3. Absence of future orientation for the UN's technical cooperation 4. Inadequate adjustment to new challenges after the East-West conflict
Structure and policy level	1. Proliferation of UN agencies and fragmentation of tasks 2. Overlapping of lines of authority and mandates 3. Inadequate political guidance of UN development cooperation 4. Poor coordination of UN development cooperation by UN bodies 5. Insufficient coordination between the UN and its specialized agencies 6. Poor coordination within the UN member states' administrations 7. Inadequate financing mechanisms and limited financial volume
Administration and implementation level	1. Poor quality and significance of measures 2. Coordination problems at implementation level 3. Administrative inefficiency 4. Poor cost awareness 5. Skill shortages and overstaffing

the UN are overstaffed. It is estimated that the staff complement could be reduced by 10 - 15% (Deen 1996, p. 4). An aspect to which little attention has been paid in this context is the political pressure that many governments exert on the UN to fill certain posts with their nationals or specific individuals ("providing for" former politicians or senior civil servants, etc.). This must be seen as one of the main causes of the current problems in the staff sphere.

1.3.2 Reform Concepts and Initiatives

There have been numerous reform concepts and initiatives in the history of the United Nations. Many partly, predominantly or wholly concern the question whether and, if so, how the UN should reorganize or reform its operational activities in the development cooperation field. It is not possible in this study to outline all the proposals or to undertake an accurate analysis of all the reform debates. Instead, important aspects of current reform concepts and initiatives, especially in the 1990s, will be briefly discussed.

Generally speaking, the substantive objectives of reform concepts and initiatives have taken two directions. Firstly, the documents and efforts concerned may be geared to questioning UN development cooperation. This is true of only a minority of reform efforts. The US Heritage Foundation, which sometimes exercises considerable influence on opinion-forming in the administration and Congress in the USA, is one of the most important exceptions. It was successful in this respect in the 1980s (Dicke 1991, p. 667). Secondly, there is a wide range of reform concepts and initiatives aimed at strengthening or stabilizing UN development cooperation. By far the most ideas and concepts follow this line.

Although most reform concepts and initiatives take, in principle, a positive view of UN development cooperation, different positions can be identified as regards the scale - "big bang" or "patchwork" (Singer / Jolly 1995, p. 2) - and pace of the proposed reforms. On the basis of a different world order that he considers possible and desirable one of the best known participants in the reform debate, Maurice Bertrand, advocates, for example, a

> "... *radical or 'constitutionalist' approach that provides for the creation of a 'third-generation' world organization ...*" (Bertrand 1995, p. 142)

A similar argument is advanced by Puchala, who calls for the present reform thinking to be abandoned because of the incapacity for reform that has been demonstrated:

> *"This leaves the world with a limping organization that does not work very well, cannot be improved very much, and will probably remain the subject of reformers' recommendations, and the source of their frustrations, up to the millennium and beyond. (...) But because it is now reasonably clear that the United Nations either cannot or will not be effectively reformed, the time has come to think anew."* (Puchala 1996, p. 242)

Others, on the other hand, consider fundamental and comprehensive reforms of the existing UN possible and desirable.

The most important analyses, reform initiatives and reform concepts relating to the UN's development cooperation (and, to some extent, other areas of UN activity) over the years include:

- the 1969 Jackson Report,[42]
- the 1985 Bertrand Report (JIU/REP/85/9; A/40/988),
- the 1986 report of the Group of 18 (A/41/49),
- the 1988 report of the USA's United Nations Association (UNA) entitled "A Successor Vision: The United Nations of Tomorrow" (UNA-USA 1987),
- the various Nordic UN Project reports, especially those appearing in 1991 and 1996,[43]

- the 1991 Stockholm Initiative (Stiftung Entwicklung und Frieden (ed.) 1991),
- the 1991 Stanley Foundation report (Stanley Foundation 1991),
- the various reports and initiatives of Childers and Urquhart[44] in the 1990s (e.g. "Renewing the United Nations System"),
- the 1995 report entitled "The United Nations in its Second Half-Century" by the Independent Working Group on the Future of the United Nations (1995),
- the 1995 report entitled "Our Global Neighbourhood" by the Commission on Global Governance (1995),
- the initiative of the Group of 7 (G7), particularly in connection with the summit meeting held in Lyon in 1996,[45]
- the Speth proposal of 1996 (Speth 1996),
- the proposals put forward by the European Union in 1996 (EU 1996).

Of the above very heterogeneous reform concepts and initiatives proposed before the end of the 1980s, two are particularly important: the 1969 Jackson Report and the 1985 Bertrand Report.

The Jackson Report[46] "A Study of the Capacity of the United Nations Development System", was drawn up for UNDP's Governing Council and contains a comprehensive analysis of and recommendations on structural, organizational and financial aspects of UN development cooperation. It was especially critical of the absence of overarching structures and adequate overall responsibility.

The recommendations concerned in particular the strengthening of UNDP, calling for it to be transformed and upgraded to a central, coordinating body. The Jackson Report formed an important basis for the Consensus Resolution (Resolution 2699 (XXV)).

The Bertrand Report (JIU/REP/85/9; A/40/988) attracted attention because of its fundamental criticism and radical recommendations. It proposed a "third-generation world organization", which would also entail extensive changes for the economic and social field. Where operational development activities were concerned, the sectoral structures should give way to regional and subregional development agencies. The report also proposed that the UN's more effective security structures should be joined by more powerful economic structures, possibly in the form of an economic security council.

The 1990s saw a new wave of analyses and proposals for reforms. Despite the specific lines taken in these reports and studies, most of the proposals for reforms have many objectives and recommendations in common:

- A major concern expressed in almost all the documents is that development issues should not be deemed less important than other topics within the UN after the end of the East-West conflict.
- The aim should be a stronger substantive focus, possibly sustainable human development or poverty alleviation.
- Stronger conceptual and institutional links need to be forged between the UN's humanitarian assistance and development cooperation.
- A lasting improvement in operational activities should be achieved by really strengthening of UNDP and/or merging programmes and funds. This might also defuse the coordination problems within the UN member states' administrations.
- UN coordination in the developing countries should be improved. Ideally, this would be ensured through a standardized UN office.
- Financing instruments should be reformed, the aim being an adequate, continuous and appropriate financial endowment.
- Incentives and mechanisms that promote accountability within the various agencies should play a greater part in all areas of UN development cooperation.
- The skills of staff entrusted with operational development activities should be improved.

- An effective and binding new ("economic security council") or thoroughly reformed (ECOSOC) UN body should be developed for the economic and social fields.
- There should be effective involvement of the specialized agencies in the UN's coordination efforts. This is primarily true of the World Bank group and the International Monetary Fund.

1.3.3 Past Reform Measures

Over the years the UN has launched a wide range of reform efforts in the economic and social field and implemented various reform measures. Although a number of resolutions on reforms have been adopted, many have never been adequately implemented.[47]

Past reform efforts and measures have not constituted a "big bang" or a review of the UN Charter as provided for in Article 109. Almost all the reform measures have been accomplished without the UN Charter being amended. The only exceptions were the Charter amendments (under Article 108) in 1963 and 1971 to increase the number of ECOSOC members.[48]

In the first 40 - 50 years of the UN's existence reforms relating to the economic and social field can be detected particularly in three areas:

- In response to the growing number of new UN member states (mostly developing countries) in the 1950s, 1960s and 1970s many changes sought to ensure that they were better represented. This affected not only ECOSOC but also many other UN agencies, committees, etc. (Bertrand 1993a, p. 165).
- Similarly in response to the changing membership structure and as a result of the new tasks in the economic and social field several new UN agencies concerned with development issues were established, mainly in the 1960s and 1970s. This phase of institutional expansion is also a clear reflection of adjustment or reform efforts

(Hüfner 1991a, p. 19; Bertrand 1993b, pp. 423 ff.; Dicke 1995, pp. 1015 f.).

- UN Secretaries-General have adjusted the Secretariat time and again, or were expected to make adjustments (Bertrand 1993a, p. 165; Dicke 1995). In 1992 and 1997, for example, the sections of the Secretariat concerned with economic and social questions were reorganized (Childers / Urquhart 1994, pp. 72 ff.).

In the past decisions to undertake reforms have been taken primarily by the General Assembly or the Secretary-General (Beigbeder 1995, p. 244). Some reform proposals and initiatives have been based directly on decisions or recommendations. Thus the Jackson Report led to the General Assembly's Consensus Resolution (GA Resolution 2688, XXV), which laid down new rules on basic elements of operational development activities. Similarly, the General Assembly adopted a resolution on reforms on the basis of the 1986 report of the Group of 18 (A/RES/41/213).

As regards comprehensive reform objectives, it has hitherto been apparent that, although the General Assembly recognizes and enumerates major shortcomings, the resolutions it adopts lack the clarity and decisiveness that might enable reform measures to be implemented effectively in practice. As a rule, the member states are unable to reach the necessary consensus on practical recommendations and mandates for action[49] that would permit more fundamental changes to be made (such as the merging of UN programmes and funds) (A/RES/45/264). Experience shows that it is far easier to modify individual UN agencies than to make changes affecting several UN agencies or the whole UN system (Williams 1987, p. 53).

The General Assembly's main working groups on aspects of the reform have been bogged down since the mid-1990s. A total of five open-ended working groups are considering reform questions (in early 1997). They are:

- the Ad Hoc Open-Ended Working Group on an Agenda for Development,[50]

- the High-Level Open-Ended Working Group on the Financial Situation of the United Nations,
- the Informal Open-Ended Working Group on an Agenda for Peace,
- the Open-Ended High-Level Working Group on the Strengthening of the United Nations System,
- the Open-Ended Working Group on the Question of Equitable Representation and Increase in the Membership of the Security Council.

One of the main problems associated with UN development cooperation, the financial endowment and the structure of resources, clearly reveals the limited potential for reform and also the limited will for reform where many of the central issues are concerned: in many decisions and resolutions this problem is covered by the wording *"substantial increase for operational activities for development on a predictable, continuous and assured basis"* (A/RES/50/120); however, all the actors are obviously also aware that the main addressees of this demand - the leading contributors - are not politically inclined actually to implement the documents that are adopted.

Progress has been made in the 1990s mainly as a result of some limited reforms and adjustment efforts within individual UN institutions. The UN agencies active in the operational sphere have all made efforts to reform, but the scale and outcome of these efforts for the various agencies cannot be analysed and evaluated here. The reform documents do reveal, however, that the scale and depth of the various reforms and the sum of the adjustment efforts have tended to be limited in nature and have not been geared to questions of structure and principle.[51] The reforms hitherto undertaken mainly comprise measures relating to management, which is to be made less costly and modernized. Many measures concern the UN Secretariat and efforts to reduce budgets. Examples of this are various new management instruments (e.g. the Performance Appraisal System), the new post of Under-Secretary-

Box 4: UN Secretary-General Kofi Annan's reform efforts and initiatives

Soon after taking office on 1 January 1997, UN Secretary-General Kofi Annan announced wide-ranging reforms and reform initiatives relating, *inter alia*, to operational development activities and the whole economic and social sphere. A group of experts under Maurice Strong had been developing and discussing the reform measures and recommendations since the autumn of 1996 (i.e. when Secretary-General Boutros Boutros-Ghali was still in office).

For the reform of UN development cooperation three steps are important:

1. In January 1997 the Secretary-General set up "sector groups" based on the UN's four main areas of activity: (1) peace and security, (2) humanitarian affairs, (3) economic and social affairs and (4) development operations. The sector groups were intended to help in their respective spheres to improve coordination, to reduce duplication and to achieve greater coherence and consistency in policies and activities.

   Each group is to be headed by an executive committee composed of the appropriate representatives of the organizational units concerned and having a convenor. The following bodies and units are represented on the executive committee for development operations: UNDP, UNFPA, UNICEF, WFP, DDSMS, UNOPS, UNIFEM, UNAIDS, UNDCP and UNCHS. The Secretary-General appointed the UNDP Administrator as convenor. The executive committees also have the task of contributing to the UN reform process (identification of suitable measures, discussion of proposals for reform, etc.).[52]

2. The Secretary-General's core reform programme consists of two parts (two-track reform plan). The first part (track one) was presented on 17 March 1997 and included a number of items on UN development cooperation (A/INF/51/6 and A/51/829):

   - strengthening of the Resident Coordinator as the representative for UN development cooperation and leader of the UN country team;
   - all UN funds and programmes to be requested to draw up at country level an outline document on development cooperation (United Nations Development Assistance Framework - UNDAF);
   - increased efforts to use common premises and common services at country level;
   - merging of the three UN Secretariat divisions concerned with economic and social questions into one organizational unit.

3. The second part of the reform programme (track two) was presented on 16 July 1997 under the heading "Renewing the United Nations: A Programme for Reform" (UN 1997g). Kofi Annan described the programme as a wide-ranging and ambitious attempt thoroughly to reorganize the UN by means of a "quiet revolution".[53]

   An important point of departure for the programme for the reform of development cooperation is the statement that the existing institutional structures of the UN funds and programmes are to be maintained.

Box 4: UN Secretary-General Kofi Annan's reform efforts and initiatives (cont.)

"*The diversity, distinctiveness and specialised focus of the United Nations funds and programmes involved in development cooperation provide important benefits to the United Nations and to the developing countries. The reform process is designed to maintain and reinforce the distinctive nature of these entities while seeking to facilitate their functioning in a more unified, cooperative and coherent framework as members of the United Nations family.*" (UN 1997g, para. 148)

Far more extensive integration of the agencies operationally active in the development sphere was, on the other hand, originally sought by the reform group under Maurice Strong, but was successfully prevented from various sides.[54]

Kofi Annan's programme refers to the following reform measures and initiatives:[55]

- The sector group for development operations is replaced by the United Nations Development Group (UNDG). The executive committee is re-formed, with UNDP, UNICEF and UNFPA and, if necessary, other agencies as its members. UNDP continues to provide the convenor.
- To achieve goal-oriented cooperation, programme coherence and synergy effects, the various programmes are formulated and submitted as part of a single outline programme (United Nations Development Assistance Framework - UNDAF); the resources for the various funds and programmes continue to be shown separately.
- At country level all UN funds and programmes report to the office of the Resident Coordinator, who acts as the Secretary-General's representative and leader of the country team.
- The UN is to have common premises at country level, to be known as "UN Houses".
- The member states are recommended to consider agreements on closer integration in the political guidance of UNDP/UNFPA and UNICEF and the holding of cohesive meetings of the executive boards and joint committees.
- The Secretary-General will put forward a proposal for fairer financial burden-sharing, the aim being to increase core resources. A new financing mechanism entailing not only voluntary contributions but also negotiated pledges on a multiannual basis is also recommended.
- A new office for development financing is set up, its task being to seek innovative approaches to fund-raising.
- The Secretary-General proposes that the General Assembly should pave the way for savings achieved through measures that improve efficiency at the UN to be transferred to a special budget for development programmes ("development dividend").

General for Internal Oversight Services, the reduction of the number of Secretariat divisions from 20 to 12 and a reduction in the staff complement by 20% in the past ten years (Paschke 1996; Frankfurter Allgemeine Zeitung, 21 June 1996).

In addition, measures have been taken to clarify the tasks of the General Assembly and ECOSOC and the division of labour between these two main organs and to reorganize the bodies that supervise the UN programmes and funds (A/RES/48/162). The decisions and recommendations that have been adopted since the General Assembly's 47th session include the following:

- transformation of the Governing Councils of UNDP/UNFPA and UNICEF into smaller Executive Boards (A/RES/48/162),
- emphasis on the need to increase resources for the UN's operational activities (A/RES/50/227),
- introduction of country strategy notes (A/RES/47/199),
- confirmation of the Resident Coordinator system and rules on various aspects in this sphere (including specification of the role of the RC system in relation to the UN Coordinator for Humanitarian Assistance, follow-up to the world conferences and the selection and organizational background of the RCs) (A/RES/47/199; A/RES/50/120).

The most important General Assembly documents on the reform of the UN's economic and social field, especially in the operational sphere, are two resolutions, A/RES/47/199 and A/RES/50/120; A/RES/48/162 and A/RES/50/227 are also relevant. Various reports provide regular information on the state of the implementation of the resolutions on reforms.[56]

UN Secretary-General Kofi Annan tried to show himself to be reform-oriented in his very first months in office. Only a few days after being installed, he decided to set up new coordinating bodies (executive committees) for the UN's four main areas of responsibility (peace and security, humanitarian affairs, economic and social affairs and development activities) (UN 1997a, 1997b). As early as March 1997 he submitted his first official reform document, and in July 1997 he published his overall reform package (A/51/829; UN 1997g). Some of his reform concepts and decisions are based directly on demands from the G7 and the EU. His decisions to merge the three development divisions of the UN Secretariat, for example, accord with the G7's and EU's views. However, the Secretary-General is not expected to undertake any structure-changing reforms (e.g. the merging of UN funds and programmes), since he has yet to receive a mandate from the member states to do so.

Despite the many and varied reform efforts that have been made so far in the 1990s, there are few signs of its being possible to negotiate and adopt a comprehensive package for the reform of the UN as a whole or of its operational activities in the area of development cooperation in the foreseeable future.[57] Efforts in the coming years will therefore continue to focus on minor adjustments and changes.

1.3.4 Views on the Reform Debate

Reforms in the field of UN development cooperation very much depend on the UN's member states and also on its administration. In the various UN bodies it is the government representatives who take the decisions to initiate reforms, or are ultimately to blame if the necessary decisions are not taken; they define the reform objectives and provide the instruments and resources for their achievement. The member states are therefore also to blame if reform efforts are inadequate, inconsistent or no more than rhetorical. Although all the actors involved have in the past repeatedly declared their desire to eliminate shortcomings by undertaking reforms, their views differ most widely on the objectives to be pursued with reform measures. The most important positions of the main actors (industrialized countries, developing countries and the UN administration) can be roughly outlined as follows:

1. Among the industrialized countries two central positions can be identified. Firstly, for the USA[58] in particular much of the reform debate is a question of the "right management". Its main aim is to see "excessive costs" reduced and more rational and efficient structures installed. Most of the large contributors among the industrialized countries identify with this position, though less forcefully (Beigbeder 1995, pp. 253 f.; Bertrand 1993b, pp. 420 f.; Bertrand 1995, pp. 142 ff.; Paschke 1996, pp. 41 f.). The claim that the World Bank performs far better than the UN in the development cooperation field has been important for the attitude of this group in the past; it has also been seen as justifying a comparatively modest commitment to UN development cooperation.[59] Secondly, the Scandinavian countries in particular focus on the strengthening of the UN in the context of operational activities. To this end, structures and procedures should be reformed (Nordic UN Project 1991b, pp. 13 f.; Nordic UN Project 1996). However, there has been a more recent tendency for the Scandinavian countries to place greater emphasis on their own objectives in the multilateral organizations than they did in the past. Such "bilateralization tendencies" in UN development cooperation are to be seen, for example, in the Danish government's strategy document on multilateral development cooperation (Danida 1996a, 1996b).

   In 1996 the Group of 7 and the EU member states both presented more specific proposals and positions on the reform of the UN in the economic and social field than in previous documents.[60] This constructive approach was also reflected in the UN Secretary-General's proposals for reforms (1997).

2. The developing countries, in the form of the Group of 77, are opposed to a reductionist or "management approach" to the reform of the UN. Their position is essentially guided by their interest in obtaining as much assistance as possible with few conditions attached and in maintaining and expanding the various UN agencies as democratic fora in which they enjoy equal rights. Accordingly, they place the emphasis in the reform debate on financing (i.e. a substantial increase in resources), greater involvement and monitoring of the specialized agencies (particularly the World

Bank group and the International Monetary Fund) by ECOSOC and the preservation of the various UN funds and programmes (South Centre 1995, 1996; Beigbeder 1995, pp. 253 f.).

3. Like his predecessor, Boutros Boutros-Ghali, at the beginning of his term of office, UN Secretary-General Kofi Annan has shown himself to be very reform-oriented and has put forward some practical proposals and initiatives. As, however, many of the more radical reforms require the member states' approval, the Secretary-General depends in almost all important reform issues on the conditions created by the General Assembly and possibly the Security Council. As regards the structure of UN development cooperation it can also be assumed that the existing UN funds and programmes have a major interest in retaining their independence and are trying to maintain a separate identity.[61] Strong vested interests have become established here; this system of interests is also based on informal staffing keys for the senior levels of the various UN bodies.

1.4 Conclusions

1.4.1 Political Dimensions and Implications of the Reform Debate

It is generally accepted that UN development cooperation is in need of reform.[62] Many publications and innumerable political declarations are based on this assumption, which is rarely analysed and hardly disputed.[63] Although this consensus on the need for reform is substantively justified, it also raises problems. The main problem is that the debate on the need for the reform of the UN in the sphere of operational activities not only performs the function for the member states of indicating shortcomings and objectives for a reform: the identification of weaknesses and the notification of pending reforms also constitute a political instrument in the context of domestic debates in individual member states and in international political disputes over UN policy. The problematical aspects include the following:

1. The apparent consensus on reforms helps to conceal the opposing views of the participants in the reform debate. The member states' declaration on the UN's 50th anniversary, for example, includes a number of passages that again emphasize the need to reform the whole of the UN:

   "In order to be able to respond effectively to the challenges of the future and expectations of the United Nations held by peoples around the world, it is essential that the United Nations itself be reformed and modernized." (UN 1995, p. 9)

   On the UN's development activities it says, among other things:

   "Improve the effectiveness and efficiency of the United Nations system for development and strengthen its role in all relevant fields of international economic cooperation (...)" (UN 1995, p. 5)

   However, the words hide the fact that agreement cannot be reached on the analysis of the need for and substance of reforms, on the reform measures that should be taken and on the objectives to be pursued.[64] A decisive obstacle to reform thus lies not in the UN but in its member states.

   "But the lack among Governments of a conceptual consensus as to the nature of the most pressing problems facing the world community and the appropriate role for international institutions in seeking solutions to those problems makes it extremely difficult to redesign bodies and institutions." (Renninger 1987), p. 106)

2. Many governments go in for "UN-bashing", without suggesting any constructive reform options. In many cases at least, this approach reflects short-term national interests rather than efforts to bring about reforms. Maurice Bertrand and others have pointed out in their studies on several occasions that member states are not primarily interested in the UN's effectiveness and efficiency: the policy of the large industrialized countries in particular is often characterized by disinterest and indifference, especially towards the UN's economic and social activities.[65] The staff policy pursued

by the member states, the governments' attitude towards contributions and the vehemence with which the UN is frequently criticized are a few practical examples.

"UN-bashing" is a contributory cause of unthinking criticism, the emphasis placed on the UN's weaknesses and the disregard for its strengths.[66] Comprehensive and comparative assessments of the work of the UN compared to other international organizations and individual countries are rare.[67] As a rule, studies that attempt such comparisons are ultimately very cautious in the statements they make. They do not at least permit across-the-board fundamental criticism, like that frequently levelled at the UN and UN development cooperation.

3. The criticism of the UN overlooks the background against which the current system was developed.

"Both the United Nations system and the United Nations intergovernmental structure have developed in an incremental and ad hoc fashion, following no overall plan, although a clear concept lay behind the creation of the decentralized system. The result is a system organized quite differently from what could be called the 'textbook model' of organization ..." (Renninger 1987, pp. 96 f; emphasis as in the original text)

Although it is easy in these circumstances to criticize the organizational structures,[68] the specific conditions under which the UN evolved and the requirements for its reform are overlooked.

"The member states (...) prescribe the tasks, invented the complex procedures, demand the Secretariat's extensive and costly services for their bodies, ensure compliance with the rules - and oppose anything that affects their interests as individuals or as a group." (Paschke 1996, p. 43)

1.4.2 Analysis of the Reform Debate and Implications for UNDP

The analysis in this section also enables various conclusions to be drawn on UN development cooperation and UNDP for the reform debate. These conclusions can be summarized in four points:

1. Generally speaking, the debate on the reform of the UN's operational (and non-operational) development activities and of the whole UN system concerns various levels, with complex problems and deficiencies. These can be roughly summarized as follows:
   - poor political guidance and coordination within the UN;
   - inadequate mechanisms and instruments for coordination between the UN and the specialized agencies, making it almost impossible for the latter to be involved in overarching approaches and deliberations of the UN;
   - proliferation of UN development agencies, which has resulted in the fragmentation and duplication of tasks;
   - poor quality and inadequate cost awareness at the UN;
   - inadequate and unstable financial endowment of the UN funds and programmes.
2. UNDP plays a central role with regard to the shortcomings of UN development cooperation and the steps that need to be taken to reform it. Many of the main problems associated with operational development activities are directly linked to aspects of coordination, political guidance or financing. These aspects have a direct impact on the tasks that UNDP has to perform. A successful reform of UNDP will therefore have considerable favourable implications for the whole of the UN's development cooperation.

   Parallel, complementary reform processes are needed. The whole system of UN development cooperation must be addressed in various ways to enable UNDP to become more effective (e.g. with respect to institutional fragmentation). However, reform efforts aimed directly at UNDP will be needed, although they will not be enough on their own.[69]

3. Many useful reform concepts have been proposed, although none has so far had any significant influence in practice.

   "Yet the sad fact is that the reformers' recommendations for the United Nations are being taken no more seriously today than they ever were in the past, and, as students of the United Nations well know, the organization's past is strewn with the corpses of dead reform proposals." (Puchala 1996, p. 230)

   The main obstacle here has been the absence of an adequate consensus among the UN member states in favour of the implementation of appropriate reform measures. The political actors have not defined the necessary political prescriptions to ensure clarity on the direction, scale and pace of reform. Inadequate reforms are therefore largely due to shortcomings in the political opinion-forming and decision-making processes.

4. At present only an approach involving limited reforms seems realistic - though hardly desirable - for improving the effectiveness of UN development cooperation. In the foreseeable future it is highly unlikely that a "package" for the reform of UN development cooperation as a whole or the UN as a whole will emerge ("big bang"). Although the minor reforms that have been undertaken in the 1990s can be rated positively, the pace of reform is too slow and the intensity of reform should be increased.

   Given the limited capacity for reforming UN development cooperation comprehensively, it is extremely important that UNDP should not wait for a "big bang" but undertake reforms within its existing framework and terms of reference.

2 Need to Reform UNDP

2.1 Introduction

UNDP's history is characterized by crisis-ridden development. The debates on and analyses of UNDP in the 1970s, 1980s and, to a great extent, the 1990s have almost all detected symptoms of crisis.[1] Since its establishment UNDP has thus always been engaged in a process of attempting to cope with its own shortcomings and a fervent search for appropriate tasks and a suitable role for itself. The conclusions that have hitherto been drawn in the debate on development and policy have been varied and contentious. It is suggested in some quarters (though not often) that UNDP is superfluous, most contributions to the debate focusing on the elimination of the UNDP's current deficiencies (see, in particular, section III.3).

A statement in the report drawn up by a Task Force of the Council on Foreign Relations on "*American National Interest and the United Nations*" can be regarded as symptomatic and as an example:

> *"The Task Force spent some time discussing the role of the United Nations in promoting sustainable development but could not reach agreement. Some members argued that the role of the U.N. Development Programme (UNDP) and other U.N. agencies was important in complementing the activities of the World Bank and the International Monetary Fund (IMF), the regional banks, and bilateral programs. Others viewed U.N. efforts in this area as superfluous, and still others thought them counterproductive, while recognizing that they may be necessary to secure the support of other nations for those U.N. programs that are considered important to the United States."* (Council on Foreign Relations (ed.) 1996, pp. 7 f.)

Against this background, this section sets out to analyse the need to reform UNDP, especially for the 1990s. The levels of analysis already introduced will be used to identify and discuss the main shortcomings and problem areas.

A study of the main shortcomings is necessary and relevant for several reasons. For one thing, it forms a link with the appraisal of the debate on the reform of the whole of UN development cooperation, i.e. it will reveal parallels in the debate and in the relationship between UNDP and other UN agencies. For another, the analysis of the shortcomings forms an important basis for the classification and assessment in the following sections of reform proposals, reform measures and reforms that have not been undertaken.

This section focuses on the areas in which reforms are needed. However, the question as to the specific benefits and advantages UNDP has to offer is also legitimate and relevant to the debate on development and policy. Although an in-depth analysis of these positive aspects cannot be undertaken here, this dimension will be briefly examined at the end of the chapter. Elements of a more effective UNDP profile are also discussed at greater length in section III.5.

2.2 Need for Reform: Shortcomings

Almost all assessments of UNDP assume there to be a substantial and comprehensive need for reform: "*... it must be acknowledged that UNDP ... still faces serious challenges and presents serious weaknesses in its capability fully to fulfill its mandate.*" (Centre for Development Research 1996, p. 32) This attitude is largely shared by UNDP, which criticizes itself and emphasizes the need for its reform. Administrator Speth has stressed on several occasions that "*UNDP must change to respond to its identified weaknesses and realize the potential inherent in its mandate*". (Speth 1994a, p. 5)

The need for the reform of UNDP - compared to other UN agencies - is often rated particularly high: "*Of the institutions reviewed, UNDP seems the one needing the most substantial reform and revitalisation*

(...)" (Gwin 1995, p. 115), as, for example, Gwin of the Overseas Development Council notes in a comparative analysis. It is argued that its particular need for reform is due not only to the major requirement for change at UNDP itself but also to the effects it is assumed such reform will have on the whole operational sphere of UN development cooperation and cooperation with other actors in the development field.

Although the environment for UNDP, for the UN's operational activities and for all international development cooperation has changed constantly in the past, the need for reform suggested in UNDP's case has remained basically unchanged. The persistent criticism is both an important indicator of inadequate efforts to adjust in the past and a sign that the shortcomings affect the basic structures and are attributable to UNDP's involvement in the UN's and UN system's operational development activities (and the cumbersome reform process associated with it).

The debate on the need for reform concerns all UNDP's important spheres and functions. It embraces aspects of the substantive profile, coordination, guidance and financing. As financing and coordination are UNDP's core tasks as an agency providing guidance, serious shortcomings in these areas may also be linked to basic questions concerning UNDP's continued existence. From this a number of other deficiencies requiring reform can be deduced, further increasing the pressure for reform. In other words, many problems are closely interrelated and cannot be considered in isolation.

2.2.1 Shortcomings at Conceptual Level

Absence of a Suitable Substantive Profile / Operationalization of a Paradigm

One of the main, typical criticisms levelled at UNDP until the early 1990s was that it lacked a clear substantive profile, a focus in development policy terms and a profiled strategy (Speth 1994a; Gwin 1995, p. 107). UNDP was seen as a development agency that offered "everything", did not focus on specific target groups, sectors or other aspects and pursued a "no-strategy approach" (Kienbaum & Partners 1991, p. 12). A 1991 study, for example, notes the following:

> *"One of the principal unwritten laws of UNDP seems to be: 'Don't have a strategy.'"* (Kienbaum & Partners 1991, p. 13)

In the 1980s and the first half of the 1990s UNDP undertook development measures in a wide variety of areas at national, regional and global level. The areas included the environment, energy, the promotion of small businesses, transport infrastructure, food security, rural development, measures to combat HIV/AIDS, health, education and humanitarian assistance. Table 1 gives an overview of the sectoral breakdown of UNDP interventions and the use of its financial resources.

The absence of focal areas was largely a deliberate principle of UNDP policy in the past. It was seen as reflecting UNDP's political neutrality and the programme countries' national sovereignty in the selection of development cooperation operations.[2] UNDP thus rated neutrality and sovereignty - under the conditions of the East-West conflict - higher than a given development policy line. Its sectorally undefined, broad profile resulted in its image being unclear. The absence of strategic orientation was particularly to blame for many of the main contributors perceiving UNDP as an agency that provided funds on very soft terms and without adequate development orientation and criteria.[3]

Since the early 1990s UNDP has been making a great effort to sharpen its substantive profile and to accomplish a clear change of course (section III.4). A decisive first step towards the development of a paradigm has been the *Human Development Report* published by UNDP since 1990. The report has done much to shape UNDP's substantive image and its external profile (UNDP 1994b, p. 8; Gwin 1995, p. 107) and has stimulated debates within UNDP. Other important steps towards substantive orientation were programmatic decisions taken by the Executive Board in 1994 and 1995, which have resulted in UNDP

Table 1: Sectoral breakdown of UNDP interventions (projects and programmes based on ACC criteria, project portfolio at 31 December 1996)

Sector	Number of operations	% of total operations	Total financial outlay[a] (US $)	% of total financial outlay
Agriculture, forestry and fisheries	581	9.94	740,093,385	10.98
Communications and information	97	1.66	127,792,028	1.90
Culture	28	0.48	219,253,689	3.25
Education	226	3.87	363,348,412	5.39
Employment	156	2.67	156,562,395	2.32
Energy	106	1.81	128,633,511	1.91
Environment	447	7.65	423,186,395	6.28
General development issues	2,177	37.26	2,155,106,043	31.98
General statistics	58	0.99	63,973,319	0.95
Health	256	4.38	601,519,813	8.93
Human settlements	121	2.07	178,824,476	2.65
Humanitarian assistance and disaster management	205	3.51	178,788,095	2.65
Industry	333	5.70	296,379,389	4.40
Natural resources	296	5.07	338,427,177	5.02
Political affairs	78	1.33	108,888,786	1.62
Population	17	0.29	16,993,825	0.25
Science and technology	116	1.99	118,022,573	1.75
Social development	293	5.01	173,453,187	2.57
Trade and development	140	2.40	126,693,959	1.88
Transport	112	1.92	223,770,770	3.32
Undefined	0	0.00	0	0.00
Total	5,843	100.00	6,739,711,227	100.0

[a] including core and non-core resources

Source: UNDP (1997o), p. 38

having a core mission and a mission statement, shifting the emphasis to sustainable human development. UNDP's efforts to change and sharpen its substantive profile are considered in greater depth in section III.4.

Inadequate Account Taken of the State of the Debate on Technical Cooperation

In the past UNDP has often been criticized for the poor quality of its approaches to development and for the consequent shortcomings in the quality of its operations.[4] This criticism has been taken up by UNDP itself in the *Human Development Report*, for example:

> *"... the technical assistance programmes of the UN system, including those of UNDP, have had limited success at building up the national capacity of developing countries."* (UNDP 1992b, p. 77)

UNDP's organization is only partly to blame for the shortcomings in its technical cooperation; they are largely related to problems which also affect other donors and which have been discussed in section II.2.

In the past the most serious criticisms of UNDP's TC have concerned the following:[5]

- overly supply-driven operations,
- insufficient account taken of standards of excellence during the planning and implementation of projects and programmes,
- for too long too low a priority given in operations to capacity-building in the developing countries, to independent project management and to implementation by the recipient countries themselves (national execution); operations instead excessively focused on expatriate personnel and external implementing organizations,
- UNDP activities insufficiently adapted to the level of development in specific countries or regions,

– UNDP staff employed often inadequately qualified for the tasks concerned.

UNDP's TC debate and TC instruments in the 1990s differ from those of other donor agencies in two important respects. Firstly, since the mid-1980s UNDP has been making a deliberate attempt through the National Technical Co-operation Assessment and Programme (NaTCAP) to help developing countries to undertake a more extensive and systematic analysis of their potential local capacities. The NaTCAP was established as a means of increasing the effectiveness of TC, not just UNDP. Secondly, UNDP plays only a limited role in the implementation of its TC. Until the early or mid-1990s it in fact usually depended for the quality of implementation on the appropriate executing agencies under the tripartite approach. The tripartite mechanism is based on the following division of labour (UNDP 1993a, Sect. 0103; DP/1990/9): (1) UNDP is responsible for guiding and coordinating TC, (2) the operations concerned are integrated into the government's development efforts and (3) agencies with the appropriate skills actually implement the measures. The tripartite mechanism has now been largely abandoned, with responsibility for projects transferred to the programme countries (national execution) (section III.4).

Thought is being given within UNDP to how the recommendations made in the evaluation can and should be implemented. The first phase of the NaTCAP is now generally regarded as having been completed. Within UNDP the option of implementing the recommendations on the second phase through the adoption of an approach known as *National Capacity Policies and Programmes* (NaTCADS) is being discussed. However, there is far less interest in the NaTCAP, a modified follow-up programme and similar issues within UNDP in the second half of the 1990s than there was in the 1980s.

Box 5: National Technical Co-operation Assessment and Programme (NaTCAP)

The aim of the National Technical Co-operation Assessment and Programme (NaTCAP) initiated by UNDP in the mid-1980s is to help developing countries with the analysis of their potential local capacities. The NaTCAP is intended to help increase the independence of human and institutional skills in socioeconomic development. It is a mechanism that endeavours to increase the effectiveness of TC by undertaking an analysis of national potential and current shortcomings with regard to TC. The NaTCAP process is the responsibility of the government of the country concerned. UNDP offers assistance with methodological, organizational and financial questions (for NaTCAPs see UNDP 1991d, 1991e; 1993b, pp. 1 ff., Sect. 20101; Williams 1995b, 1995c).

The NaTCAP is divided into two phases:

- In the first phase the various countries and their experience of TC are appraised. This analysis usually results in a technical cooperation framework statement (TCPFD), which is approved by the government concerned as domestic policy.
- In the second phase (TCP - technical cooperation programming) the aim is to identify TC projects on the basis of the TCPFD and to reorient current operations by reference to the national priorities identified. The NaTCAP process also seeks to undertake cost calculations for all TC projects and to include them in the domestic budgets.

In general, the NaTCAP has proved successful in some respects. NaTCAPs have helped to enable developing countries to assess their TC potential and need for external support from bi- and multilateral donors. Berg attributes much of the information on TC and the developing countries' criticism of it to this fact:

> *"Much more is now known about the nature and performance of technical assistance at country level than was the case even a decade ago. A principal reason for this growth of information is the introduction by UNDP in the mid-1980s of the NaTCAP (...) idea (...)"* (Berg 1993, p. 4; Gwin 1995, p. 108)

While the first phase of the NaTCAP process can be regarded as largely successful in most countries, the second phase proceeds unsatisfactorily. As many problems have arisen during implementation, the interest of the governments concerned has waned, and it has been possible to integrate the NaTCAP mechanisms operationally (to some extent) in only three countries. The 1995 NaTCAP evaluation ascribes this to four main problems: (1) the excessive complexity of the project, the aim being to achieve a great deal in a short time; (2) the absence of sufficient donor commitment; (3) the absence of mainstreaming in the UNDP field offices; (4) in most countries the process was deemed to be too externally dependent and as a UNDP headquarters project.[6]

Box 5: National Technical Co-operation Assessment and Programme (NaTCAP) (cont.)

The evaluation recommended that the first phase of the NaTCAP should be discontinued and that the approach should be geared to the second phase:

> *"No further elaboration or extension of NaTCAP's phase one national TC Policy Framework Papers should be undertaken. This phase has completed its objective of identifying TC deficiencies. The task now is two-fold:*
>
> *First, it is important to deal with TC issues directly in capacity terms and follow-up on policy framework in such terms. (...)*
>
> *Second, UNDP should engage as an intermediary with the LDCs and donors concerning reform of TC practices which strengthen capacity-building, working with the Development Assistance Committee, and interested donors directly at the country level."* (Williams 1995b, p. 8)

UNDP's own evaluations permit some conclusions on the quality of TC to be drawn, albeit on a limited scale. So far UNDP has carried out three analyses (in 1992, 1994 and 1996) of general tendencies in project evaluation (project performance). The analyses evaluate different dimensions of project design and, above all, project quality (UNDP 1997d, p. 109).

Where project design is concerned, UNDP generally identifies positive tendencies. The evaluation relating to 1996 finds the design of 29% of all the projects evaluated to be very good or good. The problems detected concern, *inter alia*, the success criteria, overly optimistic project assumptions and unsuitable institutional agreements.

Table 2: Tendencies in the quality of project design (percentage of the number of projects evaluated; based on the year of project evaluation)

	1992 survey	1994 survey	1996 survey
Very good / good	20	27	29
Satisfactory	50	46	45
Unsatisfactory	30	27	26

Source: UNDP (1997d), p. 112

UNDP's evaluation of actual project quality covers the following aspects:

- relevance of projects;
- project performance:
  - efficiency;
  - achievement of results (outputs);
  - achievement of immediate objectives;
- success of projects:
  - institution-building;
  - sustainability;
  - cost-effectiveness.

Findings on these aspects can be seen in Table 3. Most projects were assigned to the middle of three evaluation categories where the quality indicators were concerned. This categorization does not, however, reveal whether evaluations or effects "tend to be positive" or "tend to be negative". The categories used by UNDP[7] are therefore of little informative value.

From the evaluation results UNDP infers a need for change primarily in three areas (UNDP 1997d, p. 116):

- improvement of the monitoring system at project level,
- closer involvement of target groups in the project cycle and
- improved assessment of the domestic institutions responsible for project management.

Table 3: Quality of UNDP projects based on evaluations studied (selected indicators; data for the surveys conducted in 1992, 1994 and 1996, %)

	Achievement of results (outputs)			Achievement of immediate objectives			Institution-building			Sustainability		
	1992	1994	1996	1992	1994	1996	1992	1994	1996	1992	1994	1996
Very good/ good or significant	13	16	18	13	16	17	15	19	21	18	20	26
Satisfactory	71	67	64	66	63	63	59	56	54	53	51	47
Unsatisfactory or poor	17	17	18	21	21	20	26	25	25	29	28	27

Source: UNDP (1997d), pp. 113 ff.

Need for Adjustment to New Political Challenges

Generally speaking, the need for development cooperation institutions to adjust to new international conditions has increased significantly since the late 1980s and early 1990s. This greater need for adjustment is primarily due to the end of the East-West conflict. UNDP has only partly adapted to the associated challenges.

The challenges are complex and relate to different areas (Speth 1994a, pp. 2 ff.; UNDP 1993d; Riddell 1996; ODI 1994):

– The "concept of entitlement" (Speth 1994b, p. 2) that was shared by the donors under the conditions of the East-West conflict, whereby UNDP almost automatically transferred resources on a given scale for political reasons, is no longer accepted or supported by the major contributing countries.

– Owing to the political upheavals in Central and Eastern Europe and the former Soviet Union there is a fresh need in this region for development cooperation and, above all, consultancy services in the form of TC.

– The need for assistance in such politically sensitive spheres as democratization, human rights and demilitarization has risen sharply (political changes in many African countries, economic and political transformation of former communist countries, etc.). Until the early 1990s international development cooperation had little know-how to offer in these specialist areas and was also very restrained. The experience gained in these areas in the meantime must be supplemented in the future.

– The UN has been far more active in the areas of peace-keeping and peace-making since the late 1980s than in previous decades. To some extent this has led to a growth of interest in expanding UNDP's activities in the context of crises and conflicts (crisis prevention, post-conflict measures, etc.).

– Widespread aid fatigue among the people and politicians of many industrialized countries has led to an increase in fundamental doubts about the purpose and benefits of development cooperation.

In many cases the role of development cooperation in the coming decades needs to be reconsidered and redefined. This is largely due to the fact that important motives for development cooperation have become irrelevant or relevant in different ways since the end of the East-West conflict (geostrategic and foreign policy interests). Furthermore, it is clear that the expectations associated with development cooperation in the past have not been adequately fulfilled.

- Aid fatigue has had a particular impact on multilateral institutions, and especially UN agencies and UNDP. The waning commitment is reflected, for example, in a decline in financial participation. The Development Assistance Committee refers to this tendency in its reports:

  "The proportion of total ODA contributed to multilateral agencies was almost 35 per cent in the early 1980s (...) The multilateral share of ODA declined to around 30 per cent in 1993-1994, partly reflecting a fall in contributions to development banks, and donors trimmed support for a number of United Nations agencies in part because of concerns about the effectiveness and accountability of some of these institutions. The fall in multilateral ODA would have been larger but for a substantial increase in donors' support for those international agencies involved in emergency and disaster relief." (OECD 1996c, p. 93)

2.2.2 Shortcomings at Structural and Policy Level

2.2.2.1 Financing[8]

Three problems in particular affect the financing of UNDP: first, an inadequate financial endowment compared to the absolute volume available; second, financing mechanisms that provide no more than an unstable base and, in some cases, permit too little flexibility in development policy terms; third, UNDP's failure to play its funding role.

Financial Endowment

UNDP has not succeeded in attracting extensive financial resources in the past. Of crucial importance in this context are the core resources, which can be earmarked for the core programme (section III.1); in 1996 they amounted to US $ 850 million. US $ 1,134 million in non-core resources was also available in 1996.

UNDP assumes the programme countries have a far greater need, which cannot be satisfied because of financial restrictions. It currently estimates financial requirements for the various country programmes to be on average four times greater than funds actually available.[9]

In terms of voluntary contributions or expenditure documented in the OECD statistics, UNDP is comparable in importance to smaller DAC countries (such as Switzerland and Australia). Other multilateral donors, such as the World Bank group, the regional development banks and the EU, have far greater financial potential. While UNDP's financial scope was similar to the IDA's and EC's in the early 1970s, it has declined almost continuously and sharply in financial significance compared to these institutions (Table 4).

Although UNDP has been able to increase its core resources in nominal terms in the past, the changes in real terms, or adjusted for inflation, show that, despite some fluctuations, UNDP's financial volume has remained largely stagnant.[10] In the first half of the 1990s revenue declined significantly even in nominal terms (Table 5 and Figure 5). From 1992 to 1996 core resources fell from US $ 1,074m to 850m; a further decline is expected to have occurred in 1997 (UN 1997c; para. 14, and Table 5).

Table 4: Net disbursements by multilateral agencies on concessional terms (in US $m and as a percentage of the total)

	1970 - 1971	1980	1990	1994	1995
Financial institutions	448 (37.9%)	2,274 (29.3%)	6,016 (44.5%)	7,564 (39.3%)	6,975 (35.8%)
thereof: IDA	225 (19.1%)	1,543 (19.9%)	3,912 (29.0%)	5,609 (19.1%)	4,928 (25.3%)
United Nations	529 (44.8%)	2,487 (32.0%)	4,496 (33.3%)	5,874 (30.5%)	5,877 (30.1%)
thereof: UNDP	219 (18.5%)	660 (8.5%)	1,130 (8.4%)	1,241 (6.4%)	1,248 (6.4%)
EC/EU Commission	203 (17.2%)	1,043 (13.4%)	2,563 (19.0%)	4,575 (23.7%)	4,723 (24.2%)
Other multilateral donors	0 (0%)	1,969 (25.3%)	435 (3.2%)	1,255 (6.5%)	1,925 (9.9%)
Total disbursements by multilateral donors on concessional terms	1,181 (100%)	7,773 (100%)	13,510 (100%)	19,268 (100%)	19,500 (100%)

Source: Based on OECD (1996a), p. A36, and OECD (1997a), p. A42

Table 5: UNDP's financial resources, revenue from 1991 to 1996 (US $m)						
	1991	1992	1993	1994	1995	1996
I. UNDP's core programme (core resources)	1,022	1,074	908	917	930	850
II. Other resources (non-core resources) thereof:	268	382	462	858	888	1,134
a) cost-sharing thereof:	242	272	383	546	664	855
- bilateral	74	87	88	83	68	143
- multilateral	12	14	13	16	16	22
- programme countries	156	170	281	447	580	690
b) trust funds thereof:	22	106	75	305	214	268
- bilateral	15	28	57	165	132	165
- multilateral	6	77	18	139	82	102
- programme countries	1	1	1	0	1	1
c) non-budgetary/other	4	4	4	7	10	11
III. Total financial resources	1,290	1,456	1,370	1,775	1,818	1,984
Source: UNDP / Division for Resources Mobilization						

The erosion of the UNDP's core resources in the first half of the 1990s coincided with a significant increase in non-core resources, which makes up for the decline to only a very limited extent (see the comments below).

In taking its decisions, UNDP's Executive Board is guided by the need to raise the resource base and also to change the financing bases and mechanisms. The Executive Board

> *"Stresses the need for a substantial increase in resources for operational activities for development on a predictable, continuous and assured basis, commensurate with the increasing needs of developing countries ..."* (Decision 95/23 of the Executive Board, reproduced in DP/1996/1; emphasis as in the original text)

For a time (especially in 1996) UNDP encountered major resource outflow problems (about US $ 600m), which resulted in a delivery crisis (DP/1997/6, pp. 60 ff.; DP/1997/16, pp. 7 f.; DP/1996/CRP.19). Some contributing countries interpreted this as meaning that additional resources could not be appropriately channelled through UNDP. The resource outflow problems were primarily due to the expectation of a greater reduction in contributions (with corresponding implications for the volume pledged), the complete replacement of the country programming system, the reduction in opportunities for guidance owing to the increase in national execution and the large number of crisis-hit countries where appropriate resource utilization could not be guaranteed.

Financing Mechanisms

In principle, two sources for the financing of UNDP activities can be distinguished:[11] (1) voluntary contributions to the core programme, with no specific restriction on utilization; these contributions are known as core resources and are received solely from governments; (2) other payments made subject to certain conditions or restrictions as to their utilization; these payments are known as non-core resources, i.e. they do not form part of the UNDP's core programme.

The distinction between core and non-core resources and non-budgetary resources is crucially important, since core resources may be used for processes and priorities specified by UNDP and its decision-making bodies. How non-core resources are used, on the other hand, largely depends on priorities set by the countries contributing them.

Both core resources, or voluntary contributions, and non-core resources pose problems for UNDP's effectiveness.

(a) Core resources/voluntary contributions

Like almost all other operational activities of the UN, the UNDP's core programme is financed by voluntary contributions[12] from the UN member countries; in UNDP practice this is the most important form of contribution whose use is not restricted.[13] The amounts contributed are specified at the annual pledging conferences held by the UN General Assembly.

The specific features of voluntary contributions pose structural problems, particularly when compared to other forms of contribution (such as those made to the International Development Association and the UN's regular budget). They include the following:

- The annual pledging cycle enables the contributing countries to pursue a policy of short-term interests through the attitude they adopt towards the budget. This seriously impairs UNDP's stability (Nordic UN Project 1991b, pp. 84, 88). The USA, for example, reduced its contribution by 55% from US $ 113.5m in 1995 to 51.0m in 1996; with core resources totalling US $ 850m, this cut had a considerable impact (Table 5 for the figures).
- A few countries account for the bulk of the money contributed. In 1996 the five largest contributing countries provided 55% of core resources, the ten largest 85%. UNDP thus depends fairly heavily on the attitude and influence of these countries. This also does a great deal to shape the reform policy.[14]
- UNDP is required to plan and promise long-term development operations even though the contributing countries enter into financial commitments for only one year. A forward-looking policy and appropriate development policy approach are hardly possible in these circumstances.

Balanced burden-sharing among the contributing countries is hampered by the system of voluntary contributions (Childers / Urquhart 1994, pp. 102 f). The system does not include any transparent rules on burden-

Table 6: Main contributors to UNDP's core resources

Main contributors (ranked by contributions for 1996)		1994		1995		1996	
		US $ m	%	US $ m	%	US $ m	%
1.	Japan	100.11	10.9	105.11	11.3	110.11	12.9
2.	Netherlands	93.71	10.2	103.07	11.1	98.09	11.5
3.	Denmark	90.37	9.9	105.43	11.4	97.85	11.5
4.	Germany	82.96	9.0	94.10	10.2	88.53	10.4
5.	Norway	69.54	7.6	78.92	8.5	77.77	9.1
6.	Sweden	77.37	8.4	65.43	7.1	69.24	8.1
7.	United States	113.44	12.4	113.50	12.2	51.00	6.0
8.	Switzerland	44.80	4.9	45.16	4.9	43.41	5.1
9.	UK	38.76	4.2	38.71	4.2	36.92	4.3
10.	Canada	39.26	4.3	31.93	3.4	31.94	3.7
11.	Italy	25.32	2.8	18.63	2.0	21.82	2.6
12.	Belgium	20.97	2.3	22.37	2.4	21.15	2.5
13.	France	44.81	4.9	19.80	2.1	18.41	2.2
14.	Australia	13.47	1.5	13.53	1.5	14.11	1.7
15.	Austria	13.40	1.5	14.00	1.5	14.00	1.6
16.	Finland	9.81	1.1	12.77	1.4	12.79	1.5
17.	Spain	6.95	0.8	10.56	1.1	9.98	1.2
18.	India	4.31	0.5	3.87	0.4	4.08	0.5
19.	China	2.89	0.3	2.93	0.3	2.93	0.3
20.	New Zealand	2.26	0.2	2.50	0.3	2.61	0.3
21.	Ireland	1.36	0.1	2.56	0.3	2.60	0.3
22.	Korea	1.57	0.2	1.67	0.2	2.58	0.3
23.	Saudi Arabia	2.00	0.2	2.00	0.2	2.00	0.2
24.	Cuba	1.83	0.1	1.83	0.2	1.35	0.2
25.	Portugal	0.60	0.1	1.00	0.1	1.20	0.1
26.	Indonesia	1.16	0.1	1.16	0.1	1.16	0.1
27.	Thailand	1.08	0.1	1.08	0.1	1.08	0.1
28.	Sri Lanka	1.03	0.1	1.03	0.1	1.03	0.1
29.	Mexico	0.50	0.1	1.00	0.1	1.00	0.1
Subtotal		905.64	98.7	915.65	98.8	840.74	98.6
Other contributing countries		11.51	1.3	11.26	1.2	11.52	1.4
Grand total		917.15	100.0	926.91	100.0	852.26	100.0

Source: UNDP, DRM data

sharing. Compared to other financing systems, such as the regular UN budget and the budgets of the international development banks, the Netherlands and the Scandinavian countries, for example, are far more heavily committed or burdened than the USA, France and the United Kingdom.

The positive effect it was originally hoped the system of voluntary contributions would have of opening the way for a rapid increase in contributions has hitherto proved to be unrealistic in practice.

(b) Non-core resources

UNDP enables operations that do not form part of the core programme to be financed. The non-core resources concerned are meant to provide the option of acquiring and using additional financial resources for specific purposes. The appropriate use of non-core resources presupposes that they are adequately integrated into the programme country's or UNDP's current operations (A/RES/44/211; UN 1997c, para. 19).

UNDP's non-core resources[15] can be divided into three categories:

- government cost-sharing: counterpart contributions by the programme countries, especially contributions to cover local costs;
- third-party cost-sharing (bi- and multilateral): contributions related to specific countries or operations, especially from bilateral donors and international development banks;
- trust funds: contributions - specified and shown separately - towards the financing of an operation or task by one or more donors; trust funds may also be used in particular to initiate specific projects (e.g. projects relating to a substantive objective or country).

From 1992 to 1996 alone non-core resources rose from US $ 382m to 1,134m. In 1996 the volume of non-core resources was thus far larger than that of core resources. While the ratio of core to non-core resources was 2.81:1 in 1992, it had fallen to 0.75:1 by 1996. This trend is also reflected in Figure 5, which shows that almost half (49.41%) of all funds committed to current operations were non-core resources.

Figure 5: Non-core resources as a proportion of total UNDP resources (1988 - 1996, related to resources committed to current operations)

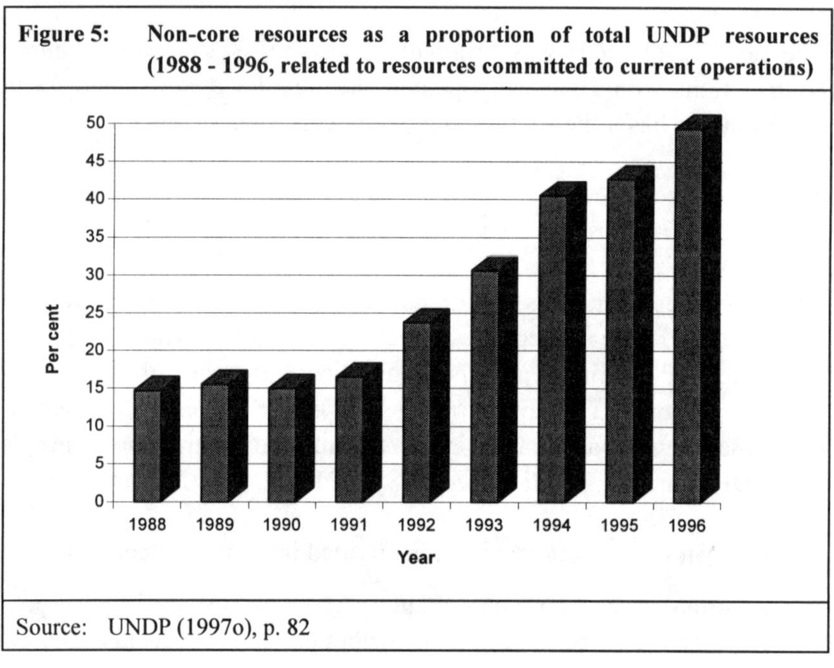

Source: UNDP (1997o), p. 82

The various categories of non-core resources underwent the following changes between 1992 and 1996:

– cost-sharing resources (total) more than tripled, from US $ 272m to 855m;

  thereof: government cost-sharing resources accounted for the largest proportion of the growth in total cost-sharing resources by quadrupling from US $ 171m to 690m;

  third-party cost-sharing resources rose significantly, from US $ 101m to 165m;

– trust funds rose two and a half times, from US $ 106m to 268m.

The trend in the 1990s has been for non-core resources to be increasingly used not as a complement to but as a substitute for core resources:

> *"(...) there has been a move away from core towards non-core resources, particularly for UNDP, whose core funding has been stagnant for the past twenty years (...)."* (ODI 1997, p. 3)

Non-core resources may have various adverse effects. In his 1994 annual report UNDP Administrator Speth therefore emphasized that non-core resources are not an appropriate alternative to core resources:

> *"To some extent, the growth in non-core resources has compensated for this erosion. However, non-core resources are, by definition, supplementary to, and not a substitute for, the core."* (The Administrator in his 1994 annual report, DP/1995/30, p. 15)

One of the main problems is that UNDP and its Executive Board have very little influence on the use of these resources. Both cost-sharing resources and trust funds give them fewer opportunities for providing guidance in the selection of substantive priorities and countries than core resources. This may have an adverse effect on principles of impartial, multilateral performance by UNDP.[16]

In the case of the trust funds in particular there is a strong tendency for the various donor countries to insist on project-related micromanagement, which is labour-intensive for UNDP. Trust funds are the clearest sign of tendencies to bilateralize UNDP, as donor countries do not really relinquish control over their financial resources.

The increase in non-core resources at the expense of core resources also has a direct influence on UNDP's funding role. With the decline in core resources, the mechanisms of the tripartite system are no longer being used in the case of interventions financed with non-core resources.[17]

Table 7: Regional distribution of UNDP resources (core and non-core) on the basis of current operations (at 31 December 1996)

	Core resources		Non-core resources		Total	
	US $m	%	US $m	%	US $m	%
Africa	1,188.8	34.9	150.0	4.5	1,338.8	19.9
Arab countries	251.6	7.4	150.4	4.5	402.0	6.0
Asia and Pacific	1,194.7	35.0	181.4	5.5	1,376.1	20.4
Europe and Commonwealth of Independent States	87.2	2.6	71.4	2.1	158.6	2.4
Latin America and Caribbean	26.4	9.6	2,709.5	81.4	3,035.9	45.1
Global	114.9	3.4	9.3	0.3	124.2	1.8
Interregional	142.8	4.2	56.8	1.7	200.0	3.0
Palestinian people	103.6	3.0	1.0	0.0	104.5	1.6
Total	3,409.9	100.0	3,329.8	100.0	6,739.7	100.0

Source: UNDP (1997o), p. 33; some calculations by the author

The growth in the programme countries' cost-sharing resources is mainly due to the fact that various economically successful developing countries have been asking themselves since the 1980s what role UNDP might play as core resources decline and whether UNDP field offices are still justified in these circumstances. A strategy based on increases in government cost-sharing resources seems to have advantages for UNDP (new tasks and additional funds) and the programme countries (UNDP's assumption of administrative functions, etc.).[18] With government cost-sharing resources rising sharply (especially for some Latin American countries[19]), there is, however, a danger that UNDP will support operations in the programme countries or provide or develop structures that are inappropriate in development terms. A situation of this kind may arise if, for example, UNDP assumes the function of bridging general bottlenecks in the public service or de facto pays salaries. This may give rise to lasting dependence or structures of a dual public service, which may above all run counter to the development objective of capacity-building.[20]

Funding Role

One of UNDP's original main tasks is the uniform and central financing of the technical cooperation (funding role) undertaken by the UN system. This calls for financial resources not to be channelled directly to the various implementing agencies of the UN system, which primarily implement measures if recipient-country governments are unable to do so, but through UNDP's structures. Appropriate endowment with core resources is essential if this task is to be performed (DP/1990/9, para. 199).

The assignment of the funding role to UNDP was specified, or confirmed, by the resolution establishing UNDP, the Consensus Resolution and a number of other resolutions. The tripartite mechanism, whereby UNDP commissions the appropriate agency of the UN system to implement a project, is based on this function.

The uniform and central financing mechanism is in principle intended to ensure a coordinated approach to the operational development cooperation activities of the UN funds and programmes and of the UN system as a whole. This is also an important feature of a multilateral approach, since the absence of a uniform financing mechanism would give the contributors greater access to the various agencies as a result of the separate contributions made to the various UN funds, programmes and specialized agencies.[21]

UNDP's funding role has been almost continuously eroded in the past. Various indicators can be cited to illustrate this trend.

- Since the 1970s UNDP's relative weight in terms of overall multilateral development cooperation, its share of technical cooperation undertaken by the whole UN system or the technical cooperation in which individual specialized agencies (especially the World

Bank) engage has declined considerably. Thus UNDP's share of total multilateral net disbursements fell from 18.5% in 1970 - 1971 to 6.9% in 1993 - 1994. Related to net disbursements solely by UN agencies, its share shrank from 41.4 to 20.2% in the same period.[22] The World Bank, whose technical cooperation was still about a quarter of UNDP's in 1969, has outstripped UNDP for several years: the World Bank group's expenditure on TC amounted to US $ 1,411m in 1993 and 1,477 in 1994, UNDP's to US $ 1,204m and 1,246m (figures according to Hüfner 1997, p. 164). The World Food Programme (at times) and such specialized agencies as the FAO show similar tendencies (Gwin 1995, p. 106; Koetz / Otte 1992, p. 190; Hüfner 1997, p. 164).

- In the 1960s UNDP was the main financial source for the non-budgetary resources of the most important specialized agencies (Edgren / Möller 1991, pp. 138 ff). Some 75% of the UN system's grant-based operational activities were financed by UNDP in the early 1970s (DP/1989/14, p. 28). The figures for the 1990s indicate that the proportion has meanwhile slipped to about 25%[23] or less.
- Finally, the shift from core to non-core resources discussed above shows that the resources which can be used freely are dwindling fast.

All in all, these tendencies have resulted in UNDP no longer being able to perform its central financing task properly. Certainly since the 1980s it has not performed its intended function of acting as one of the principal financial sources for multilateral technical cooperation. This is also obscuring the functional distinction between funding agencies and executing agencies.

> *"Although practically all UN member states recognise both the fundamental value and sheer necessity of a central agency to manage the funding and coordination of the operational side of technical cooperation, the UNDP has had to cope with serious restrictions and obstacles ever since 1970, when it was first allocated this key role."*[24]

And:

> *"Today's UNDP, contrary to General Assembly and Governing Council statements, cannot be called a 'central' funding mechanism anymore."* (Kienbaum & Partners 1991, p. 3)

Table 8: Expenditure on the UN system's grant-based operational development activities (US $m)

Origin of funds / year	1990	1992	1994
UNDP[a]	1,035.7	1,026.8	1,036.5
Funds administered by UNDP	98.0	137.6	209.8
UNFPA	179.5	128.2	201.4
UNICEF	584.3	743.8	800.6
WFP	956.4	1,575.2	1,395.1
Regular budget resources[b]	233.9	241.6	280.3
Specialized agencies and non-budget resources of other organizations	686.1	727.2	688.4
Total	3,773.9	4,580.4	4,612.1

a UNDP resources, including government cost-sharing contributions

b Largely financed with WHO resources

Source: E/1996/64/Add. 2, p. 24, Table B-1

There is no simple explanation for this problem and no single cause, especially as all concerned - the governments of the industrialized and developing countries and the United Nations - have repeatedly emphasized the need for and requested UNDP's guidance. However, various sets of explanations related in particular to institutional interests can be identified:

1. The institutions of the UN system (especially the specialized agencies, but also the various UN funds and programmes) active in the field of TC have been very reluctant in the past to commit themselves fully to coordination by UNDP (for further details see

the next few pages). Various studies have shown that the institutions' policies are geared to direct financing by the donors (through the establishment of appropriate budget instruments, such as funds for technical cooperation and trust funds). The UN institutions are thus competing for resources. Their policies are not therefore geared to close coordination with and financing by UNDP but seek a relationship with UNDP in which they remain as independent as possible. "Agency salesmanship" and "project shopping" are therefore important features of the UN system's technical cooperation.[25]

2. UNDP is increasingly vying with the World Bank for TC resources. As has been shown above, the World Bank has achieved considerable growth in this area in the 1980s and 1990s.

   "... a competitive technical cooperation market has emerged. UNDP no longer enjoys a privileged position. A proliferation of organizations are providing services. The multilateral organizations, particularly the financial institutions, have dramatically expanded their provisions of technical assistance." (Speth 1994b, p. 2)

   The World Bank's strategy document *Strategic Compact* (World Bank 1997b) emphasizes that the World Bank hopes to expand its TC further in the future.

3. A crucial factor in the collapse of the funding system has been the conduct of the donor countries, since they established and endowed the TC budgets of the various UN system institutions. Despite declarations and resolutions to the contrary, the governments have pursued an incoherent policy in the various supervisory bodies of the UN system.

   "One inconsistency, to which the DAC has in recent years given some attention, is the fact that donors who purport to endorse the central funding role of the UNDP, and who allocate large amounts to the UNDP as a proportion of their total aid, have at the same time weakened the UNDP's coordinating role by allocating large amounts to other UN

agencies in the form of trust funds and a variety of similar arrangements." (OECD 1985, p. 146)

This conduct is, in particular, evidence of a poorly coordinated approach within the donor governments (Ahlberg / Løvbraek 1985, p. 16) and also among the donor countries.

2.2.2.2 Coordination

UNDP has a wide-ranging coordinating mandate, which has, however, been carried out very poorly in the past. It stems from the Consensus Resolution and the resulting wide variety of tasks, which cover a very broad spectrum within UN development cooperation and the UN system. UNDP is also the largest agency among the UN funds and programmes and has, substantively, a multisectoral set of tasks.

The coordinating tasks to be performed by UNDP extend, in particular, to coordination with the various partner governments and agencies of the UN and UN system (Resolution 2688, XXV, especially point II.A of the Annex) and with other multilateral and bilateral donors (Resolution 2688, XXV, especially point II.A, para. 10, of the Annex). The development institutions' activities are coordinated at both headquarters and country level. At country level coordination covers not only other development institutions but above all the partner country concerned: many relevant statements by UNDP emphasize that operations are to be promoted only on the basis of the recipient country's priorities and objectives, the aim being to ensure coordination with the country's own efforts and other external contributions.

At headquarters level there are various mechanisms for coordinating overarching aspects (e.g. substantive focusing, division of labour among the various institutions, common procedures and principles, etc.). Within this framework three coordinating bodies, in which UNDP is involved without having any special authority or powers, play the most important role:

- The Administrative Committee on Co-ordination (ACC): the ACC comprises the management levels of all major agencies of the UN system.[26]
- The Consultative Committee on Programme and Operational Questions (CCPOQ): the CCPOQ also covers the whole UN system, but operates below management level and has specialized subcommittees.[27]
- The Joint Consultative Group on Policy (JCDP): the JCDP is concerned with aspects of coordination that relate only to the UN funds and programmes.

In 1997 the UN Secretary-General also set up a new coordinating body (the United Nations Development Group) for the UN funds and programmes, which is convened by the UNDP Administrator (section III.1).

Of greatest importance as regards coordination is the country level, or country-related coordination. Two elements in particular play a part in this context: first, country programming (which will be discussed in greater depth later) and, second, the Resident Representative or Resident Coordinator system.

UNDP's local representative (the Resident Representative (RR) or Resident Coordinator (RC))[28] has the task of acting as UNDP's operational arm at country level and of ensuring direct on-the-spot coordination.[29] He or she is required to be impartial in his or her dealings with the government of the programme country and also the deciding coordinating authority at country level for the agencies of the whole UN system. Within this framework the round tables arranged by UNDP play a part in country-related coordination, especially in poorer developing countries (UNDP 1996g; Cassen 1994, pp. 181 ff.).

The Consensus Resolution laid down the following principles and procedures for coordination at country level; they underline UNDP's special responsibility and overriding terms of reference in the UN system:

> *"The role of the organizations of the United Nations system in the implementation of country programmes should be that of partners, under the leadership of the Programme (UNDP - SK) in a common endeavour of the entire United Nations system. Their advice should be available to the Administrator in the implementation of all projects, as appropriate, whether executed by them or not. (...)*
>
> *There should be the maximum possible delegation of authority to the resident director (or Resident Representative - SK). His role therefore needs to be greatly strengthened. In this context, his relations with the representatives of other United Nations organizations in the field are of crucial importance. The resident director should be recognized as having full over-all responsibility for the programme in the country concerned and his role in relation to the representatives of the other United Nations organizations, where they are posted with the prior approval of the Government concerned, should be that of the leader of the team, taking into account the professional competence of these United Nations organizations and their relations with appropriate organs of the Government."* (Resolution 2688, XXV, Annex)

The country-level coordination undertaken by UNDP is generally regarded as inadequate.[30] On the one hand, UNDP has, with 136 field offices, a very good representative network; this structure of external representation is one of the greatest advantages that UNDP has as compared to other bi- and multilateral donors. On the other hand, these offices engage in little coordinating activity, and the coordinating mechanisms available and used (e.g. round tables) are often of limited importance.[31] Inadequate coordination has many adverse consequences: the programme country's institutional structures are encumbered, the various UN agencies pursue different substantive strategies, the procedures and administrative approaches differ, the structures of external representation of the various agencies give rise to costs, and competition for projects that look attractive is encouraged.

The factors that prevent the coordinating task from being performed better vary in importance:

- The most important cause of the coordination problems is the current structure of the UN system. There is a general lack of incentives and disincentives and means of imposing sanctions that might increase or even ensure the willingness of the agencies of the UN system to accept UNDP as coordinator.
- Very little of the central financing concept, or UNDP's funding role, is in fact left today. An important instrument for country programming is thus no longer available. This too must be regarded as one of the main causes of deficient coordination.
- The limited absolute volume of funds available to UNDP is a serious obstacle to the performance of coordinating tasks:

  "The view that emerges ... is that co-ordination can only be effective if organized by a donor with large resources." (Nordic UN Project 1990a, p. 27)

  In these circumstances the World Bank group, but not UNDP, is able to demonstrate sufficient relevance as a coordinator.
- The poor quality of country programmes in the past does not indicate any particular competence for coordination.
- The separate offices and representatives of different UN agencies in the partner countries impede communication and thus coordination (DP/1990/9, pp. 68 f.; Danida 1991c, p. 41; Nordic UN Project 1991b, p. 60).
- Coordination work largely depends on the quality and skills of the Resident Representative / Resident Coordinator; there are often shortcomings in this respect.[32]
- The large number of small UNDP projects makes it difficult to perform coordinating tasks, since administrative activities dominate (Kienbaum & Partners 1991, p. 29).

- UNDP is frequently seen not as impartial but as having its own interests (e.g. in project acquisition); this impairs its acceptance as a coordinator.
- As a rule, the Resident Representative is also the UN's Resident Coordinator. The different tasks he or she has to perform in his or her two capacities may give rise to conflicts or burdens that have an adverse effect on coordinating skills.

2.2.2.3 Country Programming

Country programming is the main planning and guidance instrument used by UNDP in its cooperation with the various partner countries. The original system of Indicative Planning Figures (IPFs) and the Target for Resource Assignments from the Core (TRAC) system that replaced it in 1997 form important foundations for country programming, since they are designed to provide information on the financial resources available.

The objectives which the Consensus Resolution[33] envisaged country programming would pursue were, firstly, the programming of UNDP activities on the basis of a coherent strategy paper, secondly, the coordination of all contributions made by the UN system and, thirdly, coordination with other multilateral and bilateral contributions.

UNDP has not succeeded, as originally intended, in using country programming as an effective instrument in the planning and control of TC.

> *"UNDP's **country programming** is an inadequate instrument to guide field operations, including the search for a profile in each country."* (Danida 1991c, p. i; emphasis as in the original text)

And:

> *"Whatever the original ambitions were to make the Country Programme a coherent frame-work for aid allocation, these programmes appear to be no more than a compilation of projects."* (Nordic UN Project 1990a, p. 28)

The most serious problems for country programming concern very different aspects (Danida 1996b, pp. 7 f.; Danida 1991c, pp. i f., 31 ff.; Nordic UN Project 1990a, p. 28; Koetz / Otte 1992, pp. 188 f.; Ahlberg / Løvbraek 1985, pp. 8 f.; DP/1990/9, pp. 80 f.):

- The analyses of country programmes are often inadequate and the conclusions drawn from them too general for them to be used in defining areas of main effort, etc.
- The country programmes set out in writing and the country strategies actually pursued bear little resemblance.
- Contrary to the original intention, the country programmes have not proved to be a framework document for other multilateral institutions. Many multilateral and bilateral donors are in fact guided by the World Bank's documents or now have their own country strategy papers.
- The country programmes are de facto not accepted, or not entirely accepted, by the partner countries as strategy papers for the coordination of multilateral technical cooperation.
- As the country programmes have to be approved by the Governing Council, or Executive Board as it is now known, they are subject to its political decision-making processes; this restricts the role of the UNDP Administrator.
- The IPFs have proved to be an inflexible and unreliable planning basis for the financing of country programmes. The five-year programming and financing cycles are not legally binding on UNDP's individual members (Sahlmann / Blank 1995, pp. 1286 f.). For the 5th Planning Cycle (1992 - 1996), for example, a nominal annual growth rate of 8.8% was assumed, and a total financial volume of US $ 4.4bn was made the target. A review of the unrealistic plan-

ning already resulted in a downward adjustment to 70% of the original volume (BMZ 1996c, p. 313).

- The primary function of the IPF system was to legitimize the distribution of resources for approval by the Governing Council, or Executive Board. It was essentially a rigid system of quotas for the allocation of financial resources which in fact offered no development incentives. The IPF system was largely to blame for the failure of substantive focusing efforts (Danida 1996b, p. 8).
- The various programming procedures and cycles of the UN agencies were not coordinated in the past.

In connection with the country programming instrument the Executive Board introduced some important innovations in the mid-1990s (section III.4).

2.2.2.4 Assumption of Implementing Functions

In contrast to the tasks it was originally assigned, UNDP has increasingly taken to implementing operations in the past (Kienbaum & Partners 1991, pp. 62 f.; Gwin 1995, p. 107; DP/1990/9, pp. 88 ff.). This trend too must take much of the blame for UNDP becoming less of a funding agency and more of an executing and implementing agency in many respects.

> *"The UNDP has increasingly become one of the many implementing agencies of technical cooperation projects, either directly or by actors outside the U.N. system."* (Gwin / Williams 1996, p. 123)

Until the Executive Board's decision on restructuring in 1994 (Executive Board Decision 94/12, reproduced in DP/1995/1), UNDP's Office for Project Services (OPS) performed execution tasks. Besides implementing operations financed with the non-budgetary resources of UNDP (trust funds, etc.) and other donors, the OPS carried out operations funded with resources from UNDP's core programme. Of the core programme expenditure of US $ 1,031m in 1993,[34] the OPS accounted for US $ 169m (Department of State 1994, p. 66), or 16.4%.

To prevent conflicts of interest between UNDP's coordinating and implementing roles, the OPS's status and tasks were completely redefined in the mid-1990s.[35]

2.2.2.5 Political Guidance by the Governing Council, or Executive Board

Many of UNDP's problems are directly or indirectly due to the poor political guidance it receives. Problems have been posed by the fact that the responsible political supervisory body (the Governing Council (GC) until 1994, the Executive Board (EB) thereafter) (section III.4) has proved in the past to be cumbersome, rarely innovative and largely focused on questions of detail. This generally makes it difficult for decisions to be taken and for political guidance tasks to be performed; strategic prescriptions for the UNDP administration are often lacking or unclear. This has restricted UNDP's problem-solving capacity, and adjustment and reform measures can be implemented only with difficulty.

The limited capacity for political guidance is primarily due to three factors. First, the body responsible is cumbersome. While the involvement of many member states in the various UN bodies (ECOSOC, UNDP's former Governing Council, etc.) is an important participatory means used by the United Nations to ensure compliance with vital principles (universality and political neutrality), the large number of representatives hampers and delays discussion and decision-making processes. Although the number of seats on the Governing Council, or Executive Board, has been limited (48 and 36 respectively), it still helps to make for lengthy and complex negotiating procedures. Many countries also send observers, who often exercise de facto similar rights to those of the actual members of the Governing Council, or Executive Board (speaking time, etc.).

Second, there is nothing much to distinguish the members as UNDP's Governing Council, or Executive Board (in contrast, say, to the World Bank's Board). A stronger institutional connection and more pronounced identification would probably result in the actors concerned adopting an approach that was more oriented towards problem-solving and more pragmatic. The lack of identification is due to various factors, one being that UNDP's GC, or EB, gathers only for specific meetings rather than being in permanent session, another that many members are represented not by specialists (from the capitals or UN missions) but by people from the missions who are less familiar with the subject matter.[36] A further danger inherent in this structure is that the Governing Council, or Executive Board, may act as a forum for questions of political or development principle that fall within ECOSOC's or the General Assembly's terms of reference.

Third, coordination within the governments represented in UNDP's GC, or EB, is often limited. There is frequently a lack of coordination with other representatives of the government in other UN agencies, the development banks and other international organizations. Decisions taken by different government departments therefore contain inconsistencies in many cases. Such incoherent conduct is evident, for example, from the network of external offices maintained by the various agencies, governments attaching little or no importance to decisions on the RR/RC system. They have never attempted, for instance, to force through their decision on the competence of the Resident Coordinator to act as country representative on the supervisory bodies of the various institutions (outside the UNDP).

2.2.3 Shortcomings at Administration and Implementation Level

Bureaucratic and Inefficient Structures

One of the most difficult questions is whether and to what extent the organizational and administrative structures are too bureaucratic and inefficient. UNDP has a complement of 1,045 international staff and

5,714 local staff at 136 field and liaison offices. It thus has a representational network that embraces almost all the developing countries.

The organizational and administrative structures were considered in a study by Kienbaum & Partners[37] that was completed in 1991. It refers to a wide range of sometimes serious shortcomings that encumber the organization and procedures and are costly and labour-intensive. The study gives examples of this with respect to structures at headquarters and at the field offices and communication between the two:

> *"An analysis of the administrative costs of the offices and programme disbursements reveals that some field offices cost more for the UNDP administration than UNDP project disbursements."* (Kienbaum & Partners 1991, p. 34)

And:

> *"Our analysis has shown that the procedures between field offices and HQ units are lengthy and protracted. No clear strategic guidelines and no process ownership - i.e. defined responsibility - for the 'output' of UNDP exist. Complicated administrative procedures unnecessarily consume manpower.*
>
> *We believe that UNDP HQ might become at least 30% leaner than it currently is ..."* (Kienbaum & Partners 1991, pp. MS-12)

The study also gives examples of how efficiency has deteriorated over a fairly long period in certain areas. They show that, while the number of staff at headquarters has increased, the number of projects processed by them has fallen. In 1975 an average of 14.8 projects was processed by each member of headquarters staff, as against a mere 9.4 in 1990. This tendency was accompanied by a decline in average project volume (Kienbaum & Partners 1991, p. 29).

Figure 6: UNDP ORGANIZATIONAL CHART[a]

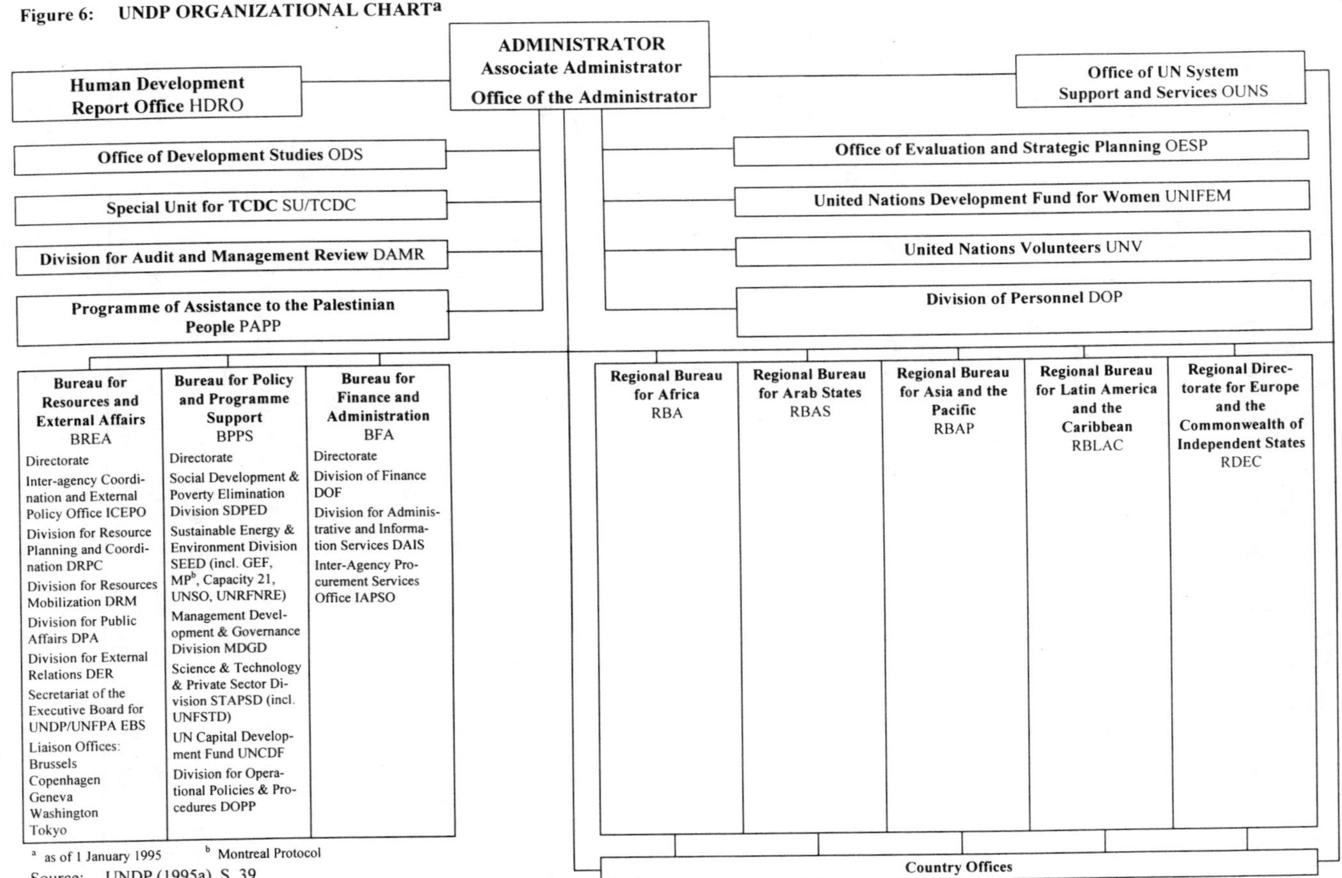

[a] as of 1 January 1995 [b] Montreal Protocol

Source: UNDP (1995a), S. 39

Besides negative examples and references to poor structures, however, the study by Kienbaum & Partners and especially other studies refer to positive aspects. Thus, despite the large representational structures in the programme countries and the existing administrative procedures at headquarters, 83% of financial resources are spent on the actual implementation of operations, the rest being used to finance the staff and the field offices (Minister for Development Cooperation 1992, p. 25). In addition, the salaries offered by UNDP are, for example, lower than those paid by many European institutions and governments (Kienbaum & Partners 1991, p. 99).

A study completed by the George Washington University in 1997 on UNDP's system of accountability[38] reached a relatively favourable conclusion. On the basis of, among other things, a comparative analysis of the best practices of five other organizations the study refers to a number of problems (e.g. unclear audit structures), but also emphasizes the functioning sides of UNDP's system of accountability:

> *"In reading this report, it is easy to focus on 'what's wrong' with the UNDP accountability system as opposed to 'what's right'. Readers should recognize that much is 'right' with the UNDP system. (...) In summary, while the UNDP accountability system is fully functional, some vital improvements are needed."* (George Washington University 1997, pp. 5 ff.)

Monitoring and Evaluation System

The system for monitoring and evaluating UNDP operations[39] is generally regarded as inadequate and poor; this also has adverse implications for the design of newly developed operations.

The most serious problems in the evaluation sphere include the following (Minister for Development Cooperation 1992, p. 26; Danida 1996b, p. 8; George Washington University 1997, p. 106):

- the organizational unit responsible for evaluations is understaffed,
- the evaluation programmes are too ambitious,
- there is no systematic follow-up to the evaluations,
- the results of evaluations tend to be too positive, or the criteria for evaluating in particular the impact and sustainability of projects are inappropriate; the evaluation of overall performance of operations is not sufficiently transparent, the marking being subjective ("high", "satisfactory" and "low").

Qualifications of UNDP Staff

Criticism similar to that expressed about the qualifications of all staff in the UN's economic and social fields can also be levelled at UNDP's staff. There are, for example, serious deficiencies in the training and experience of a large proportion of the staff (Nordic UN Project 1991b, pp. 94 ff.). Higher management posts are filled on the basis of "unwritten" nationality criteria (Kienbaum & Partners 1991, p. 58); this procedure also applies to the appointment of the UNDP Administrator, who is "traditionally" a US citizen (Urquhart / Childers 1990, pp. 34 f.). Deficient qualifications are a major feature not only of UNDP's headquarters but also of many field offices. Many studies (Centre for Development Research 1996, pp. 69 f.; Gwin 1995, p. 107; Danida 1991c, pp. 41, 44; Minister for Development Cooperation 1992, p. 26) stress the importance to be attached to the person of the Resident Representative or Resident Coordinator and to the other staff of the field offices:

> *"The personal qualities of the UNDP Resident Representatives (ResReps) are of essential importance to the effectiveness of the UNDP in recipient countries, especially since the country programmes setting out aid priorities are formally drawn up by the countries themselves."* (Minister for Development Cooperation 1992, p. 26)

Despite the importance of the RRs or RCs, their qualifications vary widely and are often inappropriate.[40] The RR or RC is usually certified as having sufficient knowledge of project administration, but his knowledge of analysis and policy-oriented conduct is deemed to be inadequate (Danida 1991c, pp. 41 and 44).

Projectitis / Dispersion

Many studies are critical of the large number and limited financial scale of the operations undertaken by UNDP (Williams 1995a) p. 199; Danida 1991c, pp. ii ff.; Nordic UN Project 1990a, pp. 15 ff.; DP/1990/9, p. 58). The main criticism is that UNDP pursues a diffuse project policy with operations that are too numerous, too small and not sufficiently focused on relevant issues. The most important outcomes of this "projectitis" are:

- time-consuming and extensive processing of projects at UNDP's headquarters and field offices,
- a project policy that is not geared to strategic development problems of the partner countries and has little impact,
- an unclear overall substantive profile in the project policy.

Since the first half of the 1990s UNDP has set itself the goal of concentration in terms of the number of operations and the average project volume. In 1996 there were 4,133 current projects, and the project volume averaged US $ 1.5m.[41]

Quality of Project Implementation and Dependence on Executing Agencies

UNDP's role in the implementation of operations is usually limited,[42] other institutions (especially the UN's specialized agencies) as a rule being entrusted with this task if it is not performed by the programme countries themselves. In the past UNDP has therefore been heavily dependent on the various executing agencies for implementation.

Although UNDP is restrained in its evaluation of the quality of the most important executing agencies and refers to methodological problems as the reason for this,[43] the quality of operations implemented by UN specialized agencies can often be described as poor:

> *"The implementation of the projects through the specialized agencies is not adequate as regards quality in general and performance of experts in particular."* (Nordic UN Project 1990a, p. 16; DP/1990/9, p. 48)

Besides quality, the question of the costs which the agencies incur during implementation and which UNDP refunds as lump sums is a contentious issue. Consequently, the form that the support-cost arrangements should take has often been very important for those concerned in the past (DP/1990/9; UNDP 1993a, Sect. 10405; UNDP 1996m). Originally, the support-cost arrangement provided for the executing agencies to be paid a lump sum equivalent to 14% (subsequently 13%) of the expenditure on a project (UNDP 1997m, Annex I). However, this gave the executing agencies a counterproductive incentive, since they had an interest in as large a project volume as possible and no interest in seeing the programme countries implement projects on their own (national execution).

From 1993 to 1995 UNDP used a total of 35 different executing agencies. Traditionally, the FAO had been the most important: in 1988 it had accounted for 19% of the financial volume, but this had fallen to a mere 4% by 1996. Other major executing agencies have been the ILO, UNIDO, UNESCO, the World Bank and WHO. Until the Office for Project Services (OPS) was transformed from a UNDP organizational unit into the independent United Nations Office for Project services (UNOPS), UNDP also had significant implementing capacities of its own (section III.4).

Table 9: UNDP's largest executing agencies, 1988 - 1996 (%)

	1988		1992		1994		1995		1996	
Executing agency	Share of number of operations	Share of volume of operations	Share of number of operations	Share of volume of operations	Share of number of operations	Share of volume of operations	Share of number of operations	Share of volume of operations	Share of number of operations	Share of volume of operations
FAO	15.6	19.0	11.9	14.4	8.1	8.8	7.4	6.5	6.2	4.5
NEX (national execution)	13.3	9.5	23.9	23.5	41.9	43.6	44.8	51.9	52.7	61.1
ILO	7.4	6.7	6.4	5.9	4.1	3.7	4.4	2.7	3.7	2.0
UNDP	12.3	9.7	14.7	12.5	17.8	15.4	0.8	0.2	2.1	0.9
UNIDO	12.8	10.3	8.3	7.1	4.6	3.5	5.0	2.9	4.4	2.1
UN	9.6	12.1	8.2	9.1	6.3	6.5	6.6	4.7	5.3	3.4
UNESCO	4.6	4.6	3.1	2.5	1.9	2.2	1.7	0.9	1.5	0.8
WB	3.1	6.7	3.7	6.2	2.3	3.7	1.5	2.9	1.1	2.4
WHO	2.8	2.2	2.2	1.7	1.6	1.5	1.1	1.2	1.0	1.3

Source:UNDP (1997o), p. 85

The traditional tripartite system, with the specific role it assigns to the executing agencies, has changed radically in the 1990s. The main reason for this has been the significant increase in projects implemented by the various countries on their own responsibility (national execution) (section III.4). As the proportion of nationally executed projects rises, so the proportion handled by the traditional executing agencies falls.

Other shortcomings concern the definition of the interface between UNDP and the executing agencies (which tasks are performed by UNDP, for which areas are the executing agencies responsible, etc.). In particular, there is inadequate overall responsibility within UNDP for the whole project cycle.[44]

2.3 Comparative Advantages

The debate on the reform of UNDP focuses on shortcomings, since the main aim is to analyse and overcome existing problems. However, UNDP's current peculiarities and comparative advantages[45] also need to be considered if there is to be an adequate overall assessment and an evaluation.

Where UNDP and its activities are concerned, reference can be made to a number of peculiarities that distinguish it primarily from bilateral development cooperation but also from other multilateral donors in some areas.

In general, the following aspects, which are discussed in greater depth in other sections of this study, can be identified as UNDP's most important comparative advantages (Gwin 1995; Gwin / Williams 1996, pp. 114 ff.; Danida 1991c; Kalderén 1991, pp. 334 ff.; DP/1990/9, pp. 47 ff.; Minister for Development Cooperation 1992, pp. 24 ff.):

– UNDP operations are characterized by a high degree of ownership in the programme countries. Unlike many other donors, UNDP enables the programme countries to have considerable influence on the distribution and use of resources and the implementation of the various operations. The Governing Council, or Executive Board, also involves them closely in the formulation of UNDP's overall policy.

- The high degree of developing-country identification with UNDP as such is evident, among other things, from the fact that developing countries contribute to its financing. Eighty-nine programme countries participate in the financing of the core resources (DP/1997/CRP.23, Chapter IV); eight developing countries each contribute over US $ 1m (UNDP 1997g), p. 12).
- UNDP is closely attached to the principle of political neutrality. This has a major effect on the choice of countries to be assisted, the development strategies, etc. (no conditionality, etc.).
- Economic self-interest and the negative aspects associated with it (tied aid, etc.) play less of a role in UNDP's work than in bilateral development cooperation.
- UNDP is itself represented by field offices in almost all the programme countries. This means in principle good conditions for close cooperation with local actors and other donors.
- UNDP's work is based on non-repayable grants and so imposes little or no financial burden[46] on the programme countries (unlike credits).
- UNDP resources can be spent on operations with a fair degree of flexibility and in a variety of sectors. They are therefore particularly suited to meeting the needs of the programme countries.

Given these advantages, UNDP operations are generally much appreciated by the programme countries.[47]

In many cases the advantages listed above have also been the main cause of some of UNDP's major weaknesses. Thus a high degree of ownership and political neutrality (taken to mean restraint even in dealings with governments that have little or no development orientation) result in poor orientation towards development policy, inadequate standards of performance and a lack of focus in many operations. The weaknesses of UNDP discussed largely confirm the experience generally gained during the debate on the effectiveness of technical cooperation, that structural shortcomings in the recipient countries are among the most important causes of limited TC effectiveness. This situation gives rise to clear conflicts among the objectives of different development policy approaches.

2.4 Conclusions

The analysis of UNDP's most important deficiencies reveals a continuing need for comprehensive reforms in the 1990s. How and to what extent UNDP and the UN have reacted to this need is examined more closely in section III.4.

A need for reform can be identified in many areas of crucial importance if UNDP is to be effective in the field of development. There are shortcomings at the conceptual level, at the structural policy level and at the administration and implementation level. The need for reform concerns UNDP's core areas and tasks: (1) the substantive profile, (2) the ability to ensure appropriate financing and to achieve adequate coordination and guidance of UN development cooperation and (3) the actual quality of work in development terms. UNDP's mandate is such that it has direct and indirect implications for the whole of the UN's development cooperation. It is therefore particularly important for current problems to be solved if the UN's development cooperation is to be effective.

Many of the deficiencies referred to above are peculiar to UNDP because of its mandate; other reforms that are needed concern the whole of the UN's development cooperation or also the development cooperation and TC of other multilateral and bilateral donors (see the last column in Figure 7). These problems, which are typical of development cooperation and of all donor organizations (quality of evaluations, concentration of resources, etc.) are to some extent overly ascribed to UN development cooperation or emphasized in this context in the political debate.

Many of UNDP's main shortcomings are structural deficiencies that already existed in the 1970s and 1980s. In some respects the environment has changed significantly. One example is the declining willingness of the main contributors to support governments with limited development orientation (e.g. corrupt regimes). Some problematical aspects, such as the ratio of core to non-core resources, are phenomena of the 1990s.

Who is responsible for the current problems or who in particular should be seeking solutions is a question to which an unequivocal answer cannot be given. The UN and UNDP administrations have contributed to the emergence of many problems; an example here is the scope which certainly exists for the concentration of resources, but which has not been adequately exploited in the past. However, it is apparent that the UNDP administration has become increasingly aware of the problems and focused its attention on them, especially in the 1990s.[48]

Most of the problems are, however, due to the UN member states themselves, since they have often delegated tasks and responsibility to UNDP without being prepared to create the instruments and conditions it needed to take action that was appropriate in development terms. The erosion of the funding role is a vivid example, as is the governments' inability in the various political supervisory bodies of the UN system to ensure that effective coordination is possible at country level through the Resident Coordinator system. Important manifestations of disintegration are also associated with UNDP's growing competition with the World Bank for TC resources. In many cases the UN and UNDP bashing to which member states have resorted is therefore misplaced.

Besides the weaknesses of UNDP that have been mentioned, it is important to note its strengths and potential (section III.5). Despite the current problems, UNDP has advantages to offer, especially when

Figure 7: UNDP's main deficiencies in the 1990s

Level	Areas		UNDP-specific (= UNDP), UN-specific (= UN) or typical of development cooperation/TC (= DC/TC)
Conceptual level	1	Substantive profile	UNDP
	2	Implementation of outcomes of debate on technical cooperation	DC/TC
	3	Adjustment to challenges after end of East-West conflict	UNDP, DC/TC
Structural and policy level	1	Financing	UNDP, UN
	1.1	Financial endowment	UNDP, UN
	1.2	Financing mechanisms	UNDP, UN
	1.3	Funding role	UNDP
	2	Coordination	UNDP
	2.1	Coordination at headquarters level	UNDP
	2.2	Coordination at country level	UNDP
	3	Country programming	UNDP, UN
	4	Assumption of implementing functions	UNDP
	5	Political guidance by Governing Council, or Executive Board	UNDP, UN
Administration and implementation level	1	Bureaucratic structures	UNDP, UN
	2	Monitoring and evaluation system	UNDP, UN, DC/TC
	3	Training of UNDP staff	UNDP, UN
	4	Projectitis	UNDP, UN, DC/TC
	5	Project implementation or heavy dependence on the various executing agencies	UNDP, UN

compared to other donors. They consist primarily in UNDP's adoption of a neutral approach that results in a strong "recipient drive". The greater opportunities the programme country receives from UNDP than other donors to exercise influence has advantages for development (e.g. extensive ownership). It is evident not least from the TC debate how important it is to seek and strengthen such approaches. In practice, however, these strengths of UNDP are often its greatest weaknesses because of conflicting objectives.

The conceptual TC debate has hitherto paid too little attention to the current conflicts of objectives. In this area UNDP has a wide range of practical experience, which has not yet attracted sufficient interest.

3 Concepts for the Reform of UNDP

3.1 Introduction

In the past there have been a number of analyses and reform initiatives relating partly or completely to UNDP. At the time of UNDP's inception the discussions on its tasks, structures and instruments were largely determined by the Jackson Report. In the 1970s, 1980s and 1990s this was followed by other studies and reform concepts, although none succeeded in carrying the same political and public weight.

This section analyses selected important documents that consider the need for UNDP's reform and put forward appropriate proposals. The main arguments and most important proposals are identified and discussed.

The analysis of the various reform concepts and initiatives is also intended to act as a basis of assessment for the following sections, so that the reform efforts of the 1990s and areas yet to be reformed may be better categorized and evaluated.

3.2 Selected Reform Concepts

A total of twelve reform concepts and initiatives published from 1969 to 1997 are considered in the following. The documents are extremely varied: some are official UN documents, others are independent studies or informal papers.

A large proportion of existing reform documents are taken into account in this section.[1] Two criteria in particular were applied in their selection: their importance for the debate on UNDP's reform[2] and their topicality, i.e. the emphasis was placed on documents compiled and published in the 1990s.

3.2.1 Jackson Report

Although the Jackson Report (DP/5) (also known as the Capacity Study) was submitted as long ago as 1969, it remains extremely important even today.[3] It identifies problems in the UN's, and especially UNDP's, operational development activities, and proposes solutions, many of which retain their validity. Many of the recommendations it contained were reflected in the 1970 Consensus Resolution (Resolution 2688, XXV) and so became an important basis for UNDP. Nonetheless, a number of structural problems identified by the Jackson Report were not, or not entirely, remedied.

The Jackson Report contains a comprehensive analysis of and recommendations on structural, organizational and financial aspects of UN development cooperation.

It attaches decisive importance to the inadequacy of the UN's capacities for guiding its development cooperation and is particularly critical of the absence of a "brain":

> *"In other words, the machine as a whole has become unmanageable in the strictest use of the word. As a result, it is*

> *becoming slower and more unwieldy, like some prehistoric monster."* (DP/5, Vol. I, p. iii)

From this the Jackson Report concludes that UNDP should become the centre of UN development cooperation:

> *"Amongst many important changes, this would require the transformation of UNDP into an effective operational organization as the centre of the United Nations development system."* (DP/5, Vol. I, pp. 18 f.)

To ensure appropriate action, which should be safeguarded by UNDP, it believes a uniform and integrated approach is needed:

> *"The first essential is to recognize that, above all else, the United Nations Development Programme must be conceived as an operation. This entails the adoption of measures designed to ensure an integrated managerial approach toward development co-operation at all levels of the UN development system, and at all phases of the operation, in order to achieve optimum results for the benefit of developing countries and maximum use of resources."* (DP/5, Vol. I, p. 22, emphasis as in the original text)

Although the report calls for better, uniform and centralized management and capacity for guidance, it also emphasizes the need to create a counterbalance to ensure flexible implementation at working level. This counterbalance should be achieved by decentralizing operational decision-making as far as possible (Righter 1995, p. 161).

To ensure that the principles set out in the report were respected, a number of practical recommendations were made. They included the following (DP/5, Vol. I, pp. 22 f.):

- introduction of a uniform programming method, embracing the whole UN system,
- effective and rapid implementation of approved projects,

- evaluation of all UNDP operations,
- effective follow-up to all projects,
- introduction of an efficient information system,
- implementation of organizational reforms at country, regional and headquarters level, the aim being to achieve both the closer integration of the various components of the UN system and an increase in decentralization to country level and in the options open to the Resident Representatives,
- appropriate staffing with qualified personnel,
- a financial framework that enables projects to be implemented without difficulty,
- the application of modern methods of management and administration,
- the greatest possible flexibility exercised by governments so that the UN's operational system may adjust quickly and effectively to new challenges.

The Jackson Report must be generally regarded as a far-sighted document, which even today is rightly seen by many as an important frame of reference in the reform debate. It can be assumed that, if its conclusions had been implemented consistently in the early 1970s, many of the structural shortcomings of UNDP and of UN development cooperation as a whole could have been avoided.

3.2.2 The Future Role of UNDP in World Development

The UNDP Administrator's report *The Future Role of UNDP in World Development*[4] published in 1975 considers fundamental aspects, procedures and instruments of technical cooperation and draws conclusions for UNDP.

The report proposes reforms (new dimensions) for technical cooperation aimed at enabling progress to be made in improving the efficiency and quality of UNDP's TC. It refers in this context to a wide range of appropriate measures for adjusting TC. The measures proposed are primarily geared to two objectives. The report calls, firstly, for a more flexible approach to TC in several respects, including more flexible interaction with financial cooperation, cooperation with other donors and the payment of local costs. Secondly, it proposes diversification in UNDP's provision of TC ("diversifying the supply base"). The list of reforms includes an increase in the number of projects implemented by the programme countries on their own responsibility (national execution), the promotion of technical cooperation among developing countries and the employment of expatriate nationals.

The report describes numerous innovative and creative approaches to technical cooperation as an instrument used by UNDP. The analysis and proposals are not only relevant to UNDP's instruments. The list of reforms includes appropriate and, in some cases, radical proposals which, though still valid, have so far been only partly implemented in UNDP's and other agencies' development cooperation.

3.2.3 *UNDP in Action*

As UNDP accounted for a large proportion of the Nordic countries' contributions to development cooperation and as little was known about what UNDP's field offices were actually doing, the governments of Denmark, Finland, Norway and Sweden jointly commissioned the study *UNDP in Action* (Ahlberg / Løvbraek 1985). The aim of this study, which was completed in 1985, was

> *"... to review the many and various UNDP activities in the field and to supply the Nordic governments with such information as to facilitate their policy decisions in the Governing Council."* (Ahlberg / Løvbraek 1985, p. 1)

The study was carried out in a total of eleven African and Asian countries. However, many of the conclusions drawn apply well beyond the examples taken for the study.

UNDP in Action arrives at a generally very favourable assessment compared to other studies. It emphasizes the comprehensive structure of the external network, the pronounced competence of the staff of the country offices, the favourable view of UNDP taken by the governments of developing countries and the sometimes helpful function of country programming (Ahlberg / Løvbraek 1985, p. 11). It is critical of the inadequate implementation of the recommendations made in the Jackson Report, the antiquated administration of the country offices, the country offices' perception of headquarters as a monitoring institution, the inflexibility of the timing of the programming cycle, UNDP's poor coordination of activities within the UN system and the lack of cooperation between UNDP and bilateral donors.

Box 6: *Failing the World's Poor* - an analysis by the Heritage Foundation

The policy paper *Failing the World's Poor*[5] published by the conservative Heritage Foundation in 1985 differs in some important respects from other analyses of UNDP and papers on its reform. This is especially true of the intention behind the document and of the criteria adopted for the analysis and evaluation.

A question of decisive importance for the document is how far UNDP complies with what are assumed to be the USA's interests.

> *"Of vastly greater importance are the political and institutional implications of UNDP programming. Is the UNDP developing, as an institution, in a direction inimical to U.S. interests?"* (Bissell 1985, p. 2)

Although the document thus conforms to the Heritage Foundation's traditional policy and its intensive efforts to bring influence to bear on the USA's policy towards the UN, it is, compared to other analyses of UNDP, very largely shaped by specific national interests that bear no direct relation to the goals and tasks of UNDP as a multilateral institution.

Consequently, the document faces a particular dilemma when analysing and evaluating UNDP:

- On the one hand, it sees UNDP as an institution with serious shortcomings:

  "... the UNDP is not satisfying the expectations of a significant proportion of its constituencies, in terms of funding sources and client-recipients of its services." (Bissell 1985, p. 2)

Box 6: *Failing the World's Poor* - an analysis by the Heritage Foundation (cont.)

Besides other problems, the document criticizes UNDP's development orientation, which is geared to the public rather than the private sector and does not therefore serve the USA's development interests (Bissell 1985, pp. 19 ff., 43 ff.). UNDP is also *"... an agency engaging in activities occasionally inimical to U.S. national interests ..."* (Bissell 1985, p. 43) An improvement in its effectiveness would not therefore necessarily be in the USA's interests:

"It is hardly sufficient to press the UNDP to use U.S. dollars more effectively, if the purposes of such expenditures are seen as contrary to U.S. interests." (Bissell 1985, p. 43)

- On the other hand, UNDP is seen as far less of a problem for the USA's policy than other UN agencies:

"The comment frequently heard when the subject of the UNDP is raised is: 'Don't look at it too critically; it's the best friend the U.S. has at the United Nations." (Bissell 1985, p. 1; see also p. 43)

Advantages are seen particularly in the strong presence of US personnel in the UNDP administration (including the Administrator), the links with the USA's foreign policy and the favourable starting position for US enterprises when UNDP awards contracts (Bissell 1985, pp. 2, 43).

In view of this dilemma *Failing the World's Poor* weighs up the costs and benefits of the USA's remaining in UNDP and withdrawing. Given the specific function performed by UNDP, the report urges it to remain a member:

"The trend over recent years has pointed to an eventual U.S. withdrawal from UNDP as from other U.N. agencies. U.S. interest has been declining, and the sense of what is accomplished through the UNDP becomes fuzzier each year. U.S. withdrawal from UNDP, however, would be premature." (Bissell 1985, p. 46)

The report also calls on the USA to give UNDP higher priority in its policy and to increase its commitment.

Besides making various detailed recommendations on procedural and organizational aspects, the study emphasizes four points in its conclusions. Firstly, it calls on the member governments to give UNDP more support in the performance of its tasks:

> *"In order to better fulfil its function as coordinator of UN system development activities, member governments should make sure it receives the moral support and the financial means to do so."* (Ahlberg / Løvbraek 1985, p. 10)

Secondly, the UN's specialized agencies should play a greater part in the programme cycle (especially in planning and evaluation) and reorganize their relationship with UNDP at country level along the lines recommended in the Consensus Resolution (i.e. tasks performed primarily by UNDP). Thirdly, UNDP documents, reports, etc. should become qualitatively more ambitious and more interesting to a larger readership. Fourthly, there should be closer cooperation between bilateral donors and UNDP.

UNDP in Action reveals the Scandinavian countries' special interest and their efforts to assess and improve UNDP's activities as early as the mid-1980s. It documents the efforts to bring about changes through constructive criticism and so represents an important basis for the Scandinavian countries' reform initiatives in the 1990s (especially the *Nordic UN Project*).

3.2.4 UNDP and World Development by the Year 2000

The report *UNDP and World Development by the Year 2000* (DP/1989/14) submitted by the UNDP Administrator in 1989 presents a broad review of aspects of direct or indirect relevance to UNDP. It considers in particular (1) important global developments in the 1980s and 1990s, (2) TC challenges for UNDP (conceptual, instrumental, etc.), (3) individual challenges and recent UNDP developments in various spheres, including evaluation, project implementation and coordination of development cooperation, (4) the financing of UNDP and (5) UNDP's organization.

Despite its forward-looking title, the report essentially underlines UNDP's tasks and activities without referring to any appreciable changes or need for adjustment:

> *"We see UNDP in the 1990s as a facilitator and catalyst for member countries, enabling them to mobilize the system's technical resources to help developing countries improve the quality of life of their citizens. The most effective way to attain this goal is to focus on enabling the developing countries to take the lead. Our approach to improving the capacity of the United Nations system to respond to the challenges of the future is to reaffirm the basic tenet of UNDP, which is one of providing assistance to sovereign Governments."* (DP/1989/ 14, p. 34)

The report lists many of the major problems facing development policy, technical cooperation and UNDP. However, it contains few self-critical or innovative and creative elements, seeking instead to ensure the continuity and consolidation of the UNDP profile and approach. *UNDP and World Development by the Year 2000* therefore primarily reflects the political conditions and minimum consensus in the UN and UNDP's Governing Council in the late 1980s, which did not permit a reform-oriented and innovative policy.

3.2.5 Kienbaum Report

The mandate of the Kienbaum Report (Kienbaum & Partners 1991), which was drawn up for UNDP in 1991, was *"... to analyze whether UNDP is still endowed with the optimal senior management structure."* (Kienbaum & Partners 1991, p. 6.) The report is therefore primarily a study of organization and management.

It begins by stating that UNDP is not performing its main tasks and has waned in significance. It goes on to say, however, that the UN system needs a development *"centerpiece"*, for which UNDP is in principle the ideal candidate (Kienbaum & Partners 1991, p. 3).

Besides a wide range of detailed findings and recommendations concerning UNDP's organization and management, the main points made and conclusions drawn in the study are as follows:

- UNDP lacks a vision, a strategy and a focus that are generally accepted and reflected in its activities. A basic feature of UNDP is in fact its "*no-strategy approach*" (Kienbaum & Partners 1991, pp. 12 ff.). This problem is one of the main causes of further shortcomings downstream.
- "*Effective governance*" in the form of the Governing Council and UNDP headquarters should concentrate on the question of how a vision, strategy and focus might be created. Instead, "*day-to-day management*" dominates (Kienbaum & Partners 1991, p. MS-2). In this situation a new "*Capacity Study*" might be an appropriate means of answering the most important questions.
- UNDP's organization should be adapted with the aim of avoiding or reducing fragmentation, micro-management and unnecessary functions. Responsibilities should be decentralized and evaluations used for the planning of future TC measures.
- The management of UNDP should take the form of a small and rather permanent Governing Council Committee. It should consider not individual measures but general strategic aspects, co-operative relations with other UN agencies and the supervision of top management.

All in all, the objectives of the Kienbaum report are such that it is not dominated by development policy. Besides covering aspects of organizational and managerial issues, it nonetheless makes some relevant references to development policy questions (e.g. UNDP's overriding objective) with helpful and critical conclusions.

3.2.6 UNDP's Effectiveness at Country Level

The study *Effectiveness of Multilateral Agencies at Country Level. UNDP in Kenya, Nepal, Sudan and Thailand* (Danida 1991c) published in 1991 was carried out by COWIconsult for the Danish Foreign Ministry's international development division (Danida). It is one of a series of studies on a total of eleven multilateral development cooperation institutions. The main aim of the overall project was to examine what these institutions were doing at country level. This was to entail, in particular, an analysis of each institutions's comparative advantages, its specific mandate and its approach (Danida 1991a, pp. 1 ff.; Danida 1991c, p. i and preface, no page number).

The part of the study that concerns UNDP divides the findings into two blocks. The first block contains a total of eight conclusions on UNDP's effectiveness at country level:

- Capacity-building in the institutions of the various recipient countries in conjunction with national execution is an increasingly important function of UNDP, complementing or replacing the original approaches.
- Country programming as undertaken by UNDP is an inappropriate instrument for guiding measures in the various countries and for developing a country profile.
- The strategies pursued in the various countries differ widely:

  "The difference is very small, however, between a constructive use of flexible gap-filling to meet the advanced technical assistance needs of specialized government bodies on the one hand, and a thin spread of technical assistance resources to meet numerous vested interests on the other." (Danida 1991c, p. ii)

- In the countries taken as examples an attempt is being made to concentrate country programming resources in three ways: (1) vertical concentration on strategic subsectors, (2) concentration on capacity-building in central government institutions and (3) concentration on the formulation of approaches and methods for the local level by means of pilot schemes. The Danida study regards the first approach as the most suitable for UNDP.
- UNDP and the governments of the programme countries are showing a growing preference for development banks and small specialized institutions rather than the UN's large specialized agencies for implementing tasks.

- UNDP should become more active in the area of programme cooperation between the specialized institutions of the government of the developing country concerned and the UN system. This might counteract projectitis and labour-intensive project cycle management.
- There are major differences in the quality of UNDP projects owing, among other things, to the different size of the projects, the types of project and the vested interests of the actors.
- In the case of project implementation the workload of the UNDP country offices is greatly increased by the tasks they take on for implementing organizations that are not represented in the country concerned.

The second block contains conclusions on UNDP's role in the multilateral donor community. They ascribe UNDP's relative strength to its close cooperation with the relevant government institutions and in the setting of priorities for capacity-building in these institutions. Its relative weaknesses consist in its dependence on other institutions for implementation, the resulting absence of a coherent strategy, an inappropriate country programming mechanism, projectitis and the underqualified and overworked staff of the country offices.

The study concludes that UNDP needs to be strengthened where four of its functions are concerned: (1) passing on technical resources from the UN specialized organizations, (2) contributing to capacity-building and national execution of UNDP projects, (3) advising the governments of developing countries and (4) promoting development cooperation and donor coordination. If these functions were strengthened, the study claims, it would be possible to react to UNDP's erosion. It was unrealistic, on the other hand, to call for a reduction in the development banks' technical cooperation so that UNDP might become more dominant in this field (Danida 1991a, p. xi).

The Danida study is, on the whole, an informative analysis of UNDP's country-related shortcomings and strengths. It has the particular merit of attempting to study and evaluate different multilateral donors with the same set of analytical criteria. This enables the statements on UNDP to be related and compared (albeit to a limited extent) to those on other donor institutions.

3.2.7 Nordic UN Project

The *Nordic UN Project* (Nordic UN Project 1991b, 1996) was launched in 1988 with the aim of developing ideas and proposals on ways in which the Nordic countries might make constructive contributions to the debate on the reform of the UN in the economic and social field. Although UNDP was not therefore the only subject of the project, it occupied a central position when it came to questions on operational activities (Nordic UN Project 1991b, p. 7).

The final report of the Nordic UN Project was completed in 1991. It was later supplemented by a further report, which was completed and published in 1996.[6]

The first report points out that a limited and uncertain financial base has prevented UNDP from performing its main funding tasks. The attitude of the donors in this respect also reflected their desire to have greater influence over project objectives. Nor had UNDP ever been granted the means to adjust its programmes to changing global and country-specific conditions (Nordic UN Project 1991b, pp. 57 f.). The report emphasizes that UNDP's role as a partner of the developing countries gives it a particular advantage over the development banks.[7]

In much the same way as the Danida study *Effectiveness of UNDP at Country Level*, the Nordic UN Project stresses that the reality of the current situation should be taken into account where UNDP's role is concerned (limited importance as a development cooperation institution, etc.). UNDP should therefore concentrate more on its comparative advantages:

> *"It should thus place greater emphasis on human resource development, institution-building and the central functions of*

> *government, policy-making, training and capacity-building."* (Nordic UN Project 1991b, p. 59)

The report also calls for the creation of a new political supervisory body and an improved financing system that includes assessed contributions, negotiated pledges and voluntary contributions.

The overall aim of the process of change was

> *"... to transform UNDP from basically a funding mechanism into a stronger development institution. It is therefore an urgent task to revitalize and reaffirm the role of the UNDP as a major and potentially effective instrument of multilateral development cooperation."* (Nordic UN Project 1991b, p. 59)

The second Nordic UN Project report essentially updates the proposals put forward in 1991. It focuses on a number of overarching aspects of the United Nations' economic and social spheres (UN representation at country level, financing of UN development cooperation, etc.) and is generally less detailed than the reports drawn up during the first phase of the Nordic UN Project; consequently, UNDP's role is considered in less depth.

On the whole, particular political importance should be attached to the Nordic UN Project, and especially its first phase. It attracted considerable attention in and outside the UN because it discussed in convincing fashion shortcomings and, above all, prospective solutions to the problem of revitalizing UN development cooperation and UNDP. It demonstrates the considerable affinity that the Scandinavian countries have with UNDP, without overlooking its weaknesses. In the early 1990s the project played a decisive part in triggering the current debate on reforms. To some extent at least, Kofi Annan's reform package also referred to the ideas produced by the Scandinavian initiative (an example being the proposals for the review of the financing mechanisms).

3.2.8 Quo Vadis, UNDP

Carlsson's study *Quo Vadis, UNDP* (Carlsson 1993), which was completed in 1993, was commissioned by the Swedish Foreign Ministry's Department of International Development Cooperation. It was carried out with the aim of contributing to the ongoing debate on UNDP's future role.

The study proceeds from the premise that the UN was established for the general purpose of considering political issues, not to organize and undertake operational development activities. Against this background and given the problems UNDP currently faces, the study believes that in principle it can take one of two directions:

> *"Should UNDP therefore,*
>
> *1) be designed to approach development primarily as a political issue and integrated into the UN political structure, or*
>
> *2) approach development as primarily a set of technical, professional issues and be further removed from the political structure of the UN."* (Carlsson 1993, p. v)

Proceeding from these assumptions, Carlsson sees three options for changing and further developing UNDP as an organization (Carlsson 1993, pp. 40 - 48). The first model, a *UN Cooperation Programme*, would place the emphasis on political functions. The tasks would extend beyond the sphere of development policy, since the Cooperation Programme would be more closely integrated into the UN Secretariat. The second model is based on the idea of a *UN agency* with a substantive focus on longer-term development activities. The agency would come close to the ideas developed in the *Capacity Study* and operate at some organizational distance from the UN Secretariat. The third model, a *UN Development Corporation*, is based on the idea of establishing an autonomous service institution financed by fees to deal with technical problems.

Carlsson emphasizes that a further option - retaining the status quo - cannot in any way be regarded as a viable basis in the long term. He calls for changes along the lines of the agency model:

> *"Among these models only the agency satisfies the requirements for both effective governance and a clear distinction between the normative role of the Secretariat and the operational activities of the UN."* (Carlsson 1993, p. vi)

Carlsson's study generally offers some interesting pointers to various options for UNDP's basic orientation. The particular merit of the analysis is therefore that it asks what UNDP's general functional tasks should be. So fundamental a redefinition of UNDP's position has not yet been sought by the UN member countries or UNDP itself.

3.2.9 *A Charter for Change*

A Charter for Change is based on a report submitted in 1993 by an internal UNDP working party (transition team) which had been set up by the UNDP Administrator. The transition team's aim was to draw up proposals on the following two subjects:[8] (1), UNDP's objectives and strategies in the context of a new development paradigm and (2) organizational changes needed if these objectives were to be achieved.

1. As regards the first task, the transition team proposes a dual mission. Firstly, countries should be assisted in their efforts to ensure *sustainable human development* (SHD). This mission is subdivided into various objectives:
   - development of domestic capacities for SHD,
   - increase in international cooperation relating to SHD and
   - support for peace and transition processes (Carlsson 1993, p. vi).

   Secondly, the UN should be supported in its efforts to achieve world peace, human safety and development, i.e. the emphasis is on UNDP's service functions. This mission too is subdivided into various objectives:

- greater coordination of the UN system to increase the effectiveness of development cooperation,
- retention of the UN system as a place for flexible responses to new and specific tasks and
- support for peace and transition processes.

2. As regards the second task - specifying the organizational requirements to be satisfied if the objectives defined are to be achieved - the report sets out proposals for the necessary organizational structures, staff requirement profiles and work processes. The proposals include the following points:
   - a new organizational structure that enables the missions to be converted into achievable objectives;
   - measures that make UNDP a stronger *"substantive organization"* (UNDP 1993e, p. 7), the aim being to transform it from a funding agency into a rather more TC- and policy-oriented institution:
   - the development of *"substantive partnerships"* (UNDP 1993e, p. 40) with the UN system and the international financial institutions;
   - the development of UNDP into a more outwardly oriented agency;
   - an increase in financial resources;
   - organizational and accountability structures and staff development questions and profiles.

On the whole, *A Charter for Change* is particularly significant, since it was drawn up by members of the UNDP staff and therefore, being highly specific, is directly applicable. Furthermore, some of the transition team's recommendations had a direct impact on the UNDP Administrator's proposals (Speth 1994a) and the Executive Board's decisions regarding UNDP's substantive profile (section III.4).

3.2.10 *A Comparative Assessment*

A Comparative Assessment, an analysis published in 1995 by the Overseas Development Council (ODC),[9] compares the UNDP, the International Monetary Fund, the World Bank and UNICEF. It starts from the premise that the conditions and therefore the tasks for the existing international development institutions have changed radically because of various factors (the end of the East-West conflict, etc.) and argues that neither the Bretton Woods institutions nor the UN development agencies are adequately prepared for these challenges.

The study sees UNDP as having both specific strengths and weaknesses. Its main strengths are (1) its close relations with the programme countries' institutions (national ownership, etc.), (2) its good external structure and (3) the conditionality and form of its technical cooperation (grant basis, South-South cooperation, etc.). UNDP's weaknesses, on the other hand, are (1) its limited and weak revenue base, (2) its lack of focus, (3) the separation of funding and execution and (4) its underqualified staff. The study detects various efforts to overcome the deficiencies, although it is not yet clear how effective they are.

The ODC study comes to a generally negative conclusion on UNDP's present situation. However, it also sees potential for international technical cooperation that might have an impact in certain circumstances:

> *"Of the institutions reviewed, UNDP seems the one needing the most substantial reform and revitalisation. Not only does it stand as the centrepiece of international technological cooperation - an area widely recognised as requiring improvement; but also, UNDP's institutional features would seem to make it potentially well-suited to take on some of the new tasks, especially in politically sensitive areas of cooperation. But if it is to play an enhanced role, its strategic purpose will need to be more sharply defined and other aspects of governance, programming, staffing and financing revised."* (Gwin 1995, p. 115)

The ODC analysis is generally more critical than the documents published by the Scandinavian countries. Nonetheless, in their analysis of UNDP's strengths and weaknesses this study and the Nordic reform concepts have much in common. The ODC study had an impact on the reform debate because it attracted the interest of, among others, the UNDP administration.

3.2.11 *Assessment of UNDP*

The Centre for Development Research completed its study *Assessment of UNDP* (Centre for Development Research 1996) in 1996. It was commissioned by Denmark, India, Sweden and the United Kingdom.

This study too is meant as a contribution to the reform debate and the process of reforming UNDP. Its declared aim is to find an appropriate link between UNDP's needs and the demands made on it on the one hand and its capacities and potential on the other (Centre for Development Research 1996, p. 1). The application-oriented recommendations are addressed primarily to the Executive Board and the UNDP Administrator.

The study proceeds from the following premises: UNDP faces many challenges in the 1990s. It has reacted to them with a number of changes and reforms. The process of change is, however, extremely demanding and is now in danger of succumbing to *reform fatigue*. Sustainable human development (SHD) is too general a development policy priority for it to be directly operationalized. The analysis and the recommendations made in the study are therefore geared to giving constructive support to the current reform process and preventing any reform fatigue from arising.

The most important conclusions are closely linked to the three main roles of UNDP identified by the study: (1) policy role, (2) technical cooperation role and (3) coordination role. Accordingly, future reforms should be arranged as follows:

- *Policy role*: UNDP can assume some important tasks at global and country level in policy analysis and policy dialogue with a view to achieving the newly developed overriding objectives (sustainable human development and, in this context, poverty alleviation).
- *Technical cooperation role*: SHD is not a sufficiently specific guide framework for setting programme priorities. UNDP should concentrate on the institutional requirements and the development of national capacity. A capacity development assistance (CDA) approach of this kind calls for adjustments to UNDP's organization and staffing.
- *Coordination role*: The coordination role primarily concerns the country level, where, by rendering appropriate services, backed by CDA, it can perform a range of tasks wanted by donors and the programme country.

The study assumes that a strategy which concentrated on the roles described above would, in some respects, have major implications for UNDP. The following aspects in particular might be affected:

- the UNDP mandate,
- representation at country level and its functions,
- the mobilization of financial resources,
- the organizational and staffing structure and
- UNDP's role in the UN system.

The *Assessment of UNDP* study contains a number of important suggestions regarding UNDP's substance. It forges many links with the current TC debate; from this it develops the CDA approach. A fundamental weakness of *Assessment of UNDP*, however, is that it focuses too heavily on the abstract objective of capacity-building.

3.2.12 Speth Initiative

UNDP Administrator Speth took the initiative in 1996 by putting forward an informal paper[10] entitled *Proposals for Reform of the United Nations in the Economic and Social Fields* (Speth 1996). The reform initiative concerns the whole operational and non-operational sphere of UN development policy. Where operational activities are concerned, UNDP plays a prominent role in the document:

> *"Briefly, in this model, UNDP would complete its current evolution towards providing the co-ordinating, integrating force for the UN's operational activities. UNDP would cease to exist as a separate programme, and the name 'UNDP' would be dropped. The former UNDP would be transformed so that it could fully provide the co-ordinating and integrating structure for the UN Alliance for people. The transformed UNDP would thus provide the much-needed 'umbrella structure' dedicated to the success of the system as a whole."* (Speth 1996, p. 8)

The proposal thus means that, while UNDP would no longer exist as a programme, it would perform overarching tasks. The Speth initiative attaches particular importance to the question of coordination by the Resident Coordinator and by integrated UN country operations. The Resident Coordinator would thus perform the function at country level of "chief of mission" for all UN institutions, including the specialized agencies. In agreement with the government of the country concerned, he would be responsible for the programming of all financial resources currently allocated to the UNDP country programmes.

The document remains vague, however, in the specific proposals it has to make concerning a future UNDP, unlike other areas of reform. Although Speth emphasizes UNDP's umbrella function, it remains unclear in many respects what requirements would have to be satisfied and what specific tasks and instruments UNDP's performance of this function would entail.

On the whole, the Speth initiative includes many sensible and far-reaching proposals. The paper takes account of decisive basic problems facing UN development cooperation and UNDP. The major weakness of the reform concept is the impression it conveys that the initiative also serves the pursuit of institutional interests. As the proposals were drawn up by the UNDP Administrator, who advocates a far stronger UNDP with a new name, the concept was seen in many quarters as having been largely prompted by personal interests and therefore failed to have any major political appeal.

3.3 Conclusions

The description and discussion of selected important reform concepts and initiatives is informative in several respects. Above all, it can be said that in the past various actors have shown an interest in the reform of UNDP with concepts of their own - though placing the emphasis on very different aspects and varying widely in the specificity of their proposals.

As to the manner in which UNDP should change or reform, the documents both differ and have a great deal in common. They differ not least because of the background against which they emerged, fundamentally different political positions and the aspect considered in each case, which are sometimes located at very different levels (i.e. overriding objectives, instruments, field offices). Many of the analyses and studies are based on initiatives of "UN-friendly" member countries, and all the documents considered here therefore reveal a more positive basic attitude than is in fact likely to be true of the political majority of the donor governments. There is no document containing proposals for reforms put forward by the programme or developing countries (section III.6). Moreover, some of the documents reveal a clear bias or specific interest. The Speth initiative, for example, reflects the UNDP Administrator's distinct interest in the upgrading of his agency and in the organizational expansion of his programme.

Most of what the documents have in common or the similarities they show concern appraisals and conclusions, with particular reference to the following:

- The reform of UNDP is generally considered necessary. It must form part of changes to the whole operational field of the UN system's development cooperation activities.
- Reforms should be undertaken with the aim of strengthening UNDP.
- The Jackson Report is still often regarded as an important frame of reference for analysing and evaluating the shortcomings and achievements of UNDP and all the UN's operational development cooperation activities.
- The recommendations made in the Jackson Report have never been properly implemented.
- The services to be provided by UNDP must be redefined.

While ideas on the tasks that UNDP should perform vary widely in some cases, many of the documents agree on the following:

- A clear focus should be sought at conceptual level.
- At structural and policy level there is a need for changes to make UNDP a high-quality technical cooperation agency and an effective coordinating agency at country and headquarters level. Among other things, an adequate and reliable financial base will be needed for this.
- Where implementation is concerned, the country level is crucial; it should be strengthened particularly with regard to its political and strategic functions and its coordinating tasks. Management and staff structures should be adjusted.

The reform concepts that have been discussed generally provide useful pointers for reform orientation and for individual reforms. The following chapters must therefore consider the proposals for reforms that have so far been taken up or implemented. The discussion will also turn to the areas in which there is an added need for reform and to the obstacles that stand in its way.

4 Measures to Reform UNDP

4.1 Introduction

Background

UNDP's history has been characterized not only by debates on reform but also by actual steps and processes undertaken to reform the organization. These adjustments have been made in an attempt to find a viable role for UNDP in international development cooperation that has majority support. The recommendations made in the Jackson Report, some of which were reiterated in the Consensus Resolution, have been the most prominent and wide-ranging example of this. A wide variety of other reform and adjustment efforts were also launched by the UN and UNDP in the 1970s and 1980s. They were intended to make it possible for UNDP's financing and coordinating tasks to be performed better or redefined to suit the prevailing environment. In the 1980s, for example, the focus was on questions relating to UNDP's analytical capacities, the round tables as coordination fora for development cooperation, the focusing of programmes, the role of the Resident Representatives/Resident Coordinators and the participation of the contributing countries and programme countries in programming and the decision-making processes (OECD 1985, p. 149).

Despite their limited success, UNDP's adjustment and reform efforts were certainly acknowledged in the 1970s and 1980s. The OECD's Development Assistance Committee, for example, described them in the mid-1980s in the following terms:

> *"The UNDP has made strong efforts to redefine its role and to render its operations more effective both as a central multila-*

> *teral source of funding and as a co-ordinator of technical assistance."* (OECD 1985, p. 149)

In the 1990s the reform and adjustment process has accelerated significantly. The General Assembly, the Secretary-General, ECOSOC, UNDP's Governing Council, or Executive Board, and the UNDP Administrator have taken a number of decisions in an attempt to trigger a process of wide-ranging and profound change. In an assessment UNDP Administrator Speth therefore comments:

> *"So, when we add this all up, the case for change in UNDP is overwhelming. The good news (...) is that UNDP is already changing, and is changing in many of the right directions (...)."* (Speth 1994a, p. 6)

Objective

The aim of this section is to analyse and evaluate measures to reform UNDP which have been initiated, are currently being implemented or have been completed in the 1990s. The intention is to review and assess the current state of the reform process and to reveal any aspects that have been overlooked or received insufficient attention in the past.

An attempt is made to give a general overview of all reform efforts directly relevant to UNDP's effectiveness in the development sphere; in other words, the analysis goes beyond the study of reform measures for which the UNDP Administrator and the Governing Council, or Executive Board, are directly responsible.

4.2 Reform Process

4.2.1 Terms of Reference

There is no single conceptual basis or overall strategy for the reform process that has been initiated and to some extent has already been completed in the 1990s. The reform process includes decisions and reform efforts by various UN organs, these being primarily the General Assembly, the Secretary-General, ECOSOC, UNDP's Governing Council, or Executive Board, and its Administrator. In accordance with their terms of reference these organs may take decisions or make suggestions regarding reforms in specific areas. Matters relating to UNDP's external structures, for example, affect the Resident Coordinator system and therefore fall within the General Assembly's and Secretary-General's terms of reference; matters relating to the distribution of UNDP's core resources among country programmes, on the other hand, are primarily the Executive Board's responsibility, while UNDP's internal administrative organization is the Administrator's responsibility.

One way of differentiating the reform measures that concern UNDP is therefore to make a distinction by the terms or reference of the various actors. Another way, which refers to the actors' powers, is to consider whether reforms affect

– the whole of the UN or UN system (e.g. the Resident Coordinator system),
– all UN funds and programmes (e.g. fora for the coordination of their activities, system of voluntary contributions) or
– solely or primarily UNDP (substantive priorities, programming criteria, internal organization, etc.).

For this study it is important that these distinctions are taken into account and made clear.

4.2.2 Foundations and Phases of Reform

Foundations of reform

The foundations on which the UNDP reform process in the 1990s is based comprises several components, which are partly interrelated:

- UN General Assembly Resolutions 47/199 and 50/120 on the reform of operational development activities[1] concern a number of substantive focus areas (capacity-building, sustainability, etc.) and especially aspects of the Resident Coordinator system, the role of the programme countries in planning and implementation (e.g. the planning documents, national execution) and the coordination of UN funds and programmes through the harmonization of work stages and procedures.
- The documents on reform drawn up by Secretary-General Kofi Annan in 1997[2] cover a wide range of substantive, structural, administrative and financial issues. Particularly important for UNDP are the initiatives relating to coordination at headquarters and country level and the mobilization of resources.
- The foundations for reform laid by the Governing Council, or Executive Board, and the UNDP Administrator:[3] this component covers matters from conception through the distribution of resources to internal organization. The foundations and stages concerned are considered in greater depth below.

Phases of reform in the 1990s

The foundations for reform laid by the Governing Council, or Executive Board, and the UNDP Administrator have so far featured two important phases of reform (initiatives for change) in the 1990s, each with its own emphasis.[4] The range, practical substance and time frame were not entirely clear when the reform process began.[5] Among other things, consultations with and the involvement of various actors (e.g. individual members of the Executive Board) have led to repeated changes and new substance for the reform process.

In the first reform period, 1994 - 1995, fundamental issues at UNDP were addressed. The emphasis was placed on substantive focusing and the setting of priorities, the programming procedure and the implementation of General Assembly Resolutions 47/199 and 50/120. Efforts were also made to create a "leaner" organization, to improve efficiency and to increase accountability. In UNDP's view the aim in this period was to launch a process of clarifying questions of principle:

> *"The aim was to reposition the organization on three fronts: (a) as an effective partner in the new environment for development cooperation emerging after the Cold War; (b) as a unifying and coordinating force to strengthen United Nations support for development; and (c) as an effective voice for a revitalized system of international development cooperation."* (DP/1997/16/Add. 7, p. 2)

The reforms were discussed frequently and intensively by various fora and groups. Special mention should be made in this context of the work and conclusions of the "transition team" (UNDP 1993d, 1993e) and the UNDP Global Meeting at Rye/New York in 1994, attended by the then UN Secretary-General and 131 UNDP Resident Representatives/Resident Coordinators), and the report on the outcome of this meeting) (UNDP 1994c).

The nature of the issues considered was such that many of the reform decisions were taken by the Executive Board,[6] i.e. the most important reform measures exceeded the Administrator's authority.

UNDP regards the 1994 - 1995 period of reform as

> *"(...) the most far-reaching development in the history of the organization since General Assembly resolution 2688 (xxv) of 11 December 1970 (the 'Consensus') (...)"* (DP/1997/16/Add. 7, p. 2)

UNDP decided the next reform period would be 1996 - 1997 and would be followed by a period of consolidation until December 1999. Even more than the first, this stage has been designed as a flexible process. It has been given the title *UNDP 2001* and sometimes *Change Management*. The main prescriptions for the second reform period were based on the conclusions drawn at a closed meeting of the UNDP management at Glen Cove in February 1996.[7] An important factor in the preparation of the second reform period was the participation of the

UNDP staff, represented by seven working groups.[8] Practical preparatory work and the coordination of *UNDP 2001* are largely the responsibility of an internal *change management committee*.

The UNDP administration sees the second reform period as the time for putting into concrete form the attempts at substantive focusing during the first period. The aim in the second period is to modify UNDP's internal functions, processes and structures so that the changes to objectives, tasks and substance approved by the Executive Board in 1994 may be put into practice.[9] To this end, five objectives were first formulated;[10] against the background of the discussion processes that had taken place UNDP referred in its documents for the Executive Board's annual general meeting to three areas which the *UNDP 2001* project should cover:

> *"1) empower country offices in order to provide quick, responsive development services to help programme countries achieve their objectives in sustainable human development (SHD); 2) enhance the quality and impact of programmes and services within the main areas of focus adopted by UNDP, drawing more fully on its experiences at the country, regional and global levels; and 3) create a more coherent, accountable and cost-effective organization with stronger leadership styles, more efficient decision-making and implementation processes and a culture of trust, professionalism and teamwork among staff."* (DP/1997/16/Add. 7, p. 1)

As the UNDP administration sees it, *UNDP 2001* differs from the first reform period as regards the question of competence in that it consists solely of reform measures which may be decided by the UNDP Administrator and do not necessarily require the Executive Board's approval. The UNDP Administrator has nonetheless sought and entered into consultation with the Executive Board at all phases of *UNDP 2001* and informed it of the current situation in various documents.[11]

4.3 Levels of Reform

The reform measures planned, initiated or implemented in the 1990s that concern UNDP's effectiveness in the development sphere are considered below on the basis of the same distinction as made in sections II.1, II.2 and III.1 between (1) the conceptual level, (2) the structural and policy level and (3) the administration and implementation level.

4.3.1 Conceptual Level

The reforms undertaken at conceptual level in the 1990s have primarily concerned substantive focusing on the goal of *sustainable human development* as part of a new *core mission* and a *mission statement.* Efforts have also been made to define new development tasks for UNDP.

Substantive Focusing: the Sustainable Human Development Concept as part of the Core Mission and Mission Statement

(a) Reform measures

At conceptual level the efforts of the UNDP administration and the Governing Council, or Executive Board, to focus and clarify the substantive objectives have been the most important innovation.

Since the mid-1990s UNDP has often been identified with the development paradigm of *sustainable human development* (SHD). The *Human Development Report* (HDR), which UNDP has published annually since 1990, began by placing the emphasis on the human dimension of development.[12] The report enabled UNDP to attract greater attention in much of the debate on development policy. The debate on human development can be seen as an indirect and frequently direct criticism of the structural adjustment policy and thus as a conceptual offensive against the policy pursued by the World Bank, especially in the 1980s.

Human development focuses not on economic growth as such but primarily on the quality of economic growth, i.e. aspects of distribution and priorities for the spending of public resources. Not least because of the development debate in the context of the UNCED conference in Rio de Janeiro (1992) UNDP too has paid greater attention to the environmental dimension of the development process; this is particularly evident from the concept of sustainable development, which was introduced into the international debate chiefly by the 1987 Brundtland Report (Schmitz 1996).

Sustainable human development is an integrating, interdisciplinary and holistic approach to development that combines the human dimension and environmental aspects.[13] In UNDP's view, which is shared by many others active in the field of development, the concept comprises the following dimensions:

> *"It is people-centred, participatory and environmentally sound. It stresses economic growth with equitable distribution, enhancement of people's capabilities and enlargement of their choices. It gives highest priority to poverty alleviation, integration of women in the development process, creation of productive and remunerative jobs, and self-reliance and self-determination of people and governments."*[14]

In the 1990s UNDP has taken two steps in particular in an attempt to establish sustainable human development as the development paradigm for its own organization and to give it conceptual shape:[15] the decisions taken by the Executive Board on (1) the *core mission* in 1994 and (2) the *mission statement* in 1996.

1. UNDP's core mission is based on Executive Board Decision 94/14, which refers to the Administrator's comments and proposal in his report *Future of the United Nations Development Programme, Initiatives for Change* (DP/1994/39). Further details were added by the progress report *Future of UNDP: Implementation of Executive Board Decision 94/14* (DP/1995/31), submitted by the Administrator in 1995. UNDP sees these conceptual efforts in 1994 and

1995 as *"pathbreaking decisions"* (UNDP 1996a, p. 1), enabling UNDP's work to become more focused and priorities to be set.

The conceptual reorientation is a complex construct with different substantive levels. It comprises a core mission, three principal goals, four focus areas and ten patterns of intervention or forms of action (see Figure 8).

The ten patterns of intervention provide indications for the operational sphere for the specification of SHD activities. The Bureau of Policy and Programme Support (BPPS) and the regional offices have been instructed to take further steps towards operationalization. They are to develop instruments and guidelines for the country level and the UNDP staff to enable SHD programmes to be identified, formulated and implemented.[16]

UNDP's conceptual deliberations focus on the concept of sustainable human development. To enable this goal to be achieved, UNDP has the task of helping countries to develop domestic capacities. In this context poverty alleviation is to have a particularly high priority for UNDP's substantive focusing.

"Of the four priority areas, we believe that poverty elimination should be the highest UNDP priority -- Job One. It has always been listed among our priority areas for a reason, and this focus on poverty is strongly grounded in the distribution of UNDP core resources among countries."[17]

Within this focus area UNDP sees its particular task as being to promote employment and incomes:

"The core of UNDP's anti-poverty work lies in empowerment of the poor, including assisting in providing the poor with access to productive assets such as credit, skills, legal rights, job opportunities, natural resources and links to national and international markets. While UNICEF and UNFPA concentrate on basic social services in health, education and family planning, UNDP initiatives centre on family livelihoods." (UNDP 1997f, p. 1)

According to UNDP, various indicators reveal a close match between substantive tasks and objectives and actual spending priorities. UNDP points out in this context that in 1994 and 1995 33% of core programme resources was spent on poverty alleviation projects, 21% on environmental measures and 32% on the development of government structures (governance) (DP/1997/16, p. 3; UNDP 1997g, pp. 1 ff). Since 1994 all project commitments have had to be compatible with the focus areas. It is claimed that operations outside the focus areas have been terminated or not extended (UNDP 1997g, p. 1), although this is not substantiated by actual data. As further evidence of the greater effort made to focus operations, reference is made to the quotas for the poorer and poorest developing countries that have been agreed under the new programming procedure, 87% of the core resources being available for countries with a low income (a per capita gross national product of less than US $ 750) and 60% for the least developed countries (LLDCs).[18]

In the mid-1990s UNDP also launched numerous initiatives relating to poverty alleviation and the other focus areas. The 1997 *Human Development Report* concentrated on the subject of poverty. In addition, various specific poverty alleviation strategies and concepts are geared to the national level. Particular reference should be made to two documents in this context: firstly, the *National Human Development Reports* (NHDRs), which are intended as a country-related complement to the HDR. In 1996 over 50 NHDRs were completed, and reports of this kind were planned for more than 100 countries by the end of 1997 (DP/1997/16, p. 4; Annexes III and IV). Secondly, the *Poverty Strategy Initiative* (PSI) was launched to implement the conclusions drawn at the World Summit for Social Development held in Copenhagen in 1995. In this case UNDP is active in over 60 countries with operations in such areas as public awareness-building and the strengthening of the structures of civil society (DP/1997/16, pp. 3 f.; Annex V).

Figure 8: Elements of the UNDP core mission[a]

UNDP's core mission reads: *To assist countries in their endeavour to achieve sustainable human development* (SHD)

I. UNDP derives three principal goals from the core mission:

1. to strengthen international cooperation for SHD; UNDP intends to be a central pillar in the achievement of this goal;
2. to assist the UN family in its efforts to be a unified and effective force for SHD;
3. to focus UNDP resources on making maximum contributions to certain key dimensions of SHD in the programme countries.

II. The emphasis in this context is on four focus areas:

1. poverty alleviation (highest priority);
2. employment promotion;
3. promotion of women's rights; and
4. preservation of the environment.

III. Certain patterns of intervention can also be identified:

1. capacity-building in government administrations in the areas of (a) development management and reform of the public sector, (b) coordination of development cooperation, (c) management of the economy and market economy reforms, (d) protection of human rights, elections and democratization processes and (e) dialogue and cooperation with civil institutions;
2. support for governments in the development of operational concepts with the focus on SHD;
3. support for governments in the identification, preparation and implementation of long-term development programmes;
4. assistance with the mobilization of financial resources;
5. promotion of transfer and adaptation of and access to technologies;
6. support for technical cooperation among developing countries;
7. promotion of capacity-building for civil society (non-governmental organizations, grass-roots groups, etc.);
8. promotion of strategic projects and operations with a leverage or demonstration effect;
9. assistance with the further development of North-South relations and appropriate international agreements (Commission on Sustainable Development, UN world conferences, etc.);
10. support for national or regional processes connected with reconciliation efforts and peace-building processes and through the reintegration of troops, refugees and displaced persons.

a See UNDP (1995b), pp. 13 f., and DP/1994/39.

2. The mission statement was adopted in 1996 with Executive Board Decision 96/29.[19] It covers various substantive aspects already covered by the core mission:

   "UNDP's mission is to help countries in their efforts to achieve sustainable human development by assisting them to build their capacity to design and carry out development programmes in poverty eradication, employment creation and sustainable livelihoods, the empowerment of women and the protection and regeneration of the environment, giving first priority to poverty eradication.

   UNDP also acts to help the United Nations family to become a unified and powerful force for sustainable human development and works to strengthen international cooperation for sustainable human development." (Executive Board Decision 96/29, Annex, in: DP/1996/19, pp. 43 f.)

   The mission statement also very briefly goes into a wide range of other, very different subjects. They confirm or touch on questions of principle for the United Nations (interrelationship of "development", "peace" and "human security" tasks), basic questions on the approach to be adopted in UNDP's work (UNDP cooperates closely with the various governments and supports their priorities), UNDP's external representation (as a rule, the Resident Representative is also the Resident Coordinator), resource endowment and the commitment to improving efficiency and effectiveness.

(b) Assessment

In the 1990s UNDP has undergone an intensive process of programmatic and conceptual orientation. In an evaluation of this process, which is reflected primarily in the core mission and core statement, distinctions need to be made since new strengths and, equally, the continuation of structural weaknesses are associated with it.

One new strength to be noted is UNDP's success in designing a development paradigm that reflects the experience gained during the development debate. For the first time UNDP has thus undergone a process of setting substantive standards. UNDP's SHD concept includes the international experience of UNCED and other world conferences appropriately and adequately. With the SHD concept and the debate that preceded it, UNDP has had a major influence on the international debate (e.g. the preparations for the world social summit in Copenhagen and the "20/20 concept"). UNDP's conceptual contributions have thus done a great deal to further the development debate in the 1990s.

The substance and wording of the conceptual framework also indicate that the international debate has had a favourable influence on the orientation of technical cooperation. Thus UNDP increasingly involves civil society in deliberations on capacity-building (even in the core mission, for example).

The main weakness of the conceptual reforms consists in the difficulty of operationalizing the conceptual framework and gaining acceptance for the results within UNDP (especially the Executive Board).

Although the efforts that have been made to formulate the core mission and SHD concept have led to the definition of development objectives, focus areas and levels of intervention, it remains unclear how these dimensions can and will assume practical guidance functions in the case of UNDP's activities. The patterns of intervention cover a very wide range of possible UNDP activities, without making it clear which operations are no longer promoted. Obviously, there are very few areas that would not fall within the range of possible UNDP activities.

> *"In this context, however, it is a problem that the UNDP has not yet specified how it will operationalize SHD. Nor has the organization formulated a strategy for the implementation of SHD or been able to define its task within the broad framework of SHD, including specifying which tasks it will perform*

> *in which areas and, conversely, which tasks it will refrain from performing."* (Danida 1996b, p. 6)

On the basis of experience in eight programme countries the report entitled *Assessment of UNDP* comes to a similar conclusion:

> *"... firstly, that all country level activities are covered by some of these patterns of intervention; secondly, that UNDP cannot use the 10 intervention patterns as a means to focus their country programmes; and thirdly, that UNDP's country offices view the patterns as an authority to legitimize all intervention forms that are appropriate in the country in question."* (Centre for Development Research 1996, p. 10)

The general data on projects and programmes do not permit any adequate or informative conclusions to be drawn on UNDP's development orientation[20] or on changes in the development policy focus areas. Although UNDP has endeavoured to quantify the development orientation of its operations and uses appropriate data (DP/1997/16, p. 3; UNDP 1997g, p. 2), the data collected are too uncertain and problematical (unclear prescriptions, inadequately objectifiable criteria, overlapping categories, etc.)[21] for reliable statements actually to be made on this basis. The data concern the classification of some 2,200 UNDP interventions approved in 1994 and 1995 and capable of being assigned to one of six categories.

The shortcomings in the operationalization, enforcement and continued development of the SHD concept reveal a major dilemma. On the one hand, UNDP and its Executive Board are well aware that substantive focusing of the UNDP mandate is necessary if an adequate profile is to be demonstrated externally and internally. On the other hand, stronger focusing is bound to limit the flexibility of the programme countries concerned and their setting of priorities. Tying UNDP activities more firmly to certain development prescriptions, criteria or focus areas has not therefore been sufficiently accepted, especially by the governments of the developing countries.

Table 10: Substantive classification of UNDP projects and programmes approved in 1994 and 1995 (%)		
Focus area/sphere	Total resources	Core programme resources (IPF)
Poverty	26	33
Governance	39	32
Environment	24	21
Employment and income	5	7
Women	2	3
Other	4	4
Total	100	100
Source: UNDP (1996j), p. xviii, which also gives explanations on the table.		

The dilemma of substantive prescriptions and focusing efforts on the one hand and the maintenance of extensive flexibility in the programme countries on the other hand is reflected in UNDP's documents. The UNDP Executive Board's decision on the core mission, for example, urges the Administrator to continue his efforts to focus the UNDP programmes. However, the Executive Board also emphasizes

> *"(...) that national development priorities shall be the primary determinant of UNDP-supported programmes, which must remain country-driven (...)"* (Executive Board Decision 94/14, in: DP/1995/1)

Other statements on and interpretations of the conceptual reforms also indicate that, although a heading for UNDP activities was chosen with the core mission and the SHD concept, it is not meant to change the past practice of resource use with very few conditions attached and the absence of development criteria.

> *"Sustainable human development <u>does not imply conditionality</u> for UNDP, which remains committed to the principles of universality, political neutrality and 'no strings attached'*

> *grant assistance that have been the hallmarks of its technical cooperation since its inception.*
>
> *Sustainable human development is also not 'top down'. Respecting national sovereignty, it stresses the self-reliance and self-determination of governments and people. As the decision of the UNDP Executive Board makes clear, it reaffirms UNDP's long-standing philosophy that development cooperation can succeed only if it is driven by national priorities, and if ownership by the country and its people is assured.*
>
> *Sustainable human development provides a broad framework for development, not a common prescription for all. It must be adapted to different objective conditions, visions and priorities and the entry points will vary from country to country."* (UNDP 1995i, p. 2; emphasis as in the original text)

The emphasis placed on UNDP's fundamentally neutral role and the considerable importance attached to ownership is particularly significant not least against the background of the international debate on technical cooperation. In principle, an area of tension with development prescriptions and restrictive criteria may exist here. The arguments against stricter development conditionality are, however, unconvincing in the context of UNDP's conceptual debate in the 1990s. The formation of focus areas and efforts to achieve a higher degree of specialization are in fact required if development strategy prescriptions are to be agreed and standards set for projects and programmes.

Turning to New Aspects of Development

(a) Reform measures

In the 1990s UNDP has begun to explore new substantive areas for cooperation. This is true of various topics that touch relatively directly on politically sensitive tasks and core government functions (security, political system, etc.) in the programme countries. Although the topics can certainly be assigned to or subsumed under the SHD concept, it is legitimate and necessary, given their newness, to examine this new area of responsibility at greater length.

Figure 9: Governance

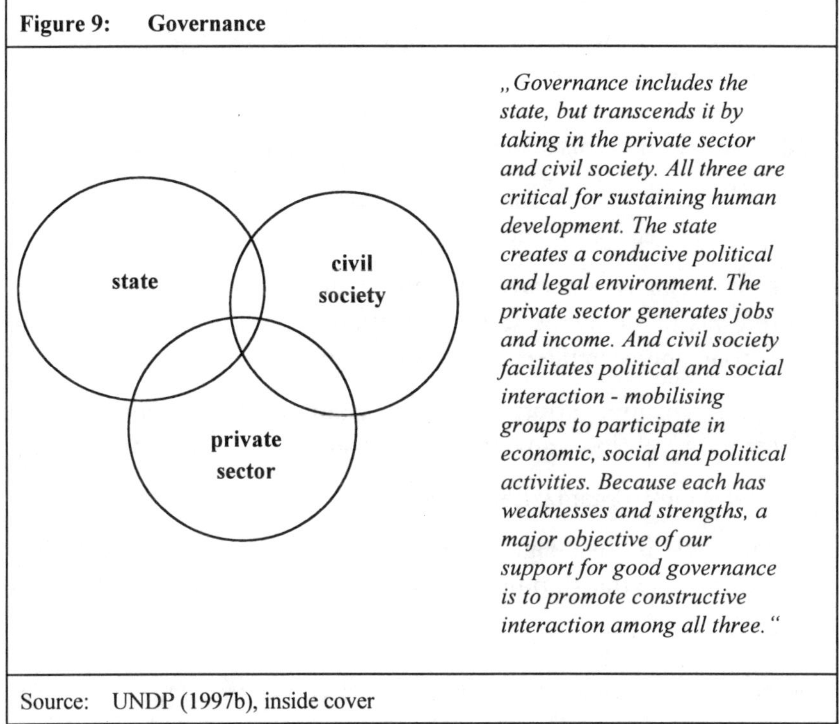

„Governance includes the state, but transcends it by taking in the private sector and civil society. All three are critical for sustaining human development. The state creates a conducive political and legal environment. The private sector generates jobs and income. And civil society facilitates political and social interaction - mobilising groups to participate in economic, social and political activities. Because each has weaknesses and strengths, a major objective of our support for good governance is to promote constructive interaction among all three."

Source: UNDP (1997b), inside cover

A greater interest in matters directly associated with *governance* and other directly political spheres can also be detected in other donors (e.g. in the context of bilateral German development cooperation). Until the late 1980s either non-governmental actors were operating in these areas (e.g. supporting human rights groups), or the topics were not considered, or considered no more than marginally, in the context of non-governmental, bi- and multilateral development cooperation.

Governance, as understood by UNDP, is a concept that goes beyond the actual government sphere in that it involves civil society and the private sector:

> *"Governance can be seen as the exercise of economic, political and administrative authority to manage a country's affairs at all levels. It comprises the mechanisms, processes and institutions through which citizens and groups articulate their interests, exercise their legal rights, meet their obligations and mediate their differences."*[22]

UNDP activities in this sphere are directed at a total of five areas:[23]

- governance institutions in the sphere of the judiciary and legislative and elected bodies,
- support for reforms affecting the public and private sectors (e.g. reforms in the public service, creation of greater transparency and accountability in the public administration),
- decentralization efforts and support for public structures below central level (local governance) (e.g. at district or municipal level),
- civil society organizations (CSOs),[24]
- countries in crisis and countries in special circumstances; UNDP includes the transforming economies of the East in the latter category.

The activities relating to countries in crisis and transforming economies cover a wide range of possible operations in the following areas among others:

- support for emergency aid activities in cooperation with other UN agencies,
- efforts to achieve reconciliation and to mediate in crisis situations,
- reintegration of demobilized troops,
- mine clearance,
- reconstruction aid.

Since the early 1990s UNDP has been concerned with the above tasks and launched activities in this sphere primarily for two reasons. Firstly, the need to monitor and support political changes (democratization, development of the organs of the rule of law, etc.) has grown since the late 1980s with the political upheavals in the transforming economies of the East and in other regions (e.g. many countries of Africa). Secondly, since the end of the East-West conflict government and international actors have had far more political scope to become active in these areas.

However, very few informative data on the areas of activity referred to above are available. UNDP puts the proportion of operations in the governance sphere approved in 1994 and 1995 at 32%.[25] It is active in the areas of reconciliation, reintegration and reconstruction in 32 countries (UNDP 1997g, p. 2).

(b) Assessment

The fact that UNDP is taking an interest in aspects of development to which the bi- and multilateral donors paid little attention before the East-West conflict came to an end is in principle to be welcomed. There is a close link between the paradigm of sustainable human development and the concept of good governance.[26] No other operational UN development agency has so direct a mandate for good governance and associated tasks as UNDP.

Matters connected with better government, greater orientation of the programme countries towards development and violent crises and conflicts are also of overriding importance and direct relevance to development cooperation. The realization that the absence of political responsibility and insufficient orientation towards development (in blatant form, for example, in the case of self-enriching dictatorships) may be the decisive obstacle to development was not appropriately or adequately reflected in development cooperation until the early 1990s. For far too long bi- and multilateral donors adopted a defensive attitude or failed to act in these areas, referring to the political sensitivity of the problems.

UNDP generally pursues a restrained policy in areas of activity relating to good governance and in the sphere of crisis prevention and conflict management. Only if requested by the government of a programme country will it take action in these (and other) spheres. Although UNDP takes *positive measures*,[27] the government of the programme country has a major influence on the nature of TC operations.[28] Here again, there is a partly latent and partly open conflict of objectives between, on the one hand, the programme country's claim to extensive influence, which is appropriate in development terms, and, on the other hand, the complete or partial failure of the government concerned to gear itself to development. In this context UNDP can and should not content itself with the principle of political neutrality and universality, but also refer to the comprehensive foundations already laid by the UN (international agreements, pacts and declarations) for all relevant aspects of good governance. Good governance is not the opposite of political neutrality and universality when it comes to the establishment of and compliance with internationally agreed rules and standards (section III.5).

Steps that go further than the *positive measures* have yet to be considered by UNDP. UNDP has not so far introduced or discussed *political conditionality* in which the volume of TC or fundamental cooperation is made dependent on progress being made in certain areas (e.g. human rights and democratization); there are, on the other hand, many declarations that place the emphasis on the principle of political neutrality.

General Assessment of Reform Measures at Conceptual Level

With some qualifications, the reform efforts hitherto undertaken at conceptual level can be rated positively. UNDP has been able to make progress particularly in formulating very general objectives. In this context the concept of sustainable human development is an important guide for UNDP itself and for the international debate on development. UNDP has also been able to make conceptual contributions in areas that have been newly explored for bi- and multilateral development co-operation in the 1990s.

The crucial deficiencies must be seen as the lack of activity or absence of political willingness to transform general findings and specific conclusions of the conceptual debates into steps and decisions that can be operationalized. UNDP has so far failed to take these steps towards defining transparent criteria and focus areas. It does not yet have a conceptual framework effective enough to enable it to rule out activities that make little or no sense in development terms. UNDP's present concept is therefore such that almost any activity may be undertaken. The most serious obstacle to progress must be seen as the absence of a majority on the Executive Board in favour of laying down development standards.

In and outside UNDP discussions on further focusing under the heading of sustainable human development continue. They are justified and should be stepped up, with the goal of achieving more practical conceptualization and developing yardsticks for practical work.

4.3.2 Structural and Policy Level

The structural and policy level has seen a number of reform measures, which are summarized in Figure 10. The reform measures in the following areas are particularly important: (1) the transformation of the Governing Council into an Executive Board, (2) coordinating mechanisms at headquarters level, (3) country-related coordinating mechanisms, (4) financial endowment and financing mechanisms and (5) the introduction of a new programming procedure.

Creation of an Executive Board

(a) Reform measures

At the beginning of 1994 the Governing Council was replaced with an Executive Board. This decision harks back to a General Assembly resolution requiring appropriate restructuring of the supervisory bodies of the UN development funds and programmes (A/RES/48/162, pp. 7 f). The resolution calls, on the one hand, for ECOSOC to be given a greater opportunity to influence the general political orientation of the funds and programmes and, on the other hand, for it to be made possible for the Executive Board to become more involved in aspects of operationalization, management and finances (Department of State 1994, p. 67; A/RES/48/162, p. 7).

On this basis the Governing Council hitherto shared by UNDP and UNFPA was reduced to a body on which there are 36 seats (previously 48). Of these seats on the Executive Board, eight are allocated to Africa, seven to Asia, four to Eastern Europe, five to Latin America and the Caribbean and 12 to Western Europe and other countries. The members are elected for a three-year term. The Executive Board holds three ordinary working meetings each year in addition to its annual meeting.

UNDP takes a generally positive view of the changes associated with the change to an Executive Board:

> *"The streamlining of the governing body of UNDP into the new Executive Board has resulted in more efficient arrangements and leaner administration."* (UNDP 1997g, p. 10)

The Executive Board and the UNDP administration are, moreover, endeavouring (e.g. through a working group on procedures and another on documentation) to make procedures as simple and flexible as possible and to improve the quality of the documents submitted to the Board.[29]

In his reform paper (July 1997) the UN Secretary-General also proposes that arrangements for closer integration of the political supervision of UNDP/UNFPA and UNICEF, the holding of consecutive or joint meetings and the setting up of joint committees should be considered.[30]

(b) Assessment

The change from Governing Council to Executive Board is, on the whole, a great improvement. It has been possible to shorten and simplify the supervisory body's procedures, thus improving its performance and the precision of the decisions it takes. Both UNDP and the members of the Executive Board agree with this evaluation.[31]

Although the changes that have been made are welcomed by all concerned, other, major structural shortcomings persist, particularly in the following areas:

- The Executive Board remains a cumbersome body, primarily because 36 is still a very high number of seats for working meetings, and the differences between members and non-members of the Executive Board are de facto slight (especially with regard to the right to speak[32]). Some Board members consider the number of meetings to be too high and the intervals between meetings too short.[33]
- The Executive Board does not concentrate on strategic questions and prescriptions relating to UNDP. It did little to initiate or monitor the reform process of the 1990s with innovative action. Many of the Board's discussions concern questions of political principle, which tend to fall within ECOSOC's or the General Assembly's terms of reference, or focus on very specific issues (*micro-management*).[34]
- Coordination with the other UN funds and programmes (and even more so with other institutions involved in development, such as the World Bank and the EU) has not hitherto been automatically

guaranteed by the political supervisory bodies. Kofi Annan's proposal, if approved by the UN's members, constitutes no more than a first step towards better coordination.

Although progress has thus been made in the area of political supervision and guidance for UNDP in the 1990s, it has not been enough to establish structures for UNDP that are characterized by sustained efficiency and effectiveness in political and development terms. Its limited ability to take action and its poor management have been the cause of the inadequacy or absence of many reform initiatives and decisions.

Coordinating Mechanisms at Headquarters Level

(a) Reform measures

In the case of reform measures taken to improve coordination at headquarters level there are two levels in particular where UNDP has the task or is pursuing the goal of overcoming coordination deficiencies: (1) its role in various coordinating mechanisms and bodies and (2) its bilateral relations above country level with other international organizations.

1. Under various headings or with different functions UNDP has been instructed by the UN Secretary-General in the 1990s to perform coordinating tasks relating to the UN's or UN system's development cooperation that go beyond country-related questions.
   - In 1994 the Secretary-General appointed the UNDP Administrator to the post of Special Coordinator for Economic and Social Development. The Administrator was instructed to assist him

     "(...) in ensuring policy coherence and enhancing coordination within the United Nations itself, in particular among headquarters departments, the regional commissions, and the funds and programmes of the Organisation." (Boutros-Ghali, quoted in UN 1996c, p. 1)

In addition, the UNDP Administrator was given the responsibility of helping the Secretary-General to improve the co-ordination of operational development activities - including the strengthening of the Resident Coordinator System - and of participating in the development of a reform agenda.

These tasks were joined by other points to be addressed by the Special Coordinator together with the managers of all units of the UN system: (a) a UN-wide action programme at country level to follow up the world conferences, (b) the launching of the special UN-wide programme for Africa (United Nations Special Initiative on Africa / UNSIA), (c) the strengthening of the Resident Coordinator system in accordance with General Assembly Resolutions 47/199 and 50/120, (d) the improvement of relations with the Bretton Woods institutions, (e) the strengthening of the links and transitions between the United Nations' development cooperation and the humanitarian, political, peace-keeping and human rights spheres, especially in the context of complex emergency situations and countries in special situations, and (f) the promotion of the reform of the UN's normative and operational functions (UN 1996c, pp. 1 f).

The Special Coordinator has considered the tasks set and results achieved in a number of reports (UN 1996b; UN 1996c).

- In 1997 the Secretary-General established the United Nations Development Group (UNDG),[35] which is headed by an executive committee. UNDP is joined on the Executive Committee by UNICEF, UNFPA and other agencies as and when necessary.[36] The Secretary-General appointed the UNDP Administrator as convenor of the Executive Committee UN 1997g, para. 153.

  The Executive Committee was initially assigned tasks connected with the preparation of the Secretary-General's reform package (1997).[37] The description of UNDG's activities in the reform programme itself covers a wide range of outstanding problems and tasks relating to UN development cooperation (e.g. avoiding duplication of effort, strengthening the decision-making processes, improving coherence).[38]

In response to the coordinating tasks assigned to UNDP by the Secretary-General in 1994 the Administrator set up a special UNDP organizational unit known as the Office of the United Nations System Support and Services (OUNS) to assist him in the performance of these tasks. The most important tasks performed by OUNS concern support for the Resident Coordinator system and other activities to promote coordination within the UN system.[39]

2. At headquarters level cooperative relations are governed by bilateral framework agreements with about 30 international organizations. UNDP emphasizes that these framework agreements are instruments for improved coordination; it particularly underlines relations with the Bretton Woods institutions in this context:

   "Partnerships with the Bretton Woods Institutions have never been stronger." (UNDP 1997g, p. 13)

   The existing agreements were joined in 1996 by a new framework agreement with the International Organization for Migration. The agreement with the World Bank was revised in the mid-1990s, the amended version being signed in 1996.

(b) Assessment

Reforms relating to coordination at headquarters level have so far been inadequate. The Secretary-general's proposals (1997) have yet to produce any fundamental changes or structural reforms. This is mainly due to the fact that, although new coordinating bodies have been created and new coordinating functions have been assigned to the UNDP Administrator (Special Coordinator, UNDG, Executive Committee), they have not been given any clear instructions regarding the form that the relationship between the various agencies and UNDP should take. In his capacity as Special Coordinator, the UNDP Administrator has essentially been able to do no more than gather the findings of the various UN agencies together and disseminate them in reports. His role as convenor of the Executive Committee has been similar; the post has so far been used solely to document the right of all the agencies to maintain their identity (UNDP 1997c). In other words, although UNDP has been given - to some extent, explicit - responsibility for coordinating tasks, it has not been equipped with any means of offering positive incentives to other agencies to submit to coordination. There are no other sanction mechanisms or instruments. UNDP has therefore been assigned a task which it cannot perform despite the reform proposals put forward by the Secretary-General in 1997. The wording used at that time in fact consolidates the institutionally fragmented situation:

> *"In providing for improved modalities of cooperation, the establishment of the UNDG will in no way dilute or compromise the distinctive character or identity of participating organizations (...)"* (UN 1997g, para. 154)

The bilateral agreements between UNDP and other international organizations are not a real innovation in cooperative efforts. They largely contain self-evident statements on the areas of activity of the parties concerned.[40] UNDP's partners do not, de facto, accept that it is playing any particular role. The agreement with the World Bank reveals that the emphasis is less on cooperation in the coordination of development cooperation[41] than on the right of both parties to take global and multisectoral action even on such coordination.[42] Above all, the various agencies concerned are unlikely to develop effective cooperative relations themselves since they are competing with one another. The coordinating tasks must therefore be performed by the members and supervisory bodies (especially ECOSOC and the General Assembly).

Country-related Coordinating Mechanisms

(a) Reform measures

The measures initiated and taken to reform the country-related coordinating mechanisms can be divided into two (related) spheres: reforms aimed at (1) strengthening the Resident Coordinator system and

(2) harmonizing, coordinating and improving the procedures and rules of the various agencies of the UN and UN system.

1. The strengthening of the Resident Coordinator system and the reaffirmation of UNDP's special role in this context form one of the main components of many reform efforts in the 1990s. Fundamental reforms have not been undertaken, however. The measures are rather geared generally to strengthening UN-wide coordination structures at country level in the form of the RCs.

   The General Assembly has expressed its views on the subject primarily in Resolutions 47/199 and 50/120;[43] these two resolutions form the most important basis for reforms in this area. Besides the general strengthening of the RC system, they call in particular for[44]

   - a clearer division of responsibilities among the RC, the UN funds and programmes and the UN specialized agencies,
   - consideration to be given to RC candidates who do not belong to UNDP,
   - greater involvement in the RC selection process of the governments of the countries in which the country offices concerned are situated,
   - a coordinated and coherent follow-up to the world conferences at country level by the *RCs,*
   - the full participation of the specialized agencies at country level in the RC system.

   The Secretary-General considered the Resident Coordinator system in his 1997 reform document and reaffirmed its main features. The document states:

   "UNDP continues as the manager and funder of the Resident Coordinator System. The Resident Coordinator System will be strengthened by the selection of Resident Coordinators from all concerned organizations. The Executive Committee on Development Operations has agreed on a series of measures designed to advance this process while identifying some areas

on which further consultations are required." (UN 1997g, para. 152)

The Secretary-General also announced that, where UN agencies shared common premises, the name "UN House" would be introduced (UN 1997g, para. 279).

In addition, UNDP's Executive Board reaffirmed the RC system and in its Decisions 94/14 and 95/23 called for further efforts to improve it.

The practical results produced by the efforts to reform the Resident Coordinator system include the following:[45]

- RCs are no longer selected solely from the UNDP pool of candidates: the choice has been widened to include the staff of other agencies. Candidates from all UN funds and programmes[46] and the four specialized agencies FAO, ILO, UNESCO and WHO are now considered (UN 1997e, para. 4). By the end of 1997 there were expected to be 17 RCs who had not been recruited directly from UNDP (DP/1997/21, Chapter VIII).
- Special new training programmes were introduced for RCs. Almost 80 country teams attended team-building courses (UN 1997e, para. 4).
- The criteria for the selection of RCs were made stricter, and orientation towards country-related requirements was increased.
- The backstopping for RCs at UNDP headquarters was improved (through the establishment of the Office of UN System Support and Services, for example).
- The UN General Assembly reaffirmed that the RC normally coordinates the UN's humanitarian assistance at country level and that UNDP's Resident Representative is also to be the Resident Coordinator (A/RES/48/209).
- There was an increase in premises shared by the UN agencies; however, the figures for this vary widely. A 1997 report by the Secretary-General refers to 34 countries with common premi-

ses (UN 1997e, para. 39), whereas UNDP speaks of 52 countries by the end of 1996 (and at least 68 by the end of 1997).[47]

2. To harmonize, coordinate and improve the policies, procedures and rules of the various agencies of the UN and UN system, the following steps directly affecting UNDP have been taken or initiated in the 1990s:

   - Country strategy notes (CSNs): CSNs were introduced by General Assembly Resolution 47/199.[48] As country strategies, they are meant to give rise to a coordinated process for the multilateral development cooperation activities of the whole UN system; in principle, they are documents of the programme countries concerned. CSNs are to act as the frame of reference for the specific country programme documents of the various UN agencies. UNDP plays a special part in this process, since the Resident Coordinators are as a rule heavily involved in the preparation of the CSNs. Information on the CSNs is available for a total of 144 countries. It shows that, of the 92 governments to have expressed an interest in CSNs, 26 have formally adopted a country strategy note, eight have completed drafts and eleven have provisional drafts.[49]
   - Harmonization of programming cycles:[50] Resolution 50/120 (para. 45) urges the various UN agencies to simplify and align their procedures and rules. Against this background the RCs are to endeavour to harmonize the programming cycles of the various institutions. This has so far been achieved in 27 countries, and in 45 it is agreed that this step should be taken by 1999 (UNDP 1997g, p. 16).
   - United Nations Development Assistance Framework (UNDAF): As item 10 on a list of measures, the reform document submitted by the Secretary-General in July 1997 includes UNDAF as an instrument for establishing country-related programme strategies:

     "(...) to achieve goal-oriented collaboration, programmatic coherence and mutual reinforcement, the United Nations programme of assistance will be formulated and

> *presented as part of a single United Nations Development Assistance Framework (UNDAF) with common objectives and time frame."* (UN 1997g, p. 38)

Although the financial resources of the various UN programmes and funds are to be shown in the UNDAF, they are not to be amalgamated.

(b) Assessment

For the quality of UNDP activities and, moreover, for all UN development cooperation the country level is of the utmost importance. It is crucial from the identification of priorities and problems through the establishment of programmes to implementation and in the assessment and evaluation of development policy. The Resident Coordinator system is the direct link between the programme country on the one hand and UNDFP and other agencies of the UN system on the other. In view of this significance intensive efforts like those launched by the UN and UNDP in the 1990s to reform the country level and especially the Resident Coordinator system are in principle appropriate and important. The RC system's close association with UNDP, which has been emphasized on several occasions in the 1990s, especially by the General Assembly, the UNDP Executive Board and the Secretary-General, plays an essential role in this context.

UNDP is increasingly attempting to demonstrate to the outside world the services it itself provides for the whole UN system. The efforts made to this end are important because the functions performed by UNDP throughout the organization are highly relevant to the success of all development cooperation in which the UN system engages. UNDP points out that the RCs devote a considerable proportion of their work capacities to the whole of the UN and its various agencies rather than UNDP. A survey has shown that on average RCs spend about half of their working hours on tasks that have nothing to do with UNDP. Activities unrelated to UNDP are tending to increase.[51] UNDP spends about US $ 100m p.a. of its core resources maintaining the Resident Coordinator system (UNDP 1997e, p. 6). All efforts so far made to persuade other agencies of the UN and UN system to share the costs incurred have failed. The attitude of the various agencies also reveals the basic dilemma of each institution wanting to remain as autonomous as possible at country level and being unwilling to relinquish responsibility to the coordination system operated by UNDP or to share the costs involved. UNDP is generally at pains to increase its legitimacy vis-à-vis the whole UN system in the area of development cooperation, its contributions being acknowledged in principle by the UN member states but not, de facto, accepted by the various UN agencies.

Many problems (such as reluctance to share premises and to accept harmonized procedures) can be traced back to this basic dilemma. A number of procedures also push the problems and needs in the programme countries too far into the background. Thus, while it is undoubtedly proper that the country strategy notes should seek to have the programme countries draw up coherent strategies (albeit with UNDP's assistance) showing how the various UN agencies can participate appropriately in an overall concept, everyday experience in the country offices indicates that many governments tend to view the country strategy notes with caution or indifference. The CSNs are drawn up primarily at the instigation of the RCs.[52]

The steps taken in the 1990s to solve the various country-related coordination problems have made progress within the existing framework; this is also true of Kofi Annan's proposal for a common programming framework (UNDAF), which has yet to be implemented. A UNDP evaluation of the RCs' work also indicates progress in coordination by the RCs at country level.[53] However, at both country and headquarters level the whole UN development cooperation system still tends to be fragmented without adequate authority or management. Although in principle it is UNDP's responsibility to overcome fragmentation at country as well as other levels, it does not have the authority or instruments for this purpose.

Financial Endowment, Financing Mechanisms and Approaches to Resource Mobilization

(a) Reform measures

UNDP's efforts to reform financing in the 1990s have concerned both the scale of resources and the financing mechanisms and resource mobilization approaches. The two dimensions, or efforts in the two areas, are closely linked.

The UNDP administration and, to some extent, the Executive Board take the volume of finance as the point of departure for reform efforts. The Administrator is backing a growth strategy in this context: *"(...) we will launch a drive for growth."* (Speth 1997a, p. 3) Other UNDP documents make similar statements:

> *"Without growth, UNDP cannot effectively support the achievement by programme countries of their objectives in SHD, nor translate into high-impact development interventions the ideas that are the foundations of its identity."* (DP/1997/16/Add. 7, p. 10)

The growth strategy propagated generally seeks to counteract any further marginalization of UNDP and the debate on reducing current UNDP services and structures.[54] Given the difficult financial situation, a question that has increasingly been raised in the 1990s is, for example, whether the dense network of country offices can be maintained.[55]

Few official, specific figures are available for the targeted scale of resources. The most important objective in the second half of the 1990s has been set by the Executive Board in the context of its decisions on the new programming system. It refers to a total of US $ 3.3bn (i.e. US $ 1.1bn p.a.) as minimum core resources for the 1997 to 1999 cycle.[56]

The available official figures on a desirable or necessary volume of resources, which may exceed the plan target of the current cycle, for example, are not complete. UNDP Administrator Speth emphasizes that UNDP could do with double the current volume of resources.[57] Estimates by UNDP also claim that four times the core resources would be needed to cover the programme priorities shown in the country cooperation frameworks (DP/1997/CRP.23, Chapter II).

For the reform of the financing mechanisms and resource mobilization approaches there are various suggestions and efforts[58] geared, on the one hand, to stabilizing and expanding the traditional mechanisms and, on the other hand, to diversifying the funding sources and mechanisms. UNDP often refers to *advocacy strategy* and *building partnerships*[59] in this context. The efforts are focused on four sources of funds:[60]

- *Traditional donor countries:* UNDP stresses the continued major importance of the donor countries on the OECD's Development Assistance Committee, who are irreplaceable.[61]
- *Emerging donors:* Reference is increasingly made to the involvement of emerging donors, and especially the successful (emerging) economies in the South, which are to play an increasingly important role as donors. They are sometimes known as *non-traditional donors*, meaning primarily the Gulf States.
- *Private sector and donations:* Efforts are to be launched and stepped up to develop partnerships with the private sector and to enable groups in civil society and individuals to be involved in resource mobilization.
- *Resource mobilization by the country offices:* The UNDP country offices are to be more heavily involved in the mobilization of resources; this applies both to the programme countries (in the context of round tables, for example) and to countries in the process of establishing themselves or expanding their role as donors (emerging donors).

UNDP has taken various steps or, in the second half of the 1990s, is taking or planning measures to this end. They include:[62]

- the improved description of UNDP activities and successes (e.g. in connection with the presentation of the *Human Development Reports* and the UNDP magazine *Choices*);
- more intensive lobbying and the development or strengthening of key constituency groups in parliaments, the non-governmental sphere, private enterprises and the academic environment;[63]
- the creation of financial conditions that enable contributions from the private sector and organizations in civil society and donations from individuals to be accepted and partnerships to be forged (Executive Board Decision 96/39 and DP/1997/24, p. 7);
- simpler and more transparent guidelines on resource mobilization (trust funds, cost-sharing resources), especially for the country offices;
- the employment of UNDP staff in the international development banks (especially the World Bank) so that relations may be expanded with a view, among other things, to mobilizing resources;
- a renewed *UNDP culture* of resource mobilization (purposeful fund-raising approaches, information work, etc.).

The reform measures and recommendations presented by UN Secretary-General Kofi Annan in 1997 also include statements on aspects of financing that concern, or might concern, UNDP. The Secretary-General recommends a new system of basic resources for UN development cooperation consisting of voluntary contributions and negotiated pledges and made available in multiannual tranches. In the summer of 1997 he held out the prospect of a report to be submitted to the UN member states for their consideration (UN 1997g, paras 165 ff.). He also proposes that savings achieved by reducing non-programme costs should be set aside for a special development budget (*development dividend*). This special budget might grow to at least US $ 200m by the year 2002 (UN 1997g, paras 57 f.); the reform programme does not otherwise explain how the resources would be used.

(b) Assessment

Of prime importance for the process of UNDP's reform is the goal of achieving a more appropriate financial endowment. This concerns both the financial volume and the financing mechanisms. By and large, then, reform efforts in this area must be considered appropriate and necessary.

In these circumstances, however, assessments of the various elements of the resource mobilization strategy adopted by UNDP are bound to differ. Three aspects are particularly important in this context. Firstly, efforts are excessively geared to resources which are subject to UNDP's priorities and control to only a limited extent (non-core resources). UNDP has sometimes been very successful in this area in the 1990s. However, the tasks cannot be performed properly on this basis, since resources of this kind can be no more than complementary and bilateralization tendencies are encouraged. On the other hand, it is to be feared that the resource mobilization target (core resources) of US $ 3.3bn for the period 1997 - 1999 cannot be achieved even though it is based on a realistic attitude rather than unjustified optimism. In 1997 the sum is likely to have been US $ 800m (DP/1997/21, Chapter VII, A), which means that in the very first year of the cycle more than 27% of planned resources were lacking because of the contributors' attitude. Secondly, the renewed efforts to form strategic groups and the increasing lobbying in the traditional donor countries is to be welcomed. These efforts are, however, still too restrained and unsystematic. In the past UNDP has been too passive in this area and has failed to pursue a long-term policy of persuading and informing. Thirdly, the attempts to involve new groups (emerging donors, the private sector) capable of making contributions are appropriate and forward-looking. At present, however, adequate conceptual foundations and practical points of departure are lacking.

A problematical aspect of the new approaches to resource mobilization is the role sought for the UNDP country offices in the efforts to attract financial resources. In principle, such efforts (including round tables organized by UNDP) seem very promising. There is, however, a danger that resource mobilization efforts at country level will not be compatible with UNDP's coordination mandate and mission.[64] In practical terms this means that a Resident Representative who, as Resident Coordinator, also undertakes UN-wide activities is at risk of no longer being considered neutral if he canvasses for financial resources for UNDP. In a situation of this kind there is likely to be a conflict of interests that will make it impossible for him to act appropriately as the representative of UN development cooperation as a whole. If UNDP intends to maintain and improve its services for the whole of the UN and UN system, efforts to mobilize resources at country level are an unsuitable means of overcoming the current financial problems.

The powers of the UNDP Administrator and Executive Board do not extend to fundamental aspects of the financing mechanisms. The Secretary-General's proposals for solving these problems are therefore important as a means of initiating a debate within the General Assembly. The proposals rightly have as their objective more reliable and more extensive funding for UN development cooperation and so for UNDP; supplementing the present voluntary contributions with negotiable pledges and multiannual tranches would be a crucial step forward in increasing effectiveness in development policy terms. The decisions needed to transform the funding bases cannot, however, be taken by the Secretary-General; this is a matter for the General Assembly. The proposals hitherto put forward for reforms in this area (especially by the Nordic UN Project) that take a similar line have been foiled by the large donor countries. The opponents of these reforms are unlikely to have changed their attitude in the meantime.

The General Assembly may agree to Kofi Annan's proposal that use should be made of a *development dividend*. The Group of Seven leading industrialized nations did at least issue a similar declaration of intent in 1996.[65] Given its core functions, it would be appropriate for UNDP to be entrusted with the task of administering the *development dividend*. The proposed *development dividend* cannot, however, make a significant contribution to solving the financial problems (because of its limited scale); it would be more in the nature of a symbol.

Programming Procedure

(a) Reform measures

The decision taken by the Executive Board in 1995 to replace the programming system then being used with a new procedure (*successor programming arrangements*) must be seen as one of the most significant reform efforts (Executive Board Decision 95/23, in: DP/1996/1, pp. 24 ff.). UNDP Administrator Speth referred in this context to *"a major turning point for UNDP"* (Speth, in: UNDP 1995a, p. 10), and the new system is frequently regarded as a "revolution" (Centre for Development Research 1996, p. 15) because of the change of principles. The old procedure, with its inflexible mechanisms and quasi-automatic country quotas, dated back to 1972; the new programming system entered into force in 1997.

The reformed programming system pursues a number of important goals simultaneously. It is meant to give the programme countries greater motivation to succeed by replacing the previous rigid allocation system with incentives to prepare and implement measures that have priority and are goal-oriented in development policy terms.[66] In addition, flexibility during programming is to be increased. The system is also so arranged that more resources are allocated to the poorer and poorest developing countries in particular.

Although the new programming concept entails many changes, the Executive Board has also reaffirmed fundamental principles of the previous procedure, especially the priority given to the programme countries in the formulation of policies and development objectives, UNDP's universality and neutrality, financing by voluntary contributions and the provision of TC on a grant basis.[67]

The most important changes in connection with the new programming system are: (1) a new document known as the *country cooperation framework* (CCF) replacing the previous *country programme*, (2) the new *Target for Resource Assignments from the Core* (TRAC) system, which replaces the *Indicative Planning Figure* (IPF), and (3) a new system for the reimbursement of costs to the implementing organizations (*support-cost arrangements*).

1. The country cooperation framework is the main guiding instrument for country-related programming. It is drawn up by the government concerned in consultation with UNDP. Once approved by the Executive Board, the document determines the distribution for the agreed period of all resources for which UNDP is responsible. The document is meant in particular to analyse the core objectives of the national development priorities against the background of the SHD focus and to identify options for support from UNDP.[68] The decisive list of criteria for assessing the quality of programmes for resource allocation comprises the following items (DP/1996/3, Annex):
   - the programme's contribution to national priorities,
   - the strengthening of national capacity,
   - thematic focus within the dimensions of sustainable human development,
   - measurable influence of the programme on sustainable human development and the life of the poor (programme leverage) and
   - the potential for mobilizing additional resources.
2. The system for allocating resources (Target for Resource Assignments from the Core - TRAC) replaces the five-year cycles with "rolling"[69] three-year cycles. It is a three-stage system that covers all the resources of the core programme for country-related allocation, or 55% of UNDP's core resources (TRAC Line 1.1); the remaining 45% of resources are allocated to regional and global measures, special programmes and activities (evaluations, etc.) and services for the UN system and the Resident Coordinators (see Table 11).

Table 11: Financing lines of the Target for Resource Assignments from the Core (TRAC) system and distribution of the resources

		Earmarkings during fifth cycle		Proposed percentage earmarkings for next period
		$ m	%	%
1.0	**Programmes/projects**			
	Country			
1.1	Target for resource assignments from core (TRAC)			
	1.1.1 Assigned immediately to countries	526	53.5	***30.0***
	1.1.2 Assigned regionally for subsequent country application	-	-	***20.0***
	1.1.3 Resources for development in countries in special situations	13	1.3	***5.0***
		539	54.8	***55.0***
	Intercountry			
1.2	Regional	56	5	***7.6***
1.3	Global, interregional and special activities	25	2.5	***4.2***
		81	8.2	***11.8***
	Other			
1.4	Evaluation	1	0.1	***0.3***
1.5	Special resources for TCDC activities	2	0.2	***0.5***
1.6	Resources for implementation	55	5.6	***3.0***
		58	5.9	***3.8***
	Subtotal	***678***	***68.9***	***70.6***
2.0	**Programme development and technical services**			
2.1	UNDP programme support and development activities (PSDA)	33	3.3	***3.0***
2.2	United Nations system for policy and programme development (SPPD)	16	1.6	***2.0***
2.3	Technical support services from United Nations specialized agencies	11	1.1	***1.6***
2.4	Other	35	3.5	-
	Subtotal	***95***	***9.5***	***6.6***
3.0	**Support to United Nations system and aid coordination**			
3.1	Programme support to the resident coordinator/aid coordination	-	-	***1.7***
3.2	Support to United Nations operational activities	43	4.4	***4.3***
	Subtotal	***43***	***4.4***	***6.0***
4.0	**Biennial budget**			
4.1	UNDP headquarters	70	7.1	***6.8***
4.2	UNDP country offices	100	10.1	***10.0***
	Subtotal	***170***	***17.2***	***16.8***
		986	**100.0**	***100.0***

Source: DP/1996/1, p. 28

The three-stage country-related TRAC system (TRAC Line 1.1) is broken down as follows:

- of the core resources are earmarked for direct assignment to individual countries. They are shared by an agreed method (TRAC Line 1.1.1). The method of distributing resources for the country programmes is determined by population, per capita gross national product, LLDC status, if appropriate, and other development indicators (DP/1996/1, p. 29; DP/1995/32, pp. 22 ff.).
- 20% of the core resources are intended for regions and are also assigned to individual countries (TRAC Line 1.1.2).
- 5% of the core resources are available for development operations in countries in special situations (TRAC Line 1.1.3).

In contrast to previous practice, an attempt is made during resource assignment to provide a more realistic picture of the financial resources available. A *resource mobilization target* (RMT) is set for this purpose. When deciding to introduce a new programming system, the Executive Board also set the first resource objective - mentioned above - for core resources for the three-year period 1997 - 1999 at US $ 3.3bn (comments in para. 7 of Deci sion 95/23).

3. The new procedure for reimbursing costs to the implementing organizations (support-cost arrangements) was adjusted with a view to simplifying the previous procedure and making it more transparent, saving costs and providing incentives for national execution. Executive Board Decision 96/31 taken in 1996 establishes the formal framework for this (Decision 96/31 in: UNDP 1996m, pp. 30 ff.).

The TRAC system provides three options for the financing of support costs (TRAC Lines 1.6, 2.2 and 2.3) (DP/1996/13, p. 3).

The new system provides for costs to be reimbursed at a flat rate not exceeding 10%.[70] The fact that the financial resources concerned are administered directly by the country offices in consultation with the programme countries encourages the latter to save costs and implement projects themselves. They can then use support costs saved as a result of national execution for additional measures.[71]

Table 12: Resources entered on TRAC Lines 1.1.1 and 1.1.2, 1997 - 1999		
	US $ m	%
Total resources on TRAC Lines 1.1.1 and 1.1.2	1,663.0	100
Assignment to countries by income:		
a) - low-income countries	1,465.7	88
- middle-income countries	197.3	12
b) - LLDCs	1,003.5	60
- non-LLDCs	659.5	40
Assignment to regional groups of countries:		
- Africa	787.3	47
- Asia and Pacific	555.9	33
- Arab countries	128.6	8
- Latin America and Caribbean	110.5	7
- Europe and Commonwealth of Independent States	80.7	5
Source: DP/1997/8, Table 1. The figures are already revised final earmarkings.		

(b) Assessment

The first country, regional and global cooperation frameworks were submitted to the Executive Board, considered and approved in 1997. As implementation did not begin until early 1997, it is virtually impossible to make an assessment that takes account of practical experience; various, more conceptual aspects of the programming system, on the other hand, can be considered in greater depth in an evaluation.

On the whole, the reformed programming system is an enormous change for UNDP. The programming procedures are the most important interface between the development paradigms and UNDP principles on the one hand and operationalization in country strategies and individual projects and programmes on the other. Operationalization in country strategies (as well as regional and global strategies) gives the Executive Board the best and most continuous opportunities for exercising influence over UNDP policy.

The sweeping changes to the procedure that applied until the end of 1996 have affected the various actors, with their different interests, in various ways. The most important questions in this context concern the development conditions attached to resources, the influence wielded by UNDP (how free are the governments of the programme countries to use resources as they wish?) and the distribution of the resources among the various TRAC lines and, above all, among the various regions and groups of countries; the considerable influence and the interests of the major implementing organizations in the allocation of operations and the reimbursement of costs should also be borne in mind.

Against this background three fundamentally positive changes or features in particular should be noted. The first improvement is that the new system attempts to operate with development incentives and so to abandon the traditional entitlement approach. If the development incentive mechanisms are applied by the Executive Board and the Administrator as they intend, they may act as a major stimulus for an improvement in the quality of development. After a country cooperation framework has been approved, it is possible for the resources to be made available in one or more instalments. The main incentive is likely to be that UNDP now has the option of making available a proportion of country-related resources (under TRAC Lines 1.1.1 and 1.1.2) amounting to at least 60%, which may, however, be greatly increased to as much as 120%. This mechanism therefore enables the programme volume available in real terms to be varied.

A second change for the better is that the influence and strong interests of the major implementing organizations have been suppressed and incentives offered to the UNDP country offices and programme countries to use or develop project management and implementation capacities of their own. It remains to be seen whether these incentives work or possibly lead to new distortions.

A third positive feature is the concentration on countries in which development cooperation measures are particularly justified by their level of development. Unlike the bilateral donors in particular, UNDP has placed distinct regional emphasis on low-income countries (88%) and LLDCs (60%) (Table 12).

Reliable statements cannot yet be made on the chances of the country strategies actually leading to stronger focusing than the former country programmes. It is doubtful, however, since the governments of the programme countries have retained considerable room for manoeuvre (even where compliance with the broad SHD concept is limited or there is no orientation towards development). Nor is any significant change to be detected in this respect in most of the practical programme documents (i.e. country cooperation frameworks as against country programmes).

Planning the use of available resources as realistically as possible remains a problem. Whether the resources actually received come relatively close to the resource mobilization target depends on several factors. Given the situation in the first half of the 1990s, the target of US $ 3.3bn set in 1995 was not unrealistic at least, but probably overoptimistic in view of the attitude of the major contributors.

Overall Assessment of the Reform Measures at Structural and Policy Level

The reforms that have been initiated at structural and policy level cannot be evaluated uniformly. Nor can more than provisional statements be made on various reform measures, since their implementation has only just begun.

The complete reform of the programming procedure is UNDP's most ambitious attempt at innovation at this level. The new procedure breaks with UNDP principles that endured for many years, especially *automatic* entitlement to certain financial resources and the associated absence of development criteria and incentives. If in practice the new programming procedure helps to create genuine development incentives, it must be described as a major success. Should the new procedure prove unsuccessful in this form after an appropriate introductory period (say, two to three years), there will again be an urgent need for reform.

The creation of the Executive Board has generally proved its worth for UNDP during the introductory period. It has become capable of taking action and decisions. With varying degrees of success so far, it has tried to improve the performance of its monitoring and decision-making functions with regard to important development questions for UNDP. The problem of the inadequately coordinated supervisory bodies for the UN's various development cooperation agencies remains.

While the reforms undertaken at headquarters and country level with a view to improving coordination have led to some progress being made in solving various problems, not enough attention has been paid to the fundamental deficiencies. The main problem here, however, is not simply the absence of coordination mechanisms, but both the unwillingness of the various UN agencies and, even more so, the UN system to submit to coordination and the failure of a majority of the UN member countries to formulate and endorse appropriate political objectives and prescriptions.

To solve the financing problems, action is needed from UNDP and the UN on various fronts. Within the given structures UNDP has far more opportunities to attract core resources or to stabilize revenue if the resource mobilization measures it has designed are adequately implemented. However, conflicts particularly between the roles played by the Resident Coordinators must be avoided. A course that promises success for the whole of the UN where the financing mechanisms are concerned has yet to be charted.

Figure 10: Reform measures at structural and policy level

Reform measures	Objectives, explanations or examples	Relevant documents and underlying decisions
Transformation of Governing Council into Executive Board	Smaller and more effective supervisory body	A/RES/48/162
Coordination at headquarters level	UNDP Administrator acts as Special Coordinator for Economic and Social Development and as convenor of the Executive Committee of the UN Development Group (UNDG)	Decisions of UN Secretary-General
	Bilateral cooperative relations with other international organizations	Bilateral agreements
Country-related coordination mechanisms	Reaffirmation and strengthening of the Resident Coordinator system, for example, through - expansion of RC pool to include various UN agencies, - special training programmes for RCs, - clearer country-related orientation to needs in appointment of RCs.	General Assembly (Resolutions 47/199 and 50/120), Secretary-General and UNDP Executive Board
	Harmonization and coordination of policies and procedures through - United Nations Development Assistance Framework (UNDAF), - country strategy notes (CSNs), - special measures to harmonize programming.	Secretary-General (UNDAF) and General Assembly (CSNs; Resolution 47/199)
Financial endowment, financing mechanisms and resource mobilization approaches	Efforts directed at - traditional donors, - emerging donors, - private sector and donations, - resource mobilization by country offices.	Executive Board and UNDP administration
Programming procedure	Incentive-oriented, more flexible and more goal-oriented programming procedure through - new programming document (country cooperation framework), - new resource assignment system (TRAC), - reorganization of support-cost arrangements.	Decisions of UNDP Executive Board

4.3.3 Administration and Implementation Level

At administration and implementation level a wide range of reforms have been initiated; some have already been completed, others are in prospect. They are summarized in Figure 12. Of these adjustment efforts, the reforms in the following spheres are of primary importance: (1) increase in national execution, (2) separation of implementing capacities, (3) programme approach and pooling of project resources, (4) measures to improve and strengthen evaluations, and (5) making the administration leaner and reorganizing structures.

Increase in National Execution

(a) Reform measures

The overriding objective of the United Nations' development cooperation is the promotion of the developing countries' self-reliance through multilateral cooperation. In this the development and strengthening of national capabilities and capacities plays a crucial part (UN 1996a, Annex 5, p. 1). As the United Nations and UNDP see it, the achievement of this objective can be promoted especially if the programme countries are given the main responsibility for the management and implementation of development cooperation projects and programmes[72] through *national execution* (NEX).[73] In the UNDP context national execution is defined as follows:

> *"Overall management, by national government authorities, of UNDP-funded development programmes and projects, along with the assumption of responsibility and accountability for the use of UNDP resources and for the production of outputs and the achievement of programme or project objectives."*[74]

Conceptually, national execution is one of the main elements if greater orientation towards the programme countries' priorities is to be achieved. Above all, this approach is intended to increase ownership of operations.

National execution has on several occasions been declared or reaffirmed as the norm by the General Assembly[75] for the whole UN system and by the Governing Council, or Executive Board, for UNDP operations.[76] Although the majority of the UN member countries call for NEX, it is a not uncontroversial principle and approach.[77]

In the past two decades the national execution of UNDP operations has grown substantially. There has been a huge increase especially in the 1990s. In the early 1980s the NEX share was well below 10%, and even in the late 1980s it was still less than 20% (UNDP 1995h, pp. 13 ff.). Since the mid-1990s the vast majority of UNDP activities have been the subject of national execution. Growth in the 1990s - in terms of project spending - has been as follows:

- 1990 - 1991: 14%,
- 1992 - 1993: 31%,
- 1994 - 1995: 56%,
- 1996 - 1997: 79%.[78]

From 1993 to 1995 alone the proportion of programme countries wanting to implement programmes or projects themselves rose from 80 to 87% of all countries (DP/1997/CRP.8, p. 2; UNDP 1997o, p. 73). Regionally, NEX is most pronounced in the two economically more advanced areas, i.e. Latin America/Caribbean and Asia/Pacific.[79]

(b) Assessment

In general, it can be said that the 1990s in particular have seen rapid movement towards compliance with the national execution norm set by the General Assembly and UNDP's Governing Council, or Executive Board. Change has thus been extremely quick.

In principle, there is much to be said in development terms - as has also been pointed out in section II.2 - for the NEX concept and its implementation. National execution makes for a very close link to the programme country's development efforts, a high level of ownership and incentives to develop or promote local capacities.

On the other hand, criticism of the NEX boom of the 1990s is not confined to the once dominant executing agencies, which are undergoing a process of profound change because of the sudden increase in national execution and can therefore certainly be regarded as "losers" as a result of NEX.[80] The main criticisms levelled at national execution and its enormous growth in the 1990s are:[81]

- the governments of the programme countries, or their institutions, may be overextended by national execution because they do not have the necessary capacities or structures;
- internal mechanisms, processes and interests in the programme countries' institutions may have an adverse effect on the objectives of the operation being implemented by causing distortion which is not desirable in development terms;
- the transparency of and accountability for operations and responsibility for the outcome of interventions may be inadequate or unclear.

In the mid-1990s the objections to and problematical aspects of NEX were considered on several occasions by UNDP's Executive Board and in various documents (DP/1997/CRP.8, DP/1997/CRP.12). Of particular interest in this context are the findings of a UNDP evaluation based on a study of 11 countries (UNDP 1995h).

The UNDP evaluation reaches a differentiated, though by and large highly favourable conclusion. It confirms (albeit with some qualifications and references to various disadvantages) many of the main positive qualities of national execution in development terms:

> *"It greatly improves and expands the sense of <u>ownership</u> of programmes. (...)*
>
> *The modality significantly increases the level of <u>self-reliance</u>. (...)*

> *NEX contributes to capacity-building, especially to the development of human resources, and in some environments to organizational capacity-building. (...)*
>
> *The greater integration of UNDP-assisted programmes into normal governmental operations, the wider participation of national persons and institutions, the stronger sense of ownership, all should enhance project sustainability, right from the beginning of the programme."* (UNDP 1995h, p. 7; emphasis as in the original text)

Particular reference should be made to two of the qualifications identified by the evaluation with respect to NEX. Firstly, greater ownership also has its price, which is often reflected in delays in implementation. Secondly, despite the use of more local know-how, the NEX approach is not as cheap as frequently assumed.

Not least because of the findings of this evaluation the process of increasing the proportion of national execution in the 1990s must be regarded as appropriate to development. It should be continued cautiously because in some cases at least problems may arise and fundamental issues have hardly been discussed so far. Above all, the process has triggered changes in the roles played by all concerned (tasks and functions of UNDP, the programme country and the traditional implementing organizations) to which not enough thought has yet been given. An important question in this context concerns UNDP's coordinating role: will it still be possible in the future for UNDP to act as coordinator vis-à-vis the large, traditional executing agencies if they cease to be clients of UNDP? It must be assumed that one of UNDP's important means of exercising influence will be lost. For the UN specialized agencies the basic question of whether and in what form they will in principle be active in the operational sphere or whether they should again concentrate more on normative tasks will, moreover, probably gain in importance.

Separation of Implementing Capacities / Establishment of UNOPS

(a) Reform measures

Until 1994 UNDP had an organizational unit (Office for Project Services - OPS)[82] for the implementation of projects. As UNDP's functions do not in principle extend to project implementation and conflicts of interest arose between its growing implementing functions and its responsibility for coordination, the Executive Board recommended (Executive Board Decisions 94/12 and 95/1, reproduced in: DP/1995/1 and DP/1996/1) that the General Assembly set up a new UN unit[83] to be known as the United Nations Office for Project Services (UNOPS) based on OPS.

The new UNOPS began work in 1995. It offers a wide range of project management services for the whole UN system; in other words, UNDP is no longer its only client:

> *"UNOPS is entirely self-financing and its clients have other choices. In a drastic departure from the previous arrangement, UNOPS has no captive market, as it had in UNDP, and UNDP no longer has a monopoly of the Office's services."* (UNOPS 1997, p. 1; emphasis as in the original text)

UNDP's share (related to core resources) of newly awarded contracts in 1996 was 37%; its share of contracts awarded by the programme countries and other UN agencies was 14%, while the international financial institutions and bilateral donors accounted for 30% (others 19%) (UNOPS Executive Director's annual report, DP/1997/19, pp. 2 f.). For its services UNOPS charges a fee which averages 7% and so, it claims, is far more favourable than the cost of comparable implementing arrangements (UNOPS 1997, p. 1).

Where project implementation is concerned, the separation of OPS has been joined by two other changes or tendencies. Firstly, UNDP is endeavouring to lay the foundations for non-governmental organizations to implement projects. In the past this was possible only indirectly and on a very small scale through subcontracting. The implementation procedures have therefore been modified in the meantime to permit NGO execution (UNDP 1997g, p. 4; NGLS 1997, pp. 117 ff.; DP/1997/16/Add. 7, pp. 4 f.; DP/1994/39, p. 15). Secondly, UNDP is tending to become less flexible now that it no longer has its own implementing capacities in the shape of OPS. UNDP stresses the need in this context to create new opportunities for implementation by the country offices.[84]

(b) *Assessment*

The transformation of OPS into UNOPS has resulted in UNDP losing the operational means that were once directly available to it. They enabled conflicts of objectives between UNDP's core tasks in coordination and financing on the one hand and implementation on the other to be resolved.

UNOPS is considered by many to be a successful reform within the UN. It differs significantly from other UN agencies in that, among other things, it uses inwardly oriented incentives in its personnel policy and operates on a profit-making basis without funding from the UN member states. In this it is in a special situation, since - unlike the UN's other development cooperation agencies - it is actually able to offer and sell services.

Business has so far developed favourably for UNOPS.[85] It is endeavouring to widen its range of clients further. The increase in operations financed by UNDP for national execution is also having an impact in this context; some of these operations are being implemented by UNOPS for programme countries.

No information is yet available on experience of operations implemented by non-governmental organizations. Some programme countries in particular continue to have considerable political reservations in this respect.[86] The earliest possible evaluation of experience of this new implementation option is necessary to determine the scale on which it has been possible to engage NGOs without the approval of the programme country's government and how far they can be involved in the future.

Programme Approach and Pooling of Project Resources

(a) Reform measures

In the 1990s UNDP has attempted at practical project or implementation level to bring about changes that permit increased pooling and concentration and thus a more goal-oriented and more strategic approach. A major part in these efforts has been played by the *programme approach*, which was introduced by the Governing Council for the UNDP[87] in 1992 and taken up by the General Assembly in the same year (A/RES/47/199, paras 12 ff.). The programme approach is an instrument that does not seek solely to concentrate development cooperation resources. The pooling of all resources (i.e. internal and external contributions), however, is almost automatically associated with the approach.

The programme approach can generally be defined as a method designed to enable governments and their development partner organizations to pursue and achieve relevant development objectives in a coherent and integrated fashion.[88] The principles and process of the programme approach therefore focus on suitable national development plans and priorities, giving prime responsibility to the programme country's government (including the coordination of development cooperation contributions) and identifying appropriate ways of involving donors. National execution is a dimension that is closely associated with the programme approach, since orientation to needs and the use or development of national capacities are important elements. NEX therefore presupposes the existence in the programme country of structures that function in much the same way as the programme approach.

The introduction of the programme approach and the raising of the limits on the resources that may be used by the Resident Representative/Resident Coordinator (DP/1995/31, p. 4) enabled concentration and pooling effects to be achieved in UNDP operations in the mid-1990s. Compared to the second half of the 1980s and the early 1990s, it has been possible to reduce the number of operations considerably and to increase the average project volume since 1992. In 1966 4,133 current UNDP operations had a total volume of US $ 6,213m and an average volume of US $ 1,503m.[89]

Table 13: Average financial volume and number of current UNDP operations

Year	Total volume (US $m)	Number of current operations	Average volume of current operations (US $)
1988	4,365	5,901	740,000
1989	4,660	6,052	770,000
1990	5,123	6,140	835,000
1991	5,420	6,189	876,000
1992	5,688	5,736	992,000
1993	5,602	5,083	1,102,000
1994	5,292	4,333	1,221,000
1995	6,167	4,701	1,312,000
1996	6,212	4,133	1,503,000

Source: UNDP (1997o), p. 84

(b) Assessment

On the whole, both the objectives associated with the programme approach and the intention to pool UNDP resources are to be welcomed in development terms. The results achieved in implementation, however, do not yet permit a clear evaluation.

The programme approach is conceptually appropriate because it seeks to achieve a strategic combination of various interventions possibly occurring in isolation and so to increase effectiveness in development terms. Ownership, capacity-building and national execution are important dimensions of the programme approach. Its application, however, raises a number of difficulties that can be attributed to its complexity and the major requirements to be satisfied.[90]

The pooling of UNDP resources is important if the fragmentation of their use and the spreading of resources too thinly over numerous subject and problem areas are to be avoided. The aim is also to relieve UNDP's immediate cooperation partners in the programme country and UNDP itself (especially the country offices) of project management activities. The concentration of resources should not, however, be equated with the promotion of large-scale operations only: the aim should be to achieve a broader impact through the use of decentralized and non-governmental structures (e.g. by reaching poor groups directly); a broad impact - possibly through small and micro operations - should therefore be sought by UNDP indirectly rather than directly.

The aggregated UNDP data on the number of current operations and the financial volume of projects and programmes should be interpreted with caution because of deficiencies in the collection and evaluation of data. It is currently impossible, for example, to make a distinction in the data between programmes and their individual components; furthermore, the collection of data on four additional types of intervention began in 1995. Nonetheless, past experience indicates that the programme approach has done a great deal to ensure that UNDP resources are pooled or at least to prevent a further rise in the number of projects (UNDP 1996j, pp. xi ff.).

Evaluations

(a) Reform measures

In the 1990s the Executive Board and the Administrator have emphasized the need to strengthen and improve the instrument of evaluation within UNDP. To this end, reforms have been initiated to strengthen the appropriate organizational unit and to improve the quality of evaluations during the preparatory stages and implementation and as the conclusions drawn are put into practice.

The main practical measures taken to strengthen and improve evaluations include the following:[91]

- reporting in the Executive Board on the findings of strategic evaluations has been increased;
- the methods of assessing and evaluating other bi- and multilateral donors have been examined and conclusions have been drawn for UNDP (UNDP 1997d);
- a database on available UNDP evaluations has been developed and also made available to the DAC;
- the transparency of the criteria for the selection of measures to be evaluated has been improved;[92]
- the provision of information by the Office of Evaluation and Strategic Planning (OESP) on evaluation experience has been improved (through the publication of the series *Lessons Learned*, for example).

(b) Assessment

As a rule, it is difficult to assess the quality of evaluations in development cooperation. There are no standards or criteria permitting relatively unequivocal statements on whether a development institution carries out or commissions high-quality or less high-quality evaluations. Nonetheless, there are some signs of an improvement in the quality and credibility of UNDP evaluations in the 1990s. Important factors in this context are the transparency created by UNDP and the debate on both appropriate methodological approaches and individual evaluations. This transparency is to be found, for example, in *Evaluation Findings* (UNDP 1995g, 1996f, 1997d), a report that has appeared annually since 1995. Many individual evaluations are also published.

Another positive change is the scale of self-criticism. Although UNDP has yet to achieve the World Bank's self-critical openness (an area in which it is well ahead of almost all other donors),[93] many UNDP evaluations still being rather restrained in their criticism, quite a number of these evaluations do make very clear references to individual shortcomings and structural problems;[94] an example is the study *Building Development Partnerships through Co-financing* (UNDP 1996i), which was not sparing in its criticism of, say, the adverse effects of government cost-sharing resources. Also to be welcomed are the consideration that UNDP gives in various evaluations to more highly aggregated issues and its study of guidance and implementation instruments that are methodologically more difficult and politically more controversial. Examples of this are the evaluations of national execution (UNDP 1995h), the work of the Resident Coordinators (UNDP 1997d, pp. 55 ff.), the NaTCAP (National Technical Cooperation Assessment and Programme) instrument (Williams 1995b, 1995c; UNDP 1991d, 1991e) and capacity-building in the area of development cooperation coordination by the programme countries (UNDP 1991b, 1991c). In these spheres UNDP now has a wealth of experience that should also be of interest to other development cooperation institutions.

Administrative Procedures, Management and Organizational Structures

(a) Reform measures

One of the UNDP Administrator's main aims in the 1990s has been to create a leaner organization and to improve accountability mechanisms. Besides concepts for the reorganization of UNDP's internal structures and functions, a wide range of other measures to reform administrative procedures are planned.

The main features of the planned reorganization (UNDP 1997h, 1997i; DP/1997/16, pp. 16 ff.; DP/1997/16/Add. 7) of UNDP from the development angle are efforts to establish decentralized structures and to improve capacities at headquarters level. Decentralization is intended to result in operational and substantive capacities being shifted to the subregional and country levels, leading to the better achievement of the SHD objectives. The Resident Representative's area of responsibility is to be appropriately wide, embracing in particular measures to ensure the success of the UNDP programme at country level, assistance for governments with the preparation of strategy documents (e.g. country cooperation frameworks), the achievement of resource mobilization targets at country level, etc. Within UNDP the Resident Representative must answer to the Bureau Regional Director. The tasks of UNDP headquarters, on the other hand, extend primarily to (1) intergovernmental mechanisms, UN procedures, the development of strategic partnerships and the provision of information for the public, (2) global resource mobilization, (3) coordination of emergency aid reactions, (4) overarching management functions and (5) compliance with organization-wide standards, checks and evaluations.

UNDP's reorganization is generally guided by the principles and objectives of modern institutions and enterprises; in other words, the emphasis is on efforts to create clear terms of reference and areas of personal responsibility. A further aim of reorganization is to reduce the

Figure 11: Outline of a new organizational structure for UNDP

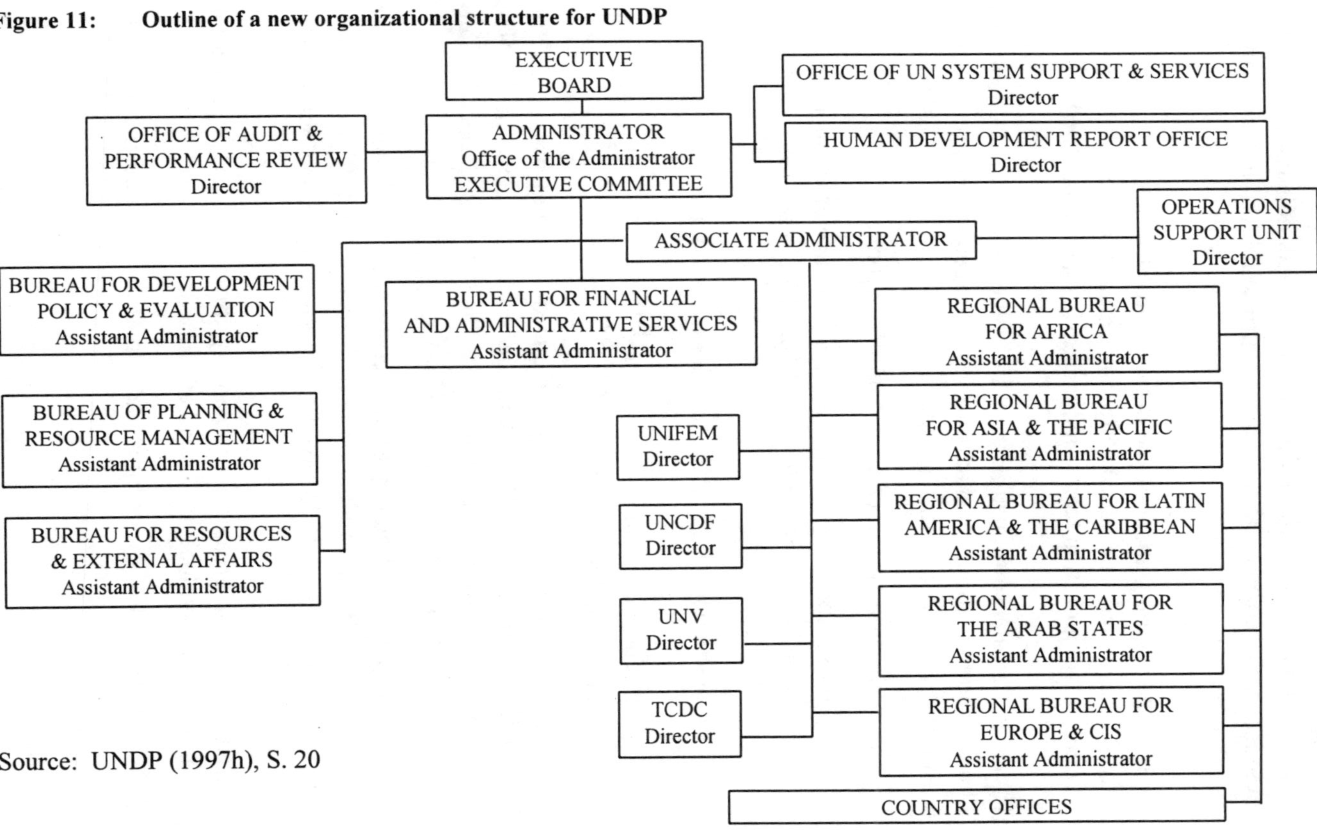

Source: UNDP (1997h), S. 20

number of units that report directly to the Administrator; it is also intended to contribute to the more purposeful linking of political decision-making processes to available evaluation experience.

Besides the rearrangement of the organizational structures, many other reforms have been launched since the mid-1990s with the aim of making the organization leaner and increasing accountability.[95]

To create greater responsibility in the spheres of development and administration, various mechanisms and management instruments have been installed or modified. They include

- the evaluation system (see the comments above),
- efforts to reform the programme performance assessment mechanisms (UNDP 1995d; DP/1997/16, pp. 16 ff.; DP/1997/16/Add. 7, pp. 13 ff.),
- the presentation of a first annual internal audit and oversight.[96]

To make the organization and procedures leaner, the following measures have also been taken or initiated:[97]

- The staff complement is being reduced. The aim was a 15% reduction from 1992 to 1997, with the number of posts at the New York headquarters suffering a 32% and thus disproportionately high reduction (DP/1996/16, p. 16).
- The proportion of administrative costs is to be reduced, the plan having been a 12% reduction in real terms from 1992 to 1997; the period 1992 - mid-1996 saw a real saving of US $ 106m in administrative costs.[98]
- There is to be greater accountability throughout the organization and from individual staff members.
- The many rules, procedures and reporting mechanisms are to be simplified.

(b) Assessment

UNDP's administrative procedures and management structures are one of the reform areas that has been undergoing a process of radical change since the mid-1990s. The UNDP administration is above all complying with demands from various major contributors (USA, Germany, etc.) in this area.

A final assessment of the effects of reorganization is not yet possible. The objectives that have been set - especially with regard to decentralization, headquarters' service functions and the stronger position of the evaluation unit - must, however, be applauded from the development angle. In principle, UNDP's internal organization and thus its reorganization are the Administrator's responsibility. It is appropriate in political and - provided that external actors have suitable experience to offer - development terms for the UN member states, or the Executive Board, to be involved in this process of change; UNDP has launched a coordination process of this kind. The debate on reorganization conducted internally and in the Executive Board also reveals a structural weakness, since the internal restructuring is being exploited by UN member states to voice interests relating to staffing policy and to bring influence to bear on the organization.[99]

The steps which, besides restructuring, were meant to lead to a leaner organization and improved accountability have on the whole made UNDP more effective administratively and in development terms. The mechanisms and procedures are comparable to the best practices of other national and international institutions.[100] In administration and personnel policy UNDP has hitherto shown a commitment to reforms that goes well beyond the willingness of other donors. Taking various examples, the UNDP administration is keen to demonstrate its willingness to take action against corruption, waste and similar undesirable factors.[101]

However, UNDP's administrative and staff reforms, which as a general rule are associated with cutbacks and redundancies, have not had entirely favourable effects (increased efficiency, simpler procedures, etc.): the reduction in staff numbers that has hitherto been effected primarily for financial reasons may lead to a loss of quality if important areas can no longer be adequately staffed. UNDP is seen as an unreliable and unattractive employer not least because of the major cuts it has made in its staff complement; a great deal more thought needs to be devoted to the question of how to keep or recruit adequately qualified personnel and how generally to avoid reform fatigue[102] among the staff.

It is therefore with some justification that the UNDP Administrator criticizes the scale of the reductions in the 1990s:

> *"The downsizing of the past six years has cut more than the fat from the UNDP budget. It has cut into the muscle and bone of the organization, leaving it weakened in numerous areas."* (DP/1997/23, p. 12)

General Assessment of the Reform Measures at Administration and Implementation Level

Wide-ranging and sometimes radical efforts have generally been made at administration and implementation level to increase the administration's effectiveness in development terms and its efficiency. The measures initiated or implemented have so far proved successful.

The changes to the implementing institutions and to direct responsibility for implementation are, on the whole, very sweeping. The separation of the operational unit (OPS) from UNDP was a wise move. The growth in national execution is generally to be welcomed in development terms; however, greater care should be taken to ensure that incentives and effects that are inappropriate in development terms are not associated with this approach. In the 1990s NEX may have suddenly expanded even in countries whose local capacities are still weak or inadequate. For UNDP's effectiveness in the development field action to improve the quality of evaluation is also very important.

Figure 12: Reform measures at administration and implementation level

Reform measures	Objectives, explanations or examples
National execution	Implementation of projects by the programme countries on their own responsibility as the norm
Separation of operational capacities from UNDP	Replacement of UNDP's Office for Project Services with a United Nations Office for Project Services
Programme orientation and pooling of resources	- Coherent and integrative approach - Reduction of the number of projects and increase in the project volume
Strengthening and improvement of evaluations	- More purposeful involvement of available evaluation experience in planning and decision-making - Improved reporting on evaluations to the Executive Board - More transparent and strategic selection of evaluations
Administrative procedures, management and organizational structures	- Reduction of proportion of administrative costs by 12% in real terms from 1992 to 1997 - Reduction of bureaucratic structures and administrative procedures - Targeted 15% reduction in total regular staff from 1992 to 1997 - 32% at headquarters level and 4% at country level (professional capacity) - Delegation of tasks to the country offices / decentralization - Creation of an organizational culture of responsibility and accountability

Comprehensive reforms of the administration, management and organizational structure have been initiated or undertaken. There is evidence to show that they are leading to a reduction in administrative costs and staff, enabling money to be saved or spent on actual operational measures. The Executive Board has so far failed to take sufficient account of the possible adverse effects, especially the loss of quality caused, for example, by the departure of qualified personnel.

4.4 Conclusions

Since the early 1990s UNDP has been undergoing a process of radical change. The scale and intensity of the adjustments and modifications are substantial in many areas. In view of the "width" and "depth" of the changes it is therefore legitimate to refer to a process of reform or a reform of UNDP.

The process of reform is relatively far advanced, but by no means complete. A number of changes have already been initiated or concluded, but experience has yet to be gained and conclusions drawn in many cases. In addition, various problems have not yet been adequately solved or considered.

The reforms that have been planned, initiated and completed address very different levels, at different times in some cases and at different speeds. They are a conglomerate of initiatives and decisions of the UN General Assembly, the UN Secretary-General, ECOSOC, the UNDP Executive Board, or Governing Council, and the UNDP Administrator. The reform measures are characterized by the fact that they form a process. The changes to UNDP do not therefore constitute *the* reform of UNDP within a clearly defined framework for the reform of the whole of UN development cooperation (*big bang*). Instead, the reform process consists of fragmented and sometimes inconsistent initiatives (e.g. staff reduction vs improved quality of development) at different speeds. In the absence of strategic instructions from the political decision-making bodies a patchwork or incremental approach can therefore be regarded as a feature of the UNDP reform process. This approach has its disadvantages primarily because there are no transparent strategic objectives or, therefore, a coherent reform package for UNDP and UN development cooperation as a whole. However, the current efforts to reform UNDP at different levels and through different actors must also be seen as the right approach, because there is as yet no satisfactory strategic approach to the reform of UN development cooperation as a whole.

The direction hitherto taken in the reform initiatives and decisions that originate from the General Assembly and the Secretary-General lacks consistency where UNDP is concerned. To some extent, functions entailing greater responsibility for coordination at headquarters and country level are being transferred to UNDP. The authority and instruments assigned to UNDP are, however, too weak and unsuitable for this.

The direction taken by the UNDP Executive Board and Administrator is clearer, but reform measures are being implemented effectively only in part. The aim of the reforms of providing high-quality services geared to sustainable human development and services for all UN development cooperation has been clearly articulated in the 1990s.

Specifically, the following dimensions can be identified as major strengths and weaknesses of the reform process so far in the 1990s:

– Strengths:

  (1) With the concept of sustainable human development UNDP has succeeded in developing a generally accepted development paradigm at a high level of abstraction.

  (2) The replacement of the previous country programming system may enable UNDP to combine its particular advantages (ownership, etc.) with more effective development incentives in the future.

  (3) The separation of the implementing unit (OPS) is enabling UNDP to improve the performance of its core tasks, which require a largely neutral framework.

  (4) The principle of national execution, programme orientation and the strengthening of evaluations have helped to integrate important findings of the TC debate into UNDP's practical project and programme work.

(5) The administrative changes have led to significant savings in costs and improved efficiency.

– Weaknesses:

(1) The development paradigm (SHD) has so far been unable to contribute to effective substantive focusing.

(2) UNDP's political guidance in the context of overall UN development cooperation continues to be poor.

(3) At headquarters level UNDP lacks effective coordination instruments.

(4) At country level the incentives to the various actors to engage in coordination under the Resident Coordinator system continue to be limited.

(5) The quality of projects and programmes in development terms continues to be unsatisfactory in some respects.

(6) The approaches to resource mobilization and the rearrangement of the financing mechanisms have so far been inadequate.

Despite the weaknesses indicated above, the reforms that have so far been undertaken are generally remarkable. This is all the truer as the political conditions for unequivocal reform objectives and expectations are inadequate and the environment of the UN reform debate is hardly conducive.

The largest role in the elimination of the current weaknesses and the protection of the reforms so far undertaken must be played by the UN member states. They must lay the necessary foundations in the decision-making bodies (General Assembly, ECOSOC, Executive Board) and support reform orientation with political commitment.

Figure 13: UNDP's most important reform measures since the beginning of the 1990s

Level	Reform measures
Conceptual level	- Substantive focusing through the definition of a core mission (*To assist countries in their endeavour to achieve sustainable human development*), three principal objectives, four focus areas and ten intervention patterns and through a mission statement - Taking up new aspects of development
Structural and policy level	- Transformation of the Governing Council into a smaller Executive Board - Expansion of the coordinating mechanisms at headquarters level - Strengthening of the coordinating mechanisms at country level - Replacement of the old programming system - Resource mobilization approaches
Administration and implementation level	- National execution as the norm - Separation of OPS and establishment of UNOPS - Programme orientation and pooling of resources - Improvement and strengthening of the evaluation instrument - Making the administration leaner and reorganizing the internal structure

5 Profile of a More Effective UNDP

5.1 Introduction

The aim of this chapter is to identify and discuss elements of a future UNDP that are appropriate or necessary if its effectiveness in the development field is to be increased. The emphasis is on the role that UNDP could and should play in development and on the conditions, environment and structures needed for this purpose.

This chapter summarizes the contents of the previous chapters. In other words, the UNDP profile to be described will be developed on the basis both of the debate on technical cooperation and of UNDP's present deficiencies, the need for adjustment, proposals for reforms and reforms that have been initiated.

The various elements and the overall picture of a more effective UNDP should be seen as forming part of an outline of an ideal type of UN agency that is appropriate and effective in the development field. Although the current political environment is important in this context, since the elements are derived from the previous chapters, it does not play a decisive role for the time being, aspects of political enforceability and implementation being considered in subsequent chapters.

5.2 Premises

The main features of the profile of a more effective UNDP which is to be developed in this chapter comply with certain premises. These premises have emerged from previous chapters and are explained here before the discussion continues. They concern the international debate on technical cooperation and the debate on the reform of the UN's and UNDP's development cooperation.

Suggestions from the international debate on technical cooperation

Many elementary suggestions for a more effective UNDP can be found in the international debate on technical cooperation. They relate both to basic issues of orientation and the instruments of TC and to specific shortcomings and functions of UNDP.

– *Capacity-building as the overriding objective:* Effective technical cooperation must be able to make a contribution to capacity-building. As a general rule, the decisive obstacles to development, especially in the poorer and poorest countries, are associated with absent and weak capacities. TC that makes an effective contribution to eliminating these shortcomings is appropriate and of the utmost importance. In principle, UNDP's tasks therefore remain relevant and are probably tending to gain in importance compared to financial cooperation.

– *Operationalization of capacity-building:* Capacity-building must be operationalized as the objective, and it must also be reflected at the level of instruments so that expectations associated with the term may be fulfilled. Evidence must be produced to show that TC is used not only to plug gaps temporarily but also to promote and develop sustainable and workable local structures.

– *Need for specialization in technical cooperation:* Technical cooperation is a complex task that should preferably be performed by specialized donors; there is no centre of excellence or think tank for TC at international level (as the World Bank is seen to be by many donor countries in the case of financial cooperation). UNDP might seek to play a far more important role in this context than it has in the past.

– *Substance of TC:* As a United Nations agency, UNDP is especially qualified to promote measures connected with participation, democracy, human rights, conflicts, civil society and other overarching aspects of *development orientation* (section III.5.3.1).

– *TC approaches and profile:* UNDP differs positively from other donors in the question of ownership and the gearing of its operations to the programme countries' priorities (national execution,

NaTCAP, etc.). This is one of UNDP's decisive advantages, and one that should be maintained in the future. As regards the quality of TC, however, it has often proved to be a disadvantage; greater efforts should be made to help resolve current conflicts of objectives.

Suggestions from the debate on the reform of the UN's and UNDP's development cooperation

The reform debate and the actual reforms of UN development cooperation and UNDP itself indicate how UNDP's effectiveness in the development field might be further increased.

- *Need for coordination:* The success of the United Nations' and UN system's operational development activities very largely depends on a coordinated approach adequately and stably endowed with resources. UNDP should assume and perform the tasks this entails.
- *Overcoming the institutional fragmentation of UN development cooperation:* The existing organizational structures of UN development cooperation should show a clear tendency to centralize and integrate the various agencies and to create manageable structures under the UNDP umbrella. The TC activities of the rest of the UN system should be carefully coordinated by UNDP.
- *Implementation requirements:* Coordination, guidance and financing tasks form UNDP's main area of activity. For this suitable instruments and enforcement mechanisms and an adequate financial endowment with a suitable structure are needed. In principle, UNDP should not therefore perform or seek to perform any implementation tasks; any private or public supplier at national and international level (local consultancies, UNOPS, etc.) who is suitable and offers value for money should be considered for the national execution of operations.
- *Quality aspects:* The quality of UNDP work should be improved further in all areas (staff, programming, etc.).

The reforms of UNDP initiated and undertaken in the 1990s and current plans for its further development should be adequately taken into account in future reform efforts. It would be politically unrealistic and counterproductive for development to call for a complete re-organization of the foundations of UNDP and to seek fundamentally new areas of activity. It is generally known how UNDP can be made more effective, and various reforms have already been launched. Reforms that still need to be undertaken should, however, be integrated into a coherent strategy, and questions regarding the political implementation of the reform strategy should be answered.

5.3 Elements of a More Effective UNDP

A reform strategy for creating a UNDP that is more effective in the development field should focus on three main elements:

- first, UNDP's substantive tasks (what causes does UNDP espouse?),
- second, functional tasks and service functions for all UN development cooperation (how can UNDP support and ensure the overall success of UN development cooperation?),
- third, elements for establishing the substantive and functional profile and ensuring high-quality development (finances, political guidance, instruments, procedures, etc.).

The reform strategy proposed here is largely based on the UNDP reform process of the 1990s and in some respects takes up the overall reform of UN development cooperation. It also includes existing analyses and proposals emanating from the UNDP reform debate (section III.3). In addition, it should be emphasized that, as the reform strategy focuses on effectiveness in the development sphere, it is not *a priori* an option adapted to the requirements of a decision-making process which would emphasize the search for a political consensus.

5.3.1 Substantive Tasks

UNDP's substantive tasks are geared to the two concepts of *sustainable human development* and *capacity-building*. The development paradigm of sustainable human development that has been introduced is in principle appropriate. Towards the end of the 1990s all the major bilateral and multilateral donors largely agree - with different terminology in some respects - on this general objective. It is therefore crucially important to put the paradigm into concrete form and to operationalize it. The majority of development cooperation institutions are also agreed on the capacity-building concept. All donors in the TC sphere accept capacity-building as a dimension that is relevant to and decisive for development.

For the implementation of the sustainable human development paradigm and the capacity-building concept there are three points of substantive emphasis for UNDP:

– good governance, crisis prevention and the consolidation of peace,
– support for the programme countries with the follow-up to the world conferences, and
– the development or promotion of mechanisms for the coordination of development cooperation by the programme countries.

These three substantive tasks are intended to have the function of specifying the areas on which UNDP is to focus. Clear substantive focusing should be sought through a narrow interpretation of these areas; no other areas should be assisted in the future. The three focus areas relate to UNDP on the basis of existing organizational structures and currently available core resources.[1]

Good governance, crisis prevention and the consolidation of peace

Good governance, crisis prevention and the consolidation of peace in the context of development cooperation can be extended well beyond their present dimensions and quality to become UNDP's most important substantive concern. Several major factors argue for this focus area.

First, good governance, crisis prevention and the consolidation of peace are of the utmost importance as substantive tasks. They are particularly relevant to development because they have a direct and essential influence on man's quality of life and opportunities in life; they are also vital as an environment (for, say, economic development). Beyond their immediate relevance to development, they are very important for international policy on peace and security. Development cooperation, which can make significant contributions to the prevention and containment of violent conflicts, is in the immediate interests of the international community. The use and further development of civil potential for crisis prevention and the consolidation of peace is of elementary interest to international policy outside development cooperation. Furthermore, measures taken in the sphere of good governance can do a great deal to help ensure that norms and values (human rights, participation, etc.) are recognized and applied.[2]

Second, no institution at international level is responsible for these tasks in the context of development cooperation. Other UN agencies operating in the field of development cooperation are concerned with given sectors or target groups; those UN agencies that are not active in development cooperation concern themselves with these issues primarily by setting standards (e.g. the General Assembly) or have little or no operational opportunity (e.g. the UN High Commissioner for Human Rights).

Third, as part of the United Nations, UNDP has - especially when compared to the bilateral approach - a particular authority to perform this set of tasks.[3] The most important international agreements relating directly or indirectly to good governance, crisis prevention and the consolidation of peace were concluded within the UN framework.[4] These documents have ensured that the many dimensions of good governance in particular have long been internationally recognized and binding when it comes to setting standards. On this basis UNDP can take action in the development sphere and, along the lines drawn in the basic documents referred to, take a clear substantive position without infringing the UN principles of political neutrality and universality.

Fourth, as a UN agency, UNDP is in the advantageous situation of co-operating closely with other UN bodies in the areas referred to and forging a link with political debates and political decisions. Although not enough experience has yet been gained in this respect, closer relations might be sought, for example, in the human rights sphere with the UN High Commissioner for Human Rights. In the long term this might make a contribution to the coherence of UN or international policy and have synergy effects.

Fifth, UNDP's very good presence at country level is a requirement particularly if it is to be able to take action on politically sensitive aspects of good governance, crisis prevention and the consolidation of peace. This is true of processes of consultation and coordination not only with the government of the programme country but also with other local actors (e.g. local non-governmental organizations) and non-governmental, bilateral and multilateral donors and embassies.

Sixth, the two areas - good governance on the one hand and crisis prevention and the consolidation of peace on the other - primarily entail technical cooperation tasks (although supplementary investment measures or commodity aid may be appropriate and necessary in certain cases). For this reason too UNDP should assume the main responsibility for these tasks.

Measures in the areas of good governance, crisis prevention and the consolidation of peace go beyond UNDP's role of merely supporting the government of a programme country, since they must include normative guidelines. They may be directed against a government's policy if it shows no more than limited development orientation; they may also be aimed at actors in civil society as such or as executing agencies and so be inconsistent with government policy. This necessary substantive attitude may lead to political conflicts with programme countries. Basic discussions on the relationship between development standards and political neutrality are therefore needed.

In principle, the development cooperation measures that can be considered in the context of good governance are those which (OECD 1995c, p. 6)

- contribute to a government's legitimation through participatory processes and the involvement of the governed,
- increase the accountability of political and other public institutions (parliaments, ministries, etc.) for their actions; this includes the transparency of decision-making processes, the freedom of the press and individual and institutional accountability mechanisms,
- strengthen the political accountability of government representatives for decision-making processes,
- improve the ability of governments to formulate appropriate policies and implement them effectively at the appropriate time,

help to protect human rights, the rule of law and the rights of individuals and groups.

Examples of measures in the area of good governance are assistance during the holding of elections, further training for judges and judicial officials on human rights issues and support for umbrella associations of non-governmental institutions.

Measures in the area of crisis prevention and the consolidation of peace are geared to the immediate and the short- to medium-term establishment and promotion of civil mechanisms for settling and resolving conflicts of interest and to the prevention or termination of violent conflicts.[5] Given these objectives, measures in the following areas may in principle be considered:[6]

- specific mediation and negotiation mechanisms,
- measures for demobilizing and reintegrating combatants,

- measures for the reintegration of other uprooted population groups (refugees and displaced persons),
- reconstruction aid,
- clearance of land mines,
- in principle, depending on the conflict situation, good governance measures.

In conceptual and practical terms the tasks connected with good governance, crisis prevention and the consolidation of peace generally represent difficult, comprehensive and sensitive challenges. However, there are now suitable foundations and some practical experience in these areas: the OECD's Development Assistance Committee adopted some helpful guidelines on *Participatory Development and Good Governance* (OECD 1995c) in 1995 and on *Conflict, Peace and Development Co-operation* (OECD 1997b) in 1997; UNDP itself has commissioned some conceptual studies (Stiefel 1994; UNDP 1997b); other non-governmental agencies, bi- and multilateral donors and research institutions have also submitted progress reports on and analyses of these topics in the 1990s (Ball 1996; Colletta / Kostner / Wiederhofer 1996; Moore 1996; Heinz 1994; Waller 1996; Wissing 1995; Mair 1997; Bredow / Jäger (eds) 1997; Tetzlaff (ed.) 1993). A qualitatively appropriate approach can be deduced from these foundations.

Support for the programme countries with follow-up to the world conferences

The UN world conferences of the 1990s have, at considerable expense, formulated a substantive consensus on many global issues and designed programmes for action. Although they have their weaknesses, the conclusions on development drawn at these conferences may form an important point of departure in the framing of policies at national as well as international level. The Copenhagen social summit, for example, defined some poverty alleviation and social development objectives that have helped to bring about practical changes (e.g. restructuring of budgets at central government level) (Gsänger 1996b).

To ensure that the objectives formulated are also achieved effectively and efficiently and remain effective in the long term, systematic follow-up at international and national level is necessary. UNDP might undertake a wider range of more purposeful activities in this context, especially at national level.

In this substantive focus area UNDP should base its approach on the past activities of the whole UN system in following up world conferences. At international level these activities are undertaken under the United Nations System Conference Follow-up Action Programme developed in 1995, which primarily consists of four substantive working groups (interagency task forces) of the Administrative Committee on Co-ordination, which are chaired by various UN agencies.[7] At country level the Resident Coordinators are responsible for ensuring coherent and coordinated UN follow-up to the conferences through thematic groups. The limited success of this follow-up process hitherto is mainly due to two factors (UN 1997e, paras 9 ff.; E/1997/54, paras 23 ff.): firstly, past activities have been excessively induced from outside and have not therefore been adequately established in the programme countries (supply-driven); secondly, the objectives of the global agendas have yet to be sufficiently operationalized and implemented for the national level.

UNDP's additional activities should not be geared to the direct implementation of the various action programmes but to assisting the programme countries with the formulation of policies and strategies. UNDP might thus take practical action at country level with a view to contributing to the implementation of the conclusions drawn at world conferences through capacity-building. There should also be purposeful follow-up to the world conferences in the context of UNDP's efforts to coordinate development cooperation at country level.

Box 7: The UN world conferences of the 1990s

The following UN world conferences[8] have been held in the 1990s:

- 1990: World Conference on Children, New York,
- 1992: Conference on Environment and Development, Rio de Janeiro,
- 1993: Second World Conference on Human Rights, Vienna,
- 1994: Third International Conference on Population and Development, Cairo,
- 1995: World Summit for Social Development, Copenhagen,
- 1995: Fourth World Conference on Women, Beijing,
- 1996: Second United Nations Conference on Human Settlements, Istanbul,
- 1996: World Food Summit, Rome.

A general assessment of the world conferences is not easy, since their substance and the documents adopted at them are too different and the defined and verifiable commitments and criteria of success are not specific enough. Despite these deficiencies, however, excessive criticism of summits that fails to take account of the positive effects they have had should be avoided. The conferences have developed, formulated or reaffirmed - albeit with differing intensity and focusing - some important common features. The main pillars of consensus for the conferences can be roughly summarized in the words *ecological viability*, *economic efficiency*, *social justice* and *political participation*.

The conferences have formulated a number of principles of an *international order* which, though often not binding, also play an important role for development cooperation (e.g. poverty alleviation as the recognized overriding objective of development cooperation). The *20/20 target* developed by UNFPA, UNICEF and UNDP and included in the action programme adopted at the World Summit for Social Development is also an example of innovation. It calls for industrialized and developing countries to agree to spend 20% of development cooperation funds and 20% of the national budget on basic social services (primary education, primary health care/family planning, water, sanitary facilities, food). For the UN the world conferences have also been an important step in its again playing a more prominent part in the international debate on development, the debates of the 1980s having been determined primarily by the World Bank.

Development or promotion of mechanisms for the coordination of development cooperation by the programme countries

In general, coordination problems at country level must be largely blamed for the poor effectiveness and efficiency of development cooperation.[9] Important aspects of the coordination problem are the poor coordination of external services (i.e. mainly for development cooperation) with national strategies and priorities and country-related coordination among the donors. The widest possible responsibility and capacity for the integration of development cooperation by the programme countries is therefore of the utmost importance. In these areas UNDP can in principle provide important services for the various programme countries and for the bi- and multilateral donors.

The coordination of development cooperation should be a focus area of UNDP activities for various reasons:

- In view of the tasks assigned to it, UNDP has a wide-ranging coordination mandate compared to other donors. The traditional donor countries have also stated in the DAC guidelines on the coordination of development cooperation, for example, that they welcome UNDP's coordinating role, particularly in connection with the round tables, and call for the mechanisms to be strengthened.[10]
- UNDP has extensive know-how in the field of coordination, derived, for example, from the round tables it organizes and from the activities of the Resident Representatives or Resident Coordinators. Much of the experience gained in this area has already been evaluated by UNDP.[11]
- The dense network of UNDP country offices provides the infrastructure needed if coordination functions requiring close and continuous on-the-spot coordination are to be assumed.
- The coordination of development cooperation (especially by the programme countries themselves) is inconsistent with the supply-oriented practical approach adopted by many donors. Given its substantive orientation and more neutral role, UNDP can take

action in a particularly suitable way to overcome the current inconsistencies and vested interests at country level. Being closer to the institutions of the country concerned, UNDP is in a better position than other donors to take on brokering and mediation roles.

In the coordination of development cooperation too the emphasis must be on local involvement to ensure ownership and sustainability; this should extend not only to the government of the programme country but explicitly to actors in civil society. As a rule, coordination of development cooperation should therefore be the task of the programme country[12] (not the donors) so that external contributions may be integrated into national or local development efforts as appropriately as possible.[13]

To improve the coordination of development cooperation, to make it as independent as possible and to bridge incapacities in the programme countries, UNDP should perform two tasks in particular (UNDP 1996g):

– Firstly, the promotion with purposeful TC measures of capacity-building to improve or develop the programme country's skills in the coordination of development cooperation. This should be one of the foremost objectives, and its achievement will be generally conducive to better development cooperation management[14] (responsibility in connection with the management and implementation of development cooperation measures). It also includes the development of transparent and participatory mechanisms for guiding development cooperation.

– Secondly, neutral services rendered directly by UNDP with a view to coordinating development cooperation. They include three functions in particular (UNDP 1996g, p. viii): (a) UNDP as a forum for the coordination of development cooperation, e.g. through round tables (general or sectoral aspects of development cooperation), (b) UNDP as an information pool (ensuring transparency of the programme country's strategies and priorities and of the many development cooperation activities of bi- and multilateral and non-governmental donors) and (c) fund-raising to fill existing financial gaps.

5.3.2 Functional Elements and Service Functions for UN Development Cooperation

Where functional tasks and service functions for the UN as a whole are concerned, the main aim is an improved and integrated approach at country level. For this reforms will be needed both at headquarters level and at country level itself. Against this background, steps relating to the institutional structure of UN development cooperation, the Resident Coordinator system and the overall programming of UN development cooperation should be taken.

Institutional structure and UNDP's position at headquarters level

As the volume of resources allocated to UN operational development cooperation is limited and the structures and approaches are fragmented, the aim at headquarters level should be the general integration of existing institutional structures. This integration should include three steps that complement each other:

- Structurally the most important measure should seek to reduce the large number of existing UN funds and programmes and to integrate them into UNDP's core programme. The underlying principle should be that at least all funds administered by UNDP and all UN funds and programmes which are not dependent on UNDP but fall within its substantive terms of reference should be amalgamated. If a review of the existing UN agencies reveals that they cannot be appropriately integrated into UNDP's task profile, they should be combined to form a maximum of two or three operational agencies (one for the environmental sphere, for example).
- UNDP should perform an effective guiding task in the period until the integration of the UN agencies and for any UN institutions remaining in the field of development cooperation. The executive

committee and the United Nations Development Group can serve as fora for this, although UNDP must be granted a decision-making power extending to all operational UN agencies in the development field if it is to be able to perform any coordinating tasks.

- The TC trust funds and the TC resources of the World Bank that are not used to back FC measures should in principle be transferred to UNDP's core programme or the remaining UN operational agencies (Gwin / Williams 1996, pp. 134 f.; Righter 1995, pp. 275 f.).

Resident Representative / Resident Coordinator system

The consolidation of UNDP's and the UN's country offices should be continued and deepened in some respects. UNDP should continue to be mainly responsible for the Resident Coordinator system in the future. The basis should be formed by a dense network of country offices in the programme countries for UN development cooperation and the whole UN system. Given the programme volume and all the other tasks performed by UNDP and the Resident Coordinator, however, it should be possible, where appropriate, to close country offices (i.e. to transfer their tasks to regional offices).

The most important features of changes that should be made are as follows:

- UN development cooperation and the UN system should in principle be represented externally by one person, the Resident Coordinator.
- By analogy with the structure at headquarters level, the Resident Coordinator should be empowered to take decisions affecting the other operational UN funds and programmes. This would ensure uniform planning, programming and implementation.
- In principle, UNDP bears direct responsibility for the Resident Coordinator system (backstopping, etc.); the candidates for Resi-

dent Coordinator posts should, however, include qualified people from agencies of the UN system that are participating in the RC system.

- Fairer cost-sharing and incentives for a stronger commitment and an improvement in quality should be achieved by requiring the agencies of the UN and UN system represented to participate in the financing of the RC system.
- In principle, the Resident Coordinator's tasks and activities (e.g. fund-raising for UNDP) should not jeopardize his neutral role vis-à-vis other UN agencies.
- The Resident Coordinators must pay sufficient attention to civil forces in the programme country. As a general rule, they should therefore consult with and advise both private and public actors.
- The foundations of the Resident Coordinator system should be clarified in a special General Assembly resolution, which should refer in particular to instruments for the effective achievement of the objectives.

Programming of UN development cooperation

A single country-related programming document for UN development cooperation, combining the current UN approaches and the programme country's strategy documents, should be formulated and submitted. It can be based on the United Nations Development Assistance Framework (UNDAF),[15] which should, however, integrate the existing framework and programming documents even more closely. The UNDAF should be a uniform document containing the country strategy notes and all programming documents of the UN funds and programmes and of other agencies of the UN system engaging in TC. The programming document might contain parts relating to specific institutions only in respect of the allocation of the tasks and financing components. UNDP should take responsibility for establishing the programming document for the UN system, but this should not reduce the role played by the programme country as the main actor.[16]

5.3.3 Elements in the Creation of the Profile and the Improvement of Quality

If the substantive and functional tasks are to be performed successfully, certain general conditions are necessary for UNDP or must be borne in mind by UNDP. Of particular importance in this context are political guidance by the Executive Board, the whole question of financing and various aspects of basic principles, instruments, procedures and implementation. These points are developed from the deficiencies discussed in the previous chapters; they should not, however, be regarded as a complete list of additional measures that are needed.

Political guidance / Executive Board

As with the integration and centralization of the UN funds and programmes, efforts need to be made to amalgamate the political supervisory bodies (Executive Boards). Reorganization should aim to create a coherent, professional, development-oriented and decisive guiding body with a self-image that gives it an identity.[17]

The Executive Board that is to be established should differ from the current Board in having the following features:

- *Decision-making powers*: Its terms of reference should extend to all UN funds and programmes. Feedback to the various capitals should be ensured, for example, by the presence of high-ranking delegates at the annual meetings so that decisions are followed by an appropriate process of implementation. The aim here would be to ensure, for instance, that decisions seeking coordination at country level and the involvement of other donors (EU, World Bank, etc.) were presented to the various supervisory bodies as a coherent policy of the government concerned.
- *Size and composition*: The number of members might be limited to about 24. The current regional composition should continue to determine the guide size. The system of the "rolling" change of

members should also be retained (a third of the members are replaced each year).

- *Representatives*: The representatives should, where possible, have specialized in development issues to some extent. Special introductory courses might be provided, particularly for UN missions with a poor financial endowment.
- *Rules*: Non-members of the Executive Board should be able to attend meetings, but - with clearly defined exceptions (participation by countries in the discussion of their country programmes, etc.) - they should not have the right to speak. The rules should also be so written that basic political declarations are not made and discussed by the Board (but by ECOSOC or the General Assembly).
- *Meetings*: The Executive Board should be able to focus on its guidance tasks as a permanent body. Fundamental issues might be discussed at an annual meeting. Annual coordination meetings should also be held at least with the World Bank and the EU to consider fundamental aspects of the division of labour or complementary activities.

Finances

Two financial aspects are particularly important: firstly, the financial volume available in absolute terms, and secondly, the financing mechanisms.

On what constitutes an appropriate and adequate financial volume there can be no more than a general statement, since the endowment would ideally be constantly adjusted to the needs of the programme countries. Under the conditions obtaining in the second half of the 1990s the need (regardless of the political means of meeting it) for core resources that should be met by UNDP is estimated as about US $ 4 - 5bn p.a. This amount largely consists of already available TC resources; it specifically includes (1) almost US $ 1bn actually available at present, (2) an estimated additional financial requirement of almost US $ 1bn[18] and (3) a World Bank TC volume of US $ 500m - 1bn that might be devoted to UNDP's work, to which can be added (4) the amounts from the other UN funds and programmes (about US $ 2bn).

The financing mechanisms should seek to ensure continuous, predictable and adequate financing. To this end, various initiatives should be launched simultaneously:

- *In the short to medium term*: The core resources can be stabilized or increased if significantly greater efforts are made to improve the information conveyed to and the lobbying of the traditional contributors (their governments, parliaments, NGOs, academic institutions, media, etc.). Hitherto these activities have played no more than a marginal role. Purposeful information work and lobbying geared to fund-raising should be directed at *emerging donors* as well as the traditional contributing countries. As their economic capacities permit, the emerging donors should be involved in a new system of international burden-sharing which does not relieve the traditional industrialized countries of their responsibility for development but includes new, potent economies in the performance and financing of global tasks.
- *In the medium term*: The system of voluntary contributions should be thoroughly reformed through additions and changes to the existing mechanism. Firstly, voluntary contributions should be made on a multiannual basis (for periods of about three years). They should be joined by a financing element based on the economic effectiveness of the country concerned. It might comprise negotiated pledges (like the IDA's endowment) or contributions based on a fixed scale.[19] Secondly, financing funds earmarked for development purposes should be established.[20] They might perform a specific task in the development field, building on the experience gained with the Global Environment Facility (GEF). This might enable additional financial resources to be acquired for important substantive purposes (e.g. democratization aid and promotion of human rights groups), but without the structural

shortcomings of trust funds (to which the financing government has access, etc.).

- *In the long term*: If there is to be adequate and secure financing for activities that are in the global interest (*global public goods*) regardless of the political conduct of individual countries, it will be appropriate and essential in the long term for a new financing base to be established. The proposals put forward since the early 1980s for *innovative international financing mechanisms* (Tobin Tax, etc.) are conceptually appropriate and should be implemented (Haq / Kaul / Grunberg 1996; Najman / d'Orville 1995; ODI 1996; Mistry / Thyness 1991; UNDP 1994d; Singer 1995). Numerous analyses and initiatives explaining and elaborating on the proposals have appeared since the Brandt Report (Brandt et al. 1980) was published (1980).

Further development of innovative TC approaches and aspects of implementation

UNDP should adjust its innovative TC principles and procedures and make them more effective in development terms. Practical action can at least be taken with respect to (1) national execution, (2) the continued development of the NaTCAP process and the capacity-building debate, and (3) greater direct involvement of non-governmental institutions in the programme countries.

1. In principle, national execution by the programme countries is an important element for ownership and capacity-building. It should therefore be retained as the norm. However, additional efforts need to be made to ensure that the approach is effective in development terms in programme countries that currently have limited and weak national capacities. It is important in this context for complementary measures that help to develop or improve management skills in this sphere (institutions relevant to capacity-building) to be taken.

In principle, all suitable candidates should be considered when practical implementing tasks are being allocated (whether or not as part of national execution); this is true, for example, both of national consultancies in the programme countries and of UNOPS and UN specialized agencies. National execution should generally be a step that contributes to the privatization of implementation, especially at national level.

2. UNDP should use and develop the outcome and conclusions of the NaTCAP process and so further encourage the international debate on capacity-building.[21] At country level it can focus on the analysis of macro policies and programmes in this context; the emphasis can and should be placed on overarching strategies and policies and less on sectoral questions. This orientation primarily covers aspects connected with
   - long-term and complex challenges (poverty alleviation, etc.),
   - government and parliament,
   - local, national and regional political actors and their interrelationship,
   - participatory development,
   - questions of principle relating to the public and private sectors and their interrelationship,
   - the role of external aid,
   - the prevention and alleviation of problems caused by development cooperation and technical cooperation (poor ownership, etc.).

   UNDP should play an important role for TC in these areas as a think tank and stimulator.

3. Existing options and the financial volume should be increased to enable civil actors to be directly involved in the implementation of UNDP operations. These actors should also receive more assistance from UNDP with the development of structures and capacities.

Graduation mechanisms

In the future UNDP should introduce graduation mechanisms to permit the country- or sector-related differentiation of conditions and so create additional incentives to improve development and efficiency. This would mean abandoning the current principle that UNDP's (and the whole UN's) TC is in principle available to all programme countries free of charge.

A future graduation mechanism would have various goals. It should be adjusted to the very different economic and financial capacities of the programme countries. Various countries, particularly in Latin America and Asia, have sufficient resources to meet at least some of the costs directly incurred. To enable better account to be taken of these differences between countries and regions, a two-tier system that could vary between a grant element for TC measures of 83.4% (i.e. the "IDA conditions") and a full grant (100%) might be introduced.

Besides the programme country's financial capacity, however, adequate account should be taken of substantive aspects. Where development justifies, it should continue to be possible to implement measures in all programme countries on a grant basis. This might be the case, for example, with measures to promote tasks in civil society if the government concerned had little or no interest in the objectives set.

The graduation mechanism might also seek to ensure that any direct financial participation improved the quality of TC and increased the programme countries' responsibility. The willingness of the programme countries to make direct financial contributions (*willingness to pay*) might have a favourable impact on operations, since it might lead to greater commitment, greater acceptance and ultimately greater ownership. The direct financial involvement of all programme countries in UNDP's TC operations should therefore be envisaged in the long term wherever possible.

Country programming

UNDP's new country programming procedure should undergo further development after its introductory phase with the aim of expanding the development incentive mechanisms. It should be asked in this context whether development criteria have led to the planned flexibility in the level of resources actually allocated or whether, as a result of political compromises and the like, resources intended to act as an incentive are causing the perpetuation of the entitlement approach (e.g. through the general acceptance of all or almost all country cooperation frameworks).

If the development-oriented incentives of the new mechanisms prove to be ineffective, the country programming procedure should again be modified. The proportion of country-related and supraregional resources determined by development criteria should then be increased, i.e. it should be possible to attune the nature (sectors, project sponsors, etc.) and scale of TC even more closely to specific countries on the basis of development standards. The programming system might also both provide for negative sanctions (which in justified exceptional cases should include the option of suspending cooperation with the government if it is not sufficiently development-oriented) and permit conditions that provide for spending on specific areas or specific implementing organizations (e.g. project responsibility and management assigned to a non-governmental body).

Linking TC measures to non-operational UN policies

UNDP might step up its efforts to forge a link with UN activities and agencies which do not directly form part of the operational sphere of development (e.g. UN human rights work). There are points of contact with almost all areas of the UN at which a link to normative activities and political decisions might be forged. UNDP might therefore make a greater effort to use its role as a UN agency to examine and develop new cooperative relations. This might increase the effectiveness of the objectives pursued by UNDP by making for a coherent policy.

Given UNDP's proposed substantive focus areas, it has options for forging links primarily in three fields. Firstly, there are the UN world conferences of the 1990s (already considered above), at which UNDP should play the most important role within the UN in matters of implementation. Secondly, few of the various UN agencies engaged in human rights work undertake operational measures that require a degree of logistics (experience of planning and programming, liaison office, etc.). UNDP could therefore do a great deal more to join with the human rights agencies in seeking practical areas and measures in which they might cooperate. Thirdly, there has hitherto been a basically restrained attitude towards the UN's peace-keeping and peace-making activities. Great care should continue to be exercised in the future in the search for approaches to cooperation in this area, since the UN's peace and security measures are primarily a matter for other policies and major political risks are involved (social support for military operations, etc.). On the other hand, cooperation might be sought in individual cases, each judged on its merits, with a view, for example, to de-escalating conflicts. Forms of cooperation ranging from the deployment of UN peace-keeping forces to UNDP activities (e.g. mediation and negotiation efforts) are conceivable in this context.

5.4 Conclusions

The profile of a more effective UNDP that has been described and discussed above shows that further areas of UNDP could appropriately be reformed. UNDP has already taken a wide range of steps that point in the direction described here. The goal should not, however, be a completely new UNDP with fundamentally modified tasks and structures. On the other hand, some important areas have not yet been addressed, or have not been addressed adequately. There continues to be considerable potential for reform here.

UNDP has in principle an important part to play in finding solutions to global challenges through development cooperation and introducing innovations into current development cooperation. If this objective is to be achieved, its profile will need to be sharpened.

UNDP is unlikely to succeed in developing as gripping and immediately comprehensible an image as some agencies have managed to do; UNICEF, for example, is able to achieve far more publicity and approval in this respect with children as its target group. Nonetheless, the UNDP task profile described above is important and indispensable for successful development in the programme countries. The substantive tasks in the areas discussed are very important, but have not yet been adequately taken into account. As the functional tasks contribute to the effectiveness of all UN development cooperation, they too should be carefully considered. For both types of task (substantive and functional) UNDP is a particularly suitable candidate, and one that already meets the legislative requirements (i.e. appropriate mandates).

With the profile described above UNDP could occupy a far more important place in the international development debate and in practical development cooperation, especially at country level. In view of the dimensions involved, there is little danger of UNDP becoming too large, even if structures are amalgamated and finances are increased. Instead, UNDP has the potential, yet to be properly tapped, to act as a *think tank*, *UN coordinator*, *mediator* and *adviser* to the programme countries. As an innovative and creative TC donor, it could exercise far more influence on important international debates and the formulation of policies. The current UNDP's concentration on selected, important topics, the pooling and integration of fragmented structures, an improvement in the quality of work and greater financial weight are crucial requirements for this.

Figure 14: Elements of a more effective UNDP	
Substantive tasks	1 – Good governance – Crisis prevention and the consolidation of peace 2 Assistance for the programme countries with follow-up to the world conferences 3 Development or promotion of mechanisms for the coordination of development cooperation by the programme countries
Functional tasks and service functions	1 – Amalgamation of UN funds and programmes under the UNDP umbrella – Increased decision-making powers for UNDP within the United Nations Development Group and on the executive committee 2 Strengthened Resident Coordinator system, with UNDP taking the main responsibility 3 Uniform and workable programming document for all UN development cooperation, with UNDP taking the responsibility (on the basis of the United Nations Development Assistance Framework)
Elements for attaining the profile and improv-ing quality	1 More effective and integrated political guidance in a transformed Executive Board 2 Larger financial volume and adapted financing mechanisms 3 Further development of innovative TC approaches (NaTCAP, national execution, etc.) 4 Country-related graduation mechanisms 5 Incentive-oriented country programming 6 Linking of TC operations to non-operational UN policies

6 Positions of the Most Important Actors on the Reform Process and on the Prospects for UNDP's Reform

6.1 Introduction

The aim of this chapter is to analyse where the most important actors stand on the role and reform of UNDP. The main features of policy towards UNDP and ideas on the prospects for reforms will be revealed. From this conclusions will be drawn as to the areas in which the various actors agree or disagree in their views.

The most important actors briefly considered here include (1) the group of industrialized countries, (2) the group of programme countries (i.e. developing countries and the transforming economies of the East) and (3) the UN system and the UN. There are sometimes major differences between these groups of countries or individual countries; sometimes positions are even found to differ between departments within a country's administration.

The main point of departure for this chapter is the conclusion that the success of UNDP's current reform process and future reforms largely depends on the member states' conduct. The attitude of the individual member states is therefore decisive when it comes to the question whether reforms are accepted and promoted, in what form and on what scale.

The positions and policies of the member states on UNDP and its reform process are often barely transparent or hardly articulated. Even on fundamental aspects of UN development cooperation basic ideas are often lacking; this is true of both the industrialized countries and (to a far greater extent) the programme countries.[1] Besides documents drawn up by the actors, some published, others not, this chapter therefore covers the interviews conducted with the members of the Executive Board for the study (see the methodological explanations in Part I).

6.2 Positions of Important Groups of Actors

6.2.1 Positions of the Industrialized Countries

Although the industrialized countries - whose principal common feature where UNDP is concerned is that they are its main contributors - do not share a view on the role and reform of UNDP, a minimum consensus to which the majority of these countries subscribe is discernible. It is evident from the declaration on the economic summit meeting of the seven leading industrialized nations (G7) and the President of the European Commission in Lyon (G7 1996) (1996) and from the European Union's 1996 reform initiative (EU 1996). In recent years the EU has increasingly become the Group of 77's negotiating partner within the United Nations (Rudischhauser 1997, p. 135) and is used by individual EU members at least (e.g. Germany) as the main vehicle for expressing views on reforms in the economic and social fields. In addition, there are - sometimes differing or more detailed - position papers put forward by individual industrialized countries[2] and the group of Scandinavian countries (Nordic UN Project 1996, 1991b). The German position is expressed primarily in the G7 and EU's documents; documents that go further are few in number.[3]

Basic position on UNDP's tasks and role

The industrialized countries share the fundamental desire to retain UN development cooperation and, in this context, UNDP.[4] UNDP is to perform a management function, although it is unclear what practical form this outstanding responsibility should take.

It seems to be agreed that the UN's operational development agencies should be brought more closely together, integration under the UNDP umbrella or into UNDP being propagated.[5] At the same time, however, this intention is qualified by the call for certain agencies to retain their identity.[6] As regards official and practical proposals for the amalgamation or integration of agencies considerable restraint can be detected in all the donor countries' initiatives; as a rule, they avoid naming UN agencies that should be amalgamated or wound up.

An important feature of the industrialized countries' initiatives is the call for an improvement in quality at country level. They place particular emphasis in this context on the Resident Coordinator system, which they believe should be strengthened. There is no suggestion that UNDP's special responsibility for the Resident Coordinator system should be reviewed (EU 1996, para. 40).

In general, a clearer profile, better performance, more accountability structures, better management and increased efficiency are expected of UNDP.

Assessment of the present reform of UNDP and expectations of further reforms

By and large, UNDP's reform process in the 1990s is rated positively by the industrialized countries. The direction the reforms are taking is considered appropriate. Some governments, however, regard the scale of the reforms (i.e. the aspects covered) as inadequate and therefore in need of expansion; the majority also consider the pace of the reforms too slow.

Various governments in this group believe the following aspects are not being addressed or not adequately addressed:

- the substantive focusing of UNDP activities on priority development tasks,
- the improvement of the quality of work at country level,
- improved management,
- the strengthening of monitoring and evaluation mechanisms,
- the achievement of greater accountability,
- improved supervisory structures through the Executive Board.

Some governments advocate the removal of further UNDP structures at headquarters level in favour of decentralized organizational units. Some countries would also like to see country offices closed[7] in advanced programme countries or countries with a limited programme volume.

The industrialized countries differ most widely on the question of financial volume and financing mechanisms. The Scandinavian countries in particular call for a far better financial endowment and a combined financing mechanism for all UN development cooperation that adds negotiated pledges and fixed contributions to the present voluntary contributions. Reforms along these lines are intended not only to ensure a larger financial volume but also fairer sharing of the financial burden among the main contributors.[8] Some countries also see a need for further discussion of innovative financing mechanisms.

Major and particularly influential industrialized countries such as the USA, France, Germany and, with qualifications, Japan take a significantly different attitude, especially on the financing issues. Some question the need for financing above the current level (referring, for example, to the disbursement problems in the mid-1990s) (section III.2). Nor is there any political will to introduce a fundamentally new financing mechanism or to discuss innovative financing options.

Assessment

The position of the industrialized countries is generally unclear. Officially, the need for UNDP is emphasized and the reform process praised. The G7's and EU's initiatives in the second half of the 1990s are particularly to be applauded in this context. Despite the public references to the importance of UNDP, the political and financial commitment is often limited (with the notable exception of the like-minded countries). A clear sign in this respect is the conduct of such donor countries as the USA and Germany with respect to contributions. They frequently give a far higher priority to the multilateral development cooperation activities of the World Bank and regional development banks and, where appropriate, to the EU's development cooperation. Added to this, policy is often poorly coordinated within the various government administrations. This results in insufficient attention being paid to overarching coordination tasks assigned to UNDP when other international organizations come to formulate their policies (e.g. the Resident Coordinator's tasks for the whole UN system). Nor are there any statements or prescriptions on the direction in which UNDP should be developed in the future, on the performance criteria that might be defined for these changes or on the financial position that a UNDP thus reformed might occupy. In this respect many governments pursue a policy that is designed not to lead to any commitments or obligations. In the 1990s this conduct has resulted de facto in surreptitious withdrawal.

The like-minded countries form an important exception in this respect. In the 1990s the Scandinavian countries in particular and, to some extent, the Netherlands have pursued an intensive strategy aimed at making UNDP more effective. This policy is symbolized by various reform initiatives. In the second half of the 1990s, however, there are also signs that this group of countries is attempting to increase UNDP's bilateralization. Indicators of this tendency are the increase in earmarked financial resources (trust funds and cost-sharing resources), which often serve the purpose of enabling UNDP to be used de facto as the implementing organization for smaller bilateral donors. This policy is reflected conceptually, for example, in the Danish document on *active multilateralism* (*Plan of Action for Active Multilateralism*) (Danida 1996a, 1996b), which concerns action deliberately taken to influence UNDP and other agencies. These bilateralization tendencies are increasingly eroding UNDP's multilateral approach.

6.2.2 Positions of the Programme Countries

The programme countries form a very heterogeneous group. Their common feature is that they qualify for UNDP operations. A common policy and attitude towards UNDP can be deduced from this to only a limited extent; a number of differences in fact determine their positions on UNDP. There are no joint declarations or documents revealing the main features of their policy towards UNDP. Nor, as a rule, do declarations of principle on the reform of the UN and on UN development cooperation contain separate comments on UNDP.[9] Clues to the position of the programme countries or individual groups of programme countries (Group of 77 and regional groups) on issues relating specifically to UNDP are to be found primarily in statements and opinions expressed in UNDP's Governing Council, or Executive Board.

Basic position on the tasks and role of UNDP

In general, the programme countries see UNDP as a particularly important institution in the area of development cooperation (Kalderén 1991, p. 327; Carlsson 1993, pp. 8 ff.). It is perceived as a neutral partner of the various governments that helps to formulate national priorities and put them into practice.[10] The programme countries see UNDP's strict orientation towards their interests and the favourable conditions attached to technical cooperation as particularly important features. They also have fairly extensive opportunities to participate at headquarters level through the Executive Board, where the principle of *one country, one vote* applies.

The contributions which the programme countries themselves make to the core resources, relatively small though they may be, are politically and symbolically very important; for this reason in particular UNDP has traditionally been seen by the developing countries as their programme. Another significant element is the network of UNDP country offices, which virtually all the programme countries want, even countries with a small programme volume and the transforming economies.

The substantive differences within the group of programme countries mainly concern the question of how far resources should be concentrated on given regions or groups of countries. The poorest countries, the more advanced countries and the transforming economies tend to differ on this question, each group pursuing its own particular interests.

Assessment of the current reform of UNDP

The reforms affecting UNDP in the 1990s are largely applauded by the programme countries. This is especially true of the measures taken to adjust country programming and make it more flexible, the strengthening of the political supervisory mechanism in the shape of the Executive Board and the administrative reforms. Various government delegations have some practical difficulty because of the many meeting sessions of the Executive Board and the limited opportunities for the government administrations in the capitals to attend them; these problems are due to the fact that the UN missions are often overworked (and small) and travel funds are limited.

The vast majority of the programme countries see reform and adjustment efforts intended to result in greater emphasis on the setting of development priorities in resource utilization as one of the main problems. It is often stressed in this context in particular that UNDP must play a universal and neutral role, which means there must be no prescribed development strategies or conditions.[11] Some governments also emphasize in this connection that measures in favour of, say, civil society groups must accord with the ideas of the programme country's government;[12] in other words, the government must continue to be the cooperation partner.

Reforms that lead to an increase in the options open to the programme countries and in their influence on the distribution and utilization of financial resources and the implementation of operations are particularly appreciated. This is especially true of the growing responsibility the countries have during the national execution of UNDP operations.

Expectations of further reforms

There is a broad consensus among the programme countries on the need for reform with respect to the financial volume and the financing mechanisms. The absolute volume of resources available to UNDP is considered far too small. As the programme countries see it, the financing instruments do not permit canvassing for additional resources or more appropriate utilization to be achieved by means of a greater degree of stability and predictability. Particular importance is generally attached to the question of financial endowment.

A highly sceptical view is taken of the question of amalgamating UN funds and programmes (under the UNDP umbrella), with the majority rejecting the suggestion. It is feared that the integration of UN agencies would eventually result in the main contributors saving resources; leaner UN structures would then have to manage with less, at the expense of the programme countries.

Assessment

Generally speaking, the programme countries have shown far less interest in the current UNDP reform processes than the industrialized countries. In many cases the programme countries act as a brake on UNDP reform. This restraint or opposition to the reform process can be ascribed to various factors. For one thing, there is a (largely understandable) fear that the whole process of reforming the UN, and thus UNDP, is merely intended to save money. An example quoted by many countries is the transformation of the Governing Council into an Executive Board. The hope (unfulfilled) here was that, if efficiency could be increased at this level, additional financial resources might be made available by the main contributing countries. In addition, various reforms have been launched with the goal of increasing UNDP's effectiveness in the development field. This in turn means that the utilization of UNDP resources, to which de facto no conditions were attached in the past, must increasingly comply with development criteria and prescriptions. As a general rule, the governments of the programme countries have no interest in seeing this happen.

The reforms of UNDP and UN development cooperation as a whole are viewed by many developing countries in the context of the overall reform of the UN. It is feared that isolated reforms of UNDP or UN development cooperation will eventually result in the weakening of the

UN's development pillar and in too little account being taken of the South in the various UN bodies (especially the Security Council). Against this background many would like to see an overall reform package for the UN.

6.2.3 Positions of the UN and UN System

Basic positions, interests and assessments of the reform of UNDP

A uniform position on the UNDP reform debate cannot be identified among the various agencies of the UN system, or UN. A distinction can be made between four important groups or lobbies in this debate.

The first group consists of the specialized agencies (especially the FAO, ILO, UNESCO, UNIDO and WHO) belonging to the UN system. These organizations have a special association with UNDP in two ways: on the one hand, they act as its implementing organizations and are particularly affected by the substantial increase in operations which they no longer implement because of national execution; on the other hand, despite their originally normative mandate (i.e. no primary tasks in the operational sphere), the specialized agencies have been able to attract TC funds over the years (Carlsson 1993, pp. 10 f.; Kalderén 1991). The funds made directly available to the specialized agencies would probably be reduced in line with UNDP's success in expanding its central financing function. These agencies therefore have a major interest in preventing reforms that further reduce their implementing role or lead to any centralization of resources in UNDP's hands at the expense of their own budgetary positions.

The second group comprises the UN funds and programmes other than UNDP. They are clearly interested - firstly - in resisting, wherever possible, any move to bring the agencies closer together (joint programme documents, concepts of integrated representation at country level, etc.) or even to amalgamate them and - secondly -in denying UNDP any particular right to act as coordinator.[13] A policy of this nature became apparent especially during the evolution of

Secretary-General Kofi Annan's reform package and the work of Maurice Strong's reform commission, when UNICEF Director-General Carol Bellamy, among others, succeeded in preventing any closer integration of the UN agencies.[14]

Thirdly, the UN Secretary-Generals have tried to play a mediating role among the various UN positions and interests. The efforts of Boutros Boutros-Ghali and especially Kofi Annan, however, clearly reveal a tendency in Secretaries-General to strengthen UNDP's role. This was evident, for example, from the proposals originally (i.e. before the intensive consultation process) put forward by the group of reform experts set up in 1996 by the Secretary-General and headed by Maurice Strong, which went well beyond the reform package eventually submitted in 1997 (Zumach 1997; Martens 1997). The Secretary-General's 1994 report on an Agenda for Development had also pointed to the need to overcome institutional fragmentation, while referring to the member states' responsibility for ensuring this happened and for bringing about appropriate decisions.[15] Furthermore, various overarching tasks (especially the office of Special Coordinator for Economic and Social Development and that of convenor of the Executive Committee of the United Nations Development Group) have been assigned to the Administrator by Secretaries-General Boutros Boutros-Ghali and Kofi Annan.

Fourthly, UNDP's position and interests are characterized mainly by a pragmatic approach to identifying within UN development cooperation and international development cooperation as a whole a task that has a fixed place and is adequately endorsed by the UN member states. To achieve this objective, UNDP has launched and implemented a reform-oriented policy in the 1990s that attempts to reconcile the various interests. Within this framework UNDP is seeking a moderate leading role for UN development cooperation, as the UNDP Administrator's 1996 reform document shows (Speth 1996). A particularly important goal is a thorough reform of the internal structures and procedures (especially in the form of thc UNDP 2001 project). The Administrator also emphasizes the need for UNDP to have a growth strategy; in other words, an increase in UNDP resources has a high priority. The deficiencies of the existing financing system also play something of a role in this context. UNDP is generally seeking to identify a new and promising niche in UN and overall international development cooperation without wishing to exclude or abandon any functions or tasks (in implementation, central funding role, etc.).

Assessment

The positions of the various actors within the UN and the UN system on UNDP are largely determined by the established structures and a policy geared to safeguarding interests. Where structure-changing approaches are developed (as in the case of the original ideas of the Strong reform group), reform efforts are neutralized and diluted by the necessary consultation processes. This policy is encouraged by the fact that appointments to the highest posts and management levels of all the agencies are largely determined by a personnel policy that attaches considerable importance to the interests of the UN member states. There is therefore no chance of the UN being able to adopt and enforce from within a clear position on reform that helps to eliminate the current shortcomings.

6.3 Conclusions

The analysis of the positions of leading actors on UNDP and its reform process shows that the very heterogeneous interests, the unclear policies and the absence of conceptual ideas on the part of many of those concerned are serious obstacles to further progress. Although success has been achieved in the 1990s where various aspects of the reforms are concerned (EU and G7 initiatives, the programme countries' approval of certain development quality standards, etc.), simple solutions cannot to be found to the remaining problems, but at least some openings for political debates and solutions can be identified:

- Both the industrialized and the programme countries need to make up their minds on what they expect and require of UNDP. In the 1990s it has become clear that, unless it has a profiled and widely accepted mission, UNDP will lack an adequate base for successful and effective operation. The main contributors must be clear about the activities that are desirable and necessary for development; the programme countries too must define a range of expectations, which should also include development standards.

- UNDP's Executive Board and the main UN organs must be prepared to lay the legislative foundations for the reforms this is bound to entail. The UN can neither accomplish this step on its own politically, nor does it have the necessary mandate to do so.

- The financing issue is a crucial aspect of UNDP's reform. It may be a key to a significant stimulation of the programme countries' commitment to reform. At the same time, efforts to increase UNDP's effectiveness are worthwhile only if it is apparent which actors are prepared to ensure adequate financing and to what extent. To clarify the questions associated with this (financing concept, necessary volume of resources, etc.), it is vital that all the actors concerned take decisions that can be relied on.

As regards the profile of a more effective UNDP developed in section III.5, it is also possible to indicate the likelihood of the elements proposed in this context being approved or rejected:

- Further specification of the substantive tasks is far more commensurate with the main contributors' ideas than the programme countries'. Developing countries and transforming economies are likely to be particularly opposed to the concentration of tasks on substantive political issues (good governance). It is doubtful, on the other hand, that the major bilateral donor countries are sufficiently prepared to make the coordination of development cooperation by the programme countries a priority task for UNDP.

- The various UN agencies whose activities would be coordinated are particularly opposed to a stronger coordinating role for UNDP at headquarters and country level and to an integrated programming document; besides this, UN development cooperation that is more focused as a result of coordination is not automatically in the programme countries' political interests, since they would then have less room for manoeuvre under the project and programme policy.

- The various UN funds and programmes and possibly certain government departments in the capitals that would lose autonomy and influence are likely to have reservations about an increase in political guidance (Executive Board).
- In some respects the further development of TC approaches is greeted with a lack of enthusiasm by industrialized countries, some of which recognize the danger of a decline in the quality of development (e.g. where it is felt that too much emphasis is being placed on the role of the programme countries, despite their weak and inadequate capacities). The increase in national execution is particularly opposed by the traditional implementing organizations.
- Graduation mechanisms are rejected or at least questioned by the programme countries, which would have to pay the price for such changes; the right to universality is particularly emphasized in this context.
- Country programming with more development conditions attached is fundamentally inconsistent with the position of the programme countries, which stress the principle of neutrality in this context.
- In the question of financial endowment, and especially of the financing mechanisms, most of the larger industrialized countries take a negative view. The main advocates of change in this area are the Scandinavian countries among the industrialized nations, the programme countries and UNDP.

On the whole, the positions adopted by the various actors show that they share a number of common assessments (especially the positive view they take of past reforms) and disagree on various basic issues. The member states have not yet shown sufficient political will to negotiate on the most important contentious issues and seek solutions.

7 Options and Scenarios for the Future Development of UNDP

7.1 Introduction

This chapter outlines and discusses possible options and scenarios for the future development of UNDP. The aim is less to make statements on the probability of certain developments, given the major uncertainties attached to forecasts. More important are the factors and conditions which are relevant in this context and outlines of the form in which UNDP might in principle take on substantive tasks and functions in international development cooperation and the implications this would have.

The first part of the chapter begins by considering premises on relevant environmental factors and then discusses five scenarios of UNDP development.

7.2 Premises on the Future Development of UNDP

A wide range of factors influence UNDP and the process of change that is taking place. It is therefore difficult to make statements on UNDP, its role, tasks and significance in the future. UNDP's environment has also been more difficult to assess and less stable in the 1990s than in previous decades. Its further development is likely to depend primarily on (1) the basic prospects for development cooperation as a whole, (2) the role and endowment of multilateral development cooperation, (3) the reform of the United Nations as a whole and (4) UNDP's reform policy. A brief assessment in the form of premises will first be made of these aspects, with tendencies indicated, so that the area in which UNDP operates may be defined.

Future of development cooperation as a whole

The question that first arises is whether development cooperation in the form in which it has existed - albeit with changes - for the past 30 - 40 years will be retained as a separate policy. Although the fundamental criticisms voiced in the past have often increased the pressure for justification of development cooperation, they have so far failed to bring it to a sudden end or change it abruptly. The view taken in this study is that development cooperation will be retained as a policy for the foreseeable future, although major adjustments appear necessary and possible. Despite the current budget problems in the traditional donor countries,[1] which are probably continuing to grow, development cooperation is likely to be used as a major instrument for influencing global challenges.

A more intensive debate on burden-sharing, i.e. increased financial commitments by the successful economies of Asia to development, is conceivable in this context. Other changes to development cooperation might consist in a further shift away from specific interventions in the form of projects and programmes and towards the promotion of certain policies and reforms (e.g. the concept of sector investment programmes), in greater emphasis being placed on the further graduation of assisted countries, together with regional concentration, and in an increase in substantive focusing on issues of particular transfrontier interest (global public goods, such as the environment, peace/war and migration).

Future of multilateral development cooperation

What role multilateral development cooperation should and will play in the future is a question of considerable importance (and one that is directly linked to the prospects for development cooperation as a whole). In general, it can be said that in the mid-1990s multilateral development cooperation came under greater pressure than that already being exerted on bilateral development (OECD 1997a, pp. 104 f.). This is likely to have been mainly due to bilateral development cooperation being more closely geared to national interests or possibly subordinated to them (e.g. because of the effects it is hoped tied aid will have on employment), the greater ease with which the parliament and public in the donor countries can be persuaded to endorse bilateral relations and the assumption by many donor governments that multilateral development cooperation is less efficient and effective. In these circumstances donor governments and parliaments are likely to reduce contributions to multilateral development cooperation disproportionately if budget problems or problems gaining political acceptance arise in the future.

Against this background it has to be asked how political and financial support for the various multilateral agencies will turn out in the future. Any answer to this question is bound to have major uncertainties attached. It can be assumed, however, that the following tendencies will be discernible or become more pronounced in the next 5 - 10 years. The international development banks - and especially the World Bank - will be able to hold their own as multilateral institutions. The main reason for this is that the leading contributors have particular confidence in them (not least because of the greater influence they can wield); the donor governments are accordingly committed to reforms. Another probable reason is that the financial commitments are longer-term than in the case of voluntary contributions to the UN's operational development activities, making a gradual withdrawal from the development banks difficult.

The prospects as regards the separation or combination of multilateral financial cooperation and technical cooperation are uncertain. Although fundamental thinking on development argues for an integrated and coherent approach (within the framework of sector investment programmes, for example), capacity-building requires a high degree of specialization, which may be impossible to achieve if investment measures are implemented or credits are allocated at the same time. Experience shows that TC activities play no more than a subordinate role when investment projects are simultaneously being implemented. The World Bank is endeavouring in this context to expand its TC activities and all its available know-how. Consequently, UN development cooperation is in growing danger of being displaced. In general, the relationship between FC and TC is likely to shift in TC's favour in the medium term.[2]

A possible variant for UN development cooperation in particular, and one to which contributing countries might increasingly resort, is *bilateralization* (by means of, say, an increase in trust funds). One element of uncertainty is whether the EU can increase its importance in development cooperation in the medium to long term. The main losers if the scale of the EU's development cooperation grew would probably be other multilateral development cooperation institutions rather than the EU Member States' bilateral development cooperation.

Reform of the United Nations

One of the main questions to be considered in this context is whether and, if so, in what form, at what speed and on what scale the United Nations or individual areas or organs of the UN can be reformed. There is currently no sign of a majority, let alone all, of the member countries agreeing to a more thorough reform of the whole UN. The history of and debate on the reform of the UN show that concepts of comprehensive and radical reform have little chance of being implemented. The only steps possible so far have been taken within the existing structures. In the question of the reform of the UN as a whole the financial dimension may be crucially important if the leading contributors forge a link between financial conduct and reforms. There is likely to be the greatest scope for practical and limited reforms concerning individual UN agencies.

Reform of UNDP

UNDP itself is also a decisive factor that can and does influence the environment and the process of change. The extent to which UNDP is able to pursue or continue pursuing an active reform policy and develops a profile which UN member states endorse and also regard as relevant is important in this context. Besides other political considerations (staffing interests, etc.), greater emphasis will be placed in the future on questions of effectiveness in the development field, efficiency and UNDP's particular advantages. The main contributing countries are therefore likely to step up their search for options that are clearly defined and offer significant benefits (specific forms of financing for global problems in the form of, say, the Global Environmental Facility).

7.3 Scenarios

In principle, very different scenarios of change to UNDP are conceivable and possible over a medium- to long-term time horizon (about 5 - 12 years). The scenarios and the form they eventually take very much depend on the environment (and thus especially the factors discussed above).

The first four scenarios developed here are based on the proposition that the UN will continue to be active in the field of development cooperation in the medium and long term and that the donor countries will continue to use multilateral institutions to a significant degree. The third scenario, however, assumes that UNDP will be transformed into an agency that performs tasks for bilateral donors. The fifth scenario assumes a process of disengagement by the leading contributing countries.

Scenario 1: Substantive focusing

The first scenario assumes that UNDP abandons functional tasks and service functions for the UN and UN system and instead develops into an agency with what is primarily a substantive mandate. This change would remove the most important qualifying difference between UNDP and the other UN funds and programmes (which derive their legitimacy from mandates relating to specific sectors or target groups).

With this thematic focusing of UNDP's purpose, two variants in particular might be considered:

- In the first variant capacity-building in general would be UNDP's purpose. The emphasis would then be on general tasks at national level or *"macro-political" aspects*.[3] At conceptual level UNDP's profile would thus be relatively broad.[4] With its tasks thus defined, UNDP would have the substantive capacity to look into a wide range of problems facing the programme countries. On the other hand, there would be a danger of capacity-building without a specific substantive mandate leading to expenditure being spread too thin (UNDP as a *jack-of-all-trades*) (Danida 1991c, p. 45).

  Substantively, this variant would probably come closest to fulfilling the programme countries' expectations, since extreme thematic focusing would not *a priori* be associated with this approach (i.e. capacity-building without a specific and predetermined objective). This definition of tasks would hardly gain the political and financial support of the main contributing countries, because it is more difficult to outline a clear objective.

- The second variant would be to place the emphasis on and attend to a matter of specific concern (advocacy functions). With the increase in the focus on global public goods on the one hand and the existing specialized institutions of international development cooperation (within the UN and beyond) on the other, these would probably be tasks with a specifically political orientation in the areas of good governance, democratization, human rights, crisis prevention and the consolidation of peace.

  Such substantive focusing would fill the present gap in the tasks of international and even bilateral agencies in the areas referred to. It would not, however, accord particularly with the wishes of the governments of many programme countries, which want to see UNDP playing as open or at least neutral a role as possible and do not regard specifically political tasks as an appropriate sphere of activity. It is impossible to say precisely how far donor countries would endorse and advocate such concentration. It is likely that the main contributing countries would, on the one hand, regard the issues as important or, on the other hand, see it as particularly difficult for bilateral development cooperation to cope with them appropriately (not least because of foreign policy and foreign trade considerations in bilateral relations, etc.); it can therefore be assumed that most of the main contributing countries would be fairly receptive to such focusing.

All the variants of focusing on substantive issues would have far-reaching consequences for UNDP and UN development cooperation as a whole. UNDP could no longer justify its present size as an organization and employer and would have to be adapted to the tasks assigned to it and so probably reduced in size considerably. At the same time other agencies would have to provide, or endeavour to provide, UNDP's overarching services: the coordinating tasks that need to be performed at headquarters level and at the country offices, especially through the Resident Coordinator system, which is operated and financed primarily by UNDP. This would mean that certain core problems due to the weakness of UNDP's coordination would not be solved by a redefinition of tasks with a substantive orientation, but merely passed on to other UN agencies (such as the UN Secretariat).[5]

Scenario 2: Functional focusing

A second scenario assumes that UNDP places the emphasis on its service functions for the UN's and UN system's development cooperation and no longer propagates and promotes specific substantive concerns. The goal would be to perform coordinating and guiding tasks at country and headquarters level as independently as possible. UNDP would play the role of an honest broker; this would presuppose greater responsibility and improved enforcement instruments for the Resident Coordinator system and overall responsibility for the UN's development cooperation and also for the technical cooperation activities of the whole UN system.

The particular advantage of this option is that it enables a more purposeful approach to be adopted to tackling and overcoming the coordination problem and related shortcomings of UN development cooperation. The main difference from the present system and UNDP's tasks would be that UNDP's role would be concentrated on UN-wide tasks. It would be able to play a more neutral role, since it would no longer be responsible for its own country programmes, the acquisition of funds, etc. This might alleviate potential conflicts of objectives (caused, for example, by the Resident Representative's or Resident Coordinator's dual role), because UNDP would be able to act more independently.

It is questionable, however, whether a UNDP limited to functional tasks would actually be able to solve the current problems satisfactorily. Its success as a coordinator should be linked to effective mechanisms for exercising influence. However, it can hardly exercise enough influence unless it is able to deploy significant financial resources, to wield decision-making powers and/or to make specialized know-how available. Furthermore, in view of the dimensions of UN development cooperation there is little justification in establishing an institution specifically for coordination matters - alongside the existing organs (especially the General Assembly, ECOSOC, the Secretariat and associated structures); in other words, the functional tasks would in this case tend to resemble those of the UN Secretariat's Department of Economic and Social Affairs.[6] UNDP's concentration on functional tasks would also result in its substantive tasks having to be transferred to an existing or new agency. The specific concerns (good governance, etc.) would then have to be transferred to another or a new UN agency.

Scenario 3: UNDP as a contractor for bilateral donors and other agencies

In a third scenario UNDP might increasingly provide services relating to the management and implementation of development cooperation measures for bilateral donors and other clients (development banks, programme countries, etc.). This scenario presupposes a growing interest in providing UNDP with earmarked financial resources in the form of trust funds and the like.

The advantage of this option might be that resources for earmarked measures are more easily acquired than for the existing core programme. A purposeful strategy and additional efforts to achieve greater flexibility (range of services, etc.) might even make further growth possible. The potential donors in this context are primarily small and medium-sized traditional donor countries and perhaps new donor countries with little or no experience in the development cooperation field which either have limited project management and implementation capacities or prefer certain development cooperation measures to be a multilateral responsibility.

The main disadvantage of this option is that it would *bilateralize* UNDP, i.e. UNDP would provide services particularly for bilateral donors without being able to introduce and exploit its own advantages as a multilateral donor. This scenario is not therefore viable as a conceptual basis and would hardly be endorsed by the traditional major donor countries. The programme countries in particular would be unlikely to accept this focused development of UNDP, since their opportunities for participating would be much reduced. It is an option, moreover, that would be bound to lead to a significant duplication of tasks with the United Nations Office for Project Services.

Scenario 4: Sharpening the substantive profile and strengthening the development services

The fourth scenario assumes that the UNDP reform process already launched will be continued and stepped up on the basis of efforts relating to substantive shaping and to UN services. It also assumes that major obstacles now standing in the way of reforms can be overcome if the following steps are taken (section III.5):

- further substantive focusing on a few, particularly important development issues (good governance, crisis prevention and the consolidation of peace; follow-up to the UN world conferences, coordination of development cooperation by the programme countries);

- amalgamation of UN funds and programmes under the UNDP umbrella;
- increased coordination of the UN system's technical cooperation under UNDP's leadership;
- improved political guidance;
- improvement in the quality of development and in the orientation of operations;
- increase in financial resources on a reliable basis.

This scenario also presupposes broad political support for the reform process from the UN member states (main contributing and programme countries), which is essential for successful adjustment and not least the financial endowment that is needed.

Under these conditions various implications can be assumed. The most important assumed outcome would be UNDP's performance of more effective development work, from which both the programme countries and the main contributing countries might derive greater benefit.

For the programme countries (taking account not only of the government in power but also of civil society and the private sector) the greatest advantages would be that the substantive focus areas would result in the purposeful promotion of sectors that are of the utmost importance for the political structures and effectiveness of the various countries. UNDP's work on political issues and structures would thus be an important pillar of development, complementing efforts in other areas (creation of economically more effective, ecologically more viable and socially more balanced structures and mechanisms). Of particular relevance in this context are efforts to assist the programme countries to improve the integration of external development cooperation activities into a coherent overall strategy (coordination of development cooperation). In addition, simplified and more effective structures for UN development cooperation - at country and headquarters level - are one of the main requirements, especially for the programme countries, if the coordination of external and internal services is to be improved and national administrative structures for the management of development cooperation are to be limited. It is also in the specific interests of the programme countries for UNDP to achieve an adequate and more reliable financial endowment by becoming more effective.

For the main contributing countries (and possibly the emerging donors) there is a serious need for progress to be made in overcoming obstacles that are to blame for losses of effectiveness and efficiency in development cooperation. There is also a growing interest in bringing influence to bear more specifically on such global interdependent problems as crises and conflicts, causes of flight, etc. within the framework of development cooperation. Substantive focusing on aspects of strategic policy therefore fills a gap that bi- and multilateral donor institutions have not been able to fill adequately and effectively in the past. An attempt is also being made to link these issues to non-operational debates on UN policy, which might enlarge development cooperation's currently limited area of influence. The major donor countries in particular believe the UN and the whole of development cooperation have problems because of fragmented and inadequately coordinated development cooperation structures. It should therefore be very much in the interests of the main contributing countries for the integration of UN agencies under the UNDP umbrella to be stepped up and for donor coordination at country level to be improved. Other challenges to which a satisfactory response has yet to be found would be coordination and cooperation with the international or regional development banks, the European Union's development cooperation activities and the bilateral donors.

Scenario 5: Disengagement of the main contributors

The fifth and final scenario proceeds from the assumption that the most important contributing countries reduce their political and financial commitment to UNDP and there are no other options for financing its activities. It also assumes that a successful UNDP reform policy is not rewarded or is ignored by most industrialized countries because, for example, budgetary factors or political preference for bilateral development cooperation or other multilateral institutions lead to disengagement.

The main contributing countries might regard a reduction in their commitment or even its termination as having the (supposed) advantage of either easing the burden on their own national budget as a result of appropriate savings or giving them a choice of options in development cooperation that promise greater benefits. Greater benefits might be sought, in the donor countries' view, with one of two possible variants:

- increased bilateral cooperation, giving them the greatest direct influence on their own development cooperation activities (e.g. in procurement issues or the choice of countries to assist and focus areas);
- the maintenance of or increase in contributions to multilateral institutions that give the donor countries greater opportunities to exercise influence and dominate the decision-making process (e.g. through voting rights linked to contributions).

Disengagement by the leading contributors at UNDP's expense would, however, give rise to substantial development costs in that important activities and tasks would be lost:

- in the programme countries there would be no mechanisms for the coordination of development cooperation as a whole, and especially the UN's activities;
- at country level the governments and civil society groups would no longer have an organization that has often been an important interlocutor;
- at headquarters level the potential for coordinating UN development cooperation and the UN system's TC would be badly weakened;
- not enough notice would be taken of aspects of the utmost importance to development which are not, or not adequately, covered by

other multilateral agencies - or by bilateral donors; this is particularly true of politically sensitive matters and macro-political issues;

- UNDP's innovative approaches in development (e.g. national execution, NaTCAP), which have emerged mainly because UNDP is firmly established in the programme countries, would no longer be available on the same scale;
- an important forum in the operational sphere of development, which gives the programme countries a large share of the responsibility through participation on an equal footing, would be lost.

7.4 Conclusions

The environment for the further development of UN development cooperation and of UNDP has been unfavourable in the 1990s. The basic debates on the justification and effectiveness of development cooperation have coincided with major budgetary difficulties in many of the donor countries; there are also specific reservations about the performance of the UN and UNDP.

Despite the difficulty of the current environment, a (partial) withdrawal by member states from UNDP would be inappropriate and counterproductive in development terms. This is all the truer as UNDP's situation in the 1990s is characterized not by the mere preservation of the status quo but by various changes and reforms for the better. The scenarios considered above show that it is plausible and worthwhile for all the governments concerned to remain committed to UNDP. A withdrawal (Scenario 5) would have obvious and directly adverse consequences for the programme countries; but for the main contributing countries too substantial (development) costs would be associated with disengagement.

The discussion of the scenarios presented also shows that most factors argue for the further development of UNDP along the lines of the fourth scenario or the profile of an effective UNDP considered in section III.5. Total concentration on substantive issues would not be a viable solution for UN development cooperation as a whole or for UNDP's real tasks; mere functional focusing would also be impracticable and hardly likely to succeed. As a contractor and manager of bilateral development cooperation resources (Scenario 3), UNDP would lose its multilateral character and thus its special features and advantages.

Although the arguments presented indicate the wisdom of the further development of UNDP along the lines of Scenario 4 and the restructuring that has begun in the 1990s, some of the elementary requirements for this option or strategy to be adequately and effectively pursued have yet to be satisfied. This is particularly true of measures to overcome some of the principal obstacles to reforms and the main contributors' and programme countries' lack of political will to give the approach to reform that has been adopted their full support. Despite a largely successful approach to and process of reform, there would appear to be every chance in the second half of the 1990s of the UN member states denying their political and financial support because of short-term interests (e.g. preference for bilateral channels because of economic self-interest, budgetary problems, the UN's public image). A delinking of capacity for reform and success in this sphere on the one hand and the donor countries' political and financial commitment on the other can be detected here.

Part IV Conclusions

1 Introduction

Conclusions on the objectives pursued and questions raised by the study are drawn in this chapter on the basis of the theoretical and conceptual discussions in sections II.1 and II.2 and the empirical findings on UN development cooperation and, above all, the reform and effectiveness of UNDP (sections III.1 to III.7). A particular aim in this context is to forge links between the findings of the various stages of the study.

2 Conclusions for the Debate on the Effectiveness of International Organizations

The debate on international organizations provided some pointers for the study of the effectiveness and reform of UNDP. While it does not offer a closed theory or conception that permits unequivocal answers to be given to the questions raised in the study, factors and levels that are, or may be, of relevance to the effectiveness of international organizations have been identified and systematized on the basis of various studies.

With the aid of the study of UN development cooperation and especially of UNDP it has been possible to show that the aspects of effectiveness which have emerged are useful at (a) conceptual level, (b) structural and policy level and (c) administration and implementation level. As analytical criteria, they have made an appropriate contribution at least to the framework of this study. It can be assumed that they might also indicate how the study of other international organizations might be structured and what analyses need to be undertaken.

Besides an analysis of transparent criteria for determining effectiveness, the question of the political weighting and appraisal of the actors is very important. The political evaluations in connection with the effectiveness and reform of UNDP show that a major and possibly decisive role is played by criteria and dimensions which have little or nothing to do with the organization's real tasks and purpose (e.g. the member states' thinking on foreign policy and staffing policy). In a study of effectiveness due account must therefore be taken not only of general criteria for the assessment of international organizations but also of the subjective or specific interests of the actors concerned. This must be seen as setting the most important limits to the analytical framework.

The structural problems connected with UN development cooperation show that considerable importance must be attached to the transparency of international organizations and the ability of their members to control them. The number of international organizations (plus insufficient responsibility for the overall system) may pose a problem for the ability to guide policy.[1] This deprives the member states of the opportunity to exercise sufficient influence and control. Owing to this lack of transparency and the members' inability to control international organizations the justification for the latter's very existence may be questioned. Institutional fragmentation may therefore trigger a crisis of legitimation for an organization.

UNDP and UN development cooperation as a whole are proof of the importance of an adequate capacity for adjustment and reform. In the long term at least this capacity is crucial for the survival of international organizations (even more so where the environment is undergoing sweeping changes and where international organizations are competing among themselves or with national organizations). Capacity for reform presupposes sufficient autonomy to be able to pursue and achieve reform objectives. The example of UNDP shows that an international organization's capacity for reform is, in the final analysis, the capacity of its members to achieve a consensus. The organization itself can create favourable conditions and, to a limited extent, initiate reforms inwardly, but its members take responsibility in decisive structural questions. An international organization's ability to undertake reforms is therefore directly dependent on the will of its members to undertake them.

3 Conclusions for the Debate on Technical Cooperation

The international debate on technical cooperation is very important in several respects. It raises questions of principle concerning development cooperation as a whole and the associated tasks and structural shortcomings. It also shows that there is extensive know-how on the relevant dimensions of TC. There is no shortage of analyses and designs for the reorganization of existing instruments and procedures. It is implementing the conclusions drawn that poses the most serious problems.

For this study the analysis of fundamental aspects of technical cooperation has provided some important pointers to and criteria for the assessment of UNDP's effectiveness in the development field. This has enabled specific features of UNDP to be placed in general categories.

In principle, the debate on development policy and the study of UNDP prove that technical cooperation performs a function of the utmost importance for development cooperation. TC must, however, concentrate on its real objectives far more than it has in the past: this means, above all else, the development and promotion of sustainable national capacities (capacity-building). Hence the need for a conscious strategy of making TC superfluous over a clearly defined period (phasing out or *aid to end aid*). If this objective is to be achieved, serious efforts need to be made to implement the conclusions that have been drawn. There is no reason and no justification in development terms for the very slow rate at which many development cooperation institutions take the findings of the debates into account in their activities. The causes may lie in other objectives (staffing interests that bilateral donors in particular may have, the donor's loss of direct influence over projects, etc.) and in interests in preserving the organizational structure of development cooperation.

Attention is increasingly turning to areas of technical cooperation that have a major impact on the political environment and good governance (democratic procedures and institutions, human rights, violent conflicts, civil society, etc.). These aspects are of strategic importance for development cooperation as a whole. Multilateral TC has several advantages where these tasks are concerned (owing to its universal structures, neutral approach, less self-interest).

To judge from the TC debate, UNDP's activities and profile are significant. UNDP began taking at least a conceptual interest in the shortcomings of TC as early as the 1970s. It can also point to successes and innovative instruments when it comes to practical implementation. The NaTCAP process was an attempt to use technical cooperation far more strategically and in a way geared far more closely to needs. National execution was developed into an important approach in the 1990s. As the programme countries wield considerable influence, a lack of ownership is not a feature of UNDP projects and programmes. The experience that UNDP has gained should therefore be taken up and discussed in far greater depth in the development debate.

The UNDP approach also shows, however, that development problems and new conflicts of objectives may well arise when the conclusions drawn in the TC debate are being implemented. There are, for example, difficulties in connection with quality standards and the orientation of development. A greater interest should also be taken in these conflicts in the conceptual debate. There are, however, no signs that fundamental doubts about the benefits of implementing the conclusions of the TC debate are justified.

It is principally due to the growing activities of the international development banks that the number of actors in the TC market is rising. In ideal circumstances increasing competition in the TC sector might lead to an improvement in quality and a reduction in costs, which would ultimately benefit the programme countries. The signs so far, however, tend to point to predatory competition, especially between the UN and the World Bank, with very few discernible advantages for the programme countries. Not least because of the poor results achieved with the World Bank's TC, the international TC debate should focus on the question whether and, if so, in what form it is still necessary for international development cooperation institutions to specialize in either financial or technical cooperation. The findings of this study indicate that such specialization is needed, since one of the main problems is that the complexity of TC tasks is underestimated. As the environment is changing so radically (the relative growth in the importance of TC being an example), there should also be a general debate on the division of labour among the development cooperation or technical cooperation institutions (relationship among the UN funds and programmes, the UN's specialized agencies, the international development banks and the EU; relationship between bi- and multilateral institutions in TC).

On the whole, it would be advisable to take a close interest in and develop further fundamental aspects of the TC debate and aspects relating to implementation. The DAC's Network on Technical Cooperation Effectiveness is an important forum for the international exchange of experience. It should be joined by a development institution to spur on the TC debate and take responsibility for it. In principle, UNDP is a suitable candidate for the task of stimulating the TC debate as a think tank and accelerating the process of implementing the conclusions drawn. It would also be very fruitful for the development debate if UNDP could play an avant-garde role in technical cooperation. To perform this task, UNDP would, however, have to make considerable efforts to expand its expertise.

4 Conclusions for the Reform and Effectiveness of UNDP and UN Development Cooperation

This study has been able to give differentiated and unequivocal answers to the initial questions concerning the UN and UNDP. It has also been able to examine aspects or raise questions that are of interest and relevance to the development debate, international relations and UN policy as a whole.

The analysis of the shortcomings in UN development cooperation as a whole has revealed a continuing need for reform. Although the debate has revived in the 1990s and efforts to reform the UN and its development cooperation have increased (Kofi Annan's reform package, the EU initiative, etc.), it is to be feared that, despite positive individual measures and the progress made towards solving some problems (UN Houses, United Nations Development Group, etc.), it has so far proved impossible to find or create an adequate basis for sustainably effective UN development cooperation. There is as yet no indication that the core problems of institutional fragmentation and financing might be satisfactorily and appropriately solved. Even if the constructive reform package put forward by Kofi Annan in 1997 was feasible in every respect and the General Assembly could take appropriate decisions, many of the deficiencies of UN development cooperation would remain or would be dealt with less than optimally. The very wide range of interests of the actors involved continues to prevent any rapprochement on decisive questions of principle with respect to UN development cooperation. The UN member states are primarily to blame for the continuing absence of a consensus on important reforms and for what is often no more than a limited commitment to reforms (*UN-bashing*, etc.).

Many areas of UNDP too are in clear need of reform. In many respects this is directly related to the weaknesses of all operational UN activities, since UNDP has not succeeded in the past in performing its coordination and guidance tasks adequately. One significant structural fault lies in the transfer of a wide variety of tasks to UNDP and its general responsibility, even though it has not been equipped with appropriate enforcement instruments and is not given sufficient political support in the performance of its tasks.

Besides UNDP's weaknesses, greater importance should be attached to its strengths with respect to the general development debate and the exchange of experience. Conceptually and in practical operational work UNDP has much to offer in the way of important approaches, experience and potential (round tables, national execution, ownership, NaTCAP, etc.).

In many respects the UNDP of the second half of the 1990s has little in common with the UNDP of about ten years ago. The mere fact that the majority of programme countries now take responsibility for a decisive proportion of implementing activities (national execution), that UNDP has lost its own operational unit (OPS), that the financing structure of core and non-core resources has changed fundamentally and that the *Human Development Report* has succeeded in changing UNDP's image in the eyes of those members of the public in many donor countries who take an interest in development is proof of a significant process of change.

The new situation reflects the wide-ranging and intensive efforts to bring about reforms and the sweeping changes in the environment (the attitude of the programme and main contributing countries towards financing, etc.). The change that is occurring is gradual, not a single event at one point in time. Since the first half of the 1990s UNDP has begun to undergo a process of conscious and intensive reform. This has been joined by a number of general UN reforms which have had an impact on UNDP. By and large, the reforms can be applauded, because they have pointed in the right direction. The successes achieved so far, however, have not been sufficiently noted and rewarded (especially by the main contributing countries). The reform process is by no means complete: it must be stepped up, become more dynamic and take in areas that have hitherto been neglected.

In the late 1990s UNDP is, on the whole, a qualitatively more effective actor than it was only a few years ago. The importance attached to it and the way it is perceived in the development debate have improved. It is now frequently identified, for example, with the concept of sustainable human development, and the 20/20 target was partly its doing. In terms of financial resources and thus opportunities for achieving and changing something at country level, however, UNDP's influence has declined substantially.

The actors (i.e. the programme and main contributing countries and UNDP, or the UN) largely take a positive view of the changes that have occurred in connection with UNDP. There is a danger nonetheless of UNDP's significance waning further in the future. The environment has changed since the 1980s and early 1990s, when UNDP had not an extensive financial base but at least greater stability with which to take action. A highly realistic scenario today is one which is in principle based on a successful approach to and process of reform, but also, paradoxically, on a dwindling commitment by the main contributors. This dilemma must be seen as one of the main problems facing UNDP in the late 1990s.

The dilemma shows how inconsistent multilateral principles (e.g. equal political influence to be exercised by the programme and main contributing countries) and enforceable mechanisms and structures of international organizations (or, specifically, UNDP) are in practice.

If this dilemma facing UNDP is to be overcome in the future, various requirements will need to be satisfied. Two aspects in particular are important in this context:

- The UN member states must state clearly how they believe UNDP (and UN development cooperation in general) should change and with what instruments. The political decisions have yet to be taken and the political mandates issued for adequate reform orientation and for structural changes. In the past the major industrialized countries have shown little commitment to UNDP; the like-minded countries have also contributed to manifestations of disintegration through micro-management and specific interests (e.g. in the form of trust funds). The positions formulated by the governments of the developing countries are characterized by excessively rigid fixation on questions of financial volume and too little willingness to incorporate standards to safeguard and monitor the quality of development.

  The country groupings within the UN and the individual member states often have no clear idea of what they expect of UNDP and UN development cooperation. The question that therefore arises is how and how far the various UN member states are prepared to support a reform process and to reward successful reforms; this concerns financial commitment as much as political support. Many member states have yet to give basic answers to these questions. The UN member states' clearly articulated desire for reforms, followed by an appropriate commitment to reforms, is also essential.

- UNDP must be able to make it even clearer what purpose it serves. It offers many important points of departure and much potential for development of which greater advantage should and could be taken in the interests of the programme countries and main contributors. If a UNDP that is more effective in the development field is to be created, past efforts must therefore be joined by reforms that follow on from the reform process of the 1990s and the overall reform of UN development cooperation. It is neither appropriate nor necessary to invent a completely new UNDP or to discover new niches: the existing approaches and the requirements emerging from the UN tasks and the development debate must be integrated into a coherent strategy.

A UNDP reform strategy should focus on three elements: (1) substantive tasks, (2) functional tasks and services for UN development cooperation as a whole and (3) elements for creating the substantive and functional profile and ensuring high-quality development.

– Proceeding from the two concepts of sustainable human development and capacity-building, UNDP might form three substantive focus areas:

  Firstly, good governance, crisis prevention and the consolidation of peace should be developed to become the most important substantive issue. This package of tasks is not only extremely important in development terms: UNDP also has special legitimacy in these areas as a UN agency; there are, moreover, links to other UN agencies (e.g. the UN High Commissioner for Human Rights) and excellent preconditions owing, among other things, to the network of country offices.

  Secondly, UNDP should help to ensure that the conclusions drawn at the UN world conferences in the 1990s are implemented effectively and efficiently; to this end, it should provide for systematic follow-up (i.e. implementation of the conclusions through purposeful capacity-building) at international and especially national level.

  Thirdly, the aim should be the most extensive possible coordination and effective management of development cooperation by the programme countries themselves; UNDP can make purposeful contributions to the development of suitable capacities.

- The emphasis in functional tasks and services for the UN is on three aspects:

  Firstly, the institutional structure of UN development cooperation and UNDP's position at headquarters level should change. Above all, it would be advisable for most UN funds and programmes (and other TC funds of the UN system) to be combined under the UNDP umbrella. It would also be appropriate for UNDP to be equipped with effective decision-making powers for its coordination tasks (especially in the United Nations Development Group).

  Secondly, the reform of the Resident Coordinator system should be stepped up and activities that make it difficult for the Resident Coordinator to undertake neutral activities (such as fund-raising specifically for UNDP) should be excluded.

  Thirdly, a single country-related programming document for UN development cooperation based on the United Nations Development Assistance Framework should be submitted as a general rule.

- In the case of the elements for creating the profile and ensuring high quality the aim should be a single Executive Board for all UN funds and programmes that is better able to take decisions, the further development of innovative TC approaches (national execution, NaTCAP, increased involvement of non-governmental actors, etc.), graduation mechanisms for the country-related differentiation of TC conditions, the expansion of development incentives in country programming and the linking of TC measures to non-operational UN policies. Adequate and reliable financing is also an essential element for reforms.

For the future of UNDP and of UN development cooperation as a whole it is crucially important that the actors concerned engage in an intensive dialogue on reforms. The UNDP profile that is the goal should be openly and thoroughly debated by the programme and main contributing countries. If adjustments are to be made to the member states' policy, the implications of inadequate reforms and of a UNDP that is further weakened must be taken into account and discussed:

- Where the programme countries are concerned, the cost of failing to sharpen the profile is especially important. In this respect it is likely to be possible for the benefits to the programme countries concerned in development terms to be significantly increased through clearer profiling, which is primarily in their interests. Unless sufficiently perceptible reforms occur, there is also a growing probability that the surreptitious or open withdrawal of the main contributing countries will continue and accelerate.
- The cost to the main contributing countries of a failure to sharpen the profile should also be openly discussed.[1] Short-term factors (supply or consultancy contracts, foreign policy considerations, etc.) can hardly play a part in this context. As regards long-term interests and global public goods, however, UNDP has considerable potential for making a constructive contribution to solving strategic problems in the programme countries (support for participatory and democracy-promoting mechanisms, civil conflict-resolving approaches, strengthening of development orientation, etc.).

  The effective and efficient use of development cooperation as a whole (its coordination by the programme countries, a coordinated UN approach, country offices that function well, etc.) should also be adequately covered during the deliberations. In the case of the functional tasks and services in particular other areas of activity might be added in the future: from the efficiency angle, for example, it would be conceivable and appropriate for the Resident Coordinator system to be able to perform functions for bilateral donors or the EU.

The question of financing may occupy a key place in the future debate on the reform of UNDP. UNDP financing is a contentious issue both among the main contributing countries (i.e. above all the like-minded countries on the one hand and the major donor countries, such as Germany and the USA, on the other) and between the programme countries and the majority of industrialized countries. If the current financing problems (absolute volume and mechanisms) prevent changes in the foreseeable future (the next 3 - 5 years), it is to be feared that the debates and reforms will hardly succeed because one of the decisive requirements will not be satisfied. Appropriate problem-solving approaches are therefore needed in this area. They should be differentiated and include both short-term and long-term strategies (section III.5). For the next few years, however, extensive and more reliable contributions from the traditional donor countries will be indispensable. This may also be a key and an incentive to reforms that have still to be undertaken. On the basis of the present level of contributions, additional contributions might be pledged for clearly defined reforms and for any successes achieved.

Other options for solving the financing problems will be essential in the future. In the medium and long term emerging donors should enter into more extensive commitments, new multilateral financing models (similar, for example, to the Global Environmental Facility) should be established, and innovative international financing instruments, such as the Tobin Tax, should be sought.

In view of the financing questions that have been raised, the present division of labour between development banks and UN agencies and the future tasks to be performed by development cooperation as a whole, the programme and donor countries should consider very carefully what the prospects and tasks of the various international development cooperation institutions could and should be. The surreptitious growth in the TC tasks assumed by the World Bank and the continuing erosion of the UN's TC are important issues in this context. A possible and appropriate model might be based on the transfer of resources for free-standing technical cooperation from the World Bank to UNDP. There are also a number of other open questions and questions of principle concerning the structures and tasks of future international development cooperation; they include the following:

- Should the UN and the development banks agree to take on certain substantive areas or approaches (e.g. "macro-political" issues for the UN, sectoral policies for the World Bank)?
- What role will the EU play in this context?

– Should bilateral development cooperation adapt to multilateral development cooperation or vice versa?

There are not yet enough fora or debates on these questions of principle.

The point of departure for all thinking on the reform of UN development cooperation must be the tasks and functions to be performed. Irrespective of the existing structures, an organizational scheme newly designed on the drawing board would require one umbrella for UN development cooperation. In the current or even new circumstances only UNDP or a similar institution can perform this function. UNDP (possibly with a different name) must or should therefore play a central role both in approaches to reform that are highly realistic (making changes within existing structures) and approaches that are characterized by utopian ideas (introducing completely new structures).

In principle, UNDP may be the most important key to the reform of the system of UN development cooperation and so to making it more effective in development terms. Given its overarching functions, it should be at the centre of changes to UN development cooperation.

It is appropriate and desirable for the international development debate and especially for practical work at country level that UNDP and UN development cooperation as a whole, with a better profile, should carry far more weight. A strengthened UNDP can make a decisive contribution to the application of multilateral principles, innovative approaches to development and more effective development cooperation.

Notes

Part I, Chapter 1

1 See, in particular, Nordic UN Project (1991b) and the more recent document Nordic UN Project (1996).

2 The discussion of principles and the criticism in the 1990s also concerns bilateral development cooperation, of course. "*Yet a chorus of criticism of foreign aid in general and multilateral aid in particular has escalated over the past ten to fifteen years.*" (Gwin / Williams (1996), p. 112)

3 In the report it published in 1997 on the current situation the DAC stated that the multilateral development organizations, which contribute almost 30% of all the aid provided by the DAC members, were under persistently heavy pressure to adjust in 1995. The report goes on to say that this pressure is likely to have been greater than at any other time in the 50-year history of these organizations. See OECD (1997a), pp. 104 f.

4 See, for example, Wapenhans, who makes the following assessment: "*Capacity for reform distinguishes the multilateral development banks from the United Nations in their favour.*" (Wapenhans (1996), p. 184)

5 Various people interviewed in connection with the study made explicit reference to this.

6 The group of "like-minded countries" is normally considered to comprise Denmark, Finland, the Netherlands, Norway, Sweden and, in some respects, Canada.

Part I, Chapter 2

1 concern efforts to focus substance, the implications of non-core resources and funding strategies (for further details see, in particular, sections III.2 and III.4). They do not, however, indicate any fundamentally new debates or reform efforts. The setting up of an "*open-ended, ad-hoc working group on the UNDP funding strategy* " (Decision 98/3) may be relevant to future reform efforts.

Part I, Chapter 3

1 See, for example, UIA (ed.) (1991).

2 See, for example, World Bank (1995b).

3 See, for example, E/1996/64 (*Progress report on the implementation of General Assembly Resolution 50/120*).

Part I, Chapter 4

1 See Glossary of Key Terms and Concepts in Development Cooperation in: OECD (1997a), pp. 175 ff.

2 See, in particular, the following: Wolfrum (1991 and 1995); Unser (1997); Simma (ed.) (1991); Ministry of Foreign Affairs and Trade (1996); Knipping / von Mangoldt / Rittberger (eds) (1995); UN (1996).

3 See UNDP (1997b), pp. 31-36, and, for more information, UNDP (1993a).

4 See, in particular, Articles 57, 63 and 64 of the UN Charter. Comments and explanations on the various articles of the UN Charter can be found in Simma (ed.) (1991).

5 The resulting structural problems are discussed in sections III.1 and III.2.

6 Chapter IX of the UN Charter is headed *"International economic and social co-operation"*.

7 See E/1996/64/Add. 2, p. 5; D'Orville (1984); Nordic UN Project (1990a), p. 1; Nordic UN Project (1996), pp. 16 ff.

8 See ODI (1997), p. 1. The UN funds and programmes referred to here sometimes perform humanitarian tasks that do not primarily have long-term development objectives.

9 See, for example, Renninger (1987), pp. 98 ff.; Trent (1995), pp. 494 ff.; Dicke (1995), pp. 1012 ff.; Martens (1989), pp. 26 f.; Unser (1997), pp. 343 ff. See also Bertrand (1993b), which makes various important substantive distinctions. For the term "reform" and various reform models (outside the UN debate) see also Haug (1997), where the definition of "reform" reads as follows: *"The concept of reform is broadly defined as an effort toward comprehensive change."* (Haug (1997), p. 418)

10 For the difference between adaptation and learning see Haas (1990), pp. 3 f.

11 For further information see, for example, the latest DAC report: OECD (1997a).

12 These terms are used not only in the UN and UNDP but also by non-governmental development groups; see, for example, their use in ICVA / Eurostep (eds) (1996). Such terms as "donor", "recipient" and "developing countries" are not without their problems, since they may have connotations no longer appropriate to the basic image of development policy in the 1990s. On the other hand, no conceptual alternatives have yet emerged to overcome these weaknesses.

Part I, Chapter 5

1 This comprises the following two organizational units: the Operational Activities for Development Unit and the Department for Policy Coordination and Sustainable Development.

2 Staff with the following functions or from the following spheres were interviewed:

- UNDP Administrator and staff of the Office of the Administrator,
- UNDP 2001 Team,
- Office of Development Studies,
- Office of UN System Support and Services,
- Office of Evaluation and Strategic Planning,
- Bureau for Resources and External Affairs (BREA),
- Executive Board Secretariat, BREA,
- Inter-Agency Coordination and External Policy Office, BREA,
- Division for Resources Planning and Coordination, BREA,
- Division for Resources Mobilization, BREA,
- Bureau for Policy and Programme Support (BPPS),
- Document and Statistics Office, BPPS,
- Division for Operational Policies and Procedure, BPPS,
- Technology Task Force, BPPS,
- Management Development and Government Division, BPPS,
- Regional Bureau for Africa,
- Bureau for Finance and Administration, Division for Administrative and Information Services.

3 The Executive Board has a total of 36 members, who are appointed in accordance with the following regional key: 8 African countries, 7 Asian countries, 4 Eastern European countries, 5 Latin American and Caribbean countries and 12 countries of Western Europe and other regions.

4 Antigua and Barbuda representing Latin America and the Caribbean.

5 Sweden representing Western Europe and other regions.

6 Romania representing Eastern Europe, Indonesia representing Asia and Zambia representing Africa.

Part II, Chapter 1

1 For the state of the research and literature see also the appropriate references in Chapter I.

2 See Bennett (1991), p. 20, and Keohane (1990), p. 738, who writes: "*The fundamental difficulty in assessing the impact of international institutions is that causal inference is difficult where experimental or statistical research designs are infeasible.*"

3 See Gallarotti (1991), p. 185; Keck (1991), p. 638. It should also be borne in mind in this context, however, that international relations as a discipline is generally accused of lacking in theory (see Meyers (1990), p. 49).

4 See, for example, Young, who points out that far less attention is paid to the effects of international organizations or regimes and the factors involved than to, say, questions about their origins: "*The ultimate justification for devoting substantial time and energy to the study of regimes must be the proposition that we can account for a good deal of the variance in collective outcomes at the international level in terms of the impact of institutional arrangements. For the most part, however, this proposition is relegated to the realm of assumptions rather than brought to the forefront as a focus for analytical and empirical investigation.*" (Young (1989), pp. 206 f.)

5 Dicke ((1994), p. 352), for example, concludes in a study "*that in theoretical conceptions of international organizations at least no criteria relating to the efficiency and effectiveness of international organizations that go beyond the political judgments of the actors in them are developed.*"

6 Young (1992), p. 164. In connection with the regime debate Kohler-Koch (1989), pp. 44 ff., refers to three different dimensions of the regime effect:

- changes of behaviour in the actors (behavioural adjustment),
- achievement of the goal pursued (goal attainment) and
- changes in the structural and functional circumstances of the international system.

See also the following definition of effectiveness in UNDP (1997b), p. 33: "*The capacity to realise organisational or individual objectives. Effectiveness requires competence; sensitivity and responsiveness to specific, concrete, human concerns; and the ability to articulate these concerns, formulate goals to address them and develop and implement strategies to realise these goals.*"

7 Referring to the 1980s, Haas (1990), p. 178, for example, comments: "*The crisis of multilateralism stems from the absence of political consensus, not from organizational malfunction.*"

8 For the question of legitimacy see, for example, Kratochwil / Ruggie, who argue: "*A regime can be perfectly rationally designed but erode because its legitimacy is undermined.*" (Kratochwil / Ruggie (1986), p. 773)

9 See Young (1995), p. 202. He continues: "*These limitations are fundamental. Organizations lacking the authority to make decisions that are binding on their members and to ensure their financial autonomy will always find themselves on a short tether in terms of their capacity for effective, much less independent, action.*" (Young (1995), p. 203)

10 See Keohane (1989), pp. 4 f. He gives the following definition: "*The extent to which the institution can alter its own rules rather than relying entirely on outside agents to do so.*"

11 For a more detailed discussion see section III.1.

12 Hannan / Freeman (1984), pp. 159 f., for example, argue: "*We think that reorganization is sometimes tantamount to creating a new organization (with a given level of resources). When reorganization is that fundamental, work groups are reshuffled, bringing strangers into contact, routines are revised, and lines of communication are reshaped. In this situation reorganization robs an organization's history of survival value. That is, reorganization reduces the reliability of performance to that of a new organization. The stability of the previous structure does not contribute to reducing variability with new sets of procedures, role relations etc.*"

13 Gallarotti (1991) analyses various aspects of this complex. A number of references to "better management" and "better administration" can also be found, for example, in Haas (1990), pp. 200 ff. A well-known example of mismanagement is UNESCO under Secretary-General Amadou Mahtar M'Bow. For a more detailed discussion of this see Rittberger (ed.) (1995).

14 Other authors who explicitly consider the adaptability of international organizations or regimes and their capacity for reform include Jönsson (1993), pp. 216 ff., and Rosenau (1986), pp. 861 ff.

15 Adaptation is a process which includes changes, but they tend to be incremental in nature and do not extend to the international organization as a whole. Learning, on the other hand, is a change which also includes the implicit theoretical assumptions and all tasks and objectives.

16 Haas formulated the following impressive theme for his study: "*If my demonstration in this book is persuasive, it will give us the tools for saying, 'If an organization of type A regularly produces certain outcomes, then this type will (or will not) serve the perceived needs of its members: therefore they will seek to design an organization of type B if they are dissatisfied or will retain type A if they are happy.'*" (Haas (1990), p. 6)

17 Reference will be made here only to Keohane (1990), who explicitly considers Haas's study in a chapter entitled "*What explains variations in institutional membership, strength, and scope?*"

18 So far the Charter has been amended only twice under Article 108, on both occasions merely to increase the number of ECOSOC members; see Mützelberg / Karl (1991); Tomuschat (1996).

Part II, Chapter 2

1 Reference will be made here only to the broader debate on the purpose of development cooperation. Important basic categories and dimensions of this debate are considered, for example, in Riddell (1987); Riddell (1996); Cassen (1994) and Raffer / Singer (1996).

2 For the NaTCAP see the comments in section III.2.

3 Berg (1993), pp. 44 ff., compares various definitions of technical cooperation.

4 "*This distinction has faded in recent years: the terms are now in most cases used interchangeably (...).*" (Berg (1993), p. 43)

5 See World Bank (1993 and 1996a). Raphaeli (1996), p. 224, describes this distinction as follows: "*(...) the World Bank has used technical cooperation as an instrument of intervention both to ensure that investment projects and policy reforms are properly designed and implemented and to assist in the creation of growth-oriented national capacity.*"

6 The abbreviation IDTA (institutional development technical assistance) is also found on occasion.

7 OECD (1995b), p. 11. See also James Gustave Speth's address at the conference (reproduced in: OECD (1995b), pp. 17 ff.).

8 The term institution-building is preferred by the World Bank, for example.

9 See, for example, DP/1993/23. The World Bank's definitions essentially share the distinctions made by UNDP. See, for example, World Bank (1993), p. 6, in which terminological distinctions from other similar terms (public sector management, business management and development management) are also explained. For the definition of capacity-building see also Mentz (1997).

10 It might be assumed that the problems usually associated with TC, which will be analysed later, do not arise where TC loans have to be repaid (because of greater cost-awareness, for example). In an interview on 25 March 1997, however, the World Bank's appropriate Technical Cooperation Adviser pointed out that corresponding differences between loans and grants could not be identified in the World Bank's TC.

11 In practical terms this means that structural adjustment policy calls for considerable potential and capacity for control in the countries concerned, which they often did not and do not have.

12 See Jacox in: OECD (1995b), p. 23, and the statistics in Bossuyt / Laporte / van Hoek (1995), pp. 84 f.

13 For further details see sections III.1 and III.2. For the data used here see E/1996/64/Add. 2.

14 In 1968, for example, the World Bank's TC volume amounted to US $ 38 million. See DP/1990/9, pp. 35 ff.

15 The Cassen Report is among the best known analyses of development cooperation and was drawn up by a task force formed by the World Bank's and IMF's Development Committee. It contains many criticisms of development cooperation and TC. In its overall appraisal of TC, however, it is comparatively restrained and cautious; see Cassen (1990), pp. 261-313.

16 As a general rule, analysing and evaluating the results achieved with TC and its weaknesses pose major methodological problems.

17 See World Bank (1996a), pp. 4 f.; see also the overview of World Bank evaluations compiled by Berg (1993), pp. 24 ff.

18 For further details see section III.2.

19 Jaycox (1993), p. d. Similar and sometimes harsher criticism is often expressed by representatives of developing countries. The only example that will be given here is an address at the OECD/World Bank/UNDP conference: "*Mr R. Sobhan (Bangladesh) mentioned severe shortcomings of TC in Bangladesh. The 2 billion dollars spent on TC since Independence in 1971 have not contributed to enhanced capacity-building and sustainable development but to a deterioration of capacities and governance.*" (OECD (1995b), p. 8)

20 For a good overview of the various studies, evaluations, information systems, etc. see, in particular, Berg (1993), pp. 1-32.

21 The list of factors is based on various studies, which cannot be discussed in greater detail here for reasons of space, but to which reference will be made as the need arises. See, in particular, Bossuyt / Laporte / van Hoek (1995), pp. 17 ff., UNDP / World Bank (1995), pp. 21 f., Berg (1993), pp. 1-32, Mitzlaff / Vermehren (1993), p. 582, and Sirleaf (1996), pp. 59. f.

22 "*In the sub-Saharan context, TC has led to fairly good results when involved with specific project goals ...*" Brigaldino (1995), p. 115. It can often be seen that, although explicitly formulated project goals can be achieved, the overriding objectives actually being pursued are not, or not adequately. Thus a project in a certain region may (temporarily) improve individual social indicators (e.g. the school enrolment rate) by bridging shortcomings and so achieve its immediate goals, yet fail to create the structures needed for sustainable and significant progress (e.g. in the education sector).

23 Many developing countries have been highly successful - albeit with significant differences among them - in the case of certain social and economic indicators in the past few decades. What part development cooperation and thus TC have played in this is essentially the real contentious issue in popular and academic discussions of development cooperation. In the position he adopts, the author of this study follows the arguments which accept that development cooperation has

made a generally positive contribution; this is not, however, to rule out the possibility of its role being marginal in many cases or of its having serious adverse effects in certain cases. The following publications, for example, describe successes in developing countries in which development cooperation has played its part: UNDP (1994d), p. 80; OECD (1996b), pp. 6 ff.

24 See, for example, the comments of the representatives of developing countries at the OECD / World Bank / UNDP conference in: OECD (1995b), pp. 8 f. However, this opinion is shared by other experts: "*Technical cooperation is donor- or supply-driven, at least in poor countries.*" (Berg (1995), p. 30)

25 To explain the useful distinction made between commitment and ownership: "*Commitment implies general support and backing. Ownership deals with direct involvement and accountability for the outcomes of a particular activity.*" (Baser / Morgan (1997), p. 9)

26 An evaluation of World Bank TC projects concluded "(...) *that borrower commitment to the intent, design and strategy of implementation of the TAL is the critical (albeit not the sole) determinant of good performance. Conversely, its absence is a virtual guarantee of ineffectiveness. In the 20 TALs under review, this correlation held to a large degree.*" (Baser / Morgan (1997), p. 9; emphasis as in the original text)

27 Sirleaf (1996), p. 60, says, for example, "(...) *that most technical co-operation projects in Africa are often not aimed at the highest priority needs* (...)".

28 For the employment of expatriate experts and advisers see the comments on the next few pages.

29 Examples of this can be found in Nordic UN Project (1990a), pp. 19 ff.

30 An interesting international round table on this subject was held in Berlin in 1995. For the conclusions see International Round Table 1995. Fundamental aspects of the subject are also discussed in the paper by Gsänger / Kampffmeyer / Otzen (1996).

31 Examples show that the cost of expatriate experts and advisers has sometimes exceeded the total salaries of the local civil servants concerned; see, for example, Berg (1993), pp. 13 f., and Bossuyt / Laporte / van Hoek (1995), p. 11.

32 Proceeding from this principle, development cooperation makes sense only in cases where external donors provide services of which the programme countries concerned cannot themselves provide.

33 See OECD (1995b). For the background to the seminar see OECD (1995c), pp. 20 ff. The network is divided into three main areas:

(1) planning and coordination mechanisms for TC, monitoring of the application of the DAC principles in specific countries, etc.,

(2) coping with sectoral problems,

(3) exchange of experience with a view to capacity-building. See OECD (1995c), pp. 23 f.

As part of the network the DAC Seminar on Technical Co-operation and Capacity Development was held in Paris on 9 and 10 December 1996. For the conclusions drawn at the seminar see Guehenno / Pio (1997).

34 An important step was the establishment in 1995 of *The International Journal of Technical Cooperation*, which gives a detailed insight into the TC debate and the positions of individual actors.

35 See, for example, OECD (1994); OECD (1995b); UNDP / World Bank (1995); World Bank (1996a), pp. 5 f.; Berg (1993), pp. 106 ff.; Sirleaf (1996), pp. 60 f.; Bossuyt / Laporte / van Hoek (1995), pp. 72 ff.; Brigaldino (1995) and Mitzlaff / Vermehren (1993).

36 UNDP Administrator Speth even proposed at the OECD / World Bank / UNDP seminar that TC should be renamed "support for national capacity-building" (Speth, in: OECD (1995b), p. 19).

37 Ownership need not necessarily be confined to government structures in the various developing countries: it may also concern non-governmental actors.

38 See, for example, the World Bank studies: "*Weak institutional development and limited capacity are major bottlenecks to the effective use of aid in many countries.*" (World Bank (1995b), p. 7)

39 For models for the employment of local experts see GTZ (1996).

40 For these examples see Berg (1993), pp. 264 ff.; Berg (1995), pp. 36 ff.; Brigaldino (1995) and Bossuyt / Laporte / van Hoek (1995), pp. 72 f.

41 For this aspect see, in particular, Raphaeli (1996), pp. 233 f.; Guehenno / Pio (1997), p. 6, and World Bank (1996d). Some deliberations on the concept of sector investment programmes are also interesting in this context; see Harrold and Associates (1995), pp. XIII and 38 ff.

42 It should be noted that the three options did not necessarily emerge as contributions to the TC debate, but nonetheless touch on many aspects of this debate.

43 See, for example, Hydén (1995); Anonymous (1995) and the examples in OECD (1997a), pp. 102 ff.

44 Harrold and Associates (1995), p. XII, thus state in their paper explaining the SIP approach: "*The most important issues relate to the in-country processing. Here, the key is full involvement of local stakeholders in project and program formulation.*"

45 See Harrold and Associates (1995). See also the following assessments of the SIP concept and some initial experience: Wolff (1996) and Wolff (1997), pp. 4 f.; Barthelt (1997); Hubert (1997) and Chiwele / Engel / Tembo (1997).

46 Guehenno / Pio (1997), p. 9, who drew up the report on the Network meeting of December 1996.

47 Reference can be made in this context to the findings of the evaluation by Baser / Morgan (1997) or to their hardly optimistic assessment of the current as well as the past situation (p. 18): "*The inability - and at times the disinterest - of the donor community to deal adequately with institutional development (ID) issues is a long-standing problem in development cooperation. (...) This lack of sustained attention to the institutional aspects of development is an important case of poor TAL performances.*"

48 See, for example, the debate on a definition of TC in the 1975 report of the UNDP Administrator "The Future Role of UNDP in World Development" (DP/114).

49 "*Capacity development is now becoming as much about creating the ability to build capacity as it is about creating capacity itself in the form of formal structures and procedures. Capacity is induced and enhanced as much as it is transferred and built. From this perspective, TA becomes more about assisting, supporting and facilitating rather than supplanting and prescribing.*" (Baser / Morgan (1997), pp. 5 f)

50 "*Despite some considerable efforts in the Bank at TA reform and performance improvement, this sobering pattern would appear to hold for Bank TA as well. A report in September 1987 analyzed most of the TA issues such as the lack of borrower commitment, the costs of TA, supply-driven TA and the special problems of institutional development that reappear in this report almost a decade later.*" (Baser / Morgan (1997), p. 3) In view of the many parallels between UNDP's earlier TC problems in the 1970s, to which reference was made, for example, in a report by the UNDP Administrator in 1976 (DP/220), and its TC problems in the 1990s, UNDP too can be said to have problems that are highly resistant to solution.

51 For a further discussion of this aspect see Cassen (1994), pp. 203 ff.; Nordic UN Project (1990a); Minister for Development Cooperation (1992) and Klingebiel (1993). Many of the aspects referred to here are considered in the next few sections as they relate to UNDP. See, in particular, sections III.2.3 and III.5.

52 This is particularly true of UNDP, the main multilateral TC institution.

53 See also the DAC's Guiding Principles for Aid-Coordination of Aid with Developing Countries, in which the special role played by the UNDP together with the World Bank in the coordination of development cooperation is considered at length (reproduced in: OECD (1992), pp. 23 ff.).

54 For a more detailed discussion of this aspect.

Part III, Chapter 1

1 See, for example, Frankfurter Allgemeine Zeitung, 29 November 1996, which contained an article headed "*Criticism of withdrawal from UNIDO. Support for application for seat on UN Security Council threatened*".

2 The literature includes a wide range of analyses of the UN's history as a mirror of world politics. See, for example, Alger (1995); Bertrand (1995), pp. 13-71; Grewe (1991); Hüfner (1991a), pp. 11-17, and Volger (1995).

3 In 1950, for example, the USA was able to bring about, through the *Uniting for Peace* resolution, UN military action in connection with the Korean war. See Nolte (1991) and UN (1986), pp. 38 f.

4 See Koschorrek (1991a), p. 49. The proportion was subsequently reduced.

5 Among other things, the Soviet Union sought to reorient its foreign policy after the death of Stalin (1953).

6 *"But the 'crisis of multilateralism' in US foreign policy in reality mirrored and also contributed to a crisis of multilateralism in the UN system itself."* (Karns / Mingst (1995), p. 410); see also Bertrand (1993b), pp. 426 ff.

7 For the arrears and the *Kassebaum Amendment* see, for example, Karns / Mingst (1995) and Koschorrek (1991a and 1991b).

8 One of the first important steps was the 1987 UN Security Council resolution on the war between Iran and Iraq. This was followed by a number of other Security Council decisions and measures relating to peace-keeping and peace-making. See, for example, Unser (1997), pp. 331 ff.

9 The *Agenda for Development* was not adopted by the UN General Assembly until 1997, after being watered down by numerous compromises.

10 A view held by Dicke (1994), pp. 281 ff., and Dicke (1991), pp. 667 ff., for example.

11 The first final report appeared in 1991, and a follow-up project was completed in 1996; see Nordic UN Project (1991b and 1996). See also Rudischhauser (1997), p. 132.

12 The resolution is reproduced in: Knipping / von Mangoldt / Rittberger (eds) (1995), pp. 670-678.

13 Resolution 2688 (XXV). The resolution is reproduced in: Knipping / von Mangoldt / Rittberger (eds) (1995), pp. 680-706.

14 UNDP's Governing Council was transformed into an Executive Board by Resolution 48/162 adopted by the General Assembly in December 1993.

15 The funds administered by UNDP form something of an exception.

16 See the General Assembly's Consensus Resolution (Resolution 2688 (XXV)), which states in paragraph 38 of the annex: *"The role of the organizations of the United Nations system in the implementation of country programmes should be that of partners, under the leadership of the Programme, in a common endeavour of the entire United Nations system."* (U.N. GAOR, 25th Sess., Supp. No. 28, at 58, U.N. DOC. A/8028 (1970))

17 See the General Assembly's Consensus Resolution (Resolution 2688 (XXV)), which states in paragraph 8 of the annex: *"In the process of country programming, efforts should be made at all levels to coordinate all sources of assistance in the United Nations system, with a view to achieving integration of the assistance at the country level."* (U.N. GAOR, 25th Sess., Supp. No. 28, at 58, U.N. DOC. A/8028 (1970))

18 For further details see Singer (1984, 1985 and 1994); Köhler (1987), pp. 342 ff., and Childers (1994). This is particularly true of the decision to locate a financing instrument with "soft" conditions not at the UN but at the World Bank, contrary to the original plans. Thus, instead of the Special United Nations Fund for Economic Development (SUNFED), the International Development Association (IDA) was established.

19 This complaint is to be heard, for example, in Dicke (1993), p. 173: *"The political organs of the UN have not yet succeeded in developing a consistent development policy conception that the UN's subsidiary organs and specialized organizations would follow."* See also, for example, Holtz (1993), p. 170, and Bertrand (1995), pp. 93 ff., where the argument of "absent priorities" is submitted to a critical analysis.

20 See Ministry for Foreign Affairs (Netherlands) (1991), p. 288, and Koetz / Otte (1992), p. 190. For the current state of the UN's conceptual debate on the role of technical cooperation and on capacity-building see the appropriate report of the UN Secretary-General: E/1997/65/Add. 3.

21 See, for example, Gwin (1995); Menon (1994) and UNDP (1994d), which states, for instance: *"The pressures of global human security and development call for a wave of creative innovations like those produced by the 1940s."* (UNDP (1994d), p. 96)

22 See, for example, the list in Koetz / Otte (1992), p. 187. A very good, systematic overview of the various UN bodies can be found in the *United Nations Handbook* (Ministry of Foreign Affairs and Trade (1996)).

23 See A/48/935, Annex III: *"Main United Nations intergovernmental and expert bodies in the economic, social and human rights fields"*.

24 See, for example, Sahlmann (1987), p. 92; Gwin (1995), pp. 99 ff.; Koetz / Otte (1992), pp. 186 f., and North South Roundtable (1991).

25 For the current debate on the reform of ECOSOC see, for example, Rudischhauser (1997), pp. 133 f.

26 The work of Hill (1978), for example, is still highly informative, especially on the various facets and backgrounds to the coordination problem; for various fundamental aspects of the subject see also McLaren (1987) and Gordenker (1995).

27 See Dicke (1994), p. 361: *"The organization's most serious shortcomings are to be found in coordination and system control. The organ provided for this purpose, ECOSOC, hardly performs its tasks in this respect, and the supervision of almost every newly established special organ with specific coordination tasks aggravates the problem rather than alleviating it."* (Emphasis as in the original text.) Puchala (1996), p. 233, summarizes this point in similar terms: *"The bulk of reformers' proposals directed toward improving the U.N.'s development performance calls for somehow improving coordination among U.N. developers."*

28 This problem has been thoroughly analysed, for example, by Haq et al. (eds) (1995); Singer (1995) and Kalderén (1991).

29 See Gwin / Williams (1996), p. 121; Sahlman (1987), p. 91, and Paschke (1996), p. 42.

30 For further details see Mistry / Thyness (1991); Unser (1997), pp. 159 ff., and Hüfner (1997).

31 The Secretary-General gives the following figures for 1992, for example: of the US $ 3,628.2 million spent on the UN's operational activities, only US $ 16.6 million came from the regular UN budget (see A/48/935, Annex II). No provision was made for voluntary contributions as a financing system when the UN was first established. See Childers / Urquhart (1994), pp. 99 ff.

32 Reference to this aspect is made in particular in the UN Secretary-General's report (UN (1997c)) and the ODI's analysis (1997).

33 See, for example, UN (1997c and 1997d) and ODI (1997). The issue is also analysed in greater depth in section III.2 as it relates to UNDP. The UN Secretary-General's report (UN (1997c)) considers the definitional details and differences among the UN agencies. For the terminology see also UNDP (1996i), pp. 91 ff.

34 See E/1995/98, pp. 14 f., and, for the figures quoted, ODI (1997), p. 3. The corresponding figures for 1982 - 1984 and 1992 - 1994 are 86.0 and 62.5% for UNDP and 70.6 and 56.3% for UNICEF. A declining tendency can also be seen in UNFPA's case.

35 Figures calculated in accordance with OECD (1997a), pp. A2 and A35.

36 This is particularly apparent from the analysis in ODI (1997).

37 For a discussion of this aspect see Nordic UN Project (1990a and 1991b) and Danida (1991a).

38 See, for example, Nordic UN project (1990a), p. 16, which comments on the gap-filling function as follows: *"This function might in some cases be warranted. But the general impression from the reports is that the donor-of-the-last-resort concept tends to focus aid less on central issues."*

39 For the current situation see UN (1996a).

40 A number of publications by the Heritage Foundation are particularly outspoken and wholesale in their criticism: *"The U.N. is a poorly managed institution plagued by corruption. It is a heaven for political patronage and suffers from a lack of management oversight."* (Cowin / Kingham (1993), p. 3)

41 For general comments on this see Nordic UN Project (1991b), pp. 94 ff.; Childers / Urquhart (1994), pp. 150 ff.; Urquhart / Childers (1990) and ODI (1987), pp. 2 f.

42 DP/5. The Jackson Report is discussed at greater length in section III.3.

43 Nordic UN Project (1991b and 1996). See also Nordic UN Project (1990a and 1991a).

44 Childers / Urquhart (1994). See also Urquhart / Childers (1990, 1991a and 1996).

45 G7 (1996). See also the outcome of the follow-up summit conference in Denver: G8 (1997).

46 DP/5. For further details see section III.3.

47 See Rudischhauser (1997), who cites Resolution 32/177 as an example.

48 The number of members was initially raised from 18 to 17 and then to 54. See Mützelburg / Karl (1991) and Tomuschat (1996).

49 The UN General Assembly has instead endorsed the maintenance of separate structures on several occasions. Resolution 50/120, for example, reads: The General Assembly

"Further stresses that, in the context of the reform of the United Nations Secretariat and the restructuring and revitalization of the intergovernmental process, the mandates of the separate sectoral and specialized entities, funds, programmes and specialized agencies should be respected and enhanced, taking into account their complementarities (...)" (A/RES/50/120, para. 16; emphasis as in the original text)

50 The Agenda for Development was adopted by the General Assembly in June 1997 (A/RES/51/240).

51 An example of this is the detailed overview of reforms drawn up by the UN's Special Coordinator for Economic and Social Development (UN (1996b)), which lists a very large number of reforms undertaken by UN agencies in the economic and social field. However, the list reveals that these tend to be patchwork reforms on a limited scale rather than a package of reforms that change structures.

52 See, for example, the second report to the Secretary-General on *Work of the Special Coordinator for Economic and Social Development* (UN (1996c)), which also covers the implementation of Resolutions A/47/199 and A/50/120. In 1977 the Secretary-General reviewed the state of the implementation of Resolution 50/120; in addition, Document E/1996/64, for example, reports on progress in the implementation of Resolutions A/RES/47/199 and A/RES/50/120.

53 For the sector groups and executive groups see UN (1997a and 1997b).

54 See, for example, the comments made by Secretary-General Kofi Annan at his press conference: SG/SM/6248/Rev. 1.

55 In this UNICEF Director Bellamy played a particularly prominent role. For the background see, for example, Zumach (1997).

56 See, in particular, the following sections of the reform document (UN (1997g)): paras 58 and 146-149.

57 Bertrand (1993b), p. 432, takes much the same view: *"But the prospects that a comprehensive conception of UN reform will gain acceptance in the near future remain slight."*

58 Reservations about multilateral development cooperation began to emerge in the USA's policy in the mid-1970s and grew under the Reagan administration in the 1980s. They principally concerned the UN with its "automatic majority" of developing countries. In 1977 the USA decided that its share of the UN's budgets would be maintained at zero growth (see Gwin / Williams (1996), pp. 111 f.). For fundamental and current aspects of the USA's UN policy see United States Department of State (1996); Clinton (1995) and Karns / Mingst (1995).

59 Bertrand (1993b), p. 433, argues along similar lines: *"The countries of the North are not much interested in most of the UN's economic and social activities and prefer to rely upon the IMF and the World Bank."*

60 See G7 (1996) and EU (1996). An assessment of both documents can be found in Rudischhauser (1997), pp. 134 ff.

61 The enormous interest in the continued existence of the various UN agencies was evident, for example, during the interviews conducted for this study in March 1997. Proposals for reforms supported by individual UN agencies or representatives are normally based on the maintenance of separate structures. See the document submitted by Speth (1996), for example. Consequently, the UN itself is hardly likely to make any attempt at reforms designed to overcome its fragmented structures (at least where the UN funds and programmes are concerned).

62 See, for example, the German Bundestag's Development Committee, which *"... considers a reform of the UN to be urgently needed ..."* (Holtz (1993), p. 170). A similar view is expressed in Dicke (1993), p. 172: *"Both the organizational and*

the substantive formulation of UN development policy indicate a major need for reform ..."

63 Favourable assessments such as the following are rare: *"The efforts the United Nations and its specialized agencies have made in the past ten years have been the equal of the programmes for bilateral cooperation and the performance of the lending institutions in effectiveness and efficiency."* (J. van Arendonk, in: Deutscher Bundestag (1991), p. 99)

64 Beigbeder (1995), p. 253, for example, writes: *"The main obstacle to significant reforms in the U.N. economic and social sector is the lack of agreement among Member States on the role of U.N. organizations in this field, and on economic objectives of U.N. activities."* A similar view is expressed by Paschke (1996), p. 41: *"It is rare for the UN to receive clear and unambiguous prescriptions from its 'supervisory board'. As each of the member countries, now 185 in number, has quite different ideas on what the world organization is actually meant to be and do, the consensus on the subject of reform is also very general; differences of opinion quickly come to light when the discussion turns to details."*

65 *"The first and most important factor in the UN's lack of realism is the relative disinterest of the superpowers and the industrialized countries in general in the UN's economic and social activities."* (Bertrand (1995), p. 76). Hüfner (1992a), p. 36, refers, for example, to the "deviousness" and "political hypocrisy of individual member states".

66 *"So much emphasis has been placed on the weaknesses of the UN system that its successes are often forgotten."* (UNDP (1994d), p. 95). Jolly (1995), for example, has listed various positive elements or strengths in his paper.

67 See, for example, the findings of the study by Kay (1980), pp. 183 ff.

68 *"It is easy to criticize the way the system has developed and the way in which it operates."* (Renninger (1987), pp. 97 f.)

69 For efforts to reform the whole of UN development cooperation and UNDP see section III.4.2.

Part III, Chapter 2

1 See, for example, the statement in a study by the conservative Heritage Foundation: *"The United Nations Development Program is in crisis."* (Bissel (1985), p. 1). Singer (1976), p. 144, identified *"symptoms of a deeper structural crisis"*, and Dubey (1977), p. 85, referred to a *"double crisis"* - a *"resource crisis"* and an *"identity crisis"*; Hüfner (1992b), p. 39, entitled his essay *"UNDP in Trouble"*.

2 The following comment on a table in a 1989 report by the UNDP Administrator is, for example, typical: *"Given the established principle of Government sovereignty in selecting the areas and priority concerns for which UNDP resources are to be*

utilized, the table does not reflect any programming emphases advocated by UNDP." (DP/1989/14, p. 11)

3 According to Danida, for example: *"The lack of clear, overall strategies and guidelines at field level, combined with the present resource distribution mechanism in which IPFs* (Indicative Planning Figures - SK) *are perceived as resource allocations, has given the impression that the developing countries largely control UNDP's programmes at will and not necessarily in accordance with the organization's objectives."* (Danida (1996b), p. 8)

4 See Williams (1995a), p. 199. Earlier UN debates and reports are also interesting in this context. As long ago as 1975 and 1976 the UNDP Administrator submitted reports on how UNDP's TC might be reoriented. The recommendations for the reorientation of TC are surprisingly similar to those emerging from the more recent TC debate and also the DAC principles for the reorientation of TC (see section II.2). See the following documents, for example: DP/114 (*"The Future Role of UNDP in World Development in the Context of the Preparations for the Seventh Special Session of the General Assembly"*) and DP/220 (*"Implementation of New Dimensions in Technical Co-operation"*).

5 See, in particular, Williams (1995a), pp. 198 ff.; Gwin (1995), pp. 107 f.; Griffin / McKinley (1996), pp. 11 ff.; Kienbaum & Partners (1991), pp. 3 f.; UNDP (1992b), p. 77; Minister for Development Cooperation (1992), pp. 25 ff.; Nordic UN Project (1990a), pp. 19 ff., and DP/1990/9.

6 See Williams (1995b), p. 7. See also the results of the evaluation "NaTCAP Guinea", in : UNDP (1995g), pp. 62-68.

7 Much the same is true of other donors' assessments of themselves. UNDP also refers to this weakness itself (see UNDP (1995g), p. 84).

8 For additional explanations of the terms used in this section (core resources, etc.) see also section III.1 and UNDP (1996i), pp. 91 ff.

9 See DP/1997/CRP.23, Chapter II. The figure is based on a provisional evaluation of the resource mobilization objectives of the country cooperation frameworks introduced in 1996. In this context it should be pointed out, however, that the resource mobilization objectives say little about a country's actual TC needs, since they are primarily UNDP commercial objectives.

10 *"In real terms the contributions to UNDP have been almost stagnant during the 1970s and 1980s."* (Nordic UN Project (1991b), p. 86) The report of the UN Secretariat on operational development activities had a similar comment to make: *"... core contributions to UNDP over the past 20 years have remained stagnant in real terms."* (E/1995/98, p. 14) See also Kolles (1994).

11 See the explanations in section III.1 and also UN (1997c), UNDP (1996i) and UNDP (1993a), Sect. 10200 - 10204. Some general reflections on the relationship between core and non-core resources can also be found in ODI (1997).

12 *"Voluntary contributions are contributions by Governments to UNDP's main resources or the central resources of other funds and programmes administered by UNDP and they are made without any restrictions."* (UNDP (1993a), Sect. 10201)

13 Although provision is also made for donations, they have hitherto been insignificant.

14 ODI (1997) and the UN Secretary-General in particular have referred to these aspects: *"The steady decline of core funding and the overwhelming dependence on a few countries indicate the potential for instability and vulnerability."* (UN (1997c), para. 14)

15 The definitions vary among the UN agencies. For the differences and other definitional questions see UN (1997c), Annex I, and UNDP (1996i), pp. 91 ff.

16 The Administrator's annual report therefore refers to the advantages of core resources. *"Core resources remain the primary means for impartial and universal multilateral assistance ..."* (DP/1997/16, p. 14)

17 For the funding role and the tripartite mechanism and for the connection between core resources and the funding role see E/1995/98, pp. 14 f.; UN (1997c) and ODI (1997).

18 For further details see UNDP (1996i). Government cost-sharing contributions may be provided in cash or kind (UNDP (1996i), pp. 94 f.).

19 In 1996 just five countries - Argentina, Colombia, Brazil, Panama and Peru - accounted for a large proportion (73%) of government cost-sharing resources (see DP/1997/24, para. 7).

20 See UNDP (1996i), pp. 6 f., where the reservations are summarized as follows: *"Two basic concerns have been voiced with regard to massive cost-sharing in the Latin American region. One is that the availability of cost-sharing may lead UNDP to approve projects to which it can make no substantive contribution. It is thus feared that UNDP may be used for purely administrative functions (i.e., a simple crown agent or* ***fiduciary role****), as a hedge against currency fluctuations, or as a convenient device to bypass national tax legislation or generally applicable limitations on public service staffing and salaries. A related concern is that cost-sharing, especially government cost-sharing combined with national execution and the use of national consultants may serve to finance ordinary government functions, generating* ***durable dependencies*** *and a two-track civil service - neither of which would be compatible with good governance and the concept of sustainability."* (Emphasis as in the original text)

21 *"This is a matter for concern, because central funding not only lies at the heart of the effectiveness of multilateralism, it is crucial to the respect of the principle of the sovereignty of recipient Governments. An important way in which the priorities of recipient Governments can be respected is to make available a central fund for allocation to these priorities."* (DP/1989/14, p. 28)

22 Author's own calculations based on data obtained from OECD (1996a), p. A36.

23 This figure is based on the data in Table 8, i.e. the volume financed by UNDP as a proportion of total expenditure. For 1994, for example, this gives a UNDP-financed share of the UN system's total grant-based operational activities of 22.47%.

24 Minister for Development Cooperation (1992), p. 26. Similar comments are made by Gwin (1995), p. 106, Danida (1991c), p. 44, and a report by a group of experts to the UNDP Administrator: *"UNDP is no longer the major source of multilateral technical co-operation funds."* (DP/1990/9, para. 199)

25 See, for example, Nordic UN Project (1990a), pp. 9-35, and Danida (1991a). Referring to the position of the programme countries on this problem, a report by a group of experts to the UNDP states: *"Governments do not want to be involved in the internal quarrels of the United Nations Organization about who should execute a project. Nor do they appreciate the salesmanship pitch that is pursued by some United Nations organizations."* (DP/1990/9, p. 48)

26 For the ACC's tasks see Ministry of Foreign Affairs and Trade (1996), p. 144.

27 For the CCPOQ's tasks see Ministry of Foreign Affairs and Trade (1996), p. 145, and UN (1996a), Part F1.

28 To enable the concepts and debate to be understood, reference should briefly be made to the following: the local UNDP representative is known as the Resident Representative (RR); the representative of the UN as a whole is the Resident Coordinator (RC). As a rule, the RR is also appointed to the office of RC, one individual thus performing different tasks (see Kulessa (1991); UN (1996a), Part B4; UNDP (1994a), Chapter XIV, and UNDP (1997e)).

29 The UNDP Organization Handbook defines the task as follows: *"The principal role of the field office network is to serve as a country-based operational arm of UNDP. In addition, this structure provides a worldwide network of information exchange, support and co-operation between the United Nations organizations, the people and governments of developing countries and the donor community."* (UNDP (1994a), Sect. 14000)

30 See, for example, Williams (1995a), p. 199, and Nordic UN Project (1990a), pp. 25 ff. See also the study by Hill (1978), which examined various aspects of this UNDP problem at a far earlier stage.

31 A recent UNDP evaluation of the work of the Resident Coordinator notes a great improvement in the performance of coordinating tasks: *"On average, coordination of United Nations operational activities has significantly improved (...)"* (UNDP (1997d), p. 56)

32 See Minister for Development Cooperation (1992), p. 26. See also the comments in Kulessa (1991), which underline the importance of the individual.

33 Owing to their great importance, the principles and explanations on country-related programming and the IPFs in the annex to the Consensus Resolution play a significant role.

34 See DP/1994/10/Add. 2, p. 8. The figure concerns *"expenditures on field programme activities"*.

35 See Executive Board Decisions 94/12 and 95/1 (reproduced in DP/1995/1 and DP/1996/1 respectively) and the UN Secretary-General's comments on the OPS: *"The overriding objective of the Secretary-General's proposal on OPS (...) was the elimination of the conflict inherent in UNDP exercising coordination responsibility in relation to the operational activities of the system while retaining through OPS, its own implementation capability."* (DP/1994/52, p. 2). See also section III.4.

36 The problems in this respect are primarily due to financial factors, especially in the case of smaller and poorer countries.

37 See Kienbaum & Partners (1991). Other studies and documents also voice these criticisms. Danida (1996b), p. 8, for example, states: *"A major element in Danish criticism of UNDP advanced by the National Auditors and followed up by the Danish Public Accounts Committee during its visit to New York in March 1994 was that a growing proportion of costs had been absorbed by administration over the past ten years."*

38 In the study accountability is defined as *"... mechanisms (internal and external) that define and monitor the overall reciprocal responsibilities of UNDP to its employees, and other stakeholders."* (George Washington University (1997), p. 2) Under this the study lists 10 different subsystems.

39 For fundamental aspects of the UNDP evaluation system see UNDP (1995g); UNDP (1996f) and UNDP (1997d). Changes or reforms in this area are discussed in greater depth in section III.4.

40 A far better view is taken by Ahlberg / Løvbraek (1985), p. 6: *"UNDP field offices are generally staffed with very competent professional staff (...)"*

41 Figures obtained from UNDP (1997o), p. 84. See also the reforms discussed in section III.4.

42 *"The responsibility for implementation rests mainly with the implementing and executing agencies."* Danida (1991c), p. 57

43 *"It is difficult to make a trend analysis for each particular agency since the number of evaluation reports (year by year) are too few to be representative."* (UNDP (1995g), p. 79)

44 *"UNDP project management suffers from the fact that there is no real 'process ownership'. No particular official is responsible for the overall success of a*

particular project." Kienbaum & Partners (1991), p. 40. See also George Washington University (1997).

45 The "like-minded" countries in particular conducted a debate in the first half of the 1990s on comparative advantages of multilateral development cooperation. See, for example, Klingebiel (1993). The UNDP Administrator discussed UNDP's advantages at length in a report entitled *Programme Planning and Implementation, Efficiency of Programming and the Comparative Advantages of UNDP* (DP/1993/28).

46 See the comments in section II.2, where the question of costs in TC is discussed in greater depth.

47 See, for example, the eight country studies carried out as part of the Nordic UN Project. They are contained in Nordic UN Project (1990a).

48 UNDP Administrator Speth comments as follows:

"The criticisms of UNDP can be grouped into three categories:

- *Weak substantive capacity; too much of a 'mailbox' function; too much of a processing function.*
- *Lack of clear mission and focus; tries to do too much; resources spread too thinly; inefficient and overstretched staff; pulled too many ways by too many forces - all of this adds to the difficulty of measuring results and having a clear sense of exactly what we are accountable for in the world.*
- *And thirdly, despite reiteration, the coordination role, our coordination assignment, is not fully accepted by the UN System as a whole, and it is not yet fully realized by UNDP, and the central funding role has not been achieved. And there has been uneven leadership capacity at headquarters and in our country offices."* (Speth (1994a), p. 5)

Part III, Chapter 3

1 See also section III.1, where other concepts and initiatives for the reform of all UN development cooperation are presented and discussed.

2 Although this is, in the final analysis, a subjective criterion, references in texts and during interviews, etc. have produced a selection of documents of outstanding importance for the debate on the reform of UNDP.

3 Its special importance can be deduced, for example, from the prominence it still enjoys in recent analyses, such as that by Righter (1995). A good analysis of the Jackson Report as seen at the time (i.e. the early 1970s) was undertaken by Kaufmann (1971).

4 DP/114. Many of the TC principles set out in the document are reiterated in a decision by UNDP's Governing Council and a resolution adopted by the UN

General Assembly in 1975. See Resolution 3405 (XXX), where the Governing Council's decision is also reproduced as an annex.

5 The author of the analysis was Richard E. Bissell (Bissell (1985)).

6 See Nordic UN Project (1991b and 1996). The 1996 report also considers which of the proposals submitted in 1991 were discussed and implemented by the UN.

7 See Nordic UN Project (1991b), p. 58, and Nordic UN Project (1990a). The final report states, for example: *"The United Nations Development Programme's approach to development cooperation is one of partnership rather than one of supplier and client."* (Nordic UN Project (1991b), p. 58)

8 See UNDP (1993d), p. 4. The transition team's report is divided into two parts to match the two parts of the task assigned to it. See UNDP (1993d and 1993e).

9 The study was made by Cathrine Gwin: Gwin (1995).

10 Although the proposal was distributed in various quarters marked *"confidential"*, it was described at great length and quoted in the UN journal *International Documents Review* (see Anonymous (1996)).

Part III, Chapter 4

1 See also section III.1. Although other UN documents have been relevant in this context in the 1990s, Resolutions 47/199 and 20/120 laid the foundations.

2 See also section III.1. His predecessor, Boutros Boutros-Ghali, also took various initiatives.

3 The main UNDP documents that provide a relatively good overview of the debate are the following: Speth (1994a), DP/1994/39, UNDP (1995c), DP/1995/31, UNDP (1996b), DP/1997/16, DP/1997/16/Add. 7 and DP/1997/CRP.16.

4 For the whole process of reform of UN development cooperation see section III.1.

5 *"UNDP recognizes that change is a process, not an event. Its action must be implemented on a wide front over time."* (UNDP (1997h), p. 2)

6 Including the following Executive Board decisions, which are considered at greater length below: 94/14 (core mission), 95/1 (conversion of OPS into UNOPS) and 95/23 (replacement of the country programming system).

7 The conclusions drawn at the closed meeting are in turn based on earlier concepts (especially the 1995 corporate plan). For the origin of the *UNDP 2001* concept see UNDP (1996b), pp. 1 ff., and DP/1997/16/Add. 7, pp. 6 ff.

8 The following topics were covered by the working groups: (1) strategic development services, (2), efficiency, results-orientation and accountability, (3)

human resources, (4) information management, (5) communication and external affairs, (6) funding strategies and partnerships and (7) management and organizational structure. The groups were active from May to November 1996.

9 DP/1997/CRP.16, p. 2 states: *"(...) the main objective of the UNDP 2001 change process is to align UNDP internal functions, processes, systems and structures with the new mandate given by the Executive Board in decision 94/14."* The new substantive mandate, or core mission, and the corresponding decisions on focusing (especially Executive Board Decision 94/14) are considered later in this section. It should be pointed out here that the many official and internal documents on the second reform period, while differing to some extent and showing some inconsistencies in their formulated and implicit objectives, are essentially similar. See, for example, UNDP (1996b and 1997g); DP/1997/16/Add. 7 and Speth (1997a).

10 *"(1) To Support Programme Countries in Their Efforts To Achieve Sustainable Human Development (SHD), and To Strengthen Country Offices and Headquarters To This End;*

(2) To Implement the New Programming Arrangements Efficiently and To Ensure Enhanced Delivery;

(3) To Play an Effective Advocacy Role, Build Constituencies and Mobilize Resources for SHD;

(4) To Strengthen UNDP's Partnerships in the UN System and Elsewhere and To Enhance UNDP's Performance in Countries in Crisis and Other Special Circumstances;

(5) To Build a Leaner, More Accountable Learning Organization." (UNDP (1996b), p. 1)

11 See, for example, the information submitted to the Executive Board on the *UNDP 2001* project in the UNDP Administrator's 1996 annual report, which urges the Executive Board to take note of the document, to encourage the Administrator to implement it and to call for reports on the progress of the reforms (DP/1997/16/Add. 7, p. 17).

12 It should be remembered that the *Human Development Report* does not necessarily reflect UNDP's opinion. The first few editions in particular attracted harsh criticism from the representatives of the developing countries.

13 For a critique of UNDP's sustainable human development approach see Nuscheler (1997).

14 UNDP (1995i), p. 2. UNDP has published a wide range of studies and papers on the development of the SHD approach. The *Human Development Reports* contain a wealth of material and suggestions on the subject; for fundamental aspects of the SHD concept see, for example, the 1994 report (UNDP (1994d)).

15 Reference can be made in this context to the decision taken by the Governing Council in 1990 (No 90/34) on six priority topics.

16 See UNDP (1995b), p. 14. For the results so far achieved see, in particular, Centre for Development Research (1996), pp. 7 ff.

17 Speth addressing the Executive Board in 1995 (quoted in: Centre for Development Research (1996), p. 9).

18 UNDP 1997g), p. 1. See the comments on the new programming procedure later in this study.

19 The mission statement is reproduced in Annex IV to this study.

20 Similar problems are, however, encountered by other donor institutions.

21 These deficiencies are mentioned by UNDP's documentation and statistics unit in this context. The explanations include the following statement: *"The exercise was rather limited because (i) it covers approximately 2,200 programmes/projects; (ii) only six categories were used; (iii) each intervention could be classified under two areas only; (iv) it was somewhat subjective as definitions were not neat and clear-cut enough; and (v) the overlap of definitions given the inter-relatedness of the themes."* (UNDP (1996j), p. xviii) A dual classification of interventions occurred where two thirds of an operation were assigned to one category and a third to another.

22 UNDP (1997b), pp. 2 f. The publication goes on to define good governance: *"Good governance is, among other things, participatory, transparent and accountable."* (p. 3)

23 See DP/1997/16, pp. 6 f. and Annex VI, and UNDP (1997b).

24 The term *civil society organization* covers only groups acting for common purposes. The definition of the term *non-governmental organization* is sometimes broader.

25 See UNDP (1997g), p. 2. For the problems associated with this figure see the comments on Table 10.

26 The relationship between sustainable human development and good governance has been examined in some depth in a study carried out for UNDP: UNDP (1997a).

27 For positive measures and political conditionality see, for example, Heinz (1994); Waller (1996) and the volume by Tetzlaff (ed.) (1993).

28 The governments of various developing countries repeatedly emphasize in this context, for example, that their permission is needed for cooperation with non-governmental organizations. Thus some delegations underlined at UNDP's 1997 annual meeting *"(...) the need to pursue linkages with civil society only at the discretion of Governments."* (DP/1997/21, p. 28)

29 See, for example, Executive Board Decision 96/25 ("*Matters relating to rules of procedure, documentation and the functioning of the Executive Board*") and the deliberations that preceded this decision in: DP/1996/19, pp. 6 ff., and UNDP (1997g), p. 10.

30 "*Recommendation: Member States are invited to consider arrangements for a closer integration of the governance oversight of UNDP/UNFPA and UNICEF with consecutive and/or joint meetings of the existing Executive Boards, and the convening of joint committees to review issues and matters of common concern.*" (UN (1997g), p. 38; emphasis as in the original text)

31 This view was expressed by the head of the Executive Board Secretariat in an interview. Almost all the Executive Board representatives interviewed confirmed this assessment. See also section III.6.

32 Although the Executive Board has only 36 members, 45 delegations spoke, for example, in the debate on the Administrator's annual report for 1995. (See DP/1996/19, p. 35.)

33 This view was expressed particularly by various representatives of developing countries during interviews; a particular problem in this context is that their missions are less well staffed than those of most industrialized countries, or the specialist staff are often unable to travel from their capitals because of the cost involved. The UNDP administration sometimes encounters difficulties in drawing up documents when the intervals between meetings are short.

34 This view was expressed especially in interviews with representatives of the "like-minded" countries.

35 UNDG's predecessor in the first half of 1997 was known as the "sector group".

36 In the first half of 1997 the membership was initially wider: UNDP, UNFPA, UNICEF, WFP, DDSMS, UNOPS, UNIFEM, UNAIDS, UNDCP and UNCHS.

37 One outcome in this context was, for example, a document containing the written opinions of the various UN agencies (UNDP (1997c)).

38 On this aspect the reform paper reads: "*The UNDG Executive Committee will further sharpen the contributions that each entity is called upon to make to the overall objectives of the Organization while helping each entity avoid duplication and build on the work and capacities of other entities; serve as a policy development and management instrument geared to contributing to, and effecting, policy, administrative and operational decisions in each entity while at the same time strengthening decision-making processes in the Organization as a whole; provide a forum for heads of entities to consult on submissions to their governing bodies on both substantive and administrative matters that have implications for other members of the Group or for the Organization as a whole; contribute to strengthening policy coherence and cost-effectiveness by avoiding duplication and by pooling resources and services so as to maximize programme impact and mini-*

mize administrative costs; share draft work programme and budget documents at a sufficiently early stage prior to their finalization and submission to the relevant governing bodies to make such consultations a meaningful phase in the programming process; and promote a more unified United Nations presence at the country level through, inter alia, providing a forum for concerted directives to Resident Coordinators and field representatives in order to ensure more integrated and consistent substantive support from headquarters for their work." (UN (1997g), para. 153)

39 OUNS has two divisions: (a) Division for Resident Coordinator System Support and (b) Division for Policy Advisory Services. OUNS' specific functions are *"(...) to (a) be the focal point for and provide support to the resident coordinators; (b) develop and support programmes for preventive and curative development; (c) handle security-related matters of UNDP country offices; (d) support the Administrator in assisting the Secretary-General in ensuring policy coherence and in enhancing coordination with the UN system."* (UN (1996a), Annex F2, p. 1) For the tasks and areas of activity see also DP/1996/CRP.3.

40 See, for example, the agreement with the International Organization for Migration.

41 The agreement is entitled: *World Bank / UNDP Aid Coordination Cooperation Agreement.*

42 The agreement states, for example: *"The World Bank and the United Nations Development Programme are the only global and multi-sectoral organizations within the UN system."* And: *"The country's preferences are to be respected with regard to the choice of consultative arrangement, and neither the CG* (Consultative Group - SK), *nor other coordination mechanism should be regarded* ***a priori*** *as the preferred mechanism."* (Emphasis as in the original text)

43 For further background information and resolutions previously adopted by the General Assembly on the RC system see, for example, UNDP (1997e). Resolution 50/120 essentially confirms Resolution 47/199, without adding any important new aspects.

44 Resolution 47/199 states:

"(a) The separate funds, programmes and specialized agencies must make a commitment to work together to integrate assistance provided by the United Nations system into the development process of the recipient countries in a fully co-ordinated manner;

(b) The United Nations system at the country level should be tailored, taking into account the views of the recipient Government, to the country's specific development needs in such a way that they correspond to ongoing and projected cooperation programmes rather than to the institutional structure of the United Nations;

(c) The separate identities and, where appropriate, representation of funds and programmes at the country level should be ensured in the framework of a clear

and improved division of labour, in accordance with their mandates (...)" (A/RES/47/199)

45 For further details see UN (1996a), Annex F2; UN (1996c), pp. 7 ff.; UNDP (1997e) and UNDP (1997n).

46 In other words, the participants in the Joint Consultative Group on Policy (JCDP).

47 See UN (1996c), p. 11. The figures relate to countries where two or more organizations participating in the JCGP share premises. Other figures - especially 45 countries sharing offices in 1997 - are also quoted in DP/1997/16/Add. 7, p. 4. Yet another figure (52) is given in DP/1997/16, p. 10.

48 Referring to the objectives of country strategy notes the resolution reads: [The General Assembly emphasizes] *"(...) that, on the basis of the priorities and plans of recipient countries, and in order to ensure the effective integration of assistance provided by the United Nations system into the development process of countries, with enhanced accountability, and to facilitate the assessment and evaluation of the impact and sustainability of that assistance, a country strategy note should be formulated by interested recipient Governments with the assistance of and in cooperation with the United Nations system under the leadership of the resident coordinator in all recipient countries where the Government so chooses (...)"* (A/RES/47/199) See also the detailed explanations on the CSN instrument in: UN (1996a), Annex A4.

49 See UN (1997e), para. 52. See also DP/1997/16/Add. 7, p. 4, and E/1996/64, p. 18. A good source of information are the RCs' reports on the state of CSN preparation, where more detailed country-related explanations are to be found. For a summary see the evaluation of the RC reports: UNDP (1996c).

50 Efforts have also been made to harmonize the presentation of the budgets of UNDP, UNFPA and UNICEF; see DP/1996/17, pp. 23 ff., and DP/1997/6, pp. 28 ff.

51 For further details see DP/1997/23, Chapter E. This source contains accurate data on assignments at the country offices, which show the RCs to have spent 48.7% of their time on UNDP activities and 51.3% on non-UNDP activities in 1997; in the case of deputy RCs, however, the division is different: 70.6% and 29.4% respectively. For both RCs and deputy RCs a significant decline in the time devoted to UNDP activities compared with the figures shown in DP/1993/45 is to be seen.

52 A positive exception in this context is the UN system at country level in India (UN System in India (1997)), where a UN System Position Statement has been developed as an alternative to the country strategy note and adopts a far more practical approach to the most important problems.

53 See UNDP (1997d), pp. 55 ff., which states (p. 56): *"On average, coordination of United Nations operational activities has significantly improved: discernible*

progress and clear results have been reported, especially since 1990. Successful mechanisms for coordination include field-level committees, the country strategy note (CSN) and any substantive or other operational collegial activity." However, the evaluation has its weaknesses when it comes to evidence in support of the optimistic view it takes.

54 See, for example, UNDP (1996n), p. 1, which states: *"Unless UNDP can increase its resource base, the organization will become marginal in the development process, will be unable to maintain the valuable network of country offices, and it will be unable to effectively advocate and implement the ideas that form the foundation of the work and the identity of the organization."*

55 See, for example, the debate at the Executive Board's 1997 annual meeting in DP/1997/21, Chapter VII.

56 The decision (95/23, reproduced in: DP/1996/1, pp. 24 ff.) states: [The Executive Board] *"Decides to adopt for planning purposes the initial figure of $ 3.3 billion for core resources for the three-year period starting in 1997 and requests the Administrator to take all necessary measures to secure at least those estimated financial resources."* (Emphasis as in the original text)

57 See the minutes of the Executive Board's 1997 annual meeting, in which Speth is recorded as saying: *"(...) UNDP could manage twice the amount of resources it had at the present time."* (DP/1997/21, Chapter VII, A)

58 Among other things, UNDP submitted a provisional paper (*Towards a Sustainable Funding Strategy for UNDP)* to the Executive Board in 1997 (DP/1997/CRP.23).

59 For these two terms see, for example, DP/1997/16, pp. 14 f. See also the comments on *substantive partnerships* in DP/1994/39, pp. 15 f., where the promotion of an *"outward-looking culture* within UNDP is discussed.

60 See DP/1997/CRP.23; DP/1997/16/Add. 7, pp. 10 f.; UNDP (1996n, 1997g and 1997l).

61 See, for example, the statements in Executive Board Decision 95/23 (especially para. 8) in: DP/1996/1, pp. 24 ff., and Speth's comments in DP/1997/21, Chapter VII, A.

62 See DP/1997/CRP.23; DP/1997/16; DP/1997/16/Add. 7, pp. 10 f.; DP/1997/24; UNDP (1996n); UNDP (1997g) and UNDP (1997l).

63 See, for example, UNDP (1997m), which reports on the various activities in the European countries. The range of measures embraces, for instance, the development of formal partnerships with national NGOs in a wide range of countries (Germany, Belgium, France, etc.), individual campaigns and information meetings with parliamentarians.

64 For this aspect see also the discussions at the Executive Board's 1997 annual meeting, reproduced in: DP/1997/21.

65 See G7 (1996), p. 635, which states: *"(...) savings resulting from increased economies should be reinvested in development programmes."*

66 UNDP referred in this context, for example, to its intention *"(...) to move from what had become an entitlement-based system to an incentive-based one."* (UNDP (1996a), p. 3)

67 Executive Board decision 95/23 states, for example: [The Executive Board] *"Reaffirms the principles of eligibility of all recipient countries on the basis of the fundamental characteristics of the operational activities of the United Nations Development System, which are, inter alia, universality, neutrality, multilateralism, the voluntary and grant nature of assistance and the capacity to respond to the needs o all recipient countries in accordance with their own policies and priorities for development (...)"* (Decision 95/23, reproduced in: DP/1996/1, pp. 24 ff.; emphasis as in the original text)

68 The various stages (e.g. preparatory documents) until the completion of the CCF cannot be considered further here. A particular feature to be borne in mind is coordination with national and other development plans and documents. CCFs must also take account of the more broadly based country strategy notes. For further explanations of the structure of CCFs and of the various procedures see DP/1996/3; DP/1995/32; UNDP (1995j and 1995k).

69 "Rolling" means that, although a plan is established for a period of three years, it is updated each year. Each year that passes is replaced with a new year in the planning chain.

70 The decision specifically states: [The Executive Board] *"Decides that the United Nations Development Programme, in order to simplify the system, should reimburse the cost of administrative and support services to the five large agencies (the Food and Agriculture Organization of the United Nations, the International Labour Organization, the United Nations Industrial Development Organization and the Department of Development Support and Management Services) and the United Nations Office of Project Services with a maximum of 10 per cent, which experience has shown is the present average reimbursement rate for various inputs. Should the actual costs fall below 10 per cent, only the actual costs incurred will be reimbursed;"* (Decision 96/31, reproduced in: UNDP (1996m), p. 31; emphasis as in the original text)

71 For the details see the Administrator's appropriate report (DP/1996/13), Executive Board Decision 96/31 (reproduced in: UNDP (1996m), pp. 30 ff.) and *Overview of Support Cost Arrangements under the Successor Programming Arrangements* (UNDP (1996m)).

72 In the other cases operations are taken over by the implementing organizations or implemented by UNDP itself in the form of direct execution. In the case of World Bank projects, most of which are, however, of a completely different nature (since they are financial cooperation measures or credits and investment projects),

operations are implemented by the governments themselves (national execution), albeit with strict prescriptions and control mechanisms (see DP/1990/9, p. 85).

73 For further details on the origins of and background to the NEX concept see DP/1990/9, UNDP (1995h) and A/50/113 (the last of these documents contains a study by the Joint Inspection Unit entitled *National Execution of Projects*).

74 A definition which is technically more accurate, though less precise in its intention in development terms, reads: *"National execution is a cooperative operational arrangement entailing, inter alia, overall responsibility for the formulation and management of programmes and projects by the recipient country as well as the latter's assumption of accountability for them."* (UN (1996a), Annex 5, p. 1; emphasis as in the original text)

75 See A/RES/47/199, para. 15, which states: *"(...) national execution should be the norm for projects and programmes supported by the United nations system (...)"*

76 See, for example, GC Decision 93/25 (reproduced in: UNDP (1995h), p. 13) and the appropriate comments in EB Decision 95/23 (para. 14) (reproduced in: DP/1996/1).

77 For the controversial issues see the comments below in the assessment and evaluation.

78 See DP/1997/CRP.8, pp. 2 f. The data concern the proportion of UNDP's total project spending. The figure for 1996 - 1997 is provisional. Data obtained with other bases of calculation produce a similar picture. See, for example, UNDP (1995h), pp. 14 f., and UNDP (1997o), p. 32.

79 See DP/1997/CRP.8, p. 3, and UNDP (1995h), pp. 14 f.; for details see the regional and country statistics on the development of NEX in: UNDP (1997o), pp. 69 ff.

80 For the effects of NEX on the executing agencies and their reactions see, for example, UNDP (1995h), pp. 54 ff.; DP/1990/9, pp. 86 f., and A/50/113, pp. 26 f. The traditional executing agencies can, however, perform important implementation tasks within the framework of national execution.

81 See George Washington University (1997), pp. 17 f., and DP/1990/9, pp. 86 f.

82 An organizational unit known as the Division for Project Execution was established as early as 1973. It was later renamed Office for Project Execution and finally Office for Project Services. See UNDP (1994a) and UNOPS (1996b), p. 4.

83 UNOPS is de facto a new UN agency. When it was established, however, an attempt was made to avoid the impression that a new UN institution was being created. Some of UNDP's administrative structures are, however, used by UNOPS. Executive Board Decision 94/12 (reproduced in: DP/1995/1) states, for example: *"(...) the Office for Project Services should become a separate and identifiable*

entity in a form that does not create a new agency and in partnership with the United Nations Development Programme and other operational entities (...)"

84 See, for example, the comments in DP/1997/CRP.8, p. 8, which states: *"There is a rapidly growing demand for implementation and other development-related services at the country level. Thanks to their proximity and coordination role, UNDP country offices are often better placed than any other United Nations entity to carry out such services, as requested by governments. Demand for country office support often occurs in situations where local services are needed in support of a loan or credit from a multilateral development bank. Currently, all UNDP cooperation must be provided in the framework of a project (...)"*

85 At the time of acquisition in 1996 a volume of US $ 534m was reached; the original target was US $ 500m (see DP/1997/19, p. 2).

86 See, for example, the comments recorded in the minutes of the Executive Board's 1997 annual meeting (DP/1997/21, Chapter VIII).

87 Governing Council Decision 92/23. See also the Administrator's comments on the programme approach in his 1992 annual report: DP/1993/10, pp. 3 f.

88 See UNDP (1997b), pp. 34 f. The common definition of the terms "programme" and "programme approach" in the UN (i.e. within the CCPOQ) is as follows:

Programme: *"A programme is a coherent set of policies, strategies, activities and investments designed to achieve a specific time-bound national development objective or set of objectives."* (UN (1996a), Annex A2, p. 4)

Programme approach: *"The pursuit of national development goals through cohesive national programmes. Such as approach by national authorities will permit United Nations system inputs to be merged with national and other external inputs in support of programmes that have been conceived by the host country with such external assistance as it may seek."* (UN (1996a), Annex A2, p. 4)

89 For further details and helpful explanations see UNDP (1996j), pp. xi-xvii, and the comments in UNDP (1997o).

90 The problems are very similar to the difficulties encountered in the context of national execution (see above). A UNDP evaluation of the programme approach carried out in 1996 described the problems as follows: *"(a) a lack of clarity and training in the subject; (b) the complexity of the instrument, including procedures for financial management; (c) a lack of guidance on how Governments should evaluate their own programmes and conduct capacity assessments in the public sector and civil society; (d) the need to harmonize procedures of donors at country level. Generally, applying the programme approach involves national execution with associated costs and benefits."* (DP/1997/16, pp. 8 f.)

91 For an overview see UNDP (1996b), pp. 13 f.; DP/1997/16, pp. 15 f.; George Washington University (1997), pp. 44 ff.; UNDP (1997d, 1996f and 1995g).

92 The selection criteria are: (1) programme or project size, (2) nature of the operation (innovative, strategic, problematic) and (3) duration of the operation. For further details see UNDP (1997d), pp. 21 ff.

93 See, for example, the evaluation by Baser / Morgan (1997) of the World Bank's development cooperation.

94 A positive tendency is also detected by many members of the Executive Board (see DP/1997/21).

95 UNDP has designed an *accountability framework*, which encompasses many more aspects than the administration and implementation level. UNDP's accountability framework includes the following: *"(a) UNDP mandate, its mission and its goals; (b) Shared values; (c) Capabilities; (d) Monitoring and learning."* (DP/1996/35, p. 3) The various elements are explained in greater detail in the document. For the question of what accountability is in the UNDP context see also George Washington University (1997).

96 The report bears the document number DP/1997/16/Add. 6. See also the Executive Board's discussions on the subject (reproduced in: DP/1997/21).

97 See UNDP (1997g), pp. 7 ff.; DP/1997/16, pp. 16 ff.; DP/1997/16/Add.7, pp. 13 ff., and UNDP (1996b).

98 See UNDP (1996a). Detailed information on UNDP's administrative costs can be found in DP/1997/23. For the expected 1998 - 1999 budget the report quotes the following figures: 21.2% is to be spent on management and administration; the financing of UNDP's core programme will account for 77.7% of the total budget, the remaining 22.3% being spent on support for the other operational activities forming part of UN development cooperation.

99 A fundamental question for governments in such discussions is, for example, whether an organizational unit headed by a national of the same country retains or loses its direct access to the UNDP management as a result of reorganization.

100 For further details see George Washington University (1997), which compares UNDP's mechanisms with those of UNICEF, the UN Secretariat, USAID, the World Bank and the Hamilton Standard Electronic Manufacturing Center.

101 See, for example, the internal investigations into overpayments in connection with construction measures which the UNDP Administrator presented at the Executive Board's meeting in March 1997. UNDP also published a press release on this on 7 March 1997 (*"UNDP Investigates Overpayments for Construction Projects"*).

102 The danger of growing reform fatigue is considered especially in Centre for Development Research (1996).

Part III, Chapter 5

1 Any integration of the existing UN funds and programmes under the UNDP umbrella should lead to an appropriate adjustment of the substantive task profile, i.e. a fixed amount of financial resources would be available in each case for other specific tasks (such as *population policy* and *children*). See also the comments below on the functional elements and service functions for UN development cooperation.

2 The intensive and heated debate on the universality of human rights cannot be discussed further here. See, for example, Tetzlaff (1993); Hanisch (ed.) (1996) and Hamm (1997).

3 For this aspect see also the documents for the conference on *Democracy and Development: The Role of International Organizations*, which was organized by UNDP and Yale University in 1997 (UNDP / Yale University (eds) (1997)). See also the papers in Hanisch (ed.) (1996) and Mair (1997).

4 In this context - and especially in the context of good governance - the important documents include the UN Charter (1945), the Universal Declaration of Human Rights (1948), the International Covenant on Civil and Political Rights (1996), the International Covenant on Economic, Social and Cultural Rights (1966) and the Declaration and Programme of Action of the Vienna World Conference on Human Rights (1993).

5 The aim is not, then, to prevent socially necessary conflicts per se but to find and promote civil problem-solving mechanisms.

6 It very much depends on the practical conditions and circumstances surrounding a conflict whether and to what extent the measures referred to here actually contribute to crisis prevention or the consolidation of peace. Measures aimed at the reintegration of former combatants or refugees, for example, do not automatically have a crisis-preventing influence, but may have these effects under specific conditions. For the various areas of action see OECD (1997b); Stiefel (1994); Wissing (1995) and DSE (1996a). For fundamental aspects of crisis prevention and the consolidation of peace see, for example, Matthies (ed.) (1997) and Vogt (ed.) (1997).

7 They are (see UN (1996c), pp. 3 f.):

- Interagency Task Force on Employment and Sustainable Livelihoods (chaired by the ILO),
- Interagency Task Force on Enabling Environment for Economic and Social Development (chaired by the World Bank),
- Interagency Task Force on Basic Social Services for All (chaired by UNFPA),
- Interagency Committee on Women and Gender Equality (chaired by the Secretary-General's Special Advisor on Gender Issues).

8 It is impossible at this juncture to do more than consider some aspects of the UN world conferences superficially. For a discussion in greater depth see, for example, Messner / Nuscheler (eds) (1996); Jolly (1995); DSE (1996b) and Gsänger (1996a and 1996b).

9 For a general discussion of this problem see, for example, Cassen (1994), pp. 174 ff.; Claus et al. (1989) and the DAC's *Guiding Principles for Aid Coordination with Developing Countries* (reproduced in: OECD (1992)).

10 See the guidelines, which are reproduced in OECD (1992).

11 See, in particular, the evaluation *Aid Coordination and Aid Management by Government: A Role for UNDP* (UNDP (1996g)), the findings of *The Aid Co-ordination Evaluation* (in: UNDP (1995g), pp. 56 ff.), the report *Capacity Building for Aid Coordination in the Least Developed Countries* (UNDP (1991b and 1991c)) and the findings of the evaluation *Strengthening the Work of the Resident Coordinators: Evolving Responses to Evolving Circumstances* (in: UNDP (1997d), pp. 55 ff.).

12 The reference to programme country here again means the participation of all actors.

13 Although the donors agree on this principle (see, for example, OECD (1997a), pp. 21 ff.), they are evidently not implementing, or trying to implement, it because that would entail a loss of control and influence.

14 See the perceptive distinction between and explanations of *aid coordination* and *aid management* in: UNDP (1996g), pp. 4 f.

15 See sections III.1 and III.4. Experience with the UNDAF should be gained and evaluated as soon as possible.

16 This means that a programme country which is sufficiently *development-oriented* and has sufficient capacities for planning should play a leading role in guiding and implementing the process. Where these requirements are not met, the Resident Coordinator or UNDP must ensure that supportive know-how is made available and/or adequate participation by civil forces is promoted by UNDP.

17 The fact that the Board of the World Bank has a relatively advanced self-image that gives it an identity may explain why work procedures clearly function better in this body.

18 UNDP assumes an amount (financial requirement) four times higher than its core resources; see DP/1997/CRP.23, Chapter II. However, as this amount, which is based on the resource mobilization targets, primarily reflects UNDP's institutional objectives, it is of little informative value as to actual TC requirements in the programme countries.

19 The Nordic countries' proposals essentially point in the right direction. See Nordic UN Project (1991b); see also DP/1997/CRP.23, Annex.

20 See also, for example, the proposals by Helmke (1993) (*Concentration on product-specific resource mobilization*) and Gwin / Williams (1996), p. 136.

21 UNDP's Management Development and Governance Division has prepared various drafts and documents on this subject. See also Centre for Development Research (1996), where these aspects are considered in depth.

Part III, Chapter 6

1 Referring to the developing countries, Carlsson writes, for example: *"There are no comprehensive reviews by developing countries as to their expectations of what to get from UNDP, nor should we expect there to be any single one."* (Carlsson (1993), p. 8). On the donor countries' position he goes on to say: *"(...) there is a lack of knowledge about UNDP among senior officials in donor countries and this is reflected in the lack of clear expectations articulated by the donor community."* (Carlsson (1993), p. 10)

2 For the USA, for example: United States Department of State (1996); for the Danish position see, for example, Danida (1996a).

3 See the Federal Government's reply to the interpellation *Reform of the United Nations* (Bundesregierung (1997)).

4 See, for example, the German government's position: *"The UN General Assembly established UNDP with the aim of creating an organization for the comprehensive planning, coordination and financing of the UN's technical cooperation. However, UNDP has not yet succeeded in playing this role to the full. The Federal Government has always advocated the strengthening of UNDP along these lines."* (Bundesregierung (1997), p. 39)

5 The G7 document, for examples, states: *"Wherever there are cogent reasons for rationalization, funds and programmes should be merged into UNDP, which would be strengthened as a result (...)"* (G7 (1996), p. 635) A US document on reforms states: *"The UN Development Program clearly has the most comprehensive range of responsibilities for operational development assistance, and should form the core of functional consolidation, whether as 'primus inter pares' among UN programs and agencies or as the principal element in a formally unified development organization."* (United States Department of State (1996), p. 18) See also Nordic UN Project (1996).

6 The USA, for instance, believes that such agencies as UNICEF should retain their identity (see United States Department of State (1996), p. 18).

7 See, for example, the minutes of the Executive Board's 1997 annual meeting: DP/1997/21, Chapter VII.

8 See, for example, the minutes of the Executive Board's 1997 annual meeting: DP/1997/21, Chapter VII.

9 See, for example, the declaration by the Group of 77 on the reform of the UN (reproduced in: South Letter, Vols 1 & 2, No 28, 1997) and the studies and discussion papers of the South Centre (which, as a permanent intergovernmental institution of the developing countries, largely formulates the current common positions): South Centre (1992a, 1992b, 1995 and 1996).

10 The African countries, for instance, are particularly grateful for the coordinating role played by UNDP in post-conflict countries. See, for example, the comments made on behalf of the group of African countries recorded in the minutes of the Executive Board's first meeting in 1997 in: DP/1997/6, pp. 57 f.

11 See, for example, the minutes of the Executive Board's 1996 annual meeting, at which the final discussions of the mission statement took place: DP/1996/19, pp. 42 f.

12 See, for example, the minutes of the Executive Board's 1997 annual meeting: DP/1997/21, Chapter VIII.

13 See, for example, the discussion papers on the reform process compiled by UNFPA, UNICEF, UNDCP, UNAIDS and others for the first meeting of the Executive Committee's Development Cooperation Sector Group in: UNDP (1997c).

14 For the background see, for example, the paper by Zumach (1997) and the UNICEF press release *"UNICEF hails United Nations reform plan"* of 16 July 1997, which states: *"Ms. Bellamy said she was gratified at the report's emphatic references to the importance of preserving the identity and distinctiveness of the United Nations Funds and Programmes. 'The Secretary-General has listened to our concerns and responded to them,' she said (...)"*

15 It states, for example: *"Over the years, the absence of clear policy guidance from the General Assembly, and the lack of effective policy coordination and control by the Economic and Social Council has resulted in an overall lack of cohesion and focus within the system. At all levels, among the central organs, the programmes and the regional commissions, there has been a steady proliferation of subsidiary bodies and an increasing lack of policy coherence."* (A/48/935, para. 227).

Part III, Chapter 7

1 That is, the members of the OECD's Development Assistance Committee.

2 See, for example, the debate on trends in the external financing of the developing countries and, in this context, the role played by official development cooperation (see, for example, OECD (1997a), pp. 57 ff.).

3 The study *Assessment of UNDP: Developing Capacity for Sustainable Human Development* advocates this orientation of UNDP; see Centre for Development Research (1996).

4 The range of aspects covered would certainly be comparable, in terms of their objectives, to German bilateral technical cooperation, like that in which the German Agency for Technical Cooperation already engages.

5 It must be assumed that, besides UNDP, the only appropriate place for the Resident Coordinator system would be the UN Secretariat. The next scenario (Scenario 2) considers a *functional UNDP*, which might in principle be entrusted with and used for this task as an organizational unit within the Secretariat.

6 This would also have a number of implications (relationship between operational development cooperation measures and other of the Secretary-General's tasks, financing of the Resident Coordinator system, encouragement of micro-management within the Secretariat, etc.), which cannot be considered in greater depth here.

Part IV, Chapter 2

1 A similar observation has been made by Jacobson / Reisinger / Mathers (1986), p. 141: "*Already there are so many IGOs that it is difficult for states to control them, which could make them progressively irrelevant or even jeopardize their existence.*"

Part IV, Chapter 4

1 See also section III.7, where the consequences of disengagement by the main contributing countries are discussed.

Annex

1 See, in particular, the following documents and sources: UNDP (1994a, 1995a, 1996j); NGLS (1997), pp. 111-124; Sahlmann / Blank (1995); Ministry for Foreign Affairs and Trade (1996), pp. 184-187; BMZ (1996a); DP/1997/16; DP/1997/24. For the origins of UNDP and its precursors (EPTA and SF) see Hill (1978), pp. 138 ff.; Kirdar (1966); Dicke (1972), pp. 38 ff.; Seth (1980) and Kaufmann (1971).

Bibliography

To keep this bibliography to a manageable size, UN documents (including those of the General Assembly, ECOSOC and UNDP)[1] published as *mimeographed documents* or *official records* have been omitted. These documents can be located with the aid of their document numbers. The form of reference used in the text is based on the UN method, which is explained by Stölken (1991) and in a special UN publication (UN, 1981).

Ahlberg, H. / A. Løvbraek (1985): *UNDP in Action. A Study on UNDP Field Offices in Selected Countries in Africa and Asia* (Utrikes-Departementet, DS UD 1985:1), Stockholm

Alger, C.F. (1995): "The United Nations in Historical Perspective", in: C.F. Alger / G.M. Lyons / J.E. Trent (eds), *The United Nations System: The Policies of Member States*, Tokyo, New York, Paris, pp. 3-40

Alger, C.F. / G.M. Lyons / J.E. Trent (eds) (1995): *The United Nations System: The Policies of Member States*, Tokyo, New York, Paris

Ameri, H. (1982): *Politics and Process in the Specialized Agencies of the United Nations*, Aldershot

Anon. (1995): Report of the Expert Consultation on the Role of Autonomous Funds as Intermediaries in Channelling Money for Social and Economic Development in Africa, in: *development dialogue*, No 2, pp. 87-94

— (1996): Speth Urges Massive Regrouping of UN Secretariat Under Five Deputy S-GS, Transformation of UNDP, in: *International Documents Review, The Weekly Newsletter of the United Nations*, Vol. 7, No 28, 22-26 July 1996, pp. 1-4

Ansari, J.A. (1986): *The Political Economy of International Economic Organization*, Boulder

Archer, C. (1992): *International Organizations*, 2nd edition, London, New York

Armstrong, D. (1982): *The Rise of International Organisation, A Short History*, London

Arndt, H.W. (1979): "Problems of the Aid Recipient Country", in: R.T. Shand / H.V. Richter (eds), *International Aid: Some Political, Administrative and Technical Realities*, Canberra, pp. 34-45

Arnold, G. (1985): *Aid and the Third World, The North/South Divide*, London

1 General Assembly documents begin with the letter "A" (= *Assembly*), ECOSOC documents with the letter "E" (= ECOSOC) and UNDP documents with the letters "DP" (= *Development Programme*).

Arnold, H. (1995): "Deutschlands Rolle in der UNO", in: *Aus Politik und Zeitgeschichte*, No 42, pp. 27-35

Auerbach, K.D. (1976): "The Distribution of Multilateral Assistance: A Five Organizations Study", in: *Social Science Quarterly*, Vol. 57, No 3, pp. 644-659

Azam, J.-P. et al. (1989): "The Impact of Macroeconomic Policies on the Rural Poor, Analytical Framework and Indicators" (UNDP Policy Discussion Paper), New York

Bäumler, J. (1972): "Illusionen und Chancen der UNDP, Länderprogrammierung am Beispiel von Kamerun", in: *Entwicklung und Zusammenarbeit*, Vol. 13, No 19, pp. 7-9

Ball, N. (1996): "The Role of the International Development Community", (ODC, Policy Essay No 18), Washington, D.C.

Banya, K. (1988): "The Role of International Organizations in Aid: A Case Study of a Teacher Education Programme in Sierra Leone", in: *International Review of Education*, Vol. 34, No 4, pp. 477-493

Barthelt, R. (1997): "Sektorinvestitionsprogramme, Eine politische Entscheidung", in: *Entwicklung und Zusammenarbeit*, Vol. 38, No 3, pp. 78 f.

Barry, A.J. (1988): "Aid Co-ordination and Aid Effectiveness, A Review of Country and Regional Experience" (Development Centre Papers of the OECD), Paris

Baser, H. / P. Morgan (1997): *Review of Technical Assistance Loans in the World Bank*

Bassin, B. (1995): "The United Nations in Global Economic and Social Policy-Making", in: K. Hüfner (ed.), *Agenda for Change, New Tasks for the United Nations*, Opladen, pp. 229-238

Beigbeder, Y. (1987): *Management in United Nations Organizations, Reform or Decline?*, London

— (1995): "Reforming the Economic and Social Sectors of the United Nations: An Incomplete Process", in: K. Hüfner (ed.), *Agenda for Change, New Tasks for the United Nations*, Opladen, pp. 239-256

Bellers, J. (1994): "Integrationstheorien", in: A. Boeckh (ed.), *Lexikon der Politik*, Vol. 6, Internationale Beziehungen, Munich, pp. 217-220

Bellers, J. / E. Häckel (1990): "Theorien internationaler Integration und internationaler Organisationen", in: V. Rittberger (ed.), *Theorien der Internationalen Beziehungen, Bestandsaufnahme und Forschungsperspektiven* (PVS Special Edition 21/1990), Opladen, pp. 286-310

Bennett, A.L. (1991): *International Organizations, Principles and Issues*, 5th edition, Englewood Cliffs

Bennis, P. (1996): *Calling the Shots, How Washington Dominates Today's UN*, New York

Berg, E.J. (1993): *Rethinking Technical Cooperation, Reforms for Capacity Building in Africa*, UNDP, New York

— (1995): "Some Key Issues in Improving Technical Cooperation", in: *The International Journal of Technical Cooperation*, Vol. 1, No 1, pp. 29-38

Berridge, G.R. / A. Jennings (eds) (1985): *Diplomacy at the UN*, Houndsmills etc.

Bertrand, M. (1986): *Refaire l'ONU, un programme pour la paix*, Geneva

— (1988): *Für eine Weltorganisation der Dritten Generation*, DGVN-Texte 38, Bonn

— (1993a): "Die Reform der UNO: Welche Schwerpunkte?", in: *Entwicklung und Zusammenarbeit*, Vol. 34, No 7, pp. 164-166

— (1993b): "The Historical Development of Efforts to Reform the UN", in: A. Roberts / B. Kingsbury (eds), *United Nations, Divided World, The UN's Roles in International Relations*, 2nd edition, Oxford, pp. 420-436

— (1995): *UNO, Geschichte und Bilanz*, Frankfurt am Main

Betz, J. (1978): *Die Internationalisierung der Entwicklungshilfe*, Baden-Baden

— (1986): "Entwicklungshilfe im System der Vereinten Nationen", in: P.J. Opitz / V. Rittberger (eds), *Forum der Welt, 40 Jahre Vereinte Nationen* (Schriftenreihe der Bundeszentrale für politische Bildung, Vol. 249), Bonn, pp. 167-175

— (1996): *Entwicklungshilfe: An Einsichten mangelt es nicht*, in: J. Betz / S. Brüne / Deutsches Übersee-Institut (eds), *Jahrbuch Dritte Welt 1997, Daten, Übersichten, Analysen*, Munich, pp. 56-66

Bissell, R.E. (1985): *The United Nations Development Program, Failing the World's Poor* (The Heritage Foundation, U.N. Studies), Washington, D.C.

BMZ (1991): "Das Entwicklungsprogramm der Vereinten Nationen, UNDP", (Ref. 210), (mimeo), Bonn

— (1992): "Informationsvermerk für den Bundestagsausschuss für wirtschaftliche Zusammenarbeit, Perspektiven der multilateralen Entwicklungszusammenarbeit einschliesslich der parlamentarischen Kontrolle" (Informationsvermerk 11/92), Bonn

— (1994): "Neue Aufgaben für das VN-Entwicklungsprogramm UNDP" (Ref. 210) (mimeo, 10 May 1994), Bonn

— (1996a): "Das Entwicklungsprogramm der Vereinten Nationen, UNDP" (Ref. 210) (mimeo), Bonn

— (1996b): "Sachstand Reform der Vereinten Nationen im Bereich der EZ" (Ref. 210) (mimeo, 4 July 1996), Bonn

— (1996c): *Journalisten-Handbuch Entwicklungspolitik 1996*, Bonn

Boeckh, A. (ed.) (1994): *Lexikon der Politik*, Vol. 6, Internationale Beziehungen, Munich

Bossuyt, J. / G. Laporte / F. van Hoek (1995): "New Avenues for Technical Co-operation in Africa, Improving the Record in Terms of Capacity Building", (European Centre for Development Policy Management, Policy Management Report Number 2), Maastricht

Bovaird, A.G. / D. Gregory / J.N. Stevens (1987a): *A Study of Multilateral Agencies, Evaluation Systems*, Vol. 1, (Evaluation Department, Overseas Development Administration), London

— (1987b): *Survey of Multilateral Agency Evaluation Systems, Comparative Tables of Individual Agency Management Practices*, Vol. 2 (Evaluation Department, Overseas Development Administration), London

— (1987c): *Survey of Multilateral Agency Evaluation Practices, Review of Individual Agencies*, Vol. 3, (Evaluation Department, Overseas Development Administration), London

Bräker, H. (1968): *Multilaterale Hilfeleistung für Entwicklungsländer*, Cologne, Opladen

Brandt, W. et al. (1980): *Der Brandt-Report, Bericht der Nord-Süd-Kommission, Frankfurt a.M.*, Berlin, Vienna

Bredow, W. von / T. Jäger (eds) (1997): *Demokratie und Entwicklung, Theorie und Praxis der Demokratisierung in der Dritten Welt*, Opladen

Brigaldino, G. (1995): "Technical Co-operation in Sub-Saharan Africa, From New Avenues to Winding Roads?", in: *Journal für Entwicklungspolitik*, Vol. 11, No 2, pp. 115-132

Browne, S. (1990): *Foreign Aid in Practice*, New York

Brüne, S. (1996): "Neuer Realismus oder Das Unbehagen an der Entwicklungshilfe", in: J. Betz / S. Brüne / Deutsches Übersee-Institut (eds), Jahrbuch Dritte Welt 1997, Daten, Übersichten, Analysen, Munich, pp. 67-77

Bundesregierung (1997): Antwort der Bundesregierung auf die Große Anfrage der Abgeordneten Gert Weisskirchen (Wiesloch), Dr. Eberhard Brecht, Brigitte Adler, weiterer Abgeordneter und der Fraktion der SPD - Drucksache 13/5055 - "Reform der Vereinten Nationen", Bundestags-Drucksache 13/6773, 15 January 1997, Bonn

Burchill, S. (1996a): "Introduction", in: S. Burchill et al., *Theories of International Relations*, Houndsmill etc., pp. 1-27

— (1996b): "Realism and Neorealism", in: S. Burchill et al., *Theories of International Relations*, Houndsmill etc., pp. 67-92

Burchill, S. / A. Linklater with R. Deevetak, M. Paterson and J. True (1996): *Theories of International Relations*, Houndsmill etc.

Buyck, B. (1991): "The Bank's Use of Technical Assistance for Institutional Development" (Policy, Research, and External Affairs Working Papers Series, WPS 578, World Bank), Washington, D.C.

Caporaso, J.A. (1992): "International Relations Theory and Multilateralism: The Search for Foundations", in: *International Organization*, Vol. 46, No 3, pp. 599-632

Carlsson, B.T. (1993): "Quo Vadis, UNDP?" A Discussion Paper on the United Nations Development Programme, Prepared for the Ministry of Foreign Affairs, Sweden, Stockholm

Cassen, R. (1990): *Entwicklungszusammenarbeit*, Berne, Stuttgart

— (1994): *Does Aid Work?*, 2nd edition, Oxford etc.

Centre for Development Research (1996): "Assessment of UNDP: Developing Capacity for Sustainable Human Development", Report prepared for the Governments of Denmark, India, Sweden, and the United Kingdom, Copenhagen

Chalker, L. (1990): "Britain's Role in the Multilateral Agencies", in: *Development Policy Review*, Vol. 8, No 4, pp. 355-364

Chapelier, G. / H. Tabatabai (1989): "Development and Adjustment, Stabilization, Structural Adjustment and UNDP Policy" (UNDP Policy Discussion Paper), New York

Chenery, H. / T.N. Srinivasan (eds) (1989a): *Handbook of Development Economics*, Vol. 1, Amsterdam etc.

— (1989b): Handbook of Development Economics, Vol. 2, Amsterdam etc.

Childers, E. (1994): "Zurück zu den Völkern. Die UN müssen im Wirtschafts- und Sozialbereich handlungsfähig werden", in: *der überblick*, Vol. 30, No 3, pp. 21-25

Childers, E. / B. Urquhart (1994): *Renewing the United Nations System* (Development Dialogue Series, No 1, Dag Hammarskjöld Foundation), Uppsala

Chiwele, D.K. / A. Engel / S. Tembo (1997): "Design and Implementation of the Agricultural Sector Investment Program (ASIP) in Zambia, A Case Study" (GTZ, mimeo), Harare, Lusaka

Claus, B. et al. (1989): *Coordination of the Development Cooperation Policies of Major OECD Donor Countries* (German Development Institute), Berlin

Clinton, B. (1995): "Fiftieth Anniversary of the United Nations, Relations between the United States and the United Nations", in: *Vital Speeches of the Day*, Vol. 51, 15 July 1995, No 18, pp. 578-581

Coate, R.A. / D.J. Puchala (1990): "Global Policies and the United Nations System: Current Assessment", in: *Journal of Peace Research*, Vol. 27, No 2, pp. 127-140

Cohen, J.M. / M.S. Grindle / S.T. Walker (1985): "Foreign Aid and Conditions Precedent: Political and Bureaucratic Dimensions", in: *World Development*, Vol. 13, No 12, pp. 1211-1230

Colletta, N.J. / M. Kostner / I. Wiederhofer (1996): "The Transition from War to Peace in Sub-Saharan Africa" (The World Bank, Directions in Development), Washington, D.C.

Commission on Global Governance (1995): *Our Global Neighbourhood, The Report of the Commission on Global Governance*, Oxford

Council on Foreign Relations (ed.) (1996): "American National Interest and the United Nations", Statement and Report of an Independent Task Force, New York

Cooper, C. / J.V. van Themaat (1989): "Dutch Aid Determinants, 1973-85: Continuity and Change", in: O. Stokke (ed.), *Western Middle Powers and Global Poverty. The Determinants of the Aid Policies of Canada, Denmark, the Netherlands, Norway and Sweden*, Uppsala, pp. 117-157

Cowin, A.J. / J. Kingham (1993): "Setting Priorities at the United Nations", in: *The Heritage Foundation, Backgrounder*, No 952, pp. 1-11

Cox, R.W. (ed.) (1969): *International Organisation: World Politics*, London etc.

Cox, R.W. / H.K. Jacobson (1978): *The Anatomy of Influence, Decision-Making in International Organizations*, New Haven, London

Czempiel, E.-O. (1994): *Die Reform der UNO, Möglichkeiten und Missverständnisse*, Munich

Danida (Department of International Cooperation, Danish Ministry of Foreign Affairs) (1991a): *Effectiveness of Multilateral Agencies at Country Level, Case Study of 11 Agencies in Kenya, Nepal, Sudan and Thailand*, Copenhagen

— (1991b): *Effectiveness of Multilateral Agencies at Country Level, EC in Kenya and Sudan*, Copenhagen

— (1991c): *Effectiveness of Multilateral Agencies at Country Level, UNDP in Kenya, Nepal, Sudan and Thailand*, Copenhagen

— (1991d): *Effectiveness of Multilateral Agencies at Country Level, UNICEF in Kenya, Nepal, Sudan and Thailand*, Copenhagen

— (1991e): *Effectiveness of Multilateral Agencies at Country Level, FAO in Kenya, Nepal, Sudan and Thailand*, Copenhagen

— (1991f): *Effectiveness of Multilateral Agencies at Country Level, ILO in Kenya, Nepal, Sudan and Thailand*, Copenhagen

— (1991g): *Effectiveness of Multilateral Agencies at Country Level, World Bank in Kenya, Nepal, Sudan and Thailand*, Copenhagen

— (1991h): *Effectiveness of Multilateral Agencies at Country Level, AfDB in Kenya and Sudan*, Copenhagen

— (1991i): *Effectiveness of Multilateral Agencies at Country Level, WHO in Kenya, Nepal, Sudan and Thailand*, Copenhagen

— (1991j): *Effectiveness of Multilateral Agencies at Country Level, UNHCR in Kenya, Sudan and Thailand*, Copenhagen

— (1996a): *Plan of Action for Active Multilateralism*, Copenhagen

— (1996b): *Strategies for Individual Organizations, Annex to the Plan of Action for Active Multilateralism*, Copenhagen

Dadzie, K. (1993): "The United Nations and the Problem of Economic Development", in: A. Roberts / B. Kingsbury (eds), *United Nations, Divided World, The UN's Roles in International Relations*, 2nd edition, Oxford, pp. 297-326

De Cooker, C. (ed.) (1990): *International Administration*, Dordrecht

Dell, S. (1989): "Relations between the United Nations and the Bretton Woods Institutions", in: *Development*, Vol. 89, No 4, pp. 27-38

— (1991): *International Development Policies, Perspectives for Industrial Countries*, Durham, London

Demongeot, P.D. (1990): "Note on Project Execution" (State Department) (mimeo), Washington, D.C.

Deen, T. (1996): "Angeschlagene Jubilarin, Die Weltorganisation an ihrem Fünfzigsten", in: *Vereinte Nationen*, Vol. 44, No 1, pp. 1-5

Department of State (USA) (1994): "United States Participation in the United Nations", Report by the President to the Congress for the Year 1993, Washington, D.C.

Deutscher Bundestag (1991): Stenographisches Protokoll der 21. Sitzung (öffentlich) des Ausschusses für wirtschaftliche Zusammenarbeit am 11. Dezember 1991, Öffentliche Anhörung von Sachverständigen zum Thema "Grundsätze und Strategien für die Entwicklungspolitik in den 90er Jahren" (Protokoll Nr. 12/21), Bonn

— (1992): Wortprotokoll der 13. Sitzung des Unterausschusses Vereinte Nationen / Weltweite Organisationen des Auswärtigen Ausschusses am 09.11.1992, Öffentliche Anhörung "Reform der Vereinten Nationen", Bonn

de Vylder, S. / E. Whist (1990a): "Bolivia", in: *Nordic UN Project 1990*, pp. 45-279

— (1990b): "Ecuador", in: *Nordic UN Project 1990*, pp. 281-316

DGVN (Deutsche Gesellschaft für die Vereinten Nationen) (ed.) (1992a): "Strukturreform der UN? Notwendigkeit, Ansätze und Handlungsspielraum einer Reform der Vereinten Nationen im Bereich der wirtschaftlichen Zusammenarbeit" (Zur Diskussion gestellt, No 42), Bonn

— (1992b): "Zukunft der Vereinten Nationen, Überlegungen zu Reformansätzen der UN" (Zur Diskussion gestellt, No 41), Bonn

Dias, C.J. (1994): "Die eigenen Standards verletzt. Die Vereinten Nationen vernachlässigen ihre Aufgaben im Entwicklungsbereich", in: *der überblick*, Vol. 30, No 3, pp. 25-28

Dicke, D.C. (1972): *Die administrative Organisation der Entwicklungshilfe durch die Vereinten Nationen*, Frankfurt a. M.

Dicke, K. (1991): "Reform der UN", in: R. Wolfrum (ed.), *Handbuch Vereinte Nationen*, 2nd edition, Munich, pp. 663-673

— (1992): "Strukturreform der Vereinten Nationen?", in: DGVN (ed.), *Strukturreform der UN? Notwendigkeit, Ansätze und Handlungsspielraum einer Reform der Vereinten Nationen im Bereich der wirtschaftlichen Zusammenarbeit* (Zur Diskussion gestellt, No 42), Bonn 1992a, pp. 4-10

— (1993): "Entwicklungspolitische Aspekte der UN-Reform", in: *Entwicklung und Zusammenarbeit*, Vol. 34, No 7, pp. 172-174

— (1994): *Effizienz und Effektivität internationaler Organisationen, Darstellung und kritische Analyse eines Topos im Reformprozeß der Vereinten Nationen*, Berlin

— (1995): "Reform of the United Nations", in: R. Wolfrum (ed.), *United Nations: Law, Policies and Practice*, 2 volumes, Munich etc., pp. 1012-1024

Dicke, K. / K. Hüfner (eds) (1987): *Die Leistungsfähigkeit des VN-Systems: Politische Kritik und wissenschaftliche Analyse*, Schriftenreihe der DGVN, Bonn

Diehl, P.F. (ed.) (1989): *The Politics of International Organizations, Patterns and Insights*, Chicago

D'Orville, H. (1984): "Die operativen Aktivitäten im Dienste der Entwicklung", in: *Vereinte Nationen*, Vol. 32, No 2, pp. 54-60

D'Orville, H. / D. Najman (1994): "Klotzen statt kleckern, Vorschläge für eine solide Finanzierung der Vereinten Nationen", in: *der überblick*, Vol. 30, No 3, pp. 46-49

DSE (Deutsche Stiftung für internationale Entwicklung) (1996a): Report, "Development Cooperation as Preventive Peace Policy, Experiences, Limitations and Scope of Action", Berlin

— (1996b): Bericht, Internationaler Round Table, "Entwicklungspolitische Bewertung der UN-Weltkonferenzen 1990 bis 1996: Ziele, Ergebnisse und Umsetzungsstrategien im Vergleich", 29 October - 1 November 1996, Berlin

Dubey, M. (1977): "The Future of the United Nations Development Programme", in: *Development Dialogue*, No 1, pp. 85-100

Edgren, G. / B. Möller (1991): "The Role of the United Nations Specialized Agencies", in: *Nordic UN Project* (1991a), pp. 115-178

Eduards, K. / G. Rosén / R. Rossborough (1991): "The Role of UN in Emergencies and ad hoc Operations", in: *Nordic UN Project* (1991a), pp. 59-114

Efinger, M. et al. (1990): "Internationale Regime und internationale Politik", in: V. Rittberger (ed.), *Theorien der Internationalen Beziehungen, Bestandsaufnahme und Forschungsperspektiven* (PVS Sonderheft 21/1990), Opladen, pp. 263-285

Elmandjra, M. (1973): *The United Nations System, An Analysis*, London

Elshorst, H.J. (1995): Institutional Development: When Can it Work?, in: *The International Journal of Technical Cooperation*, Vol. 1, No 2, pp. 296-307

Engberg-Pedersen, P. / H.K. Kuloy (1990): "Nepal", in: *Nordic UN Project* (1990), pp. 203-243

Engberg-Pedersen, P. / H.V. Pedersen (1990): "Sudan", in: *Nordic UN Project* (1990), pp. 115-163

Erickson, E.W. / D.A. Sumner (1984): "The U.N. and Economic Development", in: B.Y. Pines (ed.), *A World without a U.N* (The Heritage Foundation), pp. 1-21

EU (European Union) (1996): *Proposals of the European Union for Reform of the United Nations System in the Economic and Social Areas*

Eussner, A. (1988): *Planning for Sustainability of UNDP Country Programmes and Projects, Case Study Ethopia* (German Development Institute), Berlin

Falk, R.A. (1971): "The United Nations: Various Systems of Operation", in: L. Gordenker (ed.), *The United Nations in International Politics*, Princeton, pp. 184-230

Feld, W. / R. Jordan (1989): "Patterns of Decision Making in International Organizations", in: P.F. Diehl (ed.), *The Politics of International Organizations, Patterns and Insights*, Chicago, pp. 117-134

Finkelstein, L.S. (ed.) (1988): *Politics in the United Nations System*, Durham, London

Forss, K. (1985): "Planning and Evaluation in Aid Organizations" (Ph.D. thesis; Stockholm School of Economics, Institute of International Business / The Economic Research Institute), Stockholm

Forsse, A. / E. Jul-Larsen (1990): "Mali", in: *Nordic UN Project* (1990), pp. 69-87

Frei, D. (1982): *Internationale Zusammenarbeit, Theoretische Ansätze und empirische Beiträge*, Königstein/Ts.

— (1990): *Die Organisation der Vereinten Nationen (UNO)*, Grüsch

Freudenschuss-Reichl, I. (1994): "Gerangel um eine Vision, Der mühsame Weg zu einem Entwicklungskonzept der UN", in: *der überblick*, Vol. 30, No 3, pp. 40-42

Fukuda-Parr, S. (1995): "Redefining Technical Cooperation: Challenge for the UN or Let's Dump the 'Technical Cooperation' Mandate", in: *ids bulletin*, Vol. 26, No 4, pp. 64-67

— (1996): "Beyond Rethinking Technical Cooperation: Priorities for Capacity Building and Capacity Utilisation in Africa", in: *The International Journal of Technical Cooperation*, Vol. 2, No 2, pp. 145-157

Gallarotti, G.M. (1991): "The Limits of International Organization: Systematic Failure in the Management of International Relations", in: *International Organization*, Vol. 45, No 2, pp. 183-220

Gant, G.F. (1979): *Development Administration, Concepts, Goals, Methods*, Madison, London

Gati, T.T. (ed.) (1983): *The US, the UN, and the Management of Global Change*, New York, London

George Washington University (1997): *The UNDP System of Accountability: Review, Analysis and Recommendations for the Future*, no place

Gerson, A. (1991): *The Kirkpatrick Mission, Diplomacy Without Apology: America at the United Nations, 1981-1985*, New York

Ghazarbekian, S. (1988): "Decentralization within the United Nations System", in: *Public Administration and Development*, Vol. 8, No 2, pp. 135-150

Ghebali, V.-Y. (1985): "The Politicisation of UN Specialized Agencies: A Preliminary Analysis", in: *Millennium: Journal of International Studies*, Vol. 14, Winter 1985, No 3, pp. 317-334

Girling, R. (1985): *Multinational Institutions and the Third World*, New York

Gisle, P. / M. Vainio (1990): "Cameroon", in: *Nordic UN Project* (1990), pp. 39-67

Gitelson, S.A. (1975): *Multilateral Aid for National Development and Self-Reliance, A Case Study of the UNDP in Uganda and Tanzania*, Kampala/Nairobi, Dar es Salaam

Gordenker, L. (1976): *International Aid and National Decisions, Development Programs in Malawi, Tanzania, and Zambia*, Princeton

— (1995): "UN at 50: Institutional Development", in: *International Social Science Journal*, Vol. 47, No 2, pp. 243-260

Gordenker, L. (ed.) (1971): *The United Nations in International Politics*, Princeton

Government of Eritrea (1994): "Partnership in Development", (Mimeo), Asmara

Gref, L. et al. (1970): *Bilaterale oder multilaterale Finanzhilfen?*, Cologne, Opladen

Gregg, R.W. (1988): "The Politics of International Economic Cooperation and Development", in: L.S. Finkelstein (ed.), *Politics in the United Nations System*, Durham, London, pp. 106-147

Grewe, W.G. (1991): "Entstehung und Wandlung der Vereinten Nationen", in: B. Simma (ed.), *Charta der Vereinten Nationen, Kommentar*, Munich, pp. XXIII-XLIII

Griffin, K. / T. McKinley (1996): "New Approaches to Development Cooperation", Discussion Paper Series, No 7, UNDP, New York

Groom, A.J.R. (1988): "The Advent of International Organisation", in: P. Taylor / A.J.R. Groom (eds), *International Institutions at Work*, London, pp. 3-20

Groom, A.J.R. / P. Taylor (eds) (1990): *Frameworks for International Co-operation*, London

Group of Fifteen (1995): The Summit Level Group of Developing Countries, Issue No. 5, Genf

G8 (Group of Eight) (1997): Kommuniqué der Acht, Wirtschaftsgipfel Denver, 20.-22.06.1997, printed in: *Bulletin*, Presse- und Informationsamt der Bundesregierung (ed.), 1997, No 60, pp. 693-703

G7 (Group of Seven) (1996): Economic Communiqué, Lyon G7 Summit, 28 June 1996

Gsänger, H. (1995): "Capacity-Building for Rural Development at the Micro-, Meso-, and Macro-Levels?", in: *Journal für Entwicklungspolitik*, Vol. 11, No 2, pp. 167-177

— (1996a): "Entwicklungspolitische Bewertung der UN-Weltkonferenzen 1990-1996: Ziele, Ergebnisse und Umsetzungsstrategien im Vergleich", in: DSE (1996b), pp. 68-114

— (1996b): *Weltkonferenzen und nationale Umsetzung: Der Weltsozialgipfel und sein Folgeprozess am Beispiel Malawi und Philippinen* (German Development Institute), Berlin

Gsänger, H. / T. Kampffmeyer / U. Otzen (1996): *Stellungnahme zum Einsatz lokaler Fachkräfte in der Entwicklungszusammenarbeit* (German Development Institute), Berlin

GTZ (German Agency for Technical Cooperation) (1996): *Der Einsatz einheimischer Fachkräfte in der Technischen Zusammenarbeit, Stand und Perspektiven der Einbindung des lokalen Know-how in die Arbeit der GTZ*, Eschborn

Guehenno, M.J.-M. / A. Pio (1997): "Synthesis Report from the DAC Informal Network on Technical Co-operation", DAC Seminar on technical Co-operation and Capacity Development, 9-10 December 1996, (DCD/DAC(97)6), Paris

Guest, B. (1991): "Australia's Multilateral Aid, A Case Study" (A Report Prepared as a Contribution to a Comparative Study on Donor Countries and Multilateral Development Aid by The North-South Institute), (Australian International Development Assistance Bureau, International Development Issues No. 18), Canberra

Guina, C.S. (1991): *Perspectives on Donor Behavior under the Multilateral Aid Initiative: A Philippine View* (German Development Institute), Berlin

Gurtov, M. (1991): *Global Politics in the Human Interest*, 2nd edition, Boulder, London

Gustafsson, A. / L. Rylander (1990): "Mozambique", in: *Nordic UN Project* (1990), pp. 89-114

Guttentag, J. / R. Herring (1983): "The Lender-of-Last-Resort Function in an International Context" (Essays in International Finance, No. 151), Princeton

Gwin, C. (1993): "A Comparative Assessment of the Bretton Woods and United Nations Development Institutions", Paper Prepared for the Meeting of the North-South Roundtable on "The UN and the Bretton Woods Institutions: New Challenges for the 21st Century", Bretton Woods, 1-3 September 1993 (mimeo), (Washington, D.C.)

— (1995): "A Comparative Assessment", in: M. ul Haq et al. (ed.), *The UN and the Bretton Woods Institutions, New Challenges for the Twenty-First Century*, New York, pp. 95-116

Gwin, C. / M. Williams (1996): "The U.N. System and Sustainable Development", in: C.W. Maynes / R. Williamson (eds), *U.S. Foreign Policy and the United Nations System*, New York, London, pp. 108-139

Gygi, B. (1991): *Internationale Organisationen aus der Sicht der Neuen Politischen Ökonomie*, Heidelberg

Haas, E.B. (1964): *Beyond the Nation-State: Functionalism and International Organization*, Stanford

— (1983): "Words can hurt you; or, who said what to whom about regimes", in: S.D. Krasner (ed.), *International Regimes*, Ithaca/NY, London, pp. 23-59

— (1990): *When Knowledge is Power, Three Models of Change in International Organizations*, Berkeley, Los Angeles, Oxford

Haggard, S. / B.A. Simmons (1987): "Theories of International Regimes", in: *International Organization*, Vol. 41, No 3, pp. 491-517

Hamm, B. (1997): "Politische Menschenrechte", in: I. Hauchler / D. Messner / F. Nuscheler (eds), *Globale Trends 1998. Fakten, Analysen, Prognosen*, Frankfurt a.M., pp. 398-423

Hanisch, R. (ed.) (1996): *Demokratieexport in die Länder des Südens?*, (Schriften des Deutschen Übersee-Instituts, Nr. 35), Hamburg

Hannan, M.T. / J. Freeman (1984): "Structural Inertia and Organizational Change", in: *American Sociological Review*, Vol. 49, April 1984, No 1, pp. 149-164

Haq, M. ul (1995): "An Economic Security Council", in: *ids bulletin*, Vol. 26, No 4, pp. 20-27

Haq, M. ul et al. (eds) (1995): *The UN and the Bretton Woods Institutions, New Challenges for the Twenty-First Century*, New York

Haq, M. ul / I. Kaul / I. Grunberg (eds) (1996): *The Tobin Tax, Coping with Financial Volatility*, New York, Oxford

Harrold, P. and Associates (1995): "The Broad Sector Approach to Investment, Sector Investment Programs", (World Bank Discussion Papers No. 302), Washington, D.C.

Haug, P. (1997): "Evaluation of Government Reforms", in: *Evaluation*, Vol. 2, No 4, pp. 417-430

Helmke, R. (1993): UNDP and Development Cooperation in the Post-Cold-War Period, UNDP (mimeo), New York

Heinz, W.S. (1994): *Positive Maßnahmen zur Förderung von Demokratie und Menschenrechten als Aufgabe der Entwicklungszusammenarbeit* (German Development Institute), Berlin

Heuel, J. (1997): "Bilaterale versus multilaterale Entwicklungszusammenarbeit am Beispiel der Vereinten Nationen, Eine Analyse aus traditioneller und institutionenökonomischer Sicht" (Entwicklungsökonomische Diskussionsbeiträge, Universität Giessen, Nr. 23), Giessen

Hill, M. (1978): The United Nations System: coordinating its economic and social work (A study prepared under the auspices of the United Nations Institute for Training and Research), Cambridge etc.

Hofmann, M. (1989): Multilateral Assistance Policies of the FR of Germany (A Report as a Contribution to a Comparative Study by The North-South Institute) (mimeo), Bonn

Holsti, K.J. (1992): *International Politics, A Framework for Analysis*, 6th edition, Englewood Cliffs

Holtz, U. (1993): "Bonner Fraktionen für einen Umbau der UN", in: *Entwicklung und Zusammenarbeit*, Vol. 34, No 7, pp. 170 f.

Horberry, J. (1985): "The Accountability of Development Assistance Agencies: The Case of Environmental Policy", in: *Ecology Law Quarterly*, Vol. 12, No 4, pp. 817-869

Hoyer, W. (1995): "Die Vereinten Nationen: Die nächsten 50 Jahre", in: *KAS* (Konrad-Adenauer-Stiftung*) - Auslandsinformation*, Vol. 11, No 5, pp. 14-21

Hubert, K. (1997): "Sektorinvestitionsprogramme, Erste Erfahrungen und künftige Probleme", in: *Entwicklung und Zusammenarbeit*, Vol. 38, No 3, pp. 80 ff.

Hüfner, K. (1983): "Die freiwilligen Finanzleistungen an das UN-System", in: *German Yearbook of International Law, Jahrbuch für internationales Recht*, Vol. 26, pp. 299-342

— (1989): "The Nature and Role of Multilateral Assistance of the United Nations System", in: J.P. Renninger (ed.), *The Future Role of the United Nations in an Interdepedent World*, Dordrecht, pp. 172-190

— (1991a): Die Vereinten Nationen und ihre Sonderorganisationen, Strukturen, Aufgaben, Dokumente, Teil 1: Die Haupt- und Spezialorgane, (DGVN-Texte 40), Bonn

— (1991b): "UN-System", in: R. Wolfrum (ed.), *Handbuch Vereinte Nationen*, 2nd edition, Munich, pp. 966-973

— (1991c): "Reform der UN", in: R. Wolfrum (ed.), *Handbuch Vereinte Nationen*, 2nd edition, Munich, pp. 663-673

— (1992a): "Der ECOSOC-Kern des Unbehagens, Optionen für eine ECOSOC-Reform", in: DGVN (ed.) (1992a), *Strukturreform der UN? Notwendigkeit, Ansätze und Handlungsspielraum einer Reform der Vereinten Nationen im Bereich der wirtschaftlichen Zusammenarbeit* (Zur Diskussion gestellt, No 42), Bonn, pp. 29-39

— (1992b): "UNDP in Trouble: Financial and Political Problems", in: DGVN (ed.) (1992a), *Strukturreform der UN? Notwendigkeit, Ansätze und Handlungsspielraum einer Reform der Vereinten Nationen im Bereich der wirtschaftlichen Zusammenarbeit* (Zur Diskussion gestellt, No 42), Bonn, pp. 39-43

— (1995): "Financing the UN: Proposals for Reform", in: K. Hüfner (ed.), *Agenda for Change, New Tasks for the United Nations*, Opladen, pp. 257-268

— (1997): Die Vereinten Nationen und ihre Sonderorganisationen, Teil 3: Finanzierung des Systems der Vereinten Nationen, Teil 3A: Vereinte Nationen - Friedensoperationen - Spezialorgane (DGVN-Texte 45), Bonn

Hüfner, K. (ed.) (1994): *Die Reform der Vereinten Nationen, Die Weltorganisation zwischen Krise und Erneuerung*, Opladen

— (1995): *Agenda for Change, New Tasks for the United Nations*, Opladen

Hüfner, K. / J. Naumann (1985): "USA und UNO: Anmerkungen zur gegenwärtigen Krise", in: *Vereinte Nationen*, Vol. 33, No 3, pp. 85-90

— (1986): "Vereinte Nationen und Dritte Welt", in: Deutsches Übersee-Institut (ed.), *Jahrbuch Dritte Welt 1986*, Munich, pp. 37-48

Hüfner, K. / W. Spröte (1994): "Zur Reform des Wirtschafts- und Sozialbereichs der Vereinten Nationen", in: K. Hüfner (ed.), *Die Reform der Vereinten Nationen, Die Weltorganisation zwischen Krise und Erneuerung*, Opladen, pp. 99-118

Huntington, S.P. (1973): "Transnational Organizations in World Politics", in: *World Politics*, Vol. 15, No 3, pp. 333-368

Hurrell, A. (1993): "International Society and the Study of Regimes: A Reflective Approach", in: V. Rittberger (ed.), *Regime Theory and International Relations*, Oxford, pp. 49-72

Hydén, G. (1995): "Reforming Foreign Aid to African Development, A Proposal to Set up Politically Autonomous Development Funds", in: *development dialogue*, No 2, pp. 34-52

ICVA (International Council of Voluntary Agencies) / **Eurostep (eds)** (1996): *The Reality of Aid 1996, An Independent Review of International Aid*, London

Independent Advisory Group on U.N. Financing (1993): Financing an Effective United Nations, A Report of the Independent Advisory Group on U.N. Financing, New York

Independent Working Group on the Future of the United Nations (1995): The United Nations in its Second Half-Century, A Report of the Independent Working Group on the Future of the United Nations, New York

International Round Table (1995): Potential and Use of National Capacities and the Role of Foreign Expert in Future Development Cooperation, Edited Advance Report of Findings and Recommendations of the International Round Table, Berlin, 16-19 May 1995, in: *International Technical Cooperation*, Vol. 1, No 2, pp. 276-295

Jacobson, H.K. / W.M. Reisinger / T. Mathers (1986): "National Entanglements in International Governmental Organizations", in: *American Political Science Review*, Vol. 80, No 1, pp. 141-159

Jaycox, E.V.K. (1993): "'Capacity Building': Das fehlende Kettenglied der afrikanischen Entwicklung", reproduced in: *epd-Entwicklungspolitik*, No 18, pp. d-g

JDZB (Japanisch-Deutsches Zentrum Berlin) **(ed.)** (1991): Symposium: "The Role of the United Nations in the 1990s" (JDZB Publication, Vol. 4), Berlin

Jönsson, C. (1986): "Interorganization Theory and International Organization", in: *International Organization*, Vol. 30, No 1, pp. 39-57

— (1993): "Cognitive Factors in Explaining Dynamics", in: V. Rittberger (ed.), *Regime Theory and International Relations*, Oxford, pp. 202-222

Jolly, R. (1995): "UN Reform: Focus for Action", in: *ids bulletin*, Vol. 26, No 4, pp. 8-14

Kärre, B. / B. Svensson (1989): "The Determinants of Swedish Aid Policy", in: O. Stokke (ed.), *Western Middle Powers and Global Poverty. The Determinants of the Aid Policies of Canada, Denmark, the Netherlands, Norway and Sweden*, Uppsala, pp. 231-274

Kahn, L.K. (1989): "Nations as Organizations: Organizational Theory and International Relations", in: *Journal of Social Issues*, Vol. 45, No 2, pp. 181-194

Kaiser, K. / H.-P. Schwarz (eds) (1995): Die neue Weltpolitik, Bundeszentrale für politische Bildung, Vol. 334, Bonn

Kalderén, L. (1991): "The UN and the Bretton Woods Institutions", in: *Nordic UN Project* (1991a), pp. 323-356

Karns, M.P. / K.A. Mingst (1995): "The Past as Prologue: The United States and the Future of the UN System", in: C.F. Alger / G.M. Lyons / J.E. Trent (eds), *The United Nations System: The Policies of Member States*, Tokyo, New York, Paris, pp. 410-460

Karns, M.P. / K.A. Mingst (eds) (1990): *The United States and Multilateral Institutions, Patterns of Changing Instrumentality and Influence*, London etc.

Kaufmann, J. (1971): "The Capacity of the United Nations Development Program: The Jackson Report", in: *International Organization*, Vol. 25, No 4, pp. 938-949

— (1980): *United Nations Decision Making*, Alphen aan den Rijn, Rockville

Kaul, I. (1997): Six Proposals for UN Reform (mimeo), New York

Kay, D.A. (1980): *The Functioning and Effectiveness of Selected United Nations System Programs*, Washington, D.C.

Keck, O. (1991): "Der neue Institutionalismus in der Theorie der Internationalen Beziehungen", in: *PVS (Politische Vierteljahreszeitschrift)*, Vol. 32, No 4, pp. 635-653

Keohane, R.O. (1989): *International Institutions and State Power, Essays in International Relations Theory*, Boulder etc.

— (1990): "Multilateralism: An Agenda for Research", in: *International Journal*, Vol. 45, Autumn 1990, pp. 731-764

— (1993): "The Analysis of International Regimes: Towards a European-American Research Programme", in: V. Rittberger (ed.), *Regime Theory and International Relations*, Oxford, pp. 23-45

Kienbaum & Partners (1991): *A Strategy-Based Senior Management Structure for the United Nations Development Programme*, New York

Kinkel, K. (1995): Wir kommen unserer Verantwortung nach, Rede des deutschen Aussenministers vor der 50. UN-Generalversammlung (27.9.1995), in: *Vereinte Nationen*, Vol. 44, No 1, pp. 11-13

Kirdar, Ü. (1966): *The Structure of United Nations Economic Aid to Underdeveloped Countries*, The Hague

Khna, J. (1994): "Development Planning and Management in the OECS Countries: The Experiences of the UNDP", in: *BISS* (Bangladesh Institute of International Strategic Studies) *Journal*, Vol. 15, No 3, pp. 255-276

Klingebiel, S. (1993): "Multilaterale Entwicklungspolitik", in: *Aus Politik und Zeitgeschichte*, H. 12-13, pp. 22-28

— (1996): Entwicklungszusammenarbeit im Rahmen der Vereinten Nationen (Reihe: UN Basis Info, DGVN (Deutsche Gesellschaft für die Vereinten Nationen)), Bonn

— (1997): Wenig Lobby für mehr Multilateralismus? Deutschland und die Entwicklungszusammenarbeit der Vereinten Nationen, in: UN-williges Deutschland, Der WEED-Report zur deutschen UNO-Politik, Bonn, pp. 124-145

Knapp, M. (1991): "Die Rolle der Vereinten Nationen in den Internationalen Beziehungen", in: M. Knapp / G. Krell (eds), *Einführung in die Internationale Politik*, 2nd edition, Munich, Vienna

Knipping, F. / H. von Mangoldt / V. Rittberger (eds) (1995): *Das System der Vereinten Nationen und seine Vorläufer*, Vol. I/1, United Nations, Berne, Munich

Köhler, P.A. (1987): Sozialpolitische und sozialrechtliche Aktivitäten in den Vereinten Nationen (Studien aus dem Max-Planck-Institut für ausländisches und internationales Sozialrecht, Vol. 4), Baden-Baden

Koetz, A.G. / M. Otte (1992): "Krise und Reform der UN-Entwicklungshilfe", in: *Aussenpolitik*, Vol. 43, No 2, pp. 185-194

Kohler-Koch, B. (1989): "Zur Empirie und Theorie internationaler Regime", in: B. Kohler-Koch (ed.), *Regime in den Internationalen Beziehungen*, Baden-Baden, pp. 17-85

— (1994): "Interdependenz-Analyse", in: A. Boeckh (ed.), *Lexikon der Politik*, Vol. 6, Internationale Beziehungen, Munich, pp. 221-225

Kohler-Koch, B. (ed.) (1989): *Regime in den Internationalen Beziehungen*, Baden-Baden

Kolles, V. (1994): Freiwillige Beitragsleistungen an das System der Vereinten Nationen am Beispiel des UNDP (1970-1993) (mimeo, thesis), Berlin

Koschorreck, W. (1983): "Programmziele und finanzielle Leistungsfähigkeit im Widerstreit, Die Geschichte der Beitragsfestsetzung in den Vereinten Nationen", in: *Vereinte Nationen*, Vol. 31, No 2, pp. 51-57

— (1991a): "Beitragssystem", in: R. Wolfrum (ed.), *Handbuch Vereinte Nationen*, 2nd edition, Munich 1991, pp. 45-53

— (1991b): "Finanzkrise", in: R. Wolfrum (ed.), *Handbuch Vereinte Nationen*, 2nd edition, Munich 1991, pp. 148-155

Kotschnig, W.M. (1968): "The United Nations as an Instrument of Economic and Social Development", in: *International Organization*, Vol. 22, No 1, pp. 16-43

Krasner, S.D. (1983a): "Structural Causes and Regime Consequences: Regimes as Intervening Variables", in: S.D. Krasner (ed.), *International Regimes*, Ithaca/NY, London, pp. 1-21

— (1983b): "Regimes and the Limits of Realism: Regimes as Autonomous Variables", in: S.D. Krasner (ed.), *International Regimes*, Ithaca/NY, London, pp. 355-368

Krasner, S.D. (ed.) (1983): *International Regimes*, Ithaca/NY, London

Kratochwil, F. / J.G. Ruggie (1986): "International Organization: a State of the Art on an Art of the State", in: *International Organization*, Vol. 40, No 4, pp. 753-775

Krueger, A.O. / C. Michalopoulos / V.W. Ruttan (1989): *Aid and Development*, Baltimore, London

Kulessa, M. (1991): "Der Resident Co-ordinator", in: R. Wolfrum (ed.), *Handbuch Vereinte Nationen*, 2nd edition, Munich, pp. 686-693

Kunig, P. (1991): "Entwicklungsbanken, regionale", in: R. Wolfrum (ed.), *Handbuch Vereinte Nationen*, 2nd edition, Munich, pp. 117-123

Kydd, A. / D. Snidal (1993): "Progress in Game-Theoretical Analysis of International Regimes", in: V. Rittberger (ed.), *Regime Theory and International Relations*, Oxford, pp. 112-135

Labouisse, H.R. (1983): "Humanitäre Hilfe als Beitrag zur Entwicklung", in: *Vereinte Nationen*, Vol. 30, No 1, pp. 74-78

Lagoni, R. (1995): "ECOSOC-Economic and Social Council", in: R. Wolfrum (ed.), *United Nations: Law, Policies and Practice*, 2 volumes, Munich etc., pp. 461-469

Lavergne, R.P. (1989): "Determinants of Canadian Aid Policy", in: O. Stokke (ed.), *Western Middle Powers and Global Poverty. The Determinants of the Aid Policies of Canada, Denmark, the Netherlands, Norway and Sweden*, Uppsala, pp. 33-89

Lehmkuhl, U. (1996): *Theorien internationaler Politik*, Einführung und Texte, Munich, Vienna

Lele, U. / I. Nabi (eds) (1991): *Transitions in Development: The Role of Aid and Commercial Flows*, San Francisco

Lichtenstein, Ch.M. et al. (1986): The United Nations: Its Problems and What to Do About Them (The Heritage Foundation, United Nations Assessment Project), Washington, D.C.

Lindell, U. (1988): *Modern Multilateral Negotiation*, Lund

Luard, E. (1977): *International Agencies*, London

— (1990): *The Globalization of Politics, The Changed Focus of Political Action in the Modern World*, Houndsmill etc.

Lyons, G.M. (1995a): "Competing Visions: Proposals for UN Reform", in: C.F. Alger / G.M. Lyons / J.E. Trent (eds), *The United Nations System: The Policies of Member States*, Tokyo, New York, Paris, pp. 41-85

— (1995b): "International Organizations and National Interests", in: *International Social Science Journal*, Vol. 47, 1995, No 2, pp. 261-276

Mahajan, B.S. (1989): *Programming of Operational Activities of United Nations System*, New York

Mair, S. (1997): *Internationale Demokratisierungshilfe, Erfahrungen und Aufgaben*, (Stiftung Wissenschaft und Politik, AP 3020), Ebenhausen

Mango, A. (1988): "The Role of the Secretariats of International Institutions", in: P. Taylor / A.J.R. Groom (eds), *International Institutions at Work*, London, pp. 39-49

Mangone, G.J. (1966): "Field Administration: The United Nations Resident Representative", in: G.J. Mangone (ed.), *UN Administration of Economic and Social Programs*, New York, London, pp. 158-230

Mangone, G.J. (ed.) (1966): *UN Administration of Economic and Social Programs*, New York, London

Martens, J. (1989): Die Vereinten Nationen zwischen Krise und Erneuerung, Eine Bestandsaufnahme von vier Jahrzehnten Reformdiskussion (Diplomarbeit an der FU Berlin), Berlin

— (1997): "Annans 'stille Revolution'", in: *epd-Entwicklungspolitik*, No 15/16, pp. 24-26

Matthies, V. (ed.) (1997): *Der gelungene Frieden. Beispiele und Bedingungen erfolgreicher Konfliktbearbeitung*, Bonn

Maull, H.W. (1995): "Welche Akteure beeinflussen die Weltpolitik?", in: K. Kaiser / H.-P. Schwarz (eds), *Die neue Weltpolitik*, Bundeszentrale für politische Bildung, Vol. 334, Bonn, pp. 301-315

Mayer, P. / V. Rittberger / M. Zürn (1993): "Regime Theory: State of the Art and Perspectives", in: V. Rittberger (ed.), *Regime Theory and International Relations*, Oxford, pp. 391-430

Maynes, C.W. / R. Williamson (eds) (1996): *U.S. Foreign Policy and the United Nations System*, New York, London

McCormick, J. (1989): "Intergovernmental Organizations and Cooperation among Nations", in: P.F. Diehl (ed.), *The Politics of International Organizations, Patterns and Insights*, Chicago, pp. 83-98

McLaren, R. (1987): "Co-ordination of the United Nations System", in: *International Review of Administration Science*, Vol. 53, No 3, pp. 383-394

— (1990): "The International Network: Administrative Lessons from GESAMP", in: *International Review of Administrative Science*, Vol. 56, No 4, pp. 653-669

Meier, G.M. (1984): "The Formative Period", in: G.M. Meier / D. Seers (eds), *Pioneers in Development. A World Bank Publication*, New York etc., pp. 3-22

Meier, G.M. / D. Seers (eds) (1984): *Pioneers in Development. A World Bank Publication*, New York etc.

Meng, W. (1991): "Wirtschaftliche Zusammenarbeit unter dem UN-System", in: R. Wolfrum (ed.), *Handbuch Vereinte Nationen*, 2nd edition, Munich, pp. 1133-1142

Menon, B. (1994): "Verschleisserscheinungen, Die Vereinten Nationen in der 'midlife crisis'", in: *der überblick*, Vol. 30, No 3, pp. 5-8

Mentz, J.C.N. (1997): "Personal and Institutional Factors in Capacity Building and Institutional Development", ECDPM (European Centre for Development Policy Management) Working Paper No 14, Maastricht

Messner, D. / F. Nuscheler (1996a): "Global Governance, Organisationselemente und Säulen einer Weltordnungspolitik", in: D. Messner / F. Nuscheler (eds), *Weltkonferenzen und Weltberichte, Ein Wegweiser durch die internationale Diskussion*, Bonn, pp. 12-36

— (1996b): "Die Weltkonferenzen der 90er Jahre, Eine "Gipfelei" ohne neue Perspektiven?", in: D. Messner / F. Nuscheler (eds), *Weltkonferenzen und Weltberichte, Ein Wegweiser durch die internationale Diskussion*, Bonn, pp. 160-169

Messner, D. / F. Nuscheler (eds) (1996): *Weltkonferenzen und Weltberichte, Ein Wegweiser durch die internationale Diskussion*, Bonn

Meyers, R. (1990): "Metatheorien und methodologische Betrachtungen zur Theorie der internationalen Beziehungen", in: V. Rittberger (ed.), *Theorien der Internationalen Beziehungen, Bestandsaufnahme und Forschungsperspektiven* (PVS Sonderheft 21/1990), Opladen, pp. 48-68

— (1994): "Internationale Beziehungen als akademische Disziplin", in: A. Boeckh (ed.), *Lexikon der Politik*, Vol. 6, Internationale Beziehungen, Munich, pp. 231-241

Mezger, D. / G. Urban / H. Warth (1994): Die Instrumente der Personellen Zusammenarbeit und ihre Eignung für die Beschäftigung einheimischer Fachkräfte (Forschungsberichte des BMZ, Vol. 112), Munich etc.

Miller, J.D.B. (1979): "The Politics of International Aid", in: R.T. Shand / H.V. Richter (eds), *International Aid: Some Political, Administrative and Technical Realities*, Canberra, pp. 1-15

Miller, L.B. (1971): "International Organization and Internal Conflicts: Some Emerging Patterns of Response", in: L. Gordenker (ed.), *The United Nations in International Politics*, Princeton, pp. 130-150

Miller, L.H. (1990): *Global Order, Values and Power in International Politics*, 2nd edition, Boulder etc.

Minister for Development Cooperation (and the Minister of Finance) (Netherlands) (1992): Policy Document on Multilateral Development Cooperation. An Evaluation of the Multilateral Organisations as a Channel for Dutch Aid

Ministry of Foreign Affairs and Trade (New Zealand) (1994): *United Nations Handbook 1994*, Wellington

— (1996): *United Nations Handbook 1996*, Wellington

Ministry of Foreign Affairs (Netherlands) (1991): *A World of Difference, A New Framework for Development Cooperation in the 1990s*, The Hague

Mistry, P.S. (1991): "Multilateral Development Bank (MDB) Financing in the 1990s", in: *Nordic UN Project* (1991a), pp. 299-322

Mistry, P.S. / P. Thyness (1991): "Options for Funding the UN System and the Development Banks", in: *Nordic UN Project* (1991a), pp. 179-298

Mitzlaff, K. von / A. Vermehren (1993): "Technische Zusammenarbeit am Ende - oder am Ende einer Epoche?", in: *Nord-Süd aktuell*, Vol. 7, No 4, pp. 582-587

Moore, J. (1996): *The UN and Complex Emergencies, Rehabilitation in Third World Transitions*, Geneva

Morgenthau, H.J. (1962): "A Political Theory of Foreign Aid", in: *American Political Science Review*, Vol. 56, No 2, pp. 301-325

— (1973): *Politics among Nations, The Struggle for Power and Peace*, 5th edition, New York

Morse, B. (1977): "Zur Rolle des Entwicklungsprogramms der Vereinten Nationen, Sieben Charakteristika der multilateralen Hilfe", in: *Vereinte Nationen*, Vol. 25, No 4, pp. 104-107

Mosley, P. (1987): *Overseas Aid, Its Defence and Reform*, Brighton

Mothander, B. / K. Flodman (1989): Swedish Multilateral Development Assistance, A Report Prepared as Contribution to a Study by the North-South Institute, Ottawa, Canada, on Donor Countries and Multilateral Aid (study commissioned by the Swedish Foreign Ministry), Stockholm

Müller, J. (1994): "Zwischen Politik und Effizienz, Die Reform der Vereinten Nationen im Konflikt der Interessen", in: *der überblick*, Vol. 30, No 3, pp. 8-14

Müller, J.W. (1992): *The Reform of the United Nations*, 2 volumes, New York etc.

Müller, H. (1995): "Internationale Regime und ihr Beitrag zur Weltordnung", in: K. Kaiser / H.-P. Schwarz (eds), *Die neue Weltpolitik*, Bundeszentrale für politische Bildung, Vol. 334, Bonn, pp. 384-395

Mützelburg, B. / W. Karl (1991): "Kapitel XVIII. Änderungen", in: B. Simma (ed.), *Charta der Vereinten Nationen, Kommentar*, Munich, pp. 1108-1124.

Museveni, H.E.Y.K. (1995): "The Role of Independent Funds for Social and Economic Development in Africa", in: *development dialogue*, No 2, pp. 7-10

Myrdal, G. (1984): "International Inequality and Foreign Aid in Retrospect", in: G.M. Meier / D. Seers (eds), *Pioneers in Development. A World Bank Publication*, New York etc., pp. 151-165

Najman, D. / H. d'Orville (1995): *Towards a New Multilateralism: Funding Global Priorities, Innovative Financing Mechanisms for Internationally Agreed Programmes*, Paris, New York

Nashat, M. (1978): *National Interests and Bureaucracy versus Development Aid, A Study of United Nations Expanded Programme of Technical Assistance to the Third World*, Geneva

National Advisory Council for Development Cooperation (The Netherlands) (1996): International Funds for Cross-Border Problems, Looking for the Big Money, No. 107, The Hague

Nicol, D. / J. Renninger (1982): "The Restructuring of the UN Economic and Social System: Background and Analysis", in: *Third World Quarterly*, Vol. 4, No 4, pp. 74-92

NGLS (United Nations Non-Governmental Liaison Service) (1997): *The NGLS Handbook of UN Agencies, Programmes and Funds Working for Economic and Social Development*, 2nd edition, Geneva

Nölke, A. (1995): "Geberkoordination für die Länder Afrikas südlich der Sahara, Analyse eines interorganisatorischen Netzwerkes zwischen bi- und multilateralen Entwicklungshilfeagenturen", Konstanzer Schriften zur Politik und Verwaltungswissenschaft, Vol. 2, Baden-Baden

— (1997): "Die Vereinten Nationen im Bereich der Entwicklungszusammenarbeit: Ein Netzwerk, kein System", in: *WeltTrends, Internationale Politik und vergleichende Studien*, No 9, pp. 105-120

Nohlen, D. (ed.) (1989): *Lexikon Dritte Welt*, 3rd edition, Reinbeck

Nohlen, D. / F. Nuscheler (eds) (1992): *Handbuch der Dritten Welt*, Vol. 1, Grundprobleme, Theorien, Strategien, 3rd edition, Bonn

Nolte, B. (1991): "Uniting for Peace", in: R. Wolfrum (ed.), *Handbuch Vereinte Nationen*, 2nd edition, Munich, pp. 950-956

Norbye, O.D.K. / K. Kiljunen (1990): "Bangladesh", in: *Nordic UN Project* (1990), pp. 165-201

Nordic UN Project (1990a): *Perspectives on Multilateral Assistance*, A Review by Nordic UN Project, Stockholm

— (1990b): *The Office of UN Director-General for Development and International Economic Co-operation*, Stockholm

— (1991a): *The United Nations: Issues and Options*, Five Studies on the Role of the UN in the Economic and Social Fields Commissioned by Nordic UN Project, Stockholm

— (1991b): The United Nations in Development, Reform Issues in the Economic and Social Fields, A Nordic Perspective, Final Report by Nordic UN Project, Stockholm

— (1996): *The United Nations in Development, Strengthening the UN through Change: Fulfilling Its Economic and Social Mandate*, Oslo

Nord-Süd-Gesprächskreis (1992): Stärkung der Vereinten Nationen für die neunziger Jahre, Auszüge aus dem Bericht des Nord-Süd-Gesprächkreises, 18.-19.01.1991, Tarrytown/NY, in: DGVN (ed.) (1992b), Zukunft der Vereinten Nationen, Überlegungen zu Reformansätzen der UN (Zur Diskussion gestellt, No 41), Bonn, pp. 10-21

North South Roundtable (SID) (1991): Strengthening the United Nations for the 1990s, Report of the North South Roundtable Session on Strengthening the UN for the 1990s, New York

Nuscheler, F. (1997): "Alter Wein in neuen Schläuchen? Kritische Anmerkungen zu den UNDP-Reports", in: *SEF NEWS*, No 9 (December 1997), pp. 7-9

Nuscheler, F. / S. Klingebiel (1994): "Entwicklungspolitik, internationale", in: A. Boeckh (ed.), *Lexikon der Politik*, Vol. 6, Internationale Beziehungen, Munich, pp. 108-126

ODI (Overseas Development Institute) (1987): "The UN and the Future of Multilateralism", Briefing Paper, October 1987, London

— (1994): "Aid in Transition", Briefing Paper, November 1994, London

— (1996): "New Sources of Finance for Development", Briefing Paper, February 1996, London

— (1997): "The UN's Role in Grant-Financed Development", Briefing Paper, May 1997, London

OECD (1985): *Twenty-Five Years of Development Co-operation, A Review, Efforts and Policies of the Members of the Development Assistance Committee*, Paris

— (1992): DAC Principles for Effective Aid, Paris

— (1994): *Entwicklungshilfe-Handbuch*, DAC-Grundsätze für wirksame Entwicklungshilfe, Paris

— (1995a): "Principles for New Orientations in Technical Co-operation", in: *The International Journal of Technical Cooperation*, Vol. 1, No 1, pp. 1-17

— (1995b): "Improving the Effectiveness of Technical Cooperation in the 1990s", OECD Working Papers, No. 3, Paris

— (1995c): Participatory Development and Good Governance, (OECD, Development Co-operation Guidelines Series), Paris

— (1996a): Entwicklungszusammenarbeit, Politik und Leistungen der Mitglieder des Ausschusses für Entwicklungshilfe, Bericht 1995, Paris

— (1996b): *Shaping the 21st Century: The Contribution of Development Co-operation*, Paris

— (1996c): Development Co-operation, Efforts and Policies of the Members of the Development Assistance Committee, 1995 Report, Paris

— (1997a): Development Co-operation, Efforts and Policies of the Members of the Development Assistance Committee, 1996 Report, Paris

— (1997b): DAC Guidelines on Conflict, Peace and Development Co-operation, Paris

Opitz, P.J. / V. Rittberger (eds) (1986): *Forum der Welt, 40 Jahre Vereinte Nationen*, (Schriftenreihe der Bundeszentrale für politische Bildung, Vol. 249), Bonn

Oshiba, R. (1991): "Prospects for Restructuring World Trade and Perspectives for Multilateral Development Organizations", in: JDZB (ed.), *Symposium: "The Role of the United Nations in the 1990s"* (JDZB Publication, Vol. 4), pp. 106-114

Osmanczyk, E.J. (1985): *The Encyclopedia of the United Nations and International Agreements*, Philadelphia, London

Oye, K. (ed.) (1985): *Cooperation under Anarchy*, Princeton

Parsons, A. (1989): "The United Nations and the National Interests of States", in: A. Roberts / B. Kingsbury (eds), *United Nations, Divided World: The UN's Roles in International Relations*, Oxford, pp. 31-45

Paschke, K.T. (1996): "Innenrevision in den Vereinten Nationen - eine neue Erfahrung", in: *Vereinte Nationen*, Vol. 44, No 2, pp. 41-45

Pearson, L.B. (Vors.) (1969): Der Pearson-Bericht, Bestandsaufnahme und Vorschläge zur Entwicklungspolitik, Bericht der Kommission für Internationale Entwicklung, Vienna etc.

Pentland, C. (1989): "International Organizations and their Roles", in: P.F. Diehl (ed.), *The Politics of International Organizations, Patterns and Insights*, Chicago, pp. 5-14

Pines, B.Y. (ed.) (1984): *A World without a U.N* (The Heritage Foundation)

Pitt, D. / T.G. Weiss (eds) (1986): *The Nature of United Nations Bureaucracies*, London, Sydney

Protheroe, D.R. (1991): Canada and Multilateral Aid, A Report Prepared as a Contribution to a Comparative Study on Donor Countries and Multilateral Development Aid by the North-South Institute, Ottawa

Puchala, D.J. (1989): "American Interests and the United States", in: P.F. Diehl (ed.), *The Politics of International Organizations, Patterns and Insights*, Chicago, pp. 410-428

— (1996): "Reforming the United Nations or Going Beyond?", in: Ch.W. Maynes / R. Williamson (eds), *U.S. Foreign Policy and the United Nations System*, New York, London, pp. 229-248

Quendler, F. (1990): "Das System der UN-Sonderorganisationen und Probleme funktionaler Aussenpolitik am Beispiel Österreichs", in: *Österreichische Zeitschrift für Politikwissenschaft*, Vol. 19, No 4, pp. 397-408

Raffer, K. / H.W. Singer (1996): *The Foreign Aid Business, Economic Assistance and Development Co-operation*, Cheltenham, Brookfield

Raphaeli, N. (1996): "Technical Cooperation and the World Bank", in: *The International Journal of Technical Cooperation*, Vol. 2, No 2, pp. 224-235

Renninger, J.P. (1987): "Improving the United Nations system", in: *Development Planning*, No 17, pp. 85-111

Renninger, J.P. (ed.) (1989): *The Future Role of the United Nations in an Interdepedent World*, Dordrecht

Reymond, H. / S. Mailick (1985): International Personnel Policies and Practices, New York

Riddell, R. (1987): *Foreign Aid Reconsidered*, Baltimore

— (1996): "Aid in the 21st Century", Discussion Paper Series, No 6, UNDP, New York

Righter, R. (1995): *Utopia Lost. The United Nations and World Order*, New York

Rittberger, V. (1984): "Aufgaben und Leistungen internationaler Organisationen", in: *Universitas*, Vol. 39, No 2, pp. 183-193

— (1991a): "Theorie der Internationalen Organisationen", in: R. Wolfrum (ed.), *Handbuch Vereinte Nationen*, 2nd edition, Munich, pp. 363-372

— (1991b): "Zur Politik Deutschlands in den Vereinten Nationen", in: *Aus Politik und Zeitgeschichte*. Beilage zur Wochenzeitung *Das Parlament*, No B 36/91, pp. 14-24

— (1993): "Research on International Regimes in Germany: The Adaptive Internalization of an American Social Science Concept", in: V. Rittberger (ed.), *Regime Theory and International Relations*, Oxford, pp. 3-22

— (1994): *Internationale Organisationen, Politik und Geschichte*, Opladen

Rittberger, V. (ed.) (1990): Theorien der Internationalen Beziehungen, Bestandsaufnahme und Forschungsperspektiven, (PVS Sonderheft 21/1990), Opladen

— (1993): *Regime Theory and International Relations*, Oxford

— (1995): *Anpassung oder Austritt: Industriestaaten in der UNESCO-Krise, Ein Beitrag zur vergleichenden Aussenpolitikforschung*, Berlin

Rittberger, V. / H. Hummel (1990): "Die Disziplin 'Internationale Beziehungen' im deutschsprachigen Raum auf der Suche nach ihrer Identität: Entwicklung und Perspektiven", in: V. Rittberger (ed.), *Theorien der Internationalen Beziehungen, Bestandsaufnahme und Forschungsperspektiven* (PVS Sonderheft 21/1990), Opladen, pp. 17-47

Rittberger, V. / M. Mogler / B. Zangl (1997): *Vereinte Nationen und Weltordnung, Zivilisierung der internationalen Politik*, Opladen

Rivlin, B. (1995): "Development Dilemmas and Tensions at the UN", in: *International Social Science Journal*, Vol. 47, No 2, pp. 333-345

Roberts, A. / B. Kingsbury (eds) (1989): *United Nations, Divided World: The UN's Roles in International Relations*, Oxford

— (1993): *United Nations, Divided World, The UN's Roles in International Relations*, 2nd edition, Oxford

Roberts, A. / B. Kingsbury (1989): "Introduction: The UN's Roles in a Divided World", in: A. Roberts / B. Kingsbury (eds), *United Nations, Divided World: The UN's Roles in International Relations*, Oxford, pp. 1-29

Rochester, J.M. (1986): "The Rise and Fall of International Organization as a Field of Study", in: *International Organization*, Vol. 40, No 4, pp. 778-813

— (1990): "Global Policy and the Future of the United Nations", in: *Journal of Peace Research*, Vol. 27, No 2, pp. 141-154

Ropers, N. (1993): "Weltordnung", in: I. Hauchler (ed.), *Globale Trends 93/94, Daten zur Weltentwicklung*, Frankfurt a.M., pp. 25-47

— (1995): "Weltordnungspolitik, Chance oder Utopie?", in: I. Hauchler (ed.), *Globale Trends 1996, Fakten, Analysen, Prognosen*, Frankfurt a.M., pp. 11-35

Rose-Ackerman, S. (1997): Corruption and Good Governance, in: UNDP / Yale University (eds), Democracy and Development: The Role of International Organizations, An International Conference co-sponsored by UNDP and Yale University, Yale University, New Haven, 4-5 April 1997 (mimeo), New Haven

Rosenau, J.N. (1986): "Before Cooperation: Hegemons, Regimes, and Habit-Driven Actors in World Politics", in: *International Organization*, Vol. 40, No 4, pp. 849-894

— (1990): *Turbulence in World Politics, A Theory of Change and Continuity*, New York etc.

— (1992): *The United Nations in a Turbulent World*, Boulder

Rosenau, J.N. / E.-O. Czempiel (eds) (1992): *Governance without Government: Order and Change in World Politics*, Cambridge etc.

Rosenau, J.N. / M. Durfee (1995): *Thinking Theory Thoroughly, Coherent Approaches to an Incoherent World*, Boulder etc.

Ruckteschell, I. von (1979): "Die neue wirtschaftspolitische Spitze der Vereinten Nationen, Der Generaldirektor für Entwicklung und internationale Zusammenarbeit", in: *Vereinte Nationen*, Vol. 27, No 1, pp. 11-16

— (1984): "Erhöhung der Effizienz, Wahrung der Kontinuität, Die Empfehlungen zur Neugliederung des UN-Wirtschafts- und Sozialbereichs", in: *Vereinte Nationen*, Vol. 26, No 3, pp. 73-80

Rudischhauser, W. (1997): "Die Reform der Vereinten Nationen, ein aussichtsloses Unterfangen?", in: *Nord-Süd aktuell*, Vol. 11, No 1, pp. 132-138

Ruggie, J.G. (1989): "The United States and the United Nations: Toward a New Realism", in: P.F. Diehl (ed.), *The Politics of International Organizations, Patterns and Insights*, Chicago, pp. 396-410

— (1992): "Multilateralism: The Anatomy of an Institution", in: *International Organization*, Vol. 46, No 3, pp. 561-598

Ruggie, J.G. (ed.) (1993): *Multilateralism Matters. The Theory and Praxis of an Institutional Form*, New York

Russett, B. / H. Starr (1989): *World Politics. The Menu for Choice*, 3rd edition, New York

Russett, B. / D. Yoon (1997): A Strategy for Civil Peace: The United Nations as Peacekeeper and Democratizer, in: UNDP / Yale University (eds), Democracy and Development: The Role of International Organizations, An International Conference co-sponsored by UNDP and Yale University, Yale University, New Haven, 4-5 April 1997 (mimeo), New Haven

Sahlmann, H. (1987): "Vorschläge zur Restrukturierung im operativen Teil der Vereinten Nationen", in: K. Dicke / K. Hüfner (eds), *Die Leistungsfähigkeit des VN-Systems: Politische Kritik und wissenschaftliche Analyse*, Schriftenreihe der DGVN, Bonn, pp. 91-99

— (1991): "UNDP-Entwicklungsprogramm der Vereinten Nationen", in: R. Wolfrum (ed.), *Handbuch Vereinte Nationen*, 2nd edition, Munich, pp. 895-904

Sahlmann, H. / B. Blank (1995): "UNDP-United Nations Development Programme", in: R. Wolfrum (ed.), *United Nations: Law, Policies and Practice*, 2 volumes, Munich etc., pp. 1284-1290

Saksena, K.P. (1993): *Reforming the United Nations, The Challenge of Relevance*, New Delhi, Newbury Park, London

Schmid, H.M. (1972): "UNDP-Reorganisation. Ein Pfad durch den Dschungel", in: *Entwicklung und Zusammenarbeit*, No 10, pp. 5-9

Schmitz, A. (1996): "Sustainable Development: Paradigma oder Leerformel?", in: D. Messner / F. Nuscheler (eds), *Weltkonferenzen und Weltberichte. Ein Wegweiser durch die internationale Diskussion*, Bonn, pp. 103-119

Seib, F.G. (1974): "Die Befähigung des UN-Systems zu wirksamer Entwicklungshilfe", in: *Vereinte Nationen*, Vol. 22, No 6, pp. 179-182

Seidl-Hohenveldern, I. (1991): "Sonderorganisationen", in: R. Wolfrum (ed.), *Handbuch Vereinte Nationen*, 2nd edition, Munich, pp. 782-787

Selim, H.M. (1985): *Development Assistance Policies and the Performance of Aid Agencies*, Studies in the Performance of DAC, OPEC, the Regional Development Banks and the World Bank Group, London

Sen, S. (1980): "Farewell to Foreign Aid: At the United Nations", in: *World View*, Vol. 25, pp. 5-8

Senarclens, P. de (1995): "Reforming the United Nations: A Necessity and an Illusion", in: K. Hüfner (ed.), *Agenda for Change, New Tasks for the United Nations*, Opladen, pp. 211-228

Seth, J. (1980): "The Structural Evolution of the United Nations Development Programme", in: *Indian Journal of International Law*, Vol. 20, pp. 596-615

Shand, R.T. / H.V. Richter (eds) (1979): *International Aid: Some Political, Administrative and Technical Realities*, Canberra

Sharp, R. (1961): *Field Administration in the United Nations*, London

Sharp, W.R. (1966): "Program Coordination and the Economic and Social Council", in: G.J. Mangone (ed.), *UN Administration of Economic and Social Programs*, New York, London, pp. 102-157

Shear, D. (1988): *International Donor Coordination* (International Management & Development Group, LTD), Washington, D.C.

Siitonen, L. (1990): "Political Theories of Development Cooperation, A Study of Theories of International Cooperation" (Wider Working Papers 86), Helsinki

Silcock, T.H. (1979): "The Pearson Commission and After: National States and World Community", in: R.T. Shand / H.V. Richter (eds), *International Aid: Some Political, Administrative and Technical Realities*, Canberra, pp. 16-33

Simai, M. (1995): "The Five Decades of the United Nations: Accomplishments and Limitations", in: K. Hüfner (ed.), *Agenda for Change, New Tasks for the United Nations*, Opladen, pp. 17-38

Simma, B. (ed.) (1991): *Charta der Vereinten Nationen, Kommentar*, Munich

Singer, H.W. (1976): "Die Zukunft des Entwicklungsprogramms der Vereinten Nationen", in: *Vereinte Nationen*, Vol. 24, No 5, pp. 141-144

— (1984): "The Terms of Trade Controversy and the Evolution of Soft Financing: Early Years in the U.N", in: G.M. Meier / D. Seers (eds), *Pioneers in Development. A World Bank Publication*, New York etc., pp. 273-311

— (1985): "Der Beitrag zu wirtschaftlicher Zusammenarbeit und Entwicklung", in: *Vereinte Nationen*, Vol. 33, No 5-6, pp. 162-165

— (1994): "Ein Dollar, eine Stimme, Weltbank und Weltwährungsfonds als Teil des UN-Systems", in: *der überblick*, Vol. 30, No 3, pp. 43-45

— (1995): "Revitalizing the United Nations: Five Proposals", in: *ids bulletin*, Vol. 26, No 4, pp. 35-40

Singer, H.W. / R. Jolly (1995): "Fifty Years on: The UN and Economic and Social Development, An Overview", in: *ids bulletin*, Vol. 26, No 4, pp. 2-6

Sirleaf, E.J. (1996): "Rethinking Aid to Africa", in: *Development, Journal of SID*, No 2, pp. 59-63

Sobhan, R. (1995): "Technical Assistance to Developing Countries: The Failure of Market Forces", in: *The International Journal of Technical Cooperation*, Vol. 1, No 1, pp. 55-63

South Centre (1992a): *Enhancing the Economic Role of the United Nations*, Geneva

— (1992b): *The United Nations at a Critical Crossroads, Time for the South to Act*, Geneva

— (1992c): *Non-Alignment in the 1990s, Contributions to an Economic Agenda*, Geneva

— (1995): *Reforming the United Nations, A View from the South*, Geneva

— (1996): *For a Strong and Democratic United Nations: A South Perspective on UN Reforms*, Geneva

Speth, J.G. (1994a): Building a New UNDP: Agenda for Change, Presentation to the UNDP Executive Board, 17 February 1994, New York

— (1994b): Opening Remarks, in: UNDP 1994c, Annex II

— (1996): Proposals for Reform of the United Nations in the Economic and Social Fields (mimeo), 20 June 1996, New York

— (1997a): UNDP 2001: The Main Features of Change, Statement by James Gustave Speth, Executive Board Informals, 11 March 1997 (mimeo), New York

— (1997b): Responsible Democratization and the Struggle for Social Justice, in: UNDP / Yale University (eds), Democracy and Development: The Role of International Organizations, An International Conference co-sponsored by UNDP and Yale University, Yale University, New Haven, 4-5 April 1997 (mimeo), New Haven

Spröte, W. / H. Wünsche (eds) (1976): Die Vereinten Nationen und ihre Sonderorganisationen, Dokumente, Vol. 4, Mandate und Verfahrensregeln ökonomischer UNO-Organe, Berlin (East)

Standke, K.-H. (1984): "Die multilaterale Technische Zusammenarbeit im System der Vereinten Nationen", in: *Vereinte Nationen*, Vol. 32, No 2, pp. 50-54

Stanley Foundation (1991): The United Nations: Structure and Leadership for a New Era, 22nd UN Issues Conference 1991, Muscatine/Iowa

Steele, D.B. (1985): "The Case for Global Economic Management and UN System Reform", in: *International Organization*, Vol. 39, No 3, pp. 561-578

Stiefel, M. (1994): UNDP in Conflicts and Disaster, An Overview Report of the "Continuum Project" (mimeo), Geneva

Stiftung Entwicklung und Frieden (ed.) (1991): Gemeinsame Verantwortung in den 90er Jahren, Die Stockholmer Initiative zu globaler Sicherheit und Weltordnung (EINE Welt, Vol. 5), Bonn

— (1995): Nachbarn in Einer Welt, Der Bericht der Kommission für Weltordnungspolitik (EINE Welt, Vol. 14), Bonn

Stölken, I. (1991): "Dokumentenführer Vereinte Nationen", in: R. Wolfrum (ed.), *Handbuch Vereinte Nationen*, 2nd edition, Munich, pp. 1159-1171

Stokke, O. (1989a): "The Determinants of Aid Policies: Some Propositions Emerging from a Comparative Analysis", in: O. Stokke (ed.), *Western Middle Powers and*

Global Poverty. The Determinants of the Aid Policies of Canada, Denmark, the Netherlands, Norway and Sweden, Uppsala 1989, pp. 275-322

— (1989b): "The Determinants of Norwegian Aid Policy", in: O. Stokke (ed.), *Western Middle Powers and Global Poverty. The Determinants of the Aid Policies of Canada, Denmark, the Netherlands, Norway and Sweden*, Uppsala 1989, pp. 159-229

Stokke, O. (ed.) (1989): *Western Middle Powers and Global Poverty. The Determinants of the Aid Policies of Canada, Denmark, the Netherlands, Norway and Sweden*, Uppsala

Stoll, T. (1991): "Technische Hilfe", in: R. Wolfrum (ed.), *Handbuch Vereinte Nationen*, 2nd edition, Munich, pp. 828-838

— (1992): Wirtschaftliche Zusammenarbeit in den Vereinten Nationen, Grundlagen, Prinzipien und Strukturen, in: DGVN (ed.) (1992a), Strukturreform der UN? Notwendigkeit, Ansätze und Handlungsspielraum einer Reform der Vereinten Nationen im Bereich der wirtschaftlichen Zusammenarbeit (Zur Diskussion gestellt, No 42), Bonn, pp. 17-28

Strange, S. (1982): "Cave! hic dragones: A Critique of Regime Analysis", in: *International Organization*, Vol. 36, No 2, pp. 479-496

Streeten, P. (1989): "International Cooperation", in: H. Chenery / T.N. Srinivasan (eds), *Handbook of Development Economics*, Vol. 2, 1989b, Amsterdam etc., pp. 1153-1186

Streeter, C.L. et al. (1986): "Curriculum Development in International Coordination", in: *Journal of Social Work Education*, Vol. 22, No 1, pp. 32-40

Süssmuth, M. (1991): Multilaterale Entwicklungshilfekoordination im System der Vereinten Nationen, Kann UNDP seiner Koordinationsrolle gerecht werden? (Diplomarbeit an der Universität Konstanz, Fakultät für Verwaltungswissenschaft), Kreuzlingen

Svendsen, K.E. (1989): "Danish Aid: Old Bottles", in: O. Stokke (ed.), *Western Middle Powers and Global Poverty. The Determinants of the Aid Policies of Canada, Denmark, the Netherlands, Norway and Sweden*, Uppsala, pp. 91-115

Tassin, J. (1990): "Administrative Co-ordination in the UN-Family", in: C. De Cooker (ed.), *International Administration*, Dordrecht, pp. 1-18

Taylor, P. (1990): "A Conceptual Typology of International Organization", in: P. Taylor / A.J.R. Groom (eds), *International Institutions at Work*, London, pp. 12-26

— (1993): *International Organization in the Modern World, The Regional and the Global Process*, London

Taylor, P. / A.J.R. Groom (eds) (1988): *International Institutions at Work*, London

Tetzlaff, R. (1993): "Die 'Universalität' der Menschenrechte in Theorie und Praxis. Eine Einführung", in: R. Tetzlaff (ed.), *Menschenrechte und Entwicklung, Deutsche und internationale Kommentare und Dokumente* (Stiftung Entwicklung und Frieden, Reihe: Eine Welt, Vol. 11), Bonn, pp. 11-52

Tetzlaff, R. (ed.) (1993): *Menschenrechte und Entwicklung, Deutsche und internationale Kommentare und Dokumente* (Stiftung Entwicklung und Frieden, Reihe: Eine Welt, Vol. 11), Bonn

Tinbergen, J. (1984): "Development Cooperation as a Learning Process", in: G.M. Meier / D. Seers (eds), *Pioneers in Development. A World Bank Publication*, New York etc., pp. 313-331

Todaro, M.P. (1990): *Economic Development in the Third World*, 4th Edition, New York, London

Tomuschat, C. (1996): "Reform der Vereinten Nationen", in: *KAS* (Konrad-Adenauer-Stiftung) - *Auslandsinformation*, Vol. 12, No 5, pp. 3-16

Tooze, R. (1990): "Regimes and International Co-operation", in: A.J.R. Groom / P. Taylor (eds), *Frameworks for International Co-operation*, London, pp. 201-216

Trent, J.E. (1995): "Foreign Policy and the United Nations: National Interest in the Era of Global Politics", in: C.F. Alger / G.M. Lyons / J.E. Trent (eds), *The United Nations System: The Policies of Member States*, Tokyo, New York, Paris, pp. 463-508

UIA (Union of International Associations) (ed.) (1991): *Yearbook of International Organizations*, 1991/92, 3 volumes, 28th edition, Munich etc.

UN (1981): *United Nations Documentation, A Brief Guide*, New York

— (1986): *Everyone's United Nations, A Handbook on the Work of the United Nations*, 10th edition, New York

— (1992): *Yearbook of the United Nations 1987*, Vol. 41, Dordrecht, Boston, London

— (1995): Declaration on the Occasion of the Fiftieth Anniversary of the United Nations, 24 October 1995

— (1996a): CCPOQ (Consultative Committee on Programme and Operational Questions) Operationals Activities Reference Manual, Geneva

— (Special Coordinator for Economic and Social Development) (1996b): Managerial and Operational Reforms in the United Nations Economic and Social Sectors, New York

— (Special Coordinator for Economic and Social Development) (1996c): Second Report to the Secretary-General on the Work of the Special Coordinator for Economic and Social Development, New York

— (1997a): Inter-Office Memorandum, Policy Coordination Group, (29 January 1997), New York

— (1997b): Inter-Office Memorandum, Notes on Executive Committees of Sector Groups and on the Structure and Timetable of Reform (24 February 1997), New York

— (1997c): Operational Activities of the United Nations for International Development Cooperation, Trends in Core and Non-Core Resources, Report by the Secretary-General (unedited draft), New York

— (1997d): Operational Activities of the United Nations for International Development Cooperation, Progress on the Implementation of General Assembly Resolution 50/120, Report of the General-Secretary (revised unedited draft), New York

— (1997e): Operational Activities of the United Nations for International Development Cooperation, Field and Regional-Level Coordination, Report by the Secretary-General (unedited draft), New York

— (1997f): Restructuring and Revitalization of the United Nations in the Economic, Social and Related Fields, Report by the Secretary-General (unedited draft), New York

— (1997g): Renewing the United Nations: A Programme for Reform, Report of the Secretary-General, New York

UNA (United Nations Association of the)-USA (1987): A Successor Vision: The United Nations of Tommorrow, Final Panel Report, UNA-USA, New York

UNCDF (1991): *Information Note on the United Nations Capital Development Fund*, New York

UNDP (1986a): 1985 and Towards the 1990s, Annual Report of the United Nations Development Programme, New York

— (1989a): Entwicklung für die Städte von morgen, UNDP, Weltweite Entwicklung, Jahresbericht 1988, New York

— (1990): Vierzig Jahre der weltweiten Entwicklung, Entwicklungsprogramm der Vereinten Nationen Jahresbericht 1989, New York

— (1991a): Putting People First, UNDP 1990 Annual Report, New York

— (1991b): Capacity Building for Aid Coordination in the Least Developed Countries, A Report Commissioned by the Central Evaluation Office UNDP; Vol. I, New York

— (1991c): Capacity Building for Aid Coordination in the Least Developed Countries, A Report Commissioned by the Central Evaluation Office UNDP; Vol. II, New York

— (1991d): NaTCAP, Evaluation, Vol. I, New York

— (1991e): NaTCAP, Evaluation Reports for: Chad, Ghana, Guinea, Malawi and Zambia, Vol. II, New York

— (1992a): The Challenge of the Environment, 1991 UNDP Annual Report, New York

— (1992b): Human Development Report 1992, New York, Oxford

— (1993a): Programme and Projects Manual (PPM), Part I: The System of UNDP Technical Co-operation (loose-leaf edition; at February 1993), New York

— (1993b): Programme and Projects Manual (PPM), Part II: Programming UNDP Technical Co-operation (loose-leaf edition; at February 1993), New York

— (1993c): Programme and Projects Manual (PPM), Part III: Implementation of UNDP Technical Co-operation (loose-leaf edition; at February 1993), New York

— (1993d): UNDP: A Charter for Change, Part I: Visions and Goals, Working Paper by a Transition Team of UNDP Staff, New York

— (1993e): UNDP: A Charter for Change, Part II: Management Challenges, Working Paper by a Transition Team of UNDP Staff, New York

— (1994a): Organization Handbook (loose-leaf edition; at July 1994, New York

— (1994b): Repositioning the United Nations Development Programme: Views from the Wider Development Community, New York

— (1994c): UNDP Global Meeting, Recommendations to the Administrator, Rye/NY

— (1994d): Bericht über die menschliche Entwicklung 1994, (DGVN (Deutsche Gesellschaft für die Vereinten Nationen)), Bonn

— (1995a): Building a New UNDP, UNDP 1994/1995 Annual Report, New York

— (1995b): Strategic Management in UNDP, New York

— (1995c): Building a New UNDP, New York

— (1995d): Improving Programme Performance Assement in UNDP, A Concept Paper, New York

— (1995e): Poverty Eradication: A Policy Framework for Country Strategies, New York

— (1995f): UNDP Support for the Resident Coordinator System (mimeo, 9 November 1995), New York

— (1995g): UNDP Evaluation Findings in 1994, New York

— (1995h): National Execution: Promise and Challenges, New York

— (1995i): United Nations Development Programme (UNDP): A Force for Sustainable Human Development, New York

— (1995j): Informal Explanatory Notes on Proposed Framework for the Next Programming Period (at 7 February 1997), New York

— (1995k): Guidelines for the Implementation of the Successor Programming Arrangements in UNDP (Draft: 21 December 1995), New York

— (1996a): Change and Reform in UNDP, Highlights, Februar 1996 (mimeo), New York

— (1996b): The 1996-97 UNDP Plan, New York

— (1996c): Operational Activities for Development, Review and Analysis of 1995 Annual Reports of United Nations Resident Coordinators, Interim Report, New York

— (1996d): Management of Change in UNDP (mimeo, 5 May 1996), New York

— (1996e): Report on the Cape Town Workshop on "The Country Office of the Future", 27-31 May 1996 (Office of Evaluation and Strategic Planning), New York

— (1996f): UNDP Evaluation Findings in 1995, New York

— (1996g): Aid Coordination an Aid Management by Government: A Role for UNDP, A Study for the Bureau for Policy and Programme Support, New York

— (1996h): Building Sustainable Capacity, Challenges for the Public Sector, A Study for the Bureau for Policy and Programme Support, New York

— (1996i): Building Development Partnerships through Co-financing, New York

— (1996j): Compendium of Ongoing Projects as of 31 December 1995, New York

— (1996k): Systematic Improvement Management, Process Consultation, New York

— (1996l): Democracy, Governance and Participation: A Review of Projects in Kyrgyzstan and Ukraine, New York

— (1996m): Overview of Support Cost Arrangements under the Successor Programming Arrangements, at 23 December 1996), New York

— (1996n): Strategic Options for UNDP 2001, Team 1, UNDP Funding and Strategic Partnerships (mimeo; at 2 December 1996), New York

— (1997a): Reconceptualising Governance, (Management Develpment and Governance Division, Discussion Paper 2), New York

— (1997b): Governance for Sustainable Human Development, A UNDP Policy Document, New York

— (1997c): Executive Committee of the Development Cooperation Group (Interoffice Memorandum, OUNS, 20 March 1997), New York

— (1997d): UNDP Evaluation Findings in 1996, New York

— (1997e): The Resident Coordinator System and UNDP (mimeo), New York

— (1997f): UNDP: Redirection and Reform Highlights (mimeo), New York

— (1997g): UNDP in 1996-1997 (mimeo), New York

— (1997h): The UNDP 2001 Change Management Process, Organizational Structure and Functions, Note for Consultation with the Executive Board (mimeo), New York

— (1997i): UNDP 2001, Proposals on Organizational Structure (mimeo; at 13 March 1997), New York

— (1997j): Executive Committee of the Development Cooperation Group (mimeo; Interoffice Memorandum, 20 March 1997), New York

— (1997k): Human Development Report, Oxford

— (1997l): Designing the Future, Recommendations Arising from the UNDP 2001 Projects (mimeo; at 8 January 1997), New York

— (1997m): Building Partnerships for Sustainable Human Development, The Work of the UNDP European Office 1996, Geneva

— (1997n): The Process for the Selection and Clearance of Resident Representatives / Resident Coordinators, Note by the Director, Office of Human Resources, UNDP (mimeo), New York

— (1997o): Compendium of Ongoing Interventions as of 31 December 1996, New York

UNDP / World Bank (1995): "Toward Improving the Effectiveness of Technical Co-operation: The Issues", in: *The International Journal of Technical Cooperation*, Vol. 1, No 1, pp. 18-25

UNDP / Yale University (eds) (1997): Democracy and Development: The Role of International Organizations, An International Conference co-sponsored by UNDP and Yale University, Yale Universizty, New Haven, 4-5 April 1997 (mimeo), New Haven

United States Department of State (1996): U.S. Views on Reform Measures Necessary for Strengthening the United Nations System, A Presentation to the Open-Ended High-Level Working Group on the Strengthening of the United Nations System, February 1996, Washington, D.C.

UNOPS (1995): United Nations Office for Project Services 1994 Annual Report, New York

— (1996a): United Nations Office for Project Services 1995 Annual Report, New York

— (1996b): United Nations Office for Project Services, New York

— (1997): Reform in the United Nations: UNOPS, a Business Entity, (mimeo), New York

Unser, G. (1997): *Die UNO, Aufgaben und Strukturen der Vereinten Nationen*, 6th edition, Munich

UN System in India (1997): *UN System Position Statement-India*, New Delhi

Urquhart, B. / E. Childers (1990): A World in Need of Leadership: Tomorrow's United Nations, (Development Dialogue Series, Nos 1-2, Dag Hammarskjöld Foundation), Uppsala

— (1991a): Towards a More Effective United Nations, (Development Dialogue Series, Nos 1-2, Dag Hammarskjöld Foundation), Uppsala

— (1991b): "Reorganization of the United Nations Secretariat, A Suggested Outline of Needed Reforms", in: *idem*, 1991a, pp. 9-40

— (1991c): "Strengthening International Response to Humanitarian Emergencies", in: *idem*, 1991a, pp. 41-85

— (1996): *A World in Need of Leadership: Tomorrow's United Nations, A Fresh Appraisal*, Uppsala

USAID (United States Agency for International Development) (1995): "Technical Cooperation: A Necessary Ingredient for Sustainable Development", in: *The International Journal of Technical Cooperation*, Vol. 1, No 1, pp. 50-54

van Agt, A. (1994): The Future Role of the Global Multilateral Organisations, Report on the Conclusions and Recommendations by a High-level Group, 7-8 May 1994, The Hague

van Meerhaeghe, M.A G. (1980): *A Handbook of International Economic Institutions*, The Hague

Vente, R.E. (1961): *Die Technische Hilfe für Entwicklungsländer*, Baden-Baden, Bonn

Vogt, W.R. (ed.) (1997): *Gewalt und Konfliktbearbeitung. Befunde - Konzepte - Handeln*, Baden-Baden

Volger, H. (1994): *Die Vereinten Nationen*, Munich, Vienna

— (1995): *Geschichte der Vereinten Nationen*, Munich, Vienna

von Hauff, M. / B. Pfister-Gaspary (eds) (1982): *Internationale Sozialpolitik*, Stuttgart, New York

von Ruckteschell, I. (1979): "Die neue wirtschaftspolitische Spitze der Vereinten Nationen, Der Generaldirektor für Entwicklung und internationale Zusammenarbeit", in: *Vereinte Nationen*, No 1, pp. 11-16

Wall, D. (1973): *The Charity of Nations: the Political Economy of Foreign Aid*, London

Wallace, C.D. (1983): "United Nations Development Programme", in: R. Bernhardt (ed.), *Encyclopedia of Public International Law*, Vol. 5, pp. 307-310

Waller, P.P. (1996): "Positivmaßnahmen und politische Konditionalität", in: *Entwicklung und Zusammenarbeit*, Vol. 37, No 3, pp. 75-77

Waltz, K.N. (1979): *Theory of International Politics*, Reading/Mass.

Wamalwa, W.N. (1995): "Some Reflections on the Experience of Foreign Aid", in: *development dialogue*, No 2, pp. 11-20

Wapenhans, W.A. (1996): "Multilaterale Entwicklungsbanken, Ein interner Forderungskatalog zur Reform ihrer Arbeit", in: *Entwicklung und Zusammenarbeit*, Vol. 37, No 7, pp. 183-185.

Waters, M. (1995): *Globalization*, London, New York

Weber, H. (1991): "Entstehungsgeschichte der UN", in: R. Wolfrum (ed.), *Handbuch Vereinte Nationen*, 2nd edition, Munich, pp. 110-117

Weiter, M. (1995): "A Fresh Look at Technical Cooperation", in: *The International Technical Cooperation*, Vol. 1, No 2, pp. 308-312

Welsh, B.W.W. / P. Butorin (eds) (1990): *Dictionary of Development, Third World Economy, Environment, Society*, 2 volumes, New York, London

White, J. (1974): *The Politics of Foreign Aid*, London

Whitehead, L. (1997): Transitions to Democracy: The Role of International Organizations, in: UNDP / Yale University (eds), Democracy and Development: The Role of International Organizations, An International Conference co-sponsored by UNDP and Yale University, Yale University, New Haven, 4-5 April 1997 (mimeo), New Haven

Whittington, D. / C. Calhoun (1988): "Who Really Wants Donor Coordination?", in: *Development Policy Review*, Vol. 6, No 3, pp. 295-309

Wiegand, G. (1978): Organisatorische Aspekte der internationalen Verwaltung von Entwicklungshilfe, Ein Beitrag zur Organisationsanalyse internationaler Organisationen am Beispiel des UNDP und der Weltbank (Schriften zur Verwaltungswissenschaft, Vol. 5), Berlin

Willetts, P. (1988): "The United Nations as a Political System", in: P. Taylor / A.J.R. Groom (eds), *International Institutions at Work*, London, pp. 21-38

Williams, D. (1987): *The Specialized Agencies and the United Nations. The System in Crisis*, London

Williams, M. (1989): U.S. Multilateral Development Assistance Policy, A Report Prepared as Contribution to a Comparative Study by The North-South Institute, Ottawa, Canada on Donor Countries and Multilateral Development Aid

— (1995a): "Role of the Multilateral Agencies after the Earth Summit", in: M. ul Haq et al. (eds), *The UN and the Bretton Woods Institutions, New Challenges for the Twenty-First Century*, New York, pp. 196-209

— (1995b): Aid Coordination and NaTCAP Evaluation: UNDP's Role in AID Effectiveness, An Evaluation Commissioned by UNDP, Part I, Findings and Recommendations

— (1995c): Aid Coordination and NaTCAP Evaluation: UNDP's Role in AID Effectiveness, An Evaluation Commissioned by UNDP, Part II, Annexes

Wissing, T. (1995): *Mögliche Beiträge der Entwicklungszusammenarbeit zur Krisenprävention, Eine Literaturauswertung* (German Development Institute, Reports and Working Papers), Berlin

Wolf, K.D. (1994): "Regimeanalyse", in: A. Boeckh (ed.), *Lexikon der Politik*, Vol. 6, Internationale Beziehungen, Munich, pp. 422-429

Wolff, P. (1996): "Statt Strukturanpassung: Sektorprogramme als Entwicklungsstrategie für die ärmsten Länder?", in: *Entwicklung und Zusammenarbeit*, Vol. 37, No 1, pp. 4-5

— (1997): *Sector Investment Programs in Africa, Case Studies: Agricultural Sector Investment Program (ASIP) / Zambia, Basic Education Sector Investment Program (BESIP) / Ghana*, Berlin

Wolfrum, R. (1991a): "Die Aufgaben der Vereinten Nationen im Wandel", in: *Aus Politik und Zeitgeschichte*. Beilage zur Wochenzeitung *Das Parlament*, No B 36/91, pp. 3-13

— (1991b): Art. 55 (a,b), in: B. Simma (ed.) (1991), *Charta der Vereinten Nationen, Kommentar*, Munich, pp. 702-719

— (1991c): Art. 56, in: B. Simma (ed.) (1991), *Charta der Vereinten Nationen, Kommentar*, Munich, pp. 736-739

— (1991d): "Haushalt", in: R. Wolfrum (ed.), *Handbuch Vereinte Nationen*, 2nd edition, Munich, pp. 268-275

— (1992): Aufgaben der UN nach Art. 55 der Charta, weitreichende Ansätze und eingeschränkter Handlungsspielraum, in: DGVN (ed.) (1992a), Strukturreform der UN? Notwendigkeit, Ansätze und Handlungsspielraum einer Reform der Vereinten Nationen im Bereich der wirtschaftlichen Zusammenarbeit, (Zur Diskussion gestellt, No 42), Bonn, pp. 11-16

Wolfrum, R. (ed.) (1991): *Handbuch Vereinte Nationen*, 2nd edition, Munich

— (1995): *United Nations: Law, Policies and Practice*, 2 volumes, Munich etc.

World Bank (1990): Free-Standing Technical Assistance for Institutional Development in Sub-Saharan Africa (Report No. 8573), Washington, D.C.

— (1993): Handbook on Technical Assistance, Operations Policy Department, Washington, D.C.

— (1995a): Annual Review of Evaluation Results 1994 (Report No. 15084), Washington, D.C.

— (1995b): Strengthening the Effectiveness of Aid, Lessons for Donors, Washington, D.C.

— (1996a): Technical Assistance (Operations Evaluations Department, Lessons & Practices, No. 7), Washington, D.C.

— (1996b): Annual Review of Evaluation Results 1995, Vol. I: Main Text, Washington, D.C.

— (1996c): Annual Review of Evaluation Results 1995, Vol. II: Annexes, Washington, D.C.

— (1996d): Performance Indicators for Technical Assistance Operations, A First Edition Note, Washington, D.C.

— (1996e): Annual Report 1996, Washington, D.C.

— (1997a): World Development Report 1997, The State in a Changing World, Washington, D.C.

— (1997b): The Strategic Compact: Renewing the Bank's Effectiveness to Fight Poverty, Washington, D.C.

— (1997c): The Strategic Compact: Renewing the Bank's Effectiveness to Fight Poverty, Annexes, Washington, D.C.

Woroniecki, J. (1995): "Restructuring the United Nations: A Response to New Tasks, or a Substitute for Action?", in: K. Hüfner (Hrsg), *Agenda for Change, New Tasks for the United Nations*, Opladen, pp. 59-84

Young, O.A. (1971): "The United Nations and the International System", in: L. Gordenker (ed.), *The United Nations in International Politics*, Princeton, pp. 10-59

Young, O.R. (1989): *International Cooperation, Building Regimes for Natural Resources and the Environment*, Ithaca, London

— (1992): "The Effectiveness of International Institutions: Hard Cases and Critical Variables", in: J.N. Rosenau / E.-O. Czempiel (eds), *Governance without Government: Order and Change in World Politics*, Cambridge etc., pp. 160-194

— (1995): "System and Society in World Affairs: Implications for International Organizations", in: *International Social Science Journal*, Vol. 47, No 2, pp. 197-212

Zacher, M.W. (1990): "Toward a Theory of International Regimes", in: *Journal of International Affairs*, Vol. 44, No 1, pp. 139-157

— (1993): "Multilateral Organizations and the Institution of Multilateralism: The Development of Regimes for Nonterrestrial Spaces", in: J.G. Ruggie (ed.), *Multilateralism Matters, The Theory and Praxis of an Institutional Form*, New York, pp. 399-439

Zell, H. (1997): "Entwicklung und Staat, Die ambivalente Rolle der Entwicklungshilfe", in: W. von Bredow / T. Jäger (eds), *Demokratie und Entwicklung, Theorie und Praxis der Demokratisierung in der Dritten Welt*, Opladen, pp. 141-178

Zimmermann, H. (1963): *Öffentliche Finanzhilfen an Entwicklungsländer, Gesamtwirtschaftliche und politische Massstäbe zur Bestimmung ihrer Form*, Berlin

Zumach, A. (1997): "Allzu zaghafte UNO-Reform", in: *Entwicklung und Zusammenarbeit*, Vol. 38, No 9, pp. 237-239

Zürn, M. (1994): "Neorealistische und Realistische Schule", in: A. Boeckh (ed.), *Lexikon der Politik*, Vol. 6, Internationale Beziehungen, Munich, pp. 309-322

Annex

Annex I

UNDP: Main Features and Structures[1]

Origins

The United Nations Development Programme (UNDP) was established by the UN General Assembly in 1965 (Resolution 2029 (XX)) and began work in 1966. UNDP emerged from the combination of two existing UN entities: the *Expanded Programme of Technical Assistance* (EPTA) and the *Special Fund* (SF).

EPTA, established in 1949, had operated in the technical cooperation field primarily by assigning experts. The Special Fund, set up in 1958, had had the task of preparing major development projects. The merging of the two was intended to reduce duplication and to enable financial resources to be pooled.

In 1970 the UN General Assembly adopted what was known as the *Consensus Resolution* (Resolution 2688 (XXV)). It was based on the recommendations made in the *Capacity Study*, which had been completed in 1969 under the guidance of Sir Robert Jackson. In the Consensus Resolution the fundamental and overarching tasks (planning, coordination and financing) connected with the UN system's technical cooperation are assigned to UNDP. From the outset this met with opposition from other bodies in the UN system, each of which preferred to see itself acting as autonomously as possible.

Tasks and objectives

UNDP is the world's largest multilateral technical cooperation institution operating on the basis of grants. Its revenue base consists of the governments' annual contributions.

In principle, UNDP's task is to act as a single and central control, financing and coordinating body for the technical cooperation activities of the entire UN system.

Unlike other operational UN development institutions, UNDP is not subject to any specific substantive or sectoral restrictions (such as *children* or *population*).

Since the mid-1990s UNDP's activities have been guided by the development policy paradigm of *sustainable human development* (SHD). It has published the *Human Development Report* annually since 1990. In 1994 and 1996 its Executive Board adopted, respectively, a core mission and a mission statement, in which the emphasis is on SHD. UNDP's objective is accordingly defined as assisting countries in their efforts to achieve sustainable human development; to this end, it is to help them to develop their own capacities so that they may plan and implement development programmes, especially in the area of poverty alleviation.

Members, structure, organization and staff

All member countries of the United Nations, the UN specialized agencies and the IAEA (International Atomic Energy Agency) are free to participate in UNDP. There is no specific UNDP membership in any narrower sense of the term.

UNDP is a *subsidiary body* of the UN General Assembly. It is administered under the authority of the General Assembly and ECOSOC.

UNDP itself is composed of an Executive Board, an Administrator and its members:

- UNDP's political supervisory and controlling body is the Executive Board (formerly the Governing Council), which holds an annual meeting and, currently, three ordinary working meetings each year. One of the Executive Board's important tasks is to discuss and approve the country programmes. It also acts as the Executive Board of UNFPA.

The Executive Board has 36 members appointed in accordance with the following regional key: 8 representatives of African countries, 7 representatives of Asian countries, 4 representatives of Eastern European countries, 5 representatives of Latin America and the Caribbean and 12 representatives of Western Europe and other countries. This means that the group of developing countries has a majority in any votes taken by the Executive Board. The members of the Executive Board are elected by ECOSOC for a period of three years.

- The Administrator conducts UNDP's business. He is appointed by the UN Secretary-General after consultations with the Executive Board and confirmed by the UN General Assembly. The Administrator has always been a US national in the past, a practice which has come in for growing criticism in the 1990s. James Gustave Speth (USA) has held the post of Administrator since 1993.
- UNDP employs 892 administrative-class officials (end of 1995) at its headquarters. They are joined by about 6,000 international experts and some 17,000 local experts working on UNDP projects.

UNDP's headquarters are located in New York.

UNDP's internal organization is broken down into 5 regional units and various sectoral, implementation, administrative and financial units. A separate unit is responsible for evaluation tasks. The establishment plan in section III.2 gives a detailed insight into the organization.

UNDP administers various other UN funds and programmes of the UN system that receive separate contributions. They are:

- UNV - United Nations Volunteers,
- UNCDF - United Nations Capital Development Fund,
- UNFSTD - United Nations Fund for Science and Technology for Development,

- UNRFNRE - United Nations Revolving Fund for Natural Resources Exploration,
- UNSO - United Nations Sudano-Sahelian Office,
- UNIFEM - United Nations Development Fund for Women.

UNDP also administers the Global Environmental Facility (GEF), jointly with the World Bank and UNEP.

An important feature of UNDP is its dense network of country offices, which it maintains in some 134 countries. Its local representatives are known as Resident Representatives. As a rule, the Resident Representative and the UN Resident Coordinator appointed by the UN Secretary-General are one and the same person.

Operation and working methods

UNDP, being a financing and coordinating institution, does not as a rule play any direct part in the actual implementation of projects and programmes. Normally, the developing countries concerned are, where possible, required to take responsibility during implementation; the implementation of measures by the programme countries themselves is known as *national execution*. The proportion of projects and programmes implemented in this way has risen sharply in the 1990s (1990-1991: 14%, 1996-1997: 79%). Where programme countries are unable to perform this task themselves, it is entrusted to other implementing institutions. Traditionally, the UN's specialized agencies (the *big five*: FAO, ILO, UNESCO, UNIDO and WHO) occupy a strong position in this context. UNDP long had major implementing capacities of its own in the Office for Project Services, now largely detached from UNDP. Non-governmental organizations may also be commissioned to implement projects.

Through its country offices UNDP provides not only project and programme management but also direct consultancy services for the governments of the programme countries. These services include, in particular, the formulation and establishment of objectives and concepts of relevance to development policy and the coordination of contributions made by the various bi- and multilateral donors. In the context of donor coordination UNDP arranges *round tables*, primarily for the poorer developing countries (the World Bank has a similar instrument for most other countries: consultative group meetings).

UNDP's work centres on country-related programmes; it also has regional, interregional and global programmes. A special instrument (TCDC - technical cooperation among developing countries) is meant to contribute to South-South cooperation by promoting technical cooperation among developing countries.

Until the end of 1996 country programming pivoted on the Indicative Planning Figure (IPF). The IPF was used to calculate the TC volume for a planning cycle of five years. The criteria applied were population, gross national product per capita and other development indicators. At the beginning of 1997 the programming system was replaced with a new programming method that is based on a rolling three-year planning procedure and so gives greater flexibility. The criteria for calculating the volume of aid are guided by the indicators previously used.

Resource use and focus areas

UNDP cooperates with 176 countries. Current operations at country level number about 5,000.

Sectorally, UNDP has the following focus areas (in terms of the distribution of funds among all current operations in 1996): 1. development planning (32.0%), 2. agriculture, forestry and fisheries (11.0%), 3. health (8.9%), 4. environment (6.3%) and 5. education (5.4%).

Regionally, one of the focus areas in the fifth planning cycle (1992-1996), accounting for 87% of the country funds, was poor developing countries with a per capita GNP of less than US $ 750.

Financing

UNDP's financial resources consist of voluntary contributions. They are used to finance UNDP's core programme activities. Although the industrialized countries, and especially the *like-minded countries*, provide most of these resources, a number of developing countries also participate in the financing of the core programme; in other words, they contribute to the financing of all UNDP activities and are also direct beneficiaries.

The voluntary contributions are announced by the various governments at the annual United Nations Pledging Conference for Development Activities.

Besides the core programme, other UNDP financing mechanisms (*non-core resources*) to which UNDP and its Executive Board have only limited access are becoming increasingly important: cost-sharing by the programme countries themselves (*government cost-sharing*) and by others (*third-party cost-sharing*) and trust funds.

In 1996 core resources of US $ 852 million and non-core resources of US $ 1,124 million were available.

The Executive Board's target for core resources for the three-year period 1997 to 1999 is US $ 3.3 billion.

Annex II

Resolution 2029 (XX): Consolidation of the Special Fund and the Expanded Programme of Technical Assistance in a United Nations Development Programme

22 November 1965

Source: U. N. GAOR, 20th Sess., Supp. No. 14, at 20, U. N. Doc. A/6014 (1965).

Voting results:
In favour: 98
Against: 0
Abstaining: 9

THE GENERAL ASSEMBLY,

HAVING CONSIDERED the recommendation of the Economic and Social Council, in its resolution 1020 (XXXVII) of 11 August 1964, to combine the Special Fund and the Expanded Programme of Technical Assistance in a United Nations Development Programme,

BEING CONVINCED that such a consolidation would go a long way in streamlining the activities carried on separately and jointly by the Expanded Programme of Technical Assistance and the Special Fund, would simplify organizational arrangements and procedures, would facilitate over-all planning and needed coordination of the several types of technical cooperation programmes carried on within the United Nations system of organizations and would increase their effectiveness,

RECOGNIZING that requests for assistance on the part of the developing countries are steadily increasing in volume and in scope,

BELIEVING that a reorganization is necessary to provide a more solid basis for the future growth and evolution of the assistance programmes of the United Nations system of organizations financed from voluntary contributions,

BEING CONVINCED that the United Nations assistance programmes are designed to support and supplement the national efforts of developing countries in solving the most important problems of their economic development, including industrial development,

RECALLING AND REAFFIRMING section III of its resolution 1219 (XII) of 14 December 1957 and part C of its resolution 1240 (XIII) of 14 October 1958 concerning the decision and the conditions under which the General

Assembly shall review the scope and future activities of the Special Fund and take such action as it may deem appropriate,

REAFFIRMING that the proposed consolidation would be without prejudice to consideration of the study which the General Assembly, in its resolution 1936 (XVIII) of 11 December 1963, requested the Secretary-General to prepare on the practical steps to transform the Special Fund into a capital development fund in such a way as to include both pre-investment and investment activities, and without prejudice to the recommendation of the United Nations Conference on Trade and Development of the gradual transformation of the Special Fund, so as to include not only pre-investment but also investment proper,[1] or to the recommendation of the Economic and Social Council and of the General Assembly thereon,

TAKING NOTE of the message of the Secretary-General in which he stated, *inter alia,* that, far from limiting the possibilities of a United Nations capital investment programme, the proposals should enhance those possibilities,[2]

RECOGNIZING that the effective working of a United Nations Development Programme depends upon the full and active participation and the technical contribution of all the organizations concerned,

1. *Decides* to combine the Expanded Programme of Technical Assistance and the Special Fund in a programme to be known as the United Nations Development Programme, it being understood that the special characteristics and operations of the two programmes, as well as two separate funds, will be maintained and that, as hitherto, contributions may be pledged to the two programmes separately;

2. *Reaffirms* the principles, procedures and provisions governing the Expanded Programme of Technical Assistance and the Special Fund not inconsistent with the present resolution and declares that they shall continue to apply to relevant activities within the United Nations Development Programme;
3. *Urges* the Governing Council referred to in paragraph 4 below to consider conditions for an effective implementation of the provisions of section III of General Assembly resolution 1219 (XII) and part C of its resolution 1240 (XIII);
4. *Resolves* that a single inter-governmental committee of thirty-seven[3]

---

[1] See *Proceedings of the United Nations Conference on Trade and Development,* vol I, *Final Act and Report* (U. N. publication, Sales No.: 64.II. B.11), annex A.IV.8, p. 47.

[2] See *Official Records of the Economic and Social Council, Thirty-seventh Sesssion, Annexes,* agenda item 19, document E/3033, annex VI.

[3] See footnote 4 on p. 676.

members, to be known as the Governing Council of the United Nations Development Programme, shall be established to perform the functions previously exercised by the Governing Council of the Special Fund and the Technical Assistance Committee, including the consideration and approval of projects and programmes and the allocation of funds; in addition, it shall provide general policy guidance and direction for the United Nations Development Programme as a whole, as well as for the United Nations regular programmes of technical assistance, it shall meet twice a year and shall submit reports and recommendations thereon to the Economic and Social Council for consideration by the Council at its summer session; decisions of the Governing Council shall be made by a majority of the members present and voting;

5. *Requests* the Economic and Social Council to elect the members of the Governing Council from among States Members of the United Nations or members of the specialized agencies or of the International Atomic Energy Agency, providing for equitable and balanced representation of the economically more developed countries, on the one hand, having due regard to their contribution to the United Nations Development Programme, and of the developing countries, on the other hand, taking into account the need for suitable regional representation among the latter members and in accordance with the provisions of the annex to the present resolution, the first election to take place at the first meeting of the Economic and Social Council after the adoption of this resoltuion;
6. *Decides* to establish, in place of the Technical Assistance Board and the Consultative Board of the Special Fund, an advisory committee, to be known as the Inter-Agency Consultative Board of the United Nations Development Programme, to meet under the chairmanship of the Administrator or Co-Administrator referred to in paragraph 7 below and to include the Secretary-General of the United Nations and the executive heads of the specialized agencies and of the International Atomic Energy Agency or their representatives; the Executive Directors of the United Nations Children's Fund and the World Food Programme should be invited to participate as appropriate; in order that the participating organizations may be provided with the opportunity to take part fully in the process of decision- and policy-making in a consultative capacity, the Inter-Agency Consultative Board shall be consulted on all significant aspects of the United Nations Development Programme and in particular it shall:
   (a) Advise the management on the programmes and projects submitted by Governments, through the Resident Representative, prior to their submission to the Governing Council for approval, taking into account the programmes of technical assistance being carried out under the regular programmes of the organizations represented on

the Consultative Board, with a view to ensuring more effective co-ordination; the views of the Consultative Board, when it so requests, shall be conveyed by the Administrator to the Governing Council, together with any comments he may wish to make, when recommending for approval general policies for the Programme as a whole or for programmes and projects requested by Governments;

(b) Be consulted in the selection of agencies for the execution of specific projects, as appropriate;

(c) Be consulted on the appointment of the Resident Representatives and review annual reports submitted by them;

the Inter-Agency Consultative Board shall meet as often and for such periods as may be necessary for the performance of the foregoing functions;

7. *Decides* that, as a transitional measure, the present Managing Director of the Special Fund shall become the Administrator of the United Nations Development Programme and the present Executive Chairman of the Technical Assistance Board shall become the Co-Administrator of the Programme, each to serve until 31 December 1966 or, pending a further review of arrangements at the management level, until such later date as may be determined by the Secretary-General after consultation with the Governing Council;

8. *Decides* that the present resolution shall come into effect on 1 January 1966 and that such action as may be required in terms of this resolution shall be taken prior to that date.

Annex[4]

1. Nineteen seats on the Governing Council of the United Nations Development Programme shall be filled by developing countries and se-

[4] By General Assembly resolution 2813 (XXVI) of 14 December 1971 membership was raised to 48. 27 seats are allocated to developing countries as follows: eleven for African states, nine for Asian States and Yugoslavia, and seven seats for Latin American and Caribbean states. 21 seats are allocated to economically more advanced countries as follows: 17 for Western European and other states and four for Eastern European states. Elections to these seats are for a period of three years, 16 members being elected every year. The General Assembly decided in resolution 48/162 of 20 December 1993 that the Governing Council of the UNDP should be transformed into an Executive Board, responsible for the provision of intergovernmental support to, and supervision of, UNDP. The functions of the Executive Board are set out in that resolution. The Board meets in annual sessions with provision for additional regular meetings as the Board may determine. The Executive Board has 36 members: 8 from African States, 7 from Asian States, 4 from Eastern European States, 5 from Latin America and Caribbean States and 12 from Western European and other States.

venteen seats by economically more developed countries, subject to the following conditions:

(a) The nineteen seats allocated to developing countries of Africa, Asia and Latin America and to Yugoslavia shall be filled in the following manner: seven seats for African countries, six seats for Asian countries and six seats for Latin American countries, it being understood that agreement has been reached among the developing countries to accommodate Yugoslavia;

(b) Of the seventeen seats allocated to the economically more developed countries, fourteen shall be filled by Western European and other countries and three by Eastern European countries;

(c) Elections to these thirty-six seats shall be for a term of three years provided, however, that of the members elected at the first election the terms of twelve members shall expire at the end of the year and the terms of twelve other members at the end of two years.

2. The thirty-seventh seat shall rotate among the groups of countries mentioned in paragraph 1 above in accordance with the following nine-year cycle:

First and second years: Western European and other countries;
Third, fourth and fifth years: Eastern European countries;
Sixth year: African countries;
Seventh year: Asian countries;
Eighth year: Latin American countries;
Ninth year: Western European and other countries.

3. Retiring members shall be eligible for re-election.

Source: Knipping / von Mangoldt / Rittberger (eds) (1995), pp. 670-678

Annex III

Resolution 2688 (XXV): The Capacity of the United Nations Development System

11 December 1970

Source: U. N. GAOR, 25th Sess., Supp. No. 28, at 58, U. N. Doc. A/8028 (1970).

Voting results: Adopted.

THE GENERAL ASSEMBLY,

HAVING CONSIDERED the parts of the reports of the Governing Council of the United Nations Development Programme on its ninth[1] and tenth[2] session and of the Econonimc and Social Council[3] concerning the capacity of the United Nations development system,

TAKING NOTE of the observations and reservations made in the Governing Council of the United Nations Development Programme at its tenth session[4] and in the Economic and and Social Council at its forty-ninth session,[5]

NOTING that some questions remain to be settled within the framework of the examination of this subject,

1. *Approves* the provisions concerning the United Nations Development Programme contained in the annex to the present resolution and declares that such provisions shall apply to activities of the Programme commencing on 1 January 1971, taking into account the transitional measures in those provisions;
2. *Requests* the Governing Council of the United Nations Development Programme to prepare for consideration by the General Asssembly at its twenty-sixth session, if possible, a draft omnibus statute for the Programme, incorporating the provisions contained in the annex to the present resolution and appropriate provisions from past resolutions relating to the Programme.

---

[1] *Official Records of the Economic and Social Council, Forty-ninth Session, Supplement No. 6* (E/4782), chapter VI.

[2] Ibid., Supplement No. 6A (E/4884/Rev. 1), chapter V.

[3] *Official Records of the General Assembly, Twenty-Fifth Session, Supplement No. 3* (A/8003 and Corr. 1), chapter X, section A.

[4] *Official Records of the Economic and Social Council, Forty-ninth Session, Supplement No. 6A* (E/4884/Rev. 1), chapter V, paras. 95–106.

[5] Ibid., *Forty-ninth Session,* 1712th to 1714th meetings.

Annex

I. The United Nations Development Cooperation Cycle

1. The formulation of the United Nations Development Programme country programme is the first phase of a process which may be called the United Nations Development Cooperation Cycle. The other phases are project formulation, appraisal and approval, implementation, evaluation and follow-up. The Cycle will also include periodic reviews. The scope of the Cycle might expand as envisaged in paragraph 9 below.

II. United Nations Development Programme country programming

A. General principles

2. United Nations Development Programme country progamming means the programming of its assistance at the country level. It involves the identification of the role of Programme inputs in specified areas within the country's development objectives.

3. Country programming will be used as a means of achieving the most rational and efficient utilization of resources at the disposal of the Programme for its activities in order to have the maximum impact on the economic and social development of the developing country concerned.

4. Country programming will be based on individual national development plans or, where these do not exist, on national development priorities or objectives.

5. It is recognized that the Government of the country concerned has the exclusive responsibility for formulating its national development plan or priorities and objectives. Individual developing countries should be given, at their request, assistance from the United Nations, including the regional economic commissions and the United Nations Economic and Social Office at Beirut, in the general field of planning and from the specialized agencies in sectoral planning.

6. The programming of Programme assistance will be carried out in each country within the framework of indicative planning figures constituting an order of magnitude of the resources expected to be available from the Programme during the country programme period.

7. The country programme, based on national development plans, priorities or objectives and on the indicative planning figures, will be formulated by the Government of the recipient country in cooperation, at an appropriate stage, with representatives of the United Nations system, the latter under the leadership of the resident representative of the Programme; it should coincide, where appropriate, with the period of the country's national development plan. The formulation of the country programme should involve:

(a) A broad identification of the needs which arise out of the country's objectives in particular sectors, within the framework of its over-all development objectives, and which might appropriately be met by Programme assistance;
(b) As precise an indication as possible of the internal inputs, Programme inputs and, wherever possible, other United Nations inputs to meet these needs;
(c) A preliminary list of projects to be subsequently worked out for financing by the Programme to implement the country programme.

8. The country programme of assistance should support activities which are meaningfully related to the country's development objectives. This implies that the assistance provided constitutes a programme which receives its coherence and balance from its relationship to these national objectives.

9. In the process of country programming, efforts should be made at all levels to coordinate all sources of assistance in the United Nations system, with a view to achieving integration of the assistance at the country level.

10. It will be for the Government to take into account, while preparing the country programme, other external inputs, both multilateral and bilateral.

11. The resident representative will transmit the country programme to the Administrator of the Programme who, in turn, will submit it, with his recommendations, to the Governing Council for its consideration and approval. Approval will cover the entire period of the programme, with provision for periodic reviews aimed at possible adjustments. With the agreement of the country concerned, the Administrator, in submitting the country programme for consideration and approval, will invite the attention of the Governing Council to details of any other related programme of United Nations assistance.

12. The assistance of the Programme must be sufficiently flexible to meet unforeseen needs of recipient countries or exceptional situations, which country programmes could not take into account.

B. Indicative planning figures

13. For the purpose, among others, of establishing the indicative planning figures, any distinctions between the Technical Assistance and Special Fund components will be eliminated. The resources to be devoted to country programming will be a specified percentage of the total resources for the current year, projected over a given period of time and including a rate of growth per annum over that period, one of the assumptions being that the resources of the Programme will increase at least at the same rate as the average of the last few years.

14. The indicative country-planning figures should not be construed as representing a commitment, but as a reasonably firm indication for the purpose of forward programming.

15. The indicative planning figures will be proposed by the Administrator to Governments on the basis of the criteria and guidelines established from time to time by the Governing Council. There should be some flexibility in determining the level of resources available for indicative planning figures. After taking into account any comments which Governments may wish to make in regard to the figures, the Administrator will submit his final indicative planning figures for each country for approval by the Governing Council; wherever possible, the country programme concerned will be approved at the same time.

16. As an experimental basis for the first series of indicative planning figures, the Administrator will calculate the percentage devoted to each country of the total earmarkings of programmed resources (that is, Technical Assistance country targets plus Special Fund project earmarkings) during the five-year period from 1966 to 1970, including projects approved by the Governing Council at its eleventh session. He will apply this percentage in each case to resources estimated, in accordance with the procedure laid down in paragraph 13 above, to be available for country programming for a period of from three to five years, consistent with the period of the country's development plan or development programme, in order to obtain a preliminary indicative planning figure for each country for that period. He will scrutinize these figures in the light of existing criteria for the allocation of resources and adjust them where necessary to avoid arbitrarily projecting any exceptional present country situations, to correct any inequities due to historical circumstances and, in particular, to ensure that special consideration is given to the situation of the least developed countries and of newly independent countries whose lack of an adequate administrative infrastructure has prevented them from taking proper advantage of programme assistance.

17. The figures will be reviewed periodically by the Administrator and the Governing Council, in consultation with the Government concerned, in the light of progress in the implementation of the country programme.

C. Formulation, appraisal and approval of projects

18. Project formulation will be an on-going process and need not await the approval of the country programme. To ensure the soundness of project formulation, it will be carried out at the country level. Association of various kinds of expertise with the formulation of a particular project will be only at the specific request of the Government which, in the light of the expertise available locally, is in the best position to know the type of expertise required.

19. The appraisal of each project will be, to the fullest extent possible, an integral part of the process of formulation of the project. Thus smaller projects, up to a specified cost limit, will be appraised on behalf of the Programme by the resident representative with the assistance of competent technical expertise whenever necessary. Responsibility for the appraisal of larger projects will rest with the Administrator.

20. The Governing Council alone is empowered to approve projects submitted by countries to the Programme for consideration. The Governing Council, while retaining this authority, delegates to the Administrator for three years the authority to approve projects within country programmes. Nevertheless the Council and the requesting Government reserve the right to request the Administrator to submit particular projects of whatever magnitude to the Council for its consideration and approval. The Administrator may also bring to the Council any project which, because of its policy implications or the magnitude of its impact on the country programme as a whole, deserves the consideration and approval of the Council. The Administrator will, to the maximum extent feasible, which will be determined and indicated by him to the Governing Council in due course, delegate the authority to approve projects to the resident representatives. The Governing Council will be informed as soon as possible of all project decisions completed under its delegation of authority.

III. Intercountry Programming

21. Intercountry programming is the programming of assistance for groups of countries on a subregional, regional, interregional or global basis. Such assistance will be provided through subregional, regional, interregional and global projects at the request of at least two Governments, taking into account the equitable distribution of resources among regions.

22. The programming of such assistance will be based broadly on the same general principles as set out above for country programming, particularly in that it will be systematically related to the development priorities of the countries concerned and, as far as possible, planned in advance over a period of years.

23. The procedures for the formulation, appraisal and approval of intercountry projects will follow, in their relevant aspects, the same general lines as for projects within country programmes, and will be subject to criteria and guidelines established from time to time by the Governing Council. All global projects, however, will require specific approval by the Governing Council.

IV. Over-All disposition and management of United Nations Development Programme resources

A. Over-all disposition of resources

24. The total resources available for programming will be divided between country programming on the one hand and, on the other, intercountry programming consisting of subregional, regional, interregional and global projects.

25. Initially, and until further review by the Governing Council, at least 82 per cent of the net resources available each year, after deduction of programme support costs and administrative costs, as well as resources to meet the requirements set out in paragraph 27 below, will be set aside for country programming and, at most, 18 per cent for intercountry programming, it being understood that these proportions are intended as a planning guide.

26. Subregional, regional and interregional projects, particularly those designed by interested countries to accelerate the process of economic and social integration and to promote other forms of regional and subregional cooperation, will have the first claim on the resources for intercountry programming. Global projects will come next in the order of priority. Subject to review by the Governing Council from time to time, the amount to be allocated for global projects should not exceed 1 per cent of the net resources available for programming.

27. It will be necessary to make provision to meet unforeseen needs, to meet special needs of the least developed of the developing countries, and to finance unanticipated projects or phases of projects, particularly projects of the Special Industrial Services type, which could have a catalytic

role in the economic development of the country concerned. At the eleventh session of the Governing Council, the Administrator will make proposals on the manner in which resources to meet such requirements, as well as to maintain under present arrangements the programme of Special Industrial Services at least at the present level, will be made available.

B. Full utilization of resources and financial control

28. All financial resources of the Programme are to be available at all times to the maximum possible extent for programme purposes, subject only to the maintenance on a continuous basis of an operational reserve. After provision has been made annually for programme support and administrative costs and for replenishment of the operational reserve, all resources not otherwise committed will be utilized for project activities.

29. The purpose of the operational reserve is to guarantee in all circumstances the financial liquidity and integrity of the Programme, to compensate for uneven cash inflows and to meet such other requirements as may be decided upon by the Governing Council at a subsequent stage. The Council will keep under constant review the size and composition of the reserve, basing itself on the planning of payment authorizations and expenditures for the following financial year. At the outset, and pending receipt of a more detailed analysis from the Administrator of the financial position of the Programme up to the end of 1970, the Council, as an interim measure, authorizes the establishment of an operational reserve of $ 150 million in all categories of resources, the composition of which is to be determined and maintained by the Administrator in accordance with sound principles of financial management, this level to be reviewed by the Council at its twelfth session in the context of the financial review referred to above.

30. Full responsibility for proper utilization of funds of the Programme and for the exercise of financial and accounting controls will be borne by the Administrator. The Secretary-General will continue as custodian of Programme funds, but decisions regarding the Programme investment portfolio and currency management will be reached in agreement with the Administrator, subject to a full report on this arrangement and review by the Governing Council at its twelfth session.

31. In presenting forecasts of expenditure and requests for earmarkings to the Governing Council, the Administrator will distinguish clearly among the following types of expense: *(a)* project costs; *(b)* programme supports costs, including overhead and consultative services costs; and *(c)* administrative service costs.

C. Assessment of local costs

32. Specific recommendations will be made by the Administrator to the Governing Council at its eleventh session on the formula to be followed for the assessment of local costs, which should make provision for simplified application of full or partial waivers of local costs, taking into account those cases where undue burdens would otherwise be placed on the recipient Government.

D. Agency overhead costs

33. The Administrator will consult with the participating and executing agencies and the Advisory Committee on Administative and Budgetary Questions with a view to arriving at new methods for calculating appropriate reimbursement for project implementation and for advisory services involving programming, project formulation and policy development. The prospect of entering into general compensatory arrangements for advisory services and separate specific arrangements for the reimbursement of costs in connexion with project execution will be explored. The solution worked out should not be considered as binding until it has been submitted to the Council for consideration and approval, accompanied by a report on the kinds of services to be reimbursed.

34. The Administrator will cooperate to the fullest degree in efforts to achieve common budgeting policies and accounting systems throughout the United Nations family of organizations.

V. Implementaton of United Nations Development Programme assistance

A. Responsibility of the Governing Council[6]

35. The Governing Council has over-all responsibility for ensuring that the resources of the Programme are employed with maximum efficiency and effectiveness in assisting the development of the developing countries.

36. To this end, the principal responsibilities of the Governing Council remain as stated in the relevant resolutions of the General Assembly. In the context of the principles of country and intercountry programming set out above and of the implementation of assistance so provided, the Governing Council will consider and approve country programmes, including indicative country-planning figures, approve certain projects included in the programmes in accordance with the provisions mentioned in paragraphs 20 and 23 above, exercise effective operational control, including periodic reviews of the country programmes, and make broad allocations of resources and control their use.

---

[6] See doc. 27, footnote 4, p. 676.

B. Responsibility of the Administrator

37. In addition to the responsibilities to be delegated to him by the Governing Council, the Administrator will be fully responsible and accountable to the Governing Council for all phases and aspects of the implementation of the Programme.

C. Role of United Nations organizations in the implementation of country programmes

38. The role of the organizations of the United Nations system in the implementation of country programmes should be that of partners, under the leadership of the Programme, in a common endeavour of the entire United Nations system. Their advice should be available to the Administrator in the implementation of all projects, as appropriate, whether executed by them or not.

D. Selection and accountability of executing agents

39. The Administrator will consult the Government in each case on the selection of the agent by which Programme assistance to each project will be implemented.

40. The appropriate organizations of the United Nations system will, subject to this procedure, have first consideration as executing agents.

41. When necessary to ensure the maximum effectiveness of Programme assistance or to increase its capacity, and with due regard to the cost factor, increased use may appropriately be made of suitable services obtained from governmental and non-governmental institutions and firms, in agreement with the recipient Government concerned and in accordance with the principles of international competitive bidding. Maximum use should be made of national institutions and firms, if available, within the recipient countries.

42. In cases where expertise or services are required which are not adequately available in kind, quantity and quality within the United Nations system, the Administrator will, in agreement with the Government concerned, exercise his authority to obtain them, while inviting, in appropriate cases, the relevant United Nations organization to provide complementary support.

43. Every executing agent will be accountable to the Administrator for the implementation of Programme assistance to projects.

44. In the selection of individual experts, institutions or firms, in the procurement of equipment and supplies and in the provision of training facilities, the principle of equitable geographical distribution consistent with maximum effectiveness will be observed.

E. Availability and quality of international and national project personnel

45. The Administrator should intensify efforts in coordination with the appropriate organs of the system and should develop suitable proposals for consideration by the Governing Council, to improve the availability, briefing, refresher training and procedures for the punctual recruitment of well-qualified international project personnel. These proposals should particularly take into account the desirability of increasing the number of personnel recruited from the developing countries. The Administrator should also pay particular attention to such factors as the personal suitability of candidates, including their motivation and adaptability; the need for realistic job descriptions and reporting dates; prompt decisions on candidates by the agencies and requesting Governments; and conditions of service that will attract and retain candidates for whose services there is world-wide demand.

46. In suitable cases, qualified nationals may be designated as project managers, assisted by international specialists.

47. Where necessary, and upon the request of the recipient Government, consideration should be given by the Programme to training suitable counterpart personnel as an integral part of a Programme-assisted project, including its planning phase, so that they will be qualified to participate in and ensure effective execution of the project.

48. Since there is no set formula for the proportions of international personnel, fellowships and equipment for a particular project and no ceiling on the ratio of the value of the equipment in relation to the total cost of a project, Programme pre-investment assistance should be sufficiently flexible so that in appropriate cases it may consist of the supply of equipment alone as part of an integrated pre-investment project. In the latter case, particular attention should be given to the availability of personnel

qualified to use the equipment or to train personnel in its use in recipient countries.

F. Operational control and assessment of results

49. The monitoring of project assistance, in so far as it is required for the discharge by the Administrator of his responsibility for operational control, will normally be carried out at the country level by the resident representative.

50. Evaluation carried out within the United Nations system of Programme-assisted activities will only be made with the agreement of the Government concerned. This will be carried out jointly by the Government, the Programme, the United Nations agency concerned and, where appropriate, the executing agent outside the United Nations system.

51. Such evaluation shall be on a selective basis and restricted to the minimum essential for the improvement or follow-up of the projects concerned, for the needs of Governments and for the improvement of the Programme. With the agreement of the Government concerned, the results will be communicated to the Governing Council for its information.

G. Investment and other forms of follow-up

52. Provision for investment and other forms of follow-up to Programme-assisted projects will, when necessary, be an integral part of the programming process and of the formulation, implementation and evaluation of the projects.

53. The Government in each case will be primarily responsible for all measures which should be taken at all stages of a project to ensure effective follow-up, including follow-up investment. It will be open to the Government to seek investment assistance from all available sources. No one source of follow-up investment financing should be regarded as the only acceptable source or as a source enjoying preference over others. The Administrator will assume full responsibility within the United Nations system, as its major source of pre-investment financing, for providing assistance and advice on behalf of the United Nations system on follow-up investment, with the agreement of the Government. The Programme will develop its expertise in this matter to ensure, in consultation with the Government, early coordination, from the planning stage onwards, with potential bilateral and/or multilateral sources of finance for projects requiring follow-up investment.

VI. Timing and transitional measures

54. The principles set out above, and the procedures to give effect to them, will be progressively applied from the date of their approval by the competent legislative organs of the United Nations. The Administrator will undertake as soon as possible the necessary measures so that, if possible, some country programmes will be submitted in time for consideration by the Governing Council at its twelfth session in June 1971.

55. In the transitional period, to ensure continuity of action by the Programme in meeting Governments' requests for assistance, the appraisal and approval of projects will be carried out in accordance with existing procedures. These transitional measures may be extended in cases where the Government wishes to start its country programme later than 1972, on the understanding, however, that the total amount of assistance to be provided from 1 January 1972 will be consistent with the indicative planning figures and that the existing distinctions between the two components of the Programme will have been eliminated.

VII. Organization of the United Nations Development Programme

56. The Governing Council recognizes its responsibility for policy formulation, the determination of programme priorities, and the review of implementation in both planning and practice. The decisions of the Council on country programming and its implementation have important organizational implications. The country-programming approach implies that the Administrator will be fully accountable for the management of all aspects of the Programme. At the same time, it will be necessary to bring about, within the Programme, greater decentralization of responsibility for programming and implementation from the headquarters to the country level. The application of the twin principle of the Administrator's full accountability for the Programme and the decentralization to the country level will require certain modifications in the existing structure and procedures of the Programme. A clear definition of functions and responsibilities at all levels of the administration will therefore be necessary.

57. At the headquarters level, regional bureaux should be established to provide a direct link between the Administrator and the resident representative in all matters concerning field activities. In order to streamline channels of communication and expedite the decision-making process, the

heads of these bureaux should have direct access to the Administrator. To achieve the required degree of effectiveness of management of the bureaux, they should be headed by persons with the high qualifications and rank commensurate with their important responsibilities.

58. The country-programming approach also implies that the Programme should not only concern itself with current policy formulation, but should also be able constantly to analyse the main trends in the evolution of the Programme in order to give it new directions and to explore new possibilities for making it more effective. To meet this need, a small but highly competent long-term planning staff should be established at the headquarters level under the direction of a senior official.

59. The country-programming approach also envisages more rational and effective procedures for evaluation and follow-up. This, as well as the need to maintain close relations with other collaborating organizations of the United Nations system, must be fully reflected in the organizational restructuring at the headquarters level. The Administrator is invited to take the necessary steps in this direction and to submit further proposals to the Council.

60. The strengthening of the management of the Programme at the headquarters level, in view of the reform of the system and the expectation of a growing Programme, should be achieved by securing the services of highly qualified and experienced staff with due regard to the principle of equitable geographical distribution and to the need for economy.

61. The Administrator should continue to have the authority to appoint and administer the staff of the Programme. For this purpose, he should have authority, in consultation with the Secretary-General, to frame such staff rules, consistent with the relevant principles laid down by the General Assembly, as he considers necessary to meet the special problems which arise in the service of the Programme.

62. With respect to the organization of the Programme at the country level, the resident representative will be redesignated resident director of the Programme. His appointment by the Administrator will be subject to the prior approval of the Government concerned.

63. There should be the maximum possible delegation of authority to the resident director. His role therefore needs to be greatly strengthened. In this context, his relations with the representatives of other United

Nations organizations in the field are of crucial importance. The resident director should be recognized as having full over-all responsibility for the programme in the country concerned and his role in relation to the representatives of the other United Nations organizations, where they are posted with the prior approval of the Government concerned, should be that of the leader of the team, taking into account the professional competence of these United Nations organizations and their relations with appropriate organs of the Government. This role of leadership and over-all responsibility should extend to all contacts with the governmental authorities concerned in connexion with the programme, in regard to which he will be the principal channel of communication between the Programme and the Government. The resident director should have ultimate authority on behalf of the Administrator for all aspects of the programme at the country level and should, subject to the agreement of the organizations concerned, be the central co-ordinating authority on their behalf for the other development assistance programmes of the United Nations system. In this connexion, the organizations in the United Nations system are requested to ensure that the resident directors of the Programme are consulted on the planning and formulation of development projects with which those organizations are concerned and that they are supplied with reports on the execution of those projects, as requested by the Economic and Social Council in resolution 1453 (XLVII) of 8 August 1969.

64. The creation of new field offices or the enlargement of the existing ones should depend on the volume of Programme operations in the particular country and should be undertaken with due regard to the need for economy. In the strengthening of field offices, priority should be given to effective redeployment of existing staff.

65. The Inter-Agency Consultative Board should continue to be the forum for interagency consultation and coordination relating to the Programme. However, the Board should undertake a thorough review of its basic functions and methods of work and its relations with the Governing Council in the light of the new System of country programming of Programme assistance and the need for the efficient implementation of the country programmes.

Source: Knipping / von Mangoldt / Rittberger (eds) (1995), pp. 680-706

Annex IV

96 / 29. Mission statement of the United Nations Development Programme

The Executive Board

1. Endorses the mission statement attached as an annex to the present decision, taking into account the discussions that took place during the annual session 1996 of the Executive Board of the United Nations Development Programme and of the United Nations Population Fund, as reflected in the report on agenda item 7 of the session.

15 May 1996

Annex

MISSION STATEMENT

WE THE PEOPLES OF THE UNITED NATIONS DETERMINED
... to reaffirm faith in fundamental human rights, in the
dignity and worth of the human person, in the equal rights of
men and women and of nations large and small,
... to promote social progress and better standards of life
in larger freedom, and for these ends
... to employ international machinery for the promotion
of the economic and social advancement of all peoples,
have resolved to combine our efforts to accomplish these aims ....

From the Preamble to the Charter of the United Nations

UNDP is part of the United Nations and upholds the vision of the United Nations Charter. It is committed to the principle that development is inseparable from the quest for peace and human security and that the United Nations must be a strong force for development as well as peace.

UNDP's mission is to help countries in their efforts to achieve sustainable human development by assisting them to build their capacity to design and carry out development programmes in poverty eradication, employment creation and sustainable livelihoods, the empowerment of women and the protection and regeneration of the environment, giving first priority to poverty eradication.

UNDP also acts to help the United Nations family to become a unified and powerful force for sustainable human development and works to strengthen international cooperation for sustainable human development.

Annex

UNDP, at the request of governments and in support of its areas of focus, [illegible]sists in building capacity for good governance, popular participation, private and pub[illegible] sector development and growth with equity, stressing that national plans and prioriti[illegible] constitute the only viable frame of reference for the national programming of opera[illegible]tional activities for development within the United Nations system.

UNDP resident representatives normally serve as resident coordinators of the operational activities of the United Nations system, supporting at the request of governments the coordination of development and humanitarian assistance. Resident coordinators also help to orchestrate the full intellectual and technical resources of the United Nations system in support of national development.

UNDP strives to be an effective development partner for the United Nations relief agencies, working to sustain livelihoods while they seek to sustain lives. It acts to help countries to prepare for, avoid and manage complex emergencies and disasters.

UNDP draws on expertise from around the world, including from developing countries, United Nations specialized agencies, civil society organizations and research institutes.

UNDP supports South-South cooperation by actively promoting the exchange of experience among developing countries.

UNDP supports, within its areas of focus, technology transfer, adaptation, and access to the most effective technology.

UNDP receives voluntary contributions from nearly every country in the world. UNDP seeks to ensure a predictable flow of resources to support its programmes. It provides grant funds through criteria based on universality that strongly favour low-income countries, particularly the least developed.

UNDP is politically neutral and its cooperation is impartial. It seeks to conduct its work in a manner transparent and accountable to all its stakeholders.

UNDP is committed to a process of continuing self-evaluation and reform. It aims to improve its own efficiency and effectiveness and to assist the United Nations system in becoming a stronger force for the benefit of the people and countries of the world.

UNDP will continue to support an international development cooperation framework that responds to changing global, regional and national circumstances.

411

as-

lic

es